SUFFER

T

C

SUFFER THE LITTLE CHILDREN

Child Migration and the Geopolitics of Compassion in the United States

ANITA CASAVANTES BRADFORD

THE UNIVERSITY OF NORTH CAROLINA PRESS

Chapel Hill

This book was published with the assistance of the Thornton H. Brooks Fund of the University of North Carolina Press.

Designed by Jamison Cockerham
Set in Arno, Gotham, and Intro
by codeMantra

Cover illustration: Detail of "Sun rays illuminate people.
Silhouette immigration of people," © shutterstock/JK21.

Manufactured in the United States of America

The University of North Carolina Press has been a
member of the Green Press Initiative since 2003.

LIBRARY OF CONGRESS CATALOGING-IN-PUBLICATION DATA
Names: Casavantes Bradford, Anita, author.
Title: Suffer the little children : child migration and the geopolitics of
compassion in the United States / Anita Casavantes Bradford.
Description: Chapel Hill : University of North Carolina Press, 2022. |
Includes bibliographical references and index.
Identifiers: LCCN 2021052600 | ISBN 9781469667638 (cloth ; alk. paper) |
ISBN 9781469669175 (paperback) | ISBN 9781469667645 (ebook)
Subjects: LCSH: Unaccompanied refugee children—United States—
History. | Immigrant children—Government policy—United States. |
Immigrant children—Legal status, laws, etc.—United States.
Classification: LCC JV6455 .C34 2022 |
DDC 305.23086/9120973—dc23/eng/20211122
LC record available at https://lccn.loc.gov/2021052600

Para mi nena, Ana Sofía

CONTENTS

LIST OF ILLUSTRATIONS

ix

ACKNOWLEDGMENTS

xi

INTRODUCTION

Child Migration and the Geopolitics of
Compassion in U.S. History

1

1

AGAINST ALL ODDS

Child-Saving and Exclusion in FDR's America

17

2

COLLATERAL HUMANITARIANISM

Child-Saving during World War II

39

3

WAR ORPHANS AND CHILDREN ON DEMAND

Unaccompanied Refugee Minors and
Intercountry Adoption, 1945–1956

70

4

COLD WAR KIDS

Hungarian Unattached Youth and
Refugee Resettlement in the Eisenhower Era, 1956–1958

101

5

AN EXCEPTION WITHIN AN EXCEPTION

The Cuban Children's Program, 1960–1966

133

6

THE MOST DIFFICULT TYPE OF REFUGEE

Southeast Asian Unaccompanied Minors and the
Reinvention of U.S. Refugee Policy, 1975–1989

166

7

THE ORIGINS OF A CRISIS

Unaccompanied Refugee Minors and
Unaccompanied Alien Children, 1980–2018

197

EPILOGUE

The Right to Have Rights? Migrant Children and the
Geopolitics of Compassion in the Twenty-First Century

221

NOTES

229

INDEX

279

ILLUSTRATIONS

Gilbert and Eleanor Kraus
32

USCOM Poster
59

Hungarian Infant Refugee
108

González Family Reunion
161

Central American Adolescent UACs
207

ACKNOWLEDGMENTS

This book has benefited enormously from the support of many institutions and individuals. The University of California Critical Refugee Studies Collective provided me with generous funding support and welcomed me into its deeply committed community of refugee scholars and advocates. I am especially grateful for the friendship and guidance of the CRSC's formidable leader and matriarch of the field, Distinguished Professor Yến Lê Espiritu. I am also grateful to David FitzGerald and Warren Tam at the University of California San Diego's Center for Comparative Immigration Studies for inviting me to share findings from this book in its formative stages and providing me with logistical support to finish research and writing during the pandemic.

My sincere thanks to the eminently efficient Linnea Anderson and other staff at the University of Minnesota Social Welfare History and Immigration History archives, as well as to Amanda Moreno, Juan Antonio Villanueva, and all my old friends at the University of Miami's Cuban Heritage Collection. Similar appreciation goes out to the archivists and librarians at the National Archives in College Park, Maryland; the United States Holocaust Memorial Museum; the Eisenhower Presidential Library; Rutgers University Libraries; University of California Irvine's Southeast Asian Archives; and the Graduate Theological Union in Berkeley.

My deep appreciation to my *muy querido colega y mentor* Raúl Fernández, for providing detailed and positive feedback on every chapter. Paula Fass, John Skrentny, and Tuan Hoang also provided insightful comments on chapter drafts. Any mistakes or shortcomings in this book are the result of my failure to heed their advice. And to my dear colleague and friend Nancy Page Fernández, who so skillfully and sensitively edited every line of my meandering prose: there are no words to express my gratitude for your help in getting this book to press. I couldn't have done it without you. And to Elaine Maisner, Andreina Fernandez, and the rest of the team at the University of North Carolina Press: your impeccable professionalism is a model for how all academic presses should operate.

A few final shout-outs here. First, to my family—Mike, Ana Sofía, Tía Gaby, Tía Abi, *madrina* Cova, and *padrino* John Paul—who have encouraged and sustained me through five intense years of research and writing. Second, to my *comadres* at UCI, including Glenda Flores, Belinda Campos, Sharon Block, and the inestimable Vicki L. Ruíz, who has been my champion every step of the way. Third, to the smart, selfless, and endlessly courageous immigrant and first generation Latinx students who make UCI such a remarkable place to teach and do research: you inspire me every day.

Last but not least, I want to pay respect to the interdisciplinary community of scholars of immigration, critical refugee studies, and childhood whose work I have turned to again and again in writing this book. These include but are not limited to, Carl Bon Tempo, Jon Scanlan and the late Gil Loescher, María Cristina García, Debora Anker, Yến Lê Espiritu, Leisy Abrego, Cecilia Menjívar, Tara Zahra, Laura Briggs, Rachel Winslow, Judith Baumel-Schwartz, and Jacqueline Bhabha. This book wouldn't have been possible without your groundbreaking scholarship. I stand on your shoulders.

SUFFER THE LITTLE CHILDREN

Introduction

Child Migration and the Geopolitics
of Compassion in U.S. History

In 2015, more than 50,000 Central American minors undertook perilous solo journeys north in hopes of starting new lives in the United States. Seeking safety, freedom, and opportunity, most were apprehended, incarcerated, and summarily deported. Protesting the children's lack of legal representation and their detention in prison-like facilities designed for adults, lawmakers, lobbyists, and children's advocates asserted the United States should treat Central American boys and girls as refugees from violence and economic deprivation who have a unique age-based claim on asylum. Opponents argued the children represented an invasion of young deviants and criminals drawn by an overly generous immigration policy, epitomized by President Obama's 2012 Deferred Action for Childhood Arrivals (DACA) executive order granting temporary residence permits to undocumented youth.

As the controversy raged, students from what was then the University of California Irvine's undocumented student organization, Dreams at UCI, asked me to help them make sense of the hostile reception experienced by this group of vulnerable children from a region where many of them had family ties of their own. As Dreams at UCI's faculty advisor and as a historian of immigration and childhood, I felt a keen obligation to provide real answers to their questions. This book represents my best attempt at fulfilling that obligation.

Sadly, more than six years after I began research on this topic, the crisis of unaccompanied child migration continues to escalate. The struggle to determine the parameters of unaccompanied children's rights under American law has only intensified since President Joseph Biden took office in January 2021, as a new surge of unaccompanied Central American minors arrived at the border seeking asylum. However, ongoing controversy over the United States' legal and moral obligations to this vulnerable migrant population fails to recognize that the recent phenomenon of unaccompanied child migration to the United States—though unique in intensity—is not in fact unprecedented. Children entering the United States without a parent or responsible guardian, whether bonded or free, voluntarily or coerced, have been a large, albeit largely invisible, immigrant population since the colonial era.[1] However, only on the eve of World War II did American government officials, humanitarian leaders, and the general public begin to develop an understanding of unaccompanied child migrants as a distinct immigrant population, along with a growing (if selective) concern for and with young people migrating alone.

The first comprehensive historical analysis of unaccompanied child migration to the United States from 1930 to 2020,[2] *Suffer the Little Children*, asks a series of questions positioned at the intersections of U.S. immigration history, diplomatic history, and the history of childhood.[3] Between the 1930s and 2020, in what ways have shifting international and domestic circumstances shaped how, when, and why specific groups of children gained admission and protection in the United States? How have laws, policies, and programs devised to admit and care for those children evolved? What key players shaped the nation's response to the phenomenon of unaccompanied child migration, and how have the objectives, beliefs, and strategies of those players changed over time? How have emerging notions of refugees' and children's rights interacted with American understandings of race, class, religion, national origin, gender, and age, influencing which children were granted or denied safe harbor?

To answer these questions, I spent more than five years hunting down historical records scattered across the nation about unaccompanied child migration since the FDR era. These have included congressional records and research briefs; State Department, Department of Justice, and Department of Health, Education, and Welfare papers housed at the National Archives; U.S. Office of Refugee Resettlement reports; and documents from the Eisenhower, Kennedy, and Ford presidential libraries. I have also done extensive research in the papers of religious and secular nongovernmental organizations, including the U.S. Conference of Catholic Bishops/ Migrant and Refugee Services, Lutheran Immigration and Refugee Service, the U.S. Committee for the Care of European Children, and the American Branch of the International Social Service held at the University of Minnesota's Social Welfare History Archives. I have also made use of government and NGO memos, press releases, and other documents from the Hungarian Collection at the Rutgers Alexander Library and the Camp Kilmer Collection of the American Hungarian Foundation Archives in New Brunswick, New Jersey; the University of Miami Cuban Heritage Collection and the Monsignor Bryan O. Walsh Collection at the Barry University Archives; the Orange County and Southeast Asian Archive Center at the University of California Irvine; the Center for Migration Studies in New York City; United Nations High Commissioner for Refugees (UNHCR) and UNICEF publications; U.S. and international newspapers, periodicals, and magazines; and, of course, those few Immigration and Naturalization Service (INS) and Department of Homeland Security (DHS) records and publications that are available to the public.[4]

Read together, these sources reveal that from the 1930s through 2020, an extraordinarily wide range of organizations and actors—motivated by an equally diverse range of values, beliefs, and interests—played important roles in shaping the United States' response to unaccompanied child migration. Evolving from a series of ad hoc, voluntary agency-directed child-saving schemes targeting specific groups of endangered foreign children into a more broadly conceived set of federal laws, policies, and programs regulating the treatment of unaccompanied refugee minors (URMs) and unaccompanied alien children (UACs), this complex and deeply contingent process was linked to both the expansion of the federal government and to the emergence by the 1970s and 1980s of an international consensus about refugees' and children's rights.[5] The archives also tell a story about the remarkable power of individual Americans—including presidents, policy makers, voluntary agency staff members, consular and Border Patrol officers, parish priests, celebrities, and community leaders—to influence which children have been admitted (or excluded).

Despite the diversity of actors and interests involved—and notwithstanding official and media discourses that consistently insisted on the altruistic motives underlying successive policies and programs—I argue in this book that the United States' response to unaccompanied child migrants has been consistently driven by a "geopolitics of compassion" that selectively highlights U.S. benevolence toward suffering people outside the nation's borders while simultaneously prioritizing foreign policy and domestic political objectives over asylum seekers' best interests. Of course, as Carl Bon Tempo,

Gil Loescher, and John Scanlan have demonstrated in their foundational studies of U.S. refugee policy, this dynamic is not new.[6] Nor is the tendency to admit refugees who serve the national interest while closing the gates to less politically valuable asylum seekers specific to U.S. immigration policy. Indeed, as David FitzGerald points out in his recent book *Refuge Beyond Reach*, "measures to keep people from reaching sanctuary are as old as the asylum tradition itself."[7] However, scholars to date have failed to recognize the unique position of migrant children within this global architecture of exclusion.

Since the 1930s, the admission of carefully selected groups of unaccompanied children has provided successive administrations with a relatively low-cost means of advancing a number of foreign policy goals. In many cases, these children also became a source of evocative public relations material, as government officials and the U.S. media alike sought to exploit the propaganda value of images of suffering children to discredit the USSR, project the United States' image as a benevolent power, and confirm the superiority of the American way of life.[8] At the same time, the resettlement of unaccompanied minors has also advanced the domestic political agendas of U.S. leaders since the FDR era, serving to placate powerful political, ethnic, religious, and humanitarian lobbies demanding the nation fulfill its moral ideals and commitment to overseas allies by opening its arms to groups of suffering children uniquely deserving of American protection.

With the passage of the 1980 Refugee Act, the U.S. government adopted a set of universal criteria for the admission and care of unaccompanied refugee minors. This groundbreaking legislation, representing the culmination of almost fifty years of humanitarian, political, and legal advocacy, reflected Americans' growing acceptance of new notions of refugees' and children's rights as encoded in recent international law. Unfortunately, in practice, the new URM program has continued to be powerfully influenced by foreign policy and domestic political considerations.

The predominance of a geopolitics of compassion in determining which children were admitted or excluded became increasingly apparent during the 1980s and 1990s, when U.S. concern for emerging global security threats in Africa and transnational activism on behalf of child soldiers led to the admission of a growing number of URMs from the continent. During the 2000s, changing geopolitical and domestic circumstances contributed to further diversify the demographics of URMs to include minor refugees, asylees, and victims of trafficking and severe forms of abuse from almost fifty nations. Meanwhile, the geopolitics of compassion drove the federal government to adopt a much harsher response to growing numbers of Haitian, Mexican, and Central American children fleeing economic deprivation and state-sponsored violence and repression in their homelands during the 1980s.

During the next four decades, despite sustained advocacy by legal, religious, and grassroots organizations, the U.S. government's refusal to acknowledge the human rights violations of anti-communist allies and its disavowal of the devastating consequences of more than a century of U.S. interventions in Latin America and the Caribbean led to systematic denial of asylum to unaccompanied minors from south of the border. Mounting anti-immigrant, anti-refugee, and anti-Latino sentiment, driven by a decades-long influx of Cuban and Southeast Asian refugees, and surging unauthorized immigration from Mexico and the 9/11 attacks, have also fueled racialized hostility toward asylum seekers and public support for an increasingly punitive immigration enforcement regime. These intertwined foreign policy and domestic political contexts have shaped the reception granted to the mostly poor and non-white minors arriving alone at the border since the 1980s, who continue to be treated as "illegal" immigrants and illegitimate asylum seekers rather than children in need of protection.

In *Suffer the Little Children*, I use transnational, comparative, and relational lenses to trace and analyze the complex relationship between U.S. foreign policy, domestic politics, and the differential treatment of distinct groups of children who have migrated alone to the United States since the 1930s. I understand unaccompanied child migration as a transnational process that requires us to think about the conditions that sparked minors' emigration and the diverse forms their migration assumed. Some children, like British children during the 1940–41 Blitz and "first wave" Vietnamese minors, were evacuated directly from war zones. Others, like many Cuban "Pedro Pans," were preemptively evacuated from environments their parents viewed as a threat to physical security as well as to ideological integrity. Others, including many of the Hungarian and Southeast Asian minors that resettled in the United States, as well as Haitian, Mexican, and Central American migrant children after 1980, fled of their own volition, with or without parents' permission. Some children in these groups were inadvertently separated from relatives, while others were sent ahead by parents hoping they would later facilitate the family's resettlement in the United States. Thinking transnationally requires us to consider how the migratory paths taken by diverse groups of unaccompanied children have been shaped by their home nations' relations with the United States. And most importantly, a transnational lens requires us to keep at the front of our minds the ways in which migrant children's reception has been influenced by U.S. geopolitical interests.

Previous scholars have usually studied the migration of specific groups of unaccompanied children in isolation from one another. But a comparative and relational approach provides crucial new insight into the broader phenomenon. The archives make it surprisingly clear that the United States' widely varied responses to distinct groups of unaccompanied minors have been closely linked to one another. Many political leaders, government officials, children's advocates, and voluntary agency personnel participated in resettling more than one group of unaccompanied children; most had at least some knowledge of previous programs, from which they drew different lessons about how to handle resettlement in the future. Ongoing collaboration and competition among voluntary agencies and between voluntary agencies and the federal government also created relationships—both positive and negative—that carried over from one program to the next, shaping their character and outcomes. The American public similarly relied upon personal and collective memories of previous resettlement efforts in deciding how to feel and act toward subsequent waves of unaccompanied child migrants.

Since the federal government has been largely responsible for negotiating the foreign and domestic political interests that influenced the United States' treatment of unaccompanied migrant children, and for turning those multiple interests into laws, policies, and programs, the state takes center stage in this book's analysis. My understanding of the state draws heavily on insights and methods from cultural history, as well as scholars from political science, sociology, anthropology, and critical legal studies.[9] Rather than imagining it as a singular and static entity, I see the state, in the words of Wendy Brown, as a domain, not a thing: a "significantly unbounded terrain of powers and techniques, an ensemble of discourses, rules and practices, cohabiting in limited, tension-ridden, often contradictory relationship with one another."[10] This book thus pays close attention to how the distinct values, interests, and policy preferences of different actors and offices within the federal (and to a lesser extent, state and local level) government have shaped the United States' response to subsequent waves of unaccompanied refugee minors and alien children. Although this story has been greatly influenced by the expanded power of the executive branch over immigration and refugee policy after World War II, a wide range of state actors, including heads of federal agencies, Congress, bureaucrats, and immigration officials, have also made important decisions about which children to admit or exclude, and how to best care for them in the United States.[11]

Of course, the state doesn't operate in a vacuum; rather, the dynamic relationship between the state and civil society has played a defining role in U.S. history.[12] With that in mind, I also analyze the evolving relationship between the federal government and voluntary agencies that has driven the nation's response to unaccompanied migrant children, and explore how this relationship has led to the creation of a unique "public-private" bureaucratic infrastructure (reliant on poorly compensated female labor) through which the United States continues to regulate and care for URMs and UACs. I am not the first historian to recognize the importance of non-state actors in shaping U.S. refugee policy; in *Benevolent Empire* (2017), Stephen Porter traces the emergence of the particular form of "hybrid governance" through which American voluntary organizations and the U.S. government divided the labor of admitting and resettling refugees between World War I and the 1960s.[13] However, like other immigration historians, Porter misses the unique role child migrants have played in these processes—not simply as participants, but as *drivers* of legal, policy, and programmatic change over time.

In diving deeply into the public-private dynamic that structures child migration to the United States, I have avoided setting up a false dichotomy between a supposedly "amoral" state and "moral" nongovernmental actors. Instead, I try to demonstrate that even the most well-intended humanitarian leaders are implicated—as we all are—in the inequitable power structures that produce and reproduce the injustices they seek to remedy.[14] They are also fallible human beings. Like the rest of us, they are driven by deeply held ideals as well as their own biases and ambitions, by the desire to alleviate human suffering as well as by more pragmatic and instrumental goals.[15] The voluntary agency directors and personnel who played a leading role in the United States' response to unaccompanied child migration are no exception. Though they frequently claimed to be completely focused on the best interests of children, they often made strategic choices about which endangered children to prioritize, how to operate, and how to represent themselves in order to secure official sanction and public support for their efforts.[16] Voluntary agencies also competed with one another for power, prestige, and funding.[17] The tens of thousands of everyday Americans who have advocated for or against the admission of endangered foreign children or served as foster parents to unaccompanied minors since the 1930s similarly bore a complex blend of political, religious, and humanitarian convictions and self-interest.[18]

In addition to focusing on state-civil society relations, this book also traces how evolving notions of "refugee" and "child" have interacted with each other in U.S. history. Although the 1951 United Nations Refugee Convention defines refugees as those who are "unable or unwilling to return to their country of origin owing to a well-founded fear of being persecuted for reasons of race, religion, nationality, membership of a particular social group, or political opinion," in practice, the term encompasses a range of shifting legal and social meanings.[19] Before the passage of the 1948 Displaced Persons Act, U.S. law did not distinguish between refugees and immigrants, requiring all comers to meet the same requirements for admission. The United States adopted neither a permanent refugee law nor a universal definition of the term until 1980, preferring instead to pass a series of short-term, geographically and ideologically restrictive refugee bills that designated particular groups of people as worthy of protection in the interim. Most of the anti-communist Hungarians, Cubans, and Southeast Asians admitted before 1980 were legally designated as "parolees" rather than refugees. Government officials and the media nonetheless consistently described all these groups—many of whom would have failed to meet the United Nations criteria had they been referenced—as refugees, thereby expressing sympathy, solidarity, and discursive recognition of their claims on preferential admission. Conversely, and even after the passage of the ostensibly universal 1980 Refugee Act, people fleeing repressive right-wing regimes in Central America and the Caribbean have often been arbitrarily designated as "economic migrants," a label used to justify their legal exclusion as well as to delegitimize their claims on public sympathy.

The story told in *Suffer the Little Children* challenges the false binary between the categories of "refugee" and "economic migrant" frequently used to differentiate between groups of equally endangered people—both adults and children—that have been seeking asylum in the United States since at least the 1930s. It sheds new light on how the term refugee has served to articulate particular forms of rights deprivation while also functioning as a form of privilege, bestowing what Vietnamese refugee scholar Phuong Tran Nguyen calls a "moral belonging" on some—but not all—who need protection.[20] This book also makes clear that this "privilege" comes at a price. As Yến Lê Espiritu notes in *Body Counts: The Vietnam War and Militarized Refuge(es)*, those selected for admission to the United States as "refugees" have long been imagined by political leaders as tools of statecraft and pressed into service to support the nation's geopolitical ambitions.[21]

This way of imagining refugees necessarily frames them as passive, dependent, and voiceless, as objects of pity rather than rights-bearing subjects: exactly the way that modern Western societies imagine children. It wasn't until after the 1920s that childhood as most middle-class Americans understand it today—an idyllic and protected phase of life, free from paid labor and dedicated to school and play—became commonplace.[22] Together with new notions of children as the raw political material from which modern nation-states would be constructed, these ideas inspired a new transnational network of women-led child-saving activism, beginning with the founding of the Save the Children Fund in England in 1919.[23] Similar ideas continue to inspire humanitarian activism today. This book provides countless examples of how children's advocates since the 1930s have sought to generate support for unaccompanied minors' admission by framing them as innocent victims in need of saving by a benevolent paternal United States.[24] I also draw attention to gaps between these representations and minors' own identities and lived experiences and to the ways they have obscured the distinct capacities and needs of the adolescent boys who represent the majority of children who migrate alone. I point out how discourses and images of endangered foreign children implicitly encouraged Americans to see sympathy and humanitarian action as an alternative to the structural changes needed to remedy the human rights deprivations that fuel the ongoing crisis of unaccompanied child migration.

This book also asks a cultural historian's questions: How did changing notions of refugees and children's rights interact with Americans' shifting understandings of race, ethnicity, religion, national origin, class, gender, and age over time? How did these factors influence which unaccompanied migrant children were deemed deserving of protection and sympathy, and which were labeled "anchors" seeking to initiate a process of familial "chain migration"—or reviled as deviants and criminals? I emphasize the importance of official, media, and humanitarian discourses and images in shaping the strikingly different ways that similarly endangered groups of migrant children have been perceived by the U.S. public since the 1930s. But this book also asks a more fundamental question about the extent to which different groups of unaccompanied child migrants have been understood as individual rights-bearing subjects—and about how notions of race in particular have influenced those understandings. Like women before them, children have been considered possessions or appendages of adults. In the United States, they went unrecognized as individual subjects of immigration law until the passage of the Immigration Act of 1907, which formally prohibited children's admission without a parent or guardian (though in practice, this fell within the discretion of immigration officers at ports of entry). By the time the 1980 Refugee Act was passed, U.S. immigration law contained a number of provisions explicitly recognizing minors' unique age-based needs and interests. However, as this book reveals, decisions about which unaccompanied children to admit or exclude continued to be based on an understanding of them as extensions of their parents and communities.[25]

This implicit denial of children's individual existence facilitated the admission of some unaccompanied minors—mostly white, middle-class, European-origin, and Christian—when Americans wished to demonstrate solidarity or provide assistance to their parents or home nations. But it also worked against poor, nonwhite, and non-Christian children, whose claims on admission and protection were evaluated in light of their broader implications for refugee and immigrant flows from their homelands instead of in terms of their individual circumstances. This racialized logic of deterrence justified barring most endangered Jewish children from entering the United States in 1939, seeing them as an "entering wedge" whose admission would lead to an influx of coreligionist adult refugees. It also informed laws that forced European "half-orphans" in the 1950s and the children of American GI and Southeast Asian mothers in the 1980s to choose between lives of deprivation in their homelands or migrating to the United States alone. Between the mid-1970s and the present day, this racialized logic of deterrence has also inspired a growing number of frontline immigration officials to undercut unaccompanied Southeast Asian, Haitian, Central American, and Mexican minors' access to asylum, despite indisputable evidence of their acute need for protection.

There have, of course, been exceptions to this way of understanding specific groups of migrant children. The tragically obvious ones include those transnational adoptees whose living parents were conveniently erased, as well as today's "Dreamers," praised for their supposedly "American" work ethic and civic spirit by those who simultaneously criminalize their parents as "illegal" immigrants. This book nonetheless makes clear that the refusal to see children as individual rights-bearing subjects has played a powerful and persistent role in shaping our nation's treatment of unaccompanied minors.

Something this book does *not* do is center the lived experiences or voices of unaccompanied child migrants. I understand some readers will feel disappointed by this, especially scholars who have been arguing for more than thirty years that we need to take children seriously as historical actors in their own right.[26] It may also seem, at first glance, to disregard my argument about Americans' historical denial of children's individuality, agency, and rights. Let me go on the record, then, as saying I see unaccompanied migrant children as both individuals and members of families and communities. I also believe unaccompanied minors possess their own (albeit often limited) agency, perspectives, and voices—and that although these are often silenced, they merit our attention. I signal these commitments in the book by selectively highlighting the diversity and complexity of migrant children's experiences of displacement, family separation, flight, and resettlement. I also reflect briefly in each chapter on the trauma and suffering of successive generations of unaccompanied minors, as well as on the remarkable courage, creativity and resilience demonstrated in rebuilding their lives in the United States.

I nonetheless chose to focus this book on the adult decision makers, structures, and institutions that shaped the treatment of unaccompanied migrant children in American history. I did this because I think it is important for scholars, despite their individual analytical priorities, to recognize the predominant role of the state in shaping the experiences of forced migrants of all ages—and perhaps especially those minors deprived of state-administered rights and benefits in their homelands who seek them instead across international borders. I also hope this focus will encourage scholarly and general readers alike to reflect more deeply on adults' primary responsibility for creating the political, economic, and social conditions that compel unaccompanied minors to migrate and on the almost exclusive power they exercise over whether those children will be granted or denied protection in the United States. This book is not intended to replace studies that center unaccompanied child migrants but instead to provide historical context that will assist other scholars in critically interpreting those children's experiences, perspectives, and voices. I sincerely hope that my book will serve as a catalyst and foundation for further studies, without which our understanding of the phenomenon of unaccompanied child migration will remain incomplete.

A few words now on *Suffer the Little Children*'s organization and style. To emphasize how the United States' treatment of unaccompanied child migrants evolved over time, I organized the book into chronological chapters, each of which tells the story of a specific child evacuation or resettlement effort, from its origins to its aftermath. I use a narrative tone that seeks to be equal parts accessible and analytical. In chapter 1, I tell the story of the German Jewish Children's Aid (GJCA), an American Jewish organization that sought to bring 1,000 coreligionist children to the safety of American coreligionist foster homes after Adolf Hitler's rise to power. Against great obstacles, these early American child savers achieved a modest degree of success, wrenching the first policy accommodations for unaccompanied refugee minors from a reluctant U.S. government. Constrained by restrictive immigration laws and pervasive anti-Semitism, the GJCA (later rebranded the European Jewish Children's Aid or EJCA) ultimately provided homes for only a few hundred children fleeing Nazi terror. The operational model established by the GJCA and the principles on which it rested established the foundation upon which subsequent wartime and postwar children's evacuation programs would be built.

Chapter 2 explores child evacuation during the World War II era. It focuses on the efforts of the nonsectarian coalition originally brought together by the failed campaign to admit 20,000 endangered Jewish children to the United States through the 1939 Wagner-Rogers Bill which floundered in Congress. Rebranding themselves as the U.S. Committee for the Care of European Children (USCOM) in 1940, they coordinated spontaneous efforts to bring British children to the United States following Great Britain's entry into the war. Guided by what I call "principled opportunism," USCOM's leaders established a new working relationship with the federal government to facilitate the mostly Anglo-Saxon Protestant children's admission, while also employing policies, programs, and procedures developed to accommodate British evacuees, to continue bringing a limited number of European Jewish children to the United States. To maintain official sanction and public support, USCOM had to work within the confines of an extraordinarily strict immigration policy and to publicly obscure the racial selectivity of American sympathy for children in the war zone. Ultimately, the committee would end up practicing a kind of "collateral humanitarianism" that produced, in most cases, an ambivalent good for a small number of unaccompanied minors, while excluding many of the most endangered children from receiving the benefits of shelter and care in the United States.

Chapter 3 examines the intertwined history of efforts to resettle unaccompanied European minors and the rise of intercountry adoption in the decade after World War II. Beginning in 1946, USCOM, EJCA, and the American branch of the International Social Service (ISS) collaborated to bring a small number of European "war orphans" to the United States. Empowered by new laws that, for the first time, explicitly provided for the admission of select groups of unaccompanied refugee minors, these legacy child-saving agencies soon found themselves in competition with other voluntary organizations and individuals seeking to house European children. These included proponents of private intercountry adoption, which many Americans saw as a way to grow their families while assisting war-afflicted children and participating in the incipient struggle against communism. Established children's agencies confronted new challenges from Congress, which sought to reassert control of the nation's immigration laws by making private intercountry adoption quicker and easier while concurrently limiting the admission of unaccompanied refugee minors.

The combined efforts of restrictionist lawmakers and intercountry adoption advocates reinforced prewar tendencies to evaluate refugees of all ages for admission based on geopolitical and domestic political considerations rather than their actual protection needs, while also reinscribing notions of unaccompanied children as objects of charity rather than individual rights-bearing subjects. Despite these setbacks, voluntary agencies' continued willingness to work within the system laid the groundwork for new Cold War–era collaborations with the federal government to facilitate the admission and care of displaced and endangered children to the United States.

In chapter 4, I explore the U.S. response to the "discovery" of unattached youth among the 38,000 Hungarian escapees admitted to the United States after the failed 1956 anti-Soviet uprising. In this first federally driven refugee resettlement effort in U.S. history, approximately 800 unaccompanied minors landed in American foster homes. This unprecedented official involvement in resettling Hungarian youth represented a logical extension of emerging postwar notions of American responsibility toward endangered foreign children and of communism as a threat to young people's ideological and spiritual formation. At the same time, Americans' eagerness to open their homes to the youngest of the white Christian Hungarian children—but not to the adolescent boys who made up the majority of unattached youth—reflected the ways that race, gender, religion, and age continued to circumscribe U.S. concerns for vulnerable foreign children as well as the mixed motives of couples who hoped that fostering might be a first step toward adoption.

Agency leaders and staff, operating under extreme pressure to move refugees of all ages as quickly as possible into new homes, were pressed to subsume the unique needs of unattached Hungarian youth into the broader geopolitical objectives of Eisenhower's resettlement program. The negative consequences of these rushed placements reignited conflicts dating back to the immediate postwar period over who was best qualified to make decisions on unaccompanied refugee minors' behalf and who was responsible for them in the United States. By the time the nation's doors finally closed to Hungarian youth in March 1958, these tensions had brought about a radical renegotiation of the public-private partnership structuring previous child evacuation projects. But one key constant remained linking the Hungarian youth to the displaced children who preceded and followed them: the extent to which the children's best interests were subordinated to the nation's more pressing geopolitical and domestic political priorities.

In chapter 5, I analyze the origins and evolution of the nation's first federally directed and funded foster care program for unaccompanied refugee minors, which provided homes to more than half of the 14,000 unaccompanied minors sent from Cuba following Fidel Castro's rise to power in 1959. Reflecting a growing recognition of the importance of both refugees and young people to the nation's Cold War foreign policy goals, the convergence of a number of distinct but overlapping child evacuation efforts under the umbrella of the Cuban Children's Program represented the beginning of a new public-private partnership for the care of unaccompanied refugee minors. Beginning as a temporary child evacuation scheme to demonstrate U.S. support for Cuban parents involved in the anti-Castro underground and to safeguard the ideological and spiritual purity of the island's elite future leaders, the program quickly ballooned into a comprehensive child welfare program struggling to improvise ways to care for an undetermined period of time for thousands of increasingly diverse unaccompanied Cuban minors. Although public officials, the mainstream media, and the Cuban exile community all declared the Cuban Children's Program an unqualified success, in private, its exhausted and demoralized directors struggled to reconcile what they saw as the program's positive geopolitical outcomes with the negative consequences of children's unexpectedly prolonged stay in foster care. It nonetheless marked a new stage in the deepening collaboration between governmental and non-governmental actors in caring for unaccompanied children.

In chapter 6, I tell the story of the U.S. government's response to the approximately 25,000 unaccompanied minors among the more than 1 million Southeast Asian refugees admitted to the United States after the Vietnam War. Despite failed efforts by Republican president Gerald Ford to "walk back" the state's recently expanded commitment to refugee resettlement, a newly adversarial community of voluntary agency leaders and advocates demanded the federal government provide the same benefits to this next generation of unaccompanied minors as it had to Cuban children. These tensions spurred passage in 1980 of a Refugee Act creating a permanent program to provide priority admission and federally funded foster care to unaccompanied refugee minors of all nationalities. Representing the culmination of a process that began in 1934 with private Jewish American child-saving efforts, the creation of the new Unaccompanied Refugee Minors (URM) program enshrined in U.S. law the idea that such children possessed a unique age-based claim on priority admission and state-sponsored care.

However, unaccompanied Southeast Asian children remained vulnerable to the vicissitudes of changing foreign policy and domestic political interests. With anti-refugee and anti-immigrant sentiment again on the rise, refugee admissions declined after 1981. Even as efforts to improve the quality of care provided by the federal URM program began to bear fruit, a deeply racialized perception of unaccompanied Vietnamese youth as "anchors" led the United States to join the Association of Southeast Asian Nations (ASEAN) and the UNHCR in implementing policies that reimagined children as a tool for deterring the ongoing exodus from Southeast Asia. Proponents of this hardline approach denied a new generation of unaccompanied refugee minors the right to be evaluated for admission on the basis of their actual individual circumstances, rather than their potential impact on subsequent immigration from their homelands.

In a shorter chapter 7, I bring this story up to the present day, tracing in broad brushstrokes the evolution of the U.S. response to unaccompanied child migration in recent decades. Despite the Refugee Act's humanitarian aspirations, I argue that geopolitical and domestic political considerations have continued to disproportionately shape decisions about which children have been deemed worthy of admission and protection. I contrast the standard of care provided to a small but increasingly diverse group of URMs, including, after the mid-1990s, several hundred former African child soldiers and a highly visible contingent of Sudanese "Lost Boys," with the harsh reception offered to the growing numbers of Haitian, Mexican, and Central American children who sought security and opportunity in the United States beginning in the eighties. During sustained legal advocacy, I argue that those who have been designated UACs continue today to be confronted by an arbitrarily punitive immigration enforcement regime that treats them first as "illegals" and illegitimate asylum seekers—and only secondarily as children.

In the epilogue, I conclude with a brief reflection on what the history of unaccompanied child migration reveals about the disconnect between the United States' self-ascribed identity as a supporter of human rights, Americans' persistent racialized ambivalence to refugees and immigrants of all ages, and our continued reluctance to imagine migrant children as individual rights-bearing subjects. I also offer a few suggestions on how the United States might begin to craft a more effective and humane policy response to the growing phenomenon of unaccompanied child migration.

Suffer the Little Children shines a harsh but necessary light on the differential treatment of similarly endangered groups of unaccompanied migrant children in U.S. history from the 1930s to 2020, providing a powerful challenge to the depoliticizing humanitarian discourse through which many everyday Americans understand these children, the contexts producing them, and the policies by which their government responds. I hope to spur hard conversations about how we decide which kinds of people (and how many) are deserving of protection, as well as who counts—and doesn't count—as a child. At a time when public attention remains focused on this pressing issue, I hope my book inspires others to advocate for a more informed and compassionate policy response to this uniquely vulnerable migrant population.

With that in mind, a final word here about the meaning of the title, which refers to a moment recounted in the gospel of Matthew (19:4) when Jesus rebuked his disciples for chasing away a group of children who sought his blessing. In the King James version of this story, Christ said, "Suffer [allow] the little children, and forbid them not, to come unto me: for of such is the kingdom of heaven." While biblical scholars have offered multiple interpretations of this scripture, for me, its significance is clear. As Jesus, himself once a refugee child, reminds us: children are important members of society in their own right. Regardless of origin, identity, or citizenship status, they are uniquely entitled to care and compassion. They should be welcomed and cherished. Our collective future is in their hands.

1

Against All Odds

Child-Saving and Exclusion in FDR's America

Between 1933 and 1939, as fascism spread across Europe, concerned Americans would improvise a range of responses to the emerging threats to children's safety on the continent. The first, organized by American Jews after Adolf Hitler's rise to power, sought to bring 1,000 coreligionist children out of German to the safety of American coreligionist foster homes. During the same period, the devastating impact of the Spanish Civil War on the peninsula's youngest citizens inspired American supporters of the Spanish Republic to come together to attempt to find temporary homes for 500 Basque refugee children in the United States.

Against all odds, the first of these initiatives achieved a modest degree of success; the second, after provoking an initial flurry of media attention, collapsed before it began. They both nonetheless represent an essential part of the history of unaccompanied child migration to the United States. When considered individually and in relation to one another, they provide valuable insight into the diverse worldviews of the people that participated in or opposed early twentieth-century American child evacuation schemes, the motives behind their actions, and the approaches and strategies they employed in promoting or curtailing efforts to aid displaced children. In doing so, they shed new light on the complex and contested ways Americans imagined refugees and children during the interwar years, as well as on the ways that Americans' notions of religion, race, and culture interacted with evolving understandings of the national interest to shape immigration law and policy.

In January 1933 Adolf Hitler began to transform the collapsing German Weimar Republic, seeking to establish a National Socialist dictatorship that would dominate Europe. Convinced that Germany's military, economic, and cultural decline after World War I resulted from a communist-Jewish conspiracy and that Jewish people threatened the racial integrity of the nation, Hitler took swift action to restrict Jewish participation in national life. His actions ushered in a period of racist anti-Semitic terror and violence that eventually spilled over Germany's borders and provoked a second world war.[1]

In the months following Hitler's rise to power, American Jewish leaders organized to seek out new emigration options for coreligionists in Germany. However, current U.S. immigration laws made this almost impossible. Since 1924, the Johnson-Reed Act had strictly curtailed admissions according to a nationality-based annual quota designed to bolster the northwestern European and Protestant populations of the United States, while barring Asian immigration and drastically limiting immigration from southern and central Europe. Voted into law by an overwhelming congressional majority, the 1924 act's racialized restrictionist logic quickly became enshrined in U.S. political culture as well as the popular imagination, framing debates around immigration for the next forty years.[2]

Moreover, the 1924 act—like U.S. immigration laws before it—contained no specific provision for refugee admissions. And whereas in earlier periods laissez-faire immigration policies had facilitated the indirect admission of many victims of persecution, the new act's extraordinarily restrictive quotas, combined with rigid enforcement of visa eligibility requirements, would work together to curtail immigration *and* close the nation's doors to refuge seekers. In April 1933 Assistant Secretary of State Wilbur Carr instructed consular officials that Jews fleeing Germany must apply for visas, like any other applicants, and if qualified for admission, wait their turn for a quota number. Thus, as Nazi persecution of Jews worsened, the deliberate under-issuance of visas reduced admissions from Germany to a small percentage of their modest annual quota of 27,000.[3]

In response, a coalition of well-connected Jewish Americans, including representatives of the American Jewish Committee and the B'nai B'rith, lobbied the State Department to adjust inspection procedures to facilitate visas for German Jews. Irving Lehman, a prominent lawyer and chief judge of the New York Court of Appeals, asked his close friend President Franklin Delano Roosevelt to relax enforcement of the 1917 Immigration Act's "public charge" clause, which barred admission of any immigrant seen as likely to become dependent on taxpayer funded services.[4] A few days later, FDR charged Secretary of State Cordell Hull and Secretary of Labor Frances Perkins with looking at how visa procedures might be modified to allow admission of a "small number of prominent individuals" fleeing Nazi persecution.[5]

Giving the request serious consideration, Secretary Perkins recommended the president issue an executive order facilitating issuance of visas to German Jews. However, Secretary Hull vigorously opposed the idea, defending the State Department's rigorous admission standards and arguing Germany would see special treatment for Jews claiming religious or political persecution as unwarranted meddling in their domestic affairs.[6] Moreover, he insisted, increased immigration would antagonize labor and hurt American workers. Defending her territory, the outspoken Perkins—the first woman Cabinet member in U.S. history—retorted that labor relations and immigration's impact on the economy were HER concern and suggested that the Department of State confine its assessments of the national interest to the sphere of foreign relations.

This exchange began a prolonged turf battle between the Departments of State and Labor over the authority to regulate admission of Jewish refugees, revealing the divergent priorities of their offices as well as fundamentally incompatible understandings of the relationship between immigration and the national interest.[7] Perkins, a deeply idealistic leader whose experiences in the settlement movement convinced her of immigrants' positive impact, was determined to assist Jews fleeing Germany in every legally permissible way. The patrician southerner Hull, a former senator from Tennessee, firmly believed the nation's isolationist foreign policy rested on restrictive immigration laws. Hull's objections to Jewish refugees also reflected concerns about the negative political and economic consequences of immigration, as well as the racist anti-Semitic worldview he shared with many of the State Department's senior career officers who suspected Jews of exaggerating their suffering to unfairly circumvent U.S. immigration law.[8]

With FDR's cabinet deadlocked over the issue of Jewish refugees, American Jewish community leaders doggedly searched for ways to free up the German quota. A unique opportunity appeared in the spring of 1933 with the establishment of a department for child emigration within the Reich Agency for Jews in Germany (*Reichsvertretung der Juden in Deutschland*). The American Jewish Congress recognized that a convergence of international and domestic circumstances—the Nazi regime's desire to incentivize youth emigration combined with the availability of unused German quota visas—might make possible the evacuation of Jewish children to the United States.[9]

During the next six months, a subcommittee of representatives from the American Jewish Congress, the American Jewish Committee, and B'nai B'rith—including prominent women like Cecilia Razovsky, a first-generation Jewish American who served as assistant to the executive director of the National Refugee Service (NRS) and executive director of the National Coordinating Committee for Aid to Immigrants and Refugees from Germany—came together to envision a child evacuation plan. A subcommittee under the auspices of the National Conference of Jewish Social Workers launched its own exploration of the feasibility of such a program.[10] By early 1934, the two subcommittees joined forces to seek government approval for the admission of as many as 1,000 children to the United States.

After prolonged discussion, the subcommittees agreed to consider only children born in Germany for evacuation; they set the age limit for participants at sixteen, a decision foreshadowing later tensions between advocates for evacuation of the more endangered adolescents and those who insisted the program give preference to younger children, who were more sympathetic and easier to place. With these compromises in place, committee members created the German-Jewish Children's Aid (GJCA) to undertake fundraising, coordination of visa applications, transportation, and identification of American foster homes.

The diverse motivations underlying different organizations' participation in the GJCA's founding revealed the extraordinarily diverse Jewish American community's multivalent response to rising threats for their coreligionists in Europe. Zionist, more recently arrived, and traditionally observant Jews frequently understood child evacuation as part of broader efforts to assist all Jewish refugees, especially through relocation to Palestine. However, many elite and assimilated Jewish Americans saw child evacuation as a temporary strategy, a means of capitalizing on humanitarian concern for children even as they continued to advocate for expanded Jewish German immigration to the United States.[11] These more elite Jews—whose vision finally prevailed within the GJCA—likely understood their efforts as one of the few available means of providing assistance to German coreligionists who were either unable to leave or unwilling to surrender their homes and assets to the Nazis as a precursor to emigration.

Despite these differences, however, the GJCA's proposed program reflected American Jews' shared concern for the vulnerabilities of German Jewish children who, expelled from schools and subjected to bullying and violence, were among the first victims of Nazi anti-Semitism.[12] But the new organization's leaders quickly discovered that the legal obstacles to the admission of children were even more formidable than those confronting German Jewish adults. Unlike other areas of American jurisprudence and social policy, U.S. immigration law did not recognize children as possessing any unique age-based claim on state resources or protection.[13] It granted no special consideration to children, including those fleeing persecution or threats to their physical survival. What's more, the Immigration Act of 1917 barred unaccompanied boys and girls under sixteen from entering the United States without a special waiver from the secretary of labor—which could only be provided if they met all of the other eligibility requirements for a quota visa, including proving they would not become a public charge.[14]

But the GJCA's determined leaders discovered a loophole in immigration law that might allow for the admission of unaccompanied Jewish children. Led by retired New York State judge Joseph Proskauer, they met with representatives of the Departments of State and Labor in September 1933, requesting that—as per Section 21 of the Immigration Act of 1917—the secretary of labor accept bonds as a guarantee that the children would not become a public charge. Their request reignited the conflict between Secretaries Perkins and Hull over Jewish refugees. Although Perkins judged the bond statute inappropriate for facilitating the widespread admission of German refugees, she agreed with Jewish community leaders that minors represented an exceptional case: since they would not compete with U.S. citizens for jobs, the provision might be used to admit Jewish children. The State Department's leadership disagreed vehemently, warning that any easing of the regulations would antagonize organized labor, spark an anti-Semitic public backlash, and lead to demands that Congress pass legislation to drastically reduce existing quotas.

Reflecting Perkins' and Hull's divergent worldviews, the disagreement also pointed to a fundamental difference between the way that refugee advocates and restrictionists understood childhood. Perkins' reasoning suggests she understood refugee children as holding a unique age-based claim to sympathy and legal accommodation. In contrast, Secretary Hull and State Department senior leaders' comments suggest they saw Jewish children primarily as representatives of a racialized community, without any right *as children* to special treatment under the law. They framed objections to the children's admission in the same terms used to oppose the admission of refugees in general—the negative economic and political consequences of increased immigration. Seeing children as extensions of their inadmissible parents rather than as individuals, State Department officials believed relaxing any visa requirements would allow children to serve as an "entering wedge" and establish a dangerous precedent for policy exceptions.

In December 1933, the attorney general ruled in support of the Department of Labor's authority to grant bonds to facilitate admission of a limited number of German Jewish children.[15] A few months later, GJCA leaders met with Immigration and Naturalization Service (INS) commissioner Daniel MacCormack to work out details of the bonding procedure. Leading the delegation was GJCA executive secretary Cecilia Razovsky who, having been active in immigrant aid and resettlement work since the 1920s, was thoroughly acquainted with immigration law; a former child labor inspector for the U.S. Children's Bureau, she also enjoyed positive relationships with federal government officials.[16] In the end Commissioner MacCormack agreed to quota numbers for up to 250 boys and girls, to be placed with Jewish families approved by a U.S. Children's Bureau–certified social services agency. Foster parents would sign affidavits swearing to provide for the children's care and education until the age of twenty-one or until they married or entered military service.[17] The GJCA would also post a $500 bond for each child admitted to the United States, an additional guarantee that they would not become a public charge. Because corporations or organizations were legally barred from paying immigrants' transportation, parents or individual contributors purchased the children's passage to the United States. This initial agreement would set in motion an enduring public/private collaboration that continues into the twenty-first century to organize the nation's response to unaccompanied child migration.[18]

After more than a year of renegotiations and planning, a first group of nine Jewish children finally arrived in the United States. Nine boys aged eleven to fourteen processed by the Berlin Children's Emigration Office set sail from Cherbourg, arriving in New York on November 9 to join foster homes in the city and surrounding boroughs.[19] Despite the GJCA's best attempts at discretion, the boys' arrival provoked a burst of media attention, including coverage in the *New York Times* and *Washington Herald*. And as feared, the public response was immediately and overwhelmingly negative. Incensed by rumors that the American Jewish Congress planned to bring 20,000 children to the United States, John B. Trever, chairman of the nativist American Coalition of Patriotic, Civic and Fraternal Societies, called for a congressional investigation of purported violations of immigration law by the Labor Department. Adding fuel to the anti-Semitic racist fire, Trever further claimed the recently arrived boys came from communist families.[20]

The alarmed Department of Labor responded by reducing the total number of children authorized to enter the United States to 500, half of the number the GJCA hoped to sponsor.

The GJCA actually struggled to identify even this limited number of candidates for resettlement. Despite the increasing hardships of daily life in Germany, many Jewish parents resisted family separation, preferring to pursue emigration options together. Jewish social workers and women's associations also protested programs that separated children from their families; in November 1933, the German League of Jewish Women (*Jüdischer Frauenbund*) warned parents in a public statement about the negative psychological and social impacts for children who migrated on their own. Children themselves were profoundly ambivalent about youth evacuation schemes; although some were eager to try their luck in Palestine or America, many others refused to leave without their families.[21] GJCA representatives initially found only a small number of families willing to participate in their program—and only after convincing them that the evacuated children, upon reaching the age of majority, would secure affidavits to sponsor their parents' immigration.

In the United States the GJCA faced obstacles placing children. Fearing that a large-scale public appeal would provoke more anti-Semitic backlash, the program's directors communicated mostly through Jewish American media and community organization newsletters, appeals at synagogues, and via word of mouth. The suitability of foster families was evaluated according to the terms of the INS agreement. In accordance with child welfare laws, coreligionist homes had to be inspected by an approved child welfare agency to ensure they met standards established by the Children's Bureau. Each child must have their own bed, and no more than two children could share a bedroom. During the Great Depression, few American families enjoyed this imagined (white and middle-class) standard of living; even fewer Jewish American households met the prescribed standard. As a result, the GJCA frequently had to reject offers to care for refugee children because homes were judged inadequate. In other cases, approved foster families preferred to accept particular kinds of children, usually young, blond, blue-eyed girls instead of adolescent boys. Others withdrew their offer of a home after learning that the children were not available for adoption.

Even children with extended family in the United States proved difficult to place, since many recent immigrants' households failed to meet the prescribed standards or, if they did, were unwilling or unable to assume the economic burden of caring for the children of European relatives. A relatively more generous response came from the Orthodox Jewish community, whose commitment to charitable works among coreligionists inspired a greater number to offer shelter to refugee children without conditions; but since traditionally observant Jews were often poorer and had larger families—and therefore more crowded homes—few met the qualifications for foster homes.

The GJCA struggled from its inception with financial difficulties. By the end of 1934, less than two months after the first group of German Jewish children arrived in New York, GJCA fundraising efforts stalled. Unable to provide promised stipends to foster families and teetering on the verge of financial collapse, they requested logistical support and funding from the American Jewish Joint Distribution Committee (otherwise known as the "Joint"). The committee rejected their appeal, arguing that it was more cost effective to provide assistance to vulnerable German Jewish children in their homes—or to finance their passage to Palestine.[22] Signaling again the differences among ideologically and religiously diverse Jewish Americans over the best response to anti-Semitic violence in Nazi Germany, the Joint's refusal to support the GJCA dealt a significant blow. Lacking early and robust community support, they struggled to place 146 children between November 1934 and April 1935. By June of that year, having depleted their scarce remaining resources, the organization's American directors wired their German representatives to temporarily halt the evacuation of children.[23]

As the program faltered, conditions continued to worsen in Germany. In September 1935, the Nazi government passed the Nuremberg Laws, stripping Jews of German citizenship and forcing them out of state-regulated occupations. The new laws had a devastating economic and social impact on the already vulnerable and isolated Jewish community.[24] Despite this, between 1935 and 1937, the U.S. State Department successfully resisted every effort to liberalize immigration regulations, "quietly, selectively and without legislative approval," instructing its consuls to reduce the number of visas issued to as low as 10 percent of the authorized annual quota.[25] But because so few German Jews entered the United States between 1935 and 1937, the possibility remained—if the GJCA could find the means to reinitiate their program—that additional visas could be secured for children.

In 1937 under the leadership of Lotte Marcuse, an experienced social worker who immigrated to the United States from Germany in 1921, the GJCA did just that. After successfully petitioning the State Department for authorization to bring in five "non-Aryan" boys and girls per month, they resumed the search for foster homes. Soon the organization struggled with the same funding shortages and logistical issues they'd faced in 1934.

In addition, long-simmering tensions between the diverse worldviews and priorities of the GJCA's leaders, caseworkers, caregivers, and community supporters began to assert themselves.

The GJCA's leadership imagined evacuated children as permanent immigrants to the United States—rather than as temporary migrants who might eventually return to Europe or resettle in Palestine. They insisted that Jewish refugee children be housed to the extent possible outside of New York's Jewish enclaves, where they would live with American nuclear families, attend school with American children, and be given, according to Lotte Marcuse, "every opportunity to identify themselves with their new country which is theirs to stay."[26] This approach drove a wedge between the organization and some older children who preferred collective or semi-independent living arrangements, as well as between the GJCA and religiously observant and Zionist American Jews, who felt strongly that persecuted children belonged in group homes with others who shared their identity and experiences. Imagining the children's time in U.S. foster homes as a precursor to resettlement in Palestine, Zionist leaders advocated for a collective living environment in which Jewish children would be educated *within* and *for* their community, according to the socialist pedagogical model prevalent in interwar Europe. Group home life would also help preserve young people's linguistic and religious heritage, essential to the rebirth of the Jewish nation.[27]

Aware that selecting the most desirable ambassadors of the European Jewish community could generate greater public support for the GJCA and open the door for more Jewish children and adults behind them—Marcuse directed American caseworkers to pressure German Jewish social workers to send them the youngest, most attractive, intelligent, and "assimilable" children, and to warn them that children with physical disabilities or emotional or behavioral problems might be returned to Europe. This put the GJCA at odds with their German partners who prioritized the most at-risk children, especially teenage boys in danger of arrest, orphaned children, and Eastern European children whose parents had been deported.[28]

By early 1938, with fundraising efforts stalled, foster homes in short supply, and only 351 children under their care, the GJCA's demoralized and exhausted staff began to consider terminating the program.[29] Then the situation in Europe changed. On March 12, Hitler launched the *Anschluss*, followed immediately by mass arrests and seizure of Jewish property in the newly annexed Austrian territory; stripped of their citizenship and threatened with deportation or internment in the concentration camps at Buchenwald and Dachau, 50,000 Jews fled Austria over the next six months.[30] The takeover of the Sudetenland came next. The Nazis forced 20,000 Polish-origin Jewish residents—recently stripped of their citizenship by the Polish government—onto trains that dumped them across the border without possessions or travel documents.[31]

In Paris, seventeen-year-old Herschel Grynszpan—an unaccompanied refugee minor taken in by an impoverished aunt and uncle—learned his parents were among those stranded on the German-Polish border. On November 7, with his German reentry permit expired and his Polish passport invalidated, the now-stateless youth entered the German embassy and fatally shot Nazi consular officer Ernst vom Rath. This desperate act of protest had devastating consequences for Jews of all ages.[32] On November 9, using vom Rath's murder as a pretext, the Nazis unleashed a far-reaching campaign of anti-Jewish violence. During Kristallnacht ninety people were killed, $400 million worth of Jewish property was destroyed, and 30,000 Jewish men and boys were arrested and sent to concentration camps.[33]

FDR responded with his first unequivocal public statements support-ing Jewish refugees, condemning Nazi anti-Semitism, and recalling the U.S. ambassador from Germany, the only world leader to do so.[34] He also issued an executive order extending the visitors' visas of up to 15,000 German Jewish refugees by at least six months.[35] In a newly precarious position following the recent midterm elections—the Republicans gained eighty-one seats in the House and eight in the Senate—the president knew the congressional majority opposed liberalizing immigration.[36] Roosevelt, having concluded that war between Germany and the United States' European allies was inev-itable, had already begun angling for repeal of the Neutrality Laws block-ing American material assistance to belligerents, as well as for increases in defense spending. Calling for more robust measures to assist refugees prom-ised to inflame the public and antagonize Congress, imperiling urgent foreign policy objectives.[37]

European Jews' hopes of escaping the Reich with their families intact plummeted. German and Austrian parents, abandoning hopes of keeping their families together, found themselves competing for scarce spots in migration schemes that resettled children in the United States, Palestine, and Britain.[38] Thousands of applications flowed in each month to the GJCA Berlin office where a small, exhausted staff of Jewish social workers in fear for their own safety evaluated the urgency of each case, prioritizing adoles-cent boys whose release from concentration camps could be secured if they emigrated, as well as children whose parents had been interned or deported. At the same time, German Jewish parents flooded the GJCA office in

New York with letters begging visa priority for their own boys and girls over Austrian and Czech children.[39]

Deeply shaken by recent events, the leaders of the German Jewish Children's Aid aimed to rapidly transform a languishing child relocation effort into a child rescue operation. The GJCA successfully lobbied the Department of Labor to restart their program, receiving authorization in August to issue corporate affidavits for up to twenty Jewish children per month. They hit a roadblock in the State Department over visas. With administrative requirements eased for persecuted Jews fleeing the Nazis, the German quota—for the first time in a decade—was used up. Holding the line established in 1934, State Department officials again informed the GJCA that no special consideration would be granted to children; they must wait their turn for visas alongside adults. Efforts blocked even as need for their services skyrocketed, the GJCA evacuated only seventy-four children in 1938.[40]

Prospects for children worsened in 1939 when, by early spring, applications for visas at the U.S. consulate in Germany already exceeded the year's quota. GJCA's leaders watched helplessly as Western European and British coreligionists ramped up their efforts to save Jewish children. After Great Britain waived visa requirements to allow for the temporary admission of 5,000 Jewish children, the Kindertransport program, funded entirely by local Jewish agencies, quickly expanded to provide shelter to 20,000 refugee youth before the outbreak of war in September 1939.[41] U.S. newspapers filled with images of Jewish children being welcomed to safety in Britain were daily reminders to the GJCA of their own nation's indifference to the youngest victims of the Nazis.[42]

Kindertransport inspired other Americans to action. On December 18, 1938, Dr. Marion Kenworthy, a Jewish American psychiatrist and professor at the New York School of Social Work, hosted a meeting of individuals determined to launch a similar program in the United States. Among the guests in her home that evening was Clarence Pickett, the highly regarded director of the American Friends Service Committee, the Quaker relief organization known internationally for its work in Europe during World War I. Together the pair hatched an audacious interfaith campaign to pass legislation authorizing the admission of European refugee children to the United States, as well as developed a comprehensive plan for their selection, transportation, reception care, and foster care placement.[43]

Kenworthy and Pickett reached out to an influential circle of friends, political and philanthropic figures in New York and Washington, D.C., and received early and enthusiastic support from Secretary of Labor Perkins.[44]

Kenworthy also broached the possibility of a children's bill with Eleanor Roosevelt, a close personal friend, who discussed the idea with FDR. Offering his private support, the president gave Eleanor permission to contact Judge Justine Wise Polier, the daughter of Rabbi Stephen S. Wise, to reach out to members of both political parties to support the initiative. The president also asked Eleanor to communicate to Kenworthy and Pickett his support for their nonsectarian approach and encouraged them to seek backing from the nation's Catholic leaders and politicians which, he felt, would help neutralize public perceptions of the bill as part of a "Jewish" agenda.[45]

On January 9, 1939, fifty Catholic, Protestant, and Jewish religious leaders delivered a petition to the White House calling for the United States to open its doors to endangered European children. A month later Democratic Senator Robert Wagner, a progressive Catholic, and Republican Congresswoman Edith Nourse Rogers, a Protestant, sponsored identical bills in the U.S. House of Representatives and Senate. What became known as the Wagner-Rogers Bill proposed admission of 20,000 German refugee children under the age of fourteen per year, for a two-year period, as nonquota immigrants, to be cared for by private agencies and individuals at no expense to the federal government. The bill further stipulated that refugee children would be encouraged to return to Europe after their eighteenth birthday; if they remained in the United States, they would be counted against that year's German immigration quota.[46] Written by Clarence Pickett and others who'd met in Marion Kenworthy's home in December, the bill carefully referenced the dangers confronting "German refugee children," without reference to their religion— although it was clear most of the children admitted would, in fact, be Jewish.

On March 1, 1939, the Non-Sectarian Committee for German Refugee Children convened under the leadership of Clarence Pickett to launch their support campaign for the Wagner-Rogers Bill, the first serious attempt to liberalize the terms of the 1924 Immigration Act.[47] The bill represented a clear attack on the national origins quota system; however, supporters hoped the usual opponents of immigration exceptions might yield to endangered young people. And for a moment, it appeared that their bold strategy of organizing demands for immigration policy reform around this early articulation of at-risk children's "rights" to state just might work. During initial hearings before the joint subcommittee of the Senate and House Committees on Immigration on April 20, effusive expressions of sympathy for endangered German Jewish children provided a strong counterpoint to the anti-Semitic racism that buttressed American restrictionism.[48] Testimony in favor came from powerful and highly visible proponents, including

Immigration Commissioner James L. Houghteling and Katharine Lenroot, chief of the Children's Bureau. Actress Helen Hayes, an adoptive mother, also testified, prefiguring later celebrity involvement in refugee children's advocacy.

Public reactions to the early hearings also seemed cautiously positive. The American Federation of Labor, which had strenuously opposed easing immigration restrictions, declared themselves in favor of an age-based exception to the German quota, as economically inactive children would not add to the nation's existing unemployment problems. A number of leading Catholic clergy nationwide offered their support, as did many prominent Protestant faith leaders.[49] Although many Jewish groups, afraid of inflaming anti-Semitic backlash, avoided issuing public statements in favor of the Wagner-Rogers Bill—politically connected Jewish Americans privately communicated their support for the bill.

The bill received Eleanor Roosevelt's public endorsement. On February 13, for the first time in her six years as First Lady, Mrs. Roosevelt issued an official statement backing a piece of legislation.[50] "England, France, and the Scandinavian countries are taking their share of these children," the First Lady lauded, acknowledging inspiration by child rescue initiatives in Great Britain and Western Europe, "And I think we should, too."[51] Even former Republican president Herbert Hoover—ironically the author of the strict LPC clause (likely to become a public charge) and a Quaker with humanitarian credentials from leading famine relief efforts in Russia after World War I—endorsed the bill.

As positive momentum grew, the Non-Sectarian Committee began talks with the Children's Bureau over federal guidelines for the placement and care of German refugee children. Child welfare agencies and social workers across the country, eager to assert a role for their profession, issued their own statements of support for the Wagner-Rogers Bill and began working on plans for resettling refugee boys and girls. Paul Beisser, president of the Child Welfare League of America, pointed out that since twelve couples applied for every adoptable child in the United States, a humanitarian program to admit endangered Jewish children would also help satisfy the emotional needs of childless Americans.[52] Highlighting the blurred boundaries between the categories of foster and adoptive child in the 1930s, Beisser's comments nonetheless provided further impetus for the admission of Jewish refugee children to the United States, even as they foreshadowed the important role that the desires of American parents (and would-be parents) would play in later child rescue efforts.

Opposition to the bill also began to build. Senator Robert Reynolds (D-N.C.), an ardent restrictionist, denounced the legislation and urged his constituents to raise their own objections to easing immigration restrictions. In response the American Legion and the American Coalition of Patriotic, Civic and Fraternal Societies leapt into the fray, condemning the Wagner-Rogers Bill as an attempt to circumvent the law and demanding that overall immigration be decreased instead.[53] Rejecting the premise that children were uniquely vulnerable and, therefore, more deserving of asylum, opponents of the bill argued that breaching the quota for endangered boys and girls would open the floodgates to unrestricted immigration in the form of pressure to admit the children's families as nonquota immigrants.[54] Other critics attacked proponents' sympathy blatantly, stating the racist anti-Semitic warning that "20,000 charming children would all too soon grow into 20,000 ugly adults."[55]

Detractors raised a variety of objections grounded in children's needs. Some argued young boys and girls should not be separated from their parents; others asked that Americans' charitable impulses be directed toward the impoverished children of sharecroppers and migrant farmworkers.[56] Still others argued that if German children received special consideration, it would open the floodgates to untold numbers of endangered boys and girls around the world, and possibly to their parents.[57] The most critical detractors combined all of these objections, arguing that Jewish children represented a simultaneous ideological, cultural, and racial threat to the nation. Anti-immigration activist Alice Waters testified to that effect to Congress, declaring that "no society ... can successfully assume the tremendous responsibility of fostering thousands of motherless, embittered, persecuted children of undesirable foreigners and expect to convert these embattled souls into loyal, loving American citizens. ... If these so-called innocent, helpless children are admitted as refugees into America, I am sure they will become the leaders of revolt and deprive my children of their right to worship God, of free speech, and of life, liberty and the pursuit of happiness."[58]

Waters' argument—in effect, that traumas of displacement and lack of maternal care would convert Jewish refugee youth into sociopaths—obscured the fact that U.S. immigration law barred them from immigrating with their families, creating the need for legislation to separate 20,000 children from their parents to ensure their survival.

Opposition to the Wagner-Rogers Bill continued to mount. By spring of 1939, a *Fortune* poll revealed that 83 percent of Americans continued to oppose any increase in quotas, even for children.[59] Front page news of the

MS *St. Louis*, a ship carrying Jewish refugees turned away in Havana and now en route to the United States, stimulated new public demands for additional immigration restrictions. When the House Committee on Immigration called for additional hearings in May, INS officials who initially supported the bill now kept mum.[60]

As hopes for the Wagner-Rogers Bill dimmed, Jewish Americans desperately searched for other ways to rescue coreligionist children. In January 1939, lawyer Gilbert Kraus, representing the Philadelphia chapter of the Jewish fraternal order B'rith Sholom, arranged a meeting with Assistant Secretary of State George Messersmith to request visas for fifty European Jewish children. The order had just built a large, spacious house, complete with dining hall, swimming pool, and infirmary, in Collegeville, Pennsylvania, where it was "ready to provide a home and education" for the children. Kraus explained wealthy lodge members would supply individual affidavits of support to fulfill the law's public charge requirement. The order also possessed "ample private funds to provide transportation of the children from Germany to Philadelphia."[61] Unmoved, Messersmith insisted that the number of would-be German emigrants already exhausted the annual quota; no special priority could fast-track the children.

Kraus persistently searched for a way forward within (or around) the law, finally settling on a course of action: he would request that children be issued "dead-number visas" gone unused in the previous year and which could potentially be carried over. He and his wife Eleanor made arrangements to travel to Germany, bypassing unhelpful State Department officials in Washington, D.C., altogether to deal directly with the consular officials holding the last word on the children's fate. News of the Krauses' trip provoked alarm from some American Jews, who feared that it would provoke more anti-Semitic feelings, inflamed by prolonged debate over the Wagner-Rogers Bill. Frustrated advocates of the GJCA, whose efforts had been blocked since mid-1938, wrote to Kraus and to high-ranking officials in the State Department objecting to the B'rith Sholom child evacuation scheme as a reckless foray into an area properly left to child welfare professionals. One letter to Assistant Secretary of State Messersmith claimed the Krauses' effort was harmful "to those agencies which are properly qualified to do this work" and already "engaged in trying to bring children to this country." Discrediting the Krauses' voyage as a media stunt, the letter's author insisted that it would only generate "sensational publicity on the part of outsiders" that "would make trouble for all."[62]

Undeterred, Gilbert and Eleanor Kraus set sail for Europe in the spring of 1939, traveling from Berlin to Vienna to identify candidates for emigration.

Mr. and Mrs. Kraus and their foster charges aboard the SS *President Harding*.
Courtesy of the United States Holocaust Memorial Museum.

They returned to Berlin with fifty children in tow and applied for visas at the U.S. consul. Incredibly, Gilbert Kraus's gamble paid off: all fifty Austrian children received visas for the United States. Setting sail aboard the SS *President Harding*, the Krauses and their charges arrived in New York on June 3, 1939. By September, B'rith Sholom's members had found foster homes for all fifty children.[63]

The Krauses' successful mission, however, came at a cost; it reinforced tensions between Jewish refugee advocates over the best means of assisting European coreligionists, and it also inflamed rivalries between private philanthropists and the Jewish child welfare organizations that insisted their professional expertise was essential to children's successful resettlement. This brief but bitter turf battle reflected conflicts between individual efforts and the interests of child welfare professionals to regulate the resettlement of unaccompanied refugee minors that would shape other child migration schemes in the postwar years.

As predicted, media coverage of the Krauses' trip to Germany spurred an uproar among the Wagner-Rogers Bill's opponents. Desperate to avoid negative publicity that could finally destroy the legislation's failing chances, a spokesman for the Non-Sectarian Committee for German Refugee Children dismissed B'rith Sholom's child-saving mission as "absurd" and denounced the Philadelphia lodge for "creating the impression that Jews thought they could circumvent immigration law with money and influence."[64] But the damage had already been done. With the tide turning against the bill, the Senate Committee on Immigration proposed amending the legislation to give the 20,000 refugee children preferential admission as quota immigrants. Senator Robert Reynolds—seizing the opportunity to use the children as a pawn in his crusade to further restrict immigration—offered to support the bill in exchange for a five-year freeze on all quota immigration. Both compromises promised the admission of a small group of young people at the expense of an already highly limited number of adult refugees. For most of the bill's supporters, both were morally unacceptable.

In a last-ditch effort to save the bill, Representative Caroline O'Day (D-N.Y.) begged FDR to make a show of public support. Once again, however, the president chose not to expend his overextended political capital on refugee advocacy. Preoccupied with the looming war in Europe and unwilling to jeopardize negotiations to weaken neutrality legislation to give him greater latitude to assist America's overseas allies, he refused to comment.[65] Senator Wagner, having failed to secure the president's endorsement, withdrew the Senate bill from consideration. The House version died in committee later that month when Congress adjourned for the summer.[66] The failure of the Wagner-Rogers Bill effectively ended American efforts, lasting from 1933 to 1939, to rescue the Third Reich's youngest victims.

Meanwhile, the Spanish Civil War (1936–39) had emerged as a new threat to European children. In the winter of 1937, after sustained air and land attacks by Franco's Nationalist Army in the *País Vasco*, the autonomous Basque Country's president José Aguirre moved to evacuate noncombatant women, children, and the elderly to France.[67] Then, in April 1937, Nationalist forces joined the German Luftwaffe to bomb Gernika, viciously attacking the small Basque town's civilian population. Newspapers around the world carried images of the carnage. The Republic's supporters raised their voices, demanding the international community put aside ideological differences to aid the Basques.[68]

Supporters in the United States faced similar challenges as the GJCA. Sentiment among Americans was mixed; even those who supported the political values and reformist agenda of the Republic leaned toward maintaining distance from European conflicts.[69] Many conservatives, including leading Catholic clergy and political and civic leaders, praised Franco for restoring traditional values and defended the Nationalist cause as a war against the international forces of communism.[70] High-ranking anti-communist leaders in the State Department, Congress, and the FBI saw Communists and Social-ists in the Republic's governing coalition—as well as in U.S. Spanish Civil War aid committees—as proof of the Republican cause's illegitimacy.[71] Anx-ious to maintain the support of Catholic voters and aware of the strength of isolationist and anti-communist voices in his government, President Roo-sevelt put aside personal sympathy for the Republic and announced the United States would remain neutral in the Spanish Civil War.[72]

Concerned Americans once again looked on as European nations responded with help for Basque children. France, Belgium, Switzerland, Holland, Denmark, Sweden, Norway, Mexico, Czechoslovakia, and the USSR offered shelter to refugee boys and girls.[73] Tens of thousands of Basque parents heeded their government's urging to send their children abroad.[74]

Eager to participate in this multinational child-saving project, a newly formed committee of progressive and socialist intellectuals, journalists, and labor activists formed the American Board of Guardians for Basque Refugee Children of New York.[75] Spokesperson Gardner Jackson announced to the media that a child evacuation plan was *"now under consideration"* [italics in original] by the State Department.[76] Based upon "assurances . . . received from State Department officials that no obstacles would be placed in the way of speedy action on an application for visas" at the Bilbao consul, Jack-son continued, the board had chartered the children's passage to New York for arrival on June 19, 1937.[77] But Undersecretary of State Benjamin Sumner Welles refused to confirm any State Department discussions with the board. Maintaining the Spanish quota for 1937 was full, he conceded that State possessed "some discretion to grant six-month visitors' visas to otherwise eligible entrants,"[78] while giving no indication he was considering doing so.

Media coverage, as with the GJCA, spurred both public interest and back-lash. The Board of Guardians leadership included a number of journalists, including nationally celebrated *Tribune* columnist Dorothy Thompson, who reached out to East Coast reporters about visas for the children. Media lead-ers in New York and Washington, D.C., tended toward pro-Republican senti-ments;[79] banking on sympathy for Basque children, the board may have been using their privileged access to generate support. Stories about the proposed program moved from the middle to the front pages of national newspapers, raising a modest swell of popular enthusiasm and, among conservative Irish Catholics in Massachusetts, a "storm of protest." Led by anti-communist clergy, they denounced the Board of Guardians as leftist radicals "operating behind prominent persons as a 'front.'" The Knights of Columbus and the

League of Catholic Women similarly condemned the board's child-saving efforts as "communistic" and "propagandistic."[80]

Boston's powerful Cardinal William O'Connell took the lead in reframing Catholic opposition as concern for the children's best interests. Characterizing the Board of Guardians' plan as "ill advised," he argued the children would be unhappy in the United States, "a land so far from home, where the people speak a different language." Further, it was unnecessary, since "other means of relief so readily suggest[ed] themselves;" the children could easily be evacuated to the Basque territories of southern France where thousands of their countrymen and women had already taken shelter.[81] Irish Catholic politicians and community leaders echoed the cardinal's arguments. Joseph A. Cahalan, president of the Massachusetts Catholic Order of Foresters, telegrammed FDR directly to advise the children would be "better off" in French Basque territory where "their own people" could care for them.[82] Emphasizing refugee children's linguistic and cultural distinctiveness represented the Basque people as alien and unfamiliar, inhibiting American Catholics' ability to empathize with their suffering and constructing their endangered sons and daughters as someone else's problem.

It may appear surprising that Irish Americans in the 1930s should feel such little obligation toward a group of endangered Catholic children. Religious identity remained an important marker of identity and faith-based organizations managed most humanitarian and refugee aid. Catholic dismissals contrasted strongly with the attitude of American Jews who, although divided in their vision for child evacuation programs, generally supported efforts to rescue Jewish children fleeing Germany. The failure of intra-Catholic solidarity was linked to the distinct racial position occupied by members of both faith communities in the 1930s. Whereas "Jewishness" continues to be understood as both a religious and a racial identity, to be an American Catholic has always meant belonging to a multiethnic rather than pan-ethnic faith community, one that well into the 1960s continued to worship in ethnically distinct "national" parishes.[83] Even during the anti-Catholic fervor of the mid-1800s, a shared religious identity never bridged the racial divide between European, Hispanic/Latino, African, and Native American Catholics. By the 1930s, as Southeastern European immigrants became more fully accepted as "white," the distance between Euro-American Catholics and their coreligionists of color had only widened.[84]

Anti-Mexican sentiment during the Great Depression further reinforced the difference between white Americans and "Spanish" people—a racialized designation that at the time encompassed all U.S. residents of Hispanic and Latin American origin, seeing them as both foreign and racially inferior due to their Iberian, Indigenous, and African heritage. In this context, recently whitened Irish American Catholics may have been particularly predisposed to draw stark lines between themselves and the still imagined as nonwhite "Spanish" Catholics.[85] Despite Basques' unique linguistic and cultural heritage and their deeply ingrained sense of difference from other Spaniards, most Depression-era Americans, including Catholics, imagined them as "Spanish."[86]

As Catholic opposition to the admission of Basque children mounted, a showdown between the American Board of Guardians for Basque Refugee Children and the State Department seemed imminent. On June 25, under mounting political pressure, Eleanor Roosevelt withdrew her support, conceding that perhaps—as Cardinal O'Connell had insisted—it was "not such a good idea" to bring the children to the United States, "so far away from their homeland." The president similarly declined—as he did with the Wagner-Rogers Bill—to endorse the board's efforts. The same day, having finally received applications for the Basque children's visas, the State Department denied admission for all Basque refugee children.[87] The *New York Times* reported tersely that "the application for temporary visas for 500 Basque Children . . . has been held up by technical restrictions in Washington."[88] Belying their earlier professions of concern for the Basque children's well-being, the Catholic media wasted no time celebrating the Board of Guardians' demise. The board itself would quickly fade into obscurity, their brief moment in the media spotlight coming to an end only a month after it began. There is no evidence to suggest that board members engaged in future activities on behalf of Basque children overseas, choosing instead, as American Catholics had demanded, to leave them in the hands of "their own people." Their sudden disappearance lends unfortunate credence to suspicions that their intentions had not, in fact, been entirely humanitarian.

Between 1934 and 1938—with very little help from the American government—the German Jewish Children's Aid rescued 350 European Jewish children. The organization established the first model for a comprehensive program to identify, transport, and resettle unaccompanied refugee children in the United States. Winning the right to bring children into the United States under a corporate affidavit, they wrenched a concession from a recalcitrant federal bureaucracy that reflected the beginnings of a notion of children as possessing a unique age-based claim on refuge. Based on the notion that legal and legislative exceptions could and should be made to facilitate the admission of endangered children to the country, this unprecedented use of corporate affidavits as a way around existing visa eligibility requirements established a precedent for other agencies to bring in children under similar arrangements during the war and postwar years.

Through their close ties to the Roosevelt administration and links to the Children's Bureau and the Child Welfare League of America, the GJCA also initiated a new relationship between the U.S. government and refugee and child advocacy organizations, at a time when the state otherwise played no role in refugee resettlement. This new relationship, which created greater visibility and legitimacy for the women-led U.S. Children's Bureau and the field of social work in general, linked federal agencies with local child welfare organizations and individual caregivers in a nationwide network that made use of new "scientific" methods of casework, child psychoanalysis, and home studies to place refugee children in foster homes. This operational model and the principles upon which it rested—including the notion that unaccompanied child refugees had different needs than adult refugees and thus a greater claim on community (and later government) resources—provided the foundation upon which wartime and postwar children's evacuation initiatives would be built.

The organization's success would not have been possible without the active participation of its highly educated and politically connected patrons, backed by an ethnic voting bloc of significant value to FDR, who enjoyed close personal ties to the president. What's more, their willingness to operate discretely, exercising their influence behind the scenes and, with few exceptions, without involving the media, allowed the White House to support this first child evacuation program without risking a significant backlash. Constrained by American political leaders' isolationism, restrictionist immigration laws, and pervasive racist anti-Semitism, and weakened by internal conflicts grounded in American Jews' divergent understandings of the relationship between children, ethnic identity, and the future of the Jewish people, the GJCA struggled to sustain its efforts. Their paralysis in the face of heightening Nazi terror after 1938 sparked other initiatives, including the successful B'rith Sholom program to bring fifty children to the United States, as well as the much more ambitious but unsuccessful nonsectarian campaign to pass the Wagner-Rogers Bill. With their chances of securing more than a few visas for children definitively blocked by the failure of that legislation, the GJCA provided homes for only a few hundred children fleeing the Third Reich.

Efforts to bring endangered Basque children to the United States encountered many of the same obstacles. Opposed by the U.S. State Department, the American Board of Guardians for Basque Refugee Children's media campaign for support also provoked a rapid backlash by politically connected anti-communist Irish American Catholics. The Board of Guardians' activism on behalf of Basque refugee children proved short-lived; in the end, although as many as 25,000 unaccompanied Basque boys and girls would find shelter in refugee camps, group homes and foster families in France, Belgium, the United Kingdom, Mexico, and the USSR, none would be admitted to the United States.[89] Another group of Americans, however, would come to play an important role in the care of children displaced by the Spanish Civil War; by 1941, the American Friends Service Committee (AFSC)—led by Clarence Pickett, co-organizer of the campaign to pass the Wagner-Rogers Bill— would establish six colonies that housed as many as 600 Basque boys and girls in southern France. At the same time, the Foster Parents' Plan for Spanish Children (which would later become the Foster Parents' Plan for War Children) would be created to solicit money from long-distance American foster parents who would commit to a year's financial support to care for Spanish refugee children in France, removing them from concentration camps and placing them in Foster Parents' colony in Biarritz, France.[90] These much less-publicized efforts would help lay the foundation for later child-saving initiatives, as over time the AFSC and other American aid organizations shifted resources and expertise acquired through work with Spanish refugee children to assist boys and girls fleeing Nazi terror during World War II.

Given the geopolitical and domestic political obstacles working against admission of unaccompanied children to the United States in the 1930s, it is not surprising American children's advocates, despite their best intentions, ultimately played a minor role in world efforts to rescue children endangered by the rise of European fascism. Child-saving campaigns in FDR's America nonetheless helped create public awareness of the unique age-based vulnerabilities confronting children in conflict zones, raising for the first time the possibility of U.S. government involvement in facilitating programs to shelter children at risk in their homelands. In so doing, they would lay the groundwork for future efforts to assert children's unique claims on state protection and setting in motion what is by now almost a century-long—and still deeply geopolitically and racially fraught—public-private collaboration to bring endangered children to safety in the United States.

2

Collateral Humanitarianism

Child-Saving during World War II

Between 1940 and 1945, concerned Americans continued to improvise child evacuation programs to safeguard endangered children across the Atlantic. The nonsectarian coalition brought together to promote the Wagner-Rogers Bill regrouped and rebranded as the U.S. Committee for the Care of European Children (USCOM) to manage spontaneous efforts to bring British children to the United States following their nation's entry into the war. Buoyed by overwhelming public sympathy for the white Christian children endangered by Nazi air raids on London during the 1940–41 Blitz, USCOM's leaders established a new working relationship with the federal government to facilitate the children's admission. In doing so, they expanded on the corporate affidavit process pioneered by the German-Jewish Children's Aid (GJCA) and forged a new relationship between the Children's Bureau and voluntary organizations involved in caring for unaccompanied refugee minors. At the same time, USCOM's leaders remained deeply concerned with imperiled European Jewish children. Adopting a strategy of principled opportunism, they sought to use new policies, programs, and procedures developed by the state to accommodate British children to continue bringing a limited number of "continental" Jewish children to the United States.

After the British government halted the overseas evacuation of children, USCOM continued its efforts whenever and wherever possible. This required the committee to take a delicate approach to public relations, underlining the nonsectarian nature of its work to appeal to generalized sympathy for child victims of the war—and its new association with white British children—while obscuring the specific religious and ethnic origins of the rescued children. To maintain its privileged relationship with the U.S. government, USCOM also had to work within the confines of an extraordinarily strict immigration policy—sometimes having to publicly obscure its injustice and operate in ways that served foreign policy and domestic political interests at the expense of children's needs.

In order to harmonize their interests with the geopolitics of compassion underlying the FDR administration's approach to the burgeoning European refugee crisis, USCOM ended up practicing a kind of "collateral humanitarianism" that produced, in most cases, an ambivalent good for a small number of children, while excluding many of the most desperately needy children from the benefits of shelter and care in the United States. When contrasted with the hundreds of thousands of European Jewish children who died in death camps, the story of the small number of children USCOM brought to the country highlights the extent to which decisions about the fate of refugee minors continued during the war years to be decided in terms of geopolitical and domestic political objectives rather than humanitarian concern for boys and girls whose lives were imperiled by war.

After Nazi forces invaded Poland on September 1, 1939, and the United Kingdom and France declared war against Germany, the British government prepared for fighting on its soil by hastily organizing a program to evacuate children from English cities to the countryside.[1] By the end of the war, as many as 4 million young people—47 percent of all British school age children, along with hundreds or perhaps thousands of European Jewish refugee children who had been granted temporary asylum in Britain through the Kindertransport—had been relocated for some period of time to rural foster homes.[2] Forcing millions of young people into a jarringly intimate encounter with the intertwined religious and class-based prejudices rampant in prewar British society, the evacuation compounded the homesickness, loneliness, and pain of separation for working-class children and their parents. At the same time, more privileged urban Britons arranged privately to send their children to live with relatives or friends among the rural landed gentry. This emergence of a two-tier evacuation system further added to the latent class-based bitterness and resentment stirred up by the removal of children from their homes.[3] During the first few months following the declaration of war, as the anxiously anticipated outbreak of hostilities on British soil failed to arrive, as many as 80 percent of the first wave of child evacuees returned home.[4]

After the fall of Dunkirk in May 1940, when the evacuation of British troops from the European continent opened the way for a German invasion of France, England found itself newly vulnerable to a land-based invasion. Geoffrey Shakespeare, MP, was appointed head of the newly formed Children's Overseas Reception Board (CORB), tasked with coordinating and facilitating the government-sponsored evacuation of children to British overseas dominions and the United States. In the next two weeks, British parents registered more than 200,000 children for emigration, and 32,000 of those families expressed a preference to evacuate their children to the United States.[5] In response, U.S. ambassador Joseph P. Kennedy called for the establishment of an American Committee for the Evacuation of British Children, composed of American businessmen residing in London and chaired by Lawrence L. Tweedy, president of the U.S. Chamber of Commerce in London, to facilitate the selection and processing of children for departure for the United States.[6]

In the United States, Britain's entry into the war was quickly followed by public expressions of concern for the island's young people. As early as September 1939, letters and telegrams offering temporary American homes to British children began pouring into the British Foreign Office in Washington, D.C. Businesses and labor unions, fraternal organizations, and private schools also offered to provide shelter and safety for the children.[7] In Rochester, New York, the Eastman Kodak Company prepared homes for 150 "Kodakids," the children of workers from the company's London factory. *Washington Post* publisher Eugene Meyer offered to open his Virginia farm to a group of British nursery school students.[8] By June 1940, a Gallup Poll indicated that 58 percent of Americans believed that (white and Christian) British women and children should be permitted to seek asylum in the United States until the end of the war.[9]

While this support reflected genuine concern for endangered British citizens, it was also inseparably entangled with America's foreign policy and domestic political interests on the eve of the Second World War. Many Americans (and their Congress) were determined to stay out of the war. At the same time, they felt frustrated by strict neutrality laws that prevented the United States from providing more direct material support for the fight against Hitler. France's defeat in the summer of 1940 and news of the impending air battle for Britain only strengthened public desire to provide aid to the endangered island nation.[10] Americans' support for asylum represented both a tangible offer of assistance to families concerned for their survival and a symbolic gesture of support for the embattled British nation.

Race, religion, and national origin continued to powerfully shape American humanitarian sentiment. Enthusiasm for the evacuation of British citizens contrasted sharply with public opinion over the rescue of endangered Basque and European Jewish children, and despite long U.S. missionary record in the East, no corresponding campaign emerged to offer American homes to the hundreds of thousands of children imperiled by the Japanese war against China.[11] Letters from prospective American foster parents revealed how their racialized identification with the white Anglo-Saxon Protestant majority in the United Kingdom was crucial to their support of the overseas evacuation program. For example, Mary Fitzpatrick of San Francisco offered to open her home to a "healthy, intelligent" English child of a "good hereditary background," while other writers, primarily from middle-class Anglo-origin families in Massachusetts, New York, and Ohio, extended their hospitality to British children of "pure stock."[12]

Asserting cultural and class ties to the British elite also appears to have motivated some more privileged Americans to support the evacuation of British children to the United States. The headmaster of the New York Cambridge Tutoring School—likely named for the renowned British university—wrote directly to Prime Minister Winston Churchill, offering reduced tuition for one hundred British boys from the most cultured backgrounds, especially the "sons of army and navy officers and professionals."[13] At Yale University, a faculty committee determined to save "at least some of the children of the intellectuals before the storm breaks" secured 300 offers of homes for Oxford and Cambridge faculty members' children. Cambridge ultimately declined, citing parents' fears that participation might be seen as unfair class privilege and as evidence of a lack of patriotic resolve.[14]

The complex range of motives underlying American support for the evacuation of British children sheds light on both the similarities and differences between the ways that British and European Jewish children were imagined in the United States in 1940. Public discourse in the years leading up to the war tended to de-emphasize the unique age-based identities and vulnerabilities of Jewish boys and girls, framing them instead as representatives of the Semitic race. In contrast, U.S. leaders and the media regularly depicted British children as innocent victims of the war whose tender years entitled them to special sympathy and concern—*and* as symbolic representatives of their embattled (white) nation. In neither case, however, were children's claims on asylum evaluated primarily in terms of their individual circumstances. Sympathy for British children remained closely linked to Americans' admiration for and identification with their Anglo-Saxon mothers and fathers—who were also imagined as desirable immigrants and were eligible under the undersubscribed British quota. American opposition to the admission of Jewish refugee children similarly turned upon the children's relationship to their parents; however, in this case, this association served as a barrier to their admission, inasmuch as it was widely understood that offering a safe haven to child victims of Nazism would draw attention to their racially undesirable parents' equally pressing need for asylum.

By June 1940, efforts by a determined network of European organizations and individuals to save European Jewish children from the Nazis had increased—as had Americans' growing preoccupation with the impending threat to the United Kingdom's youngest subjects.[15] Observing the rapid proliferation of local committees offering American foster homes to British boys and girls, leading members of the Non-Sectarian Committee for German Refugee Children, led by executive secretary of the American Friends Service Committee Clarence Pickett and Jewish American professor of social work Marion Kenworthy, intuited that the United Kingdom's impending entrance into hostilities represented both a crisis and opportunity. Concerned over an uncoordinated and unregulated arrival of British boys and girls to the United States, they recognized the need to immediately establish a national organization to oversee foster home placements and provide for contingencies and disruptions in the children's care.

This was an unprecedented proposition; as of the 1930s, needy domestic children were provided for through a haphazard tangle of local arrangements run by religious associations and charities, public authorities, and individuals and families.[16] The members of the now dormant Non-Sectarian Committee, by virtue of their professional expertise, prominence within national refugee advocacy and child welfare circles, and close relationships with a network of high-ranking government officials, were uniquely prepared for the task. Dr. Kenworthy and Pickett invited representatives from the American Friends Service Committee and the German-Jewish Children's Aid, along with delegates from national child welfare agencies and local British child-saving committees, to a historic July 19, 1940, meeting at First Lady Eleanor Roosevelt's New York City home.

The assembly established a new committee to provide national leadership for the evacuation of British children to the United States, as well as: "obtain and provide lawful refuge and asylum in the United States or elsewhere for children who desire or are required to depart from European countries because of war, political or social conditions, racial or religious intolerance of the opinions held by them or their parents or other relatives; to furnish financial aid or assistance to individuals, groups, corporations, organizations, religious bodies, governments, and governmental agencies of all kinds, domestic and foreign, in obtaining or providing such asylum and refuge, and in selecting, caring for and supporting the children."[17]

The United States Committee for the Care of European Children articles of incorporation made clear the founders' expansive vision of the committee as a vehicle not only for overseeing the placement of British children in American foster homes but also as a means of reinitiating efforts, through "all means . . . permitted by applicable law," to rescue imperiled European Jewish children.[18] The choice of using "European" rather than "British" in the committee's name marked a similarly strategic choice. To reestablish their leadership of American child-saving efforts, founding committee members temporarily redirected energy away from rescuing endangered Jewish boys and girls and toward the more immediately feasible goal of evacuating British children to the United States. Framing their committee's concern for all European children as a response to wartime dangers and deprivation, irrespective of religious affiliation, they sought to shift an anti-Semitic public toward supporting the effort to rescue any and all imperiled children in the war zone. This approach enabled the creation of a platform from which efforts to rescue Jewish children from the war zones might be reinvigorated.[19]

USCOM's founders recruited a highly visible and emphatically nonsectarian coalition of religious, business, academic, philanthropic, and political leaders to participate on the committee. After inviting Eleanor Roosevelt to serve as "honorary president," they appointed Chicago department store magnate Marshall Field to the roles of acting president and spokesman. Prominent Jewish Americans—including Albert Einstein, Zionist Reform Rabbi Stephen S. Wise, and labor activist Dorothy Bellanca, who also served on the national Maternal and Child Welfare Committee convened by Secretary of Labor Frances Perkins—joined the committee. Episcopal bishop Reverend Henry St. George Tucker and Presbyterian minister Reverend Samuel McCrea Cavert, who also served on the new President's Advisory Committee on Political Refugees, were members, as was Catholic Cardinal Francis Spellman. Other members included philanthropist John D. Rockefeller III; chairman of the board of Chase National Bank Winthrop W. Aldrich (whom FDR would appoint president of the National War Fund); newspaper baron William Randolph Hearst; University of Chicago president Robert Maynard Hutchins; General John J. Pershing; New York governor Herbert Lehman; and actress Helen Hayes.[20]

With its membership set, USCOM announced its formation to the media on June 20, 1940. Seeking to immediately assert the committee's national leadership role, President Marshall Field explained that USCOM's executive board had come together in response to "the imperative demand from the American people for a unified policy and plan to meet the present emergency" occasioned by the impending German attack on Britain. Anticipating objections from individuals and child welfare organizations already launching local efforts to place British children in U.S. homes, as well as critics insisting America's poor children come first, Field continued:

> Many of us have been closely identified with efforts to better the situation of American children throughout the country. We have undertaken this added responsibility in the deep conviction that the mobilizing of the spontaneous desire to rescue at least some of Europe's children from the fearful fate of bombs and shell fire that awaits them can in no way detract from or diminish efforts to meet the needs of American youth. There must be no slackening of the services to American children—governmental and private—which must be maintained and expanded wherever they are inadequate.[21]

Highlighting committee members' leading role and ongoing commitment in domestic child welfare, USCOM's statement undercut objections while simultaneously reinforcing the legitimacy of the child welfare profession and its claims on government and private resources. They next worked to co-opt rival interests by recruiting experienced child welfare workers from a range of leading agencies to staff their newly established New York City headquarters. USCOM's board invited Sybil Foster, director of the Foster Home program at the New York Children's Aid Society and a former director of the Child Welfare League, to serve as a founding member on the Subcommittee on Child Welfare, thereby ensuring a collegial relationship between USCOM and the nation's most influential association of child welfare professionals.[22]

USCOM's carefully crafted media statements also worked to co-opt the social capital accrued from earlier Jewish child refugee advocacy while simultaneously obscuring its relationship to those efforts. Acknowledging that the Non-Sectarian Foundation for Refugee Children had "placed its resources and personnel at the disposal of the Committee, and become an integral part of it," USCOM's spokespersons affirmed that the "organization and individuals who have joined together in this movement represent a cross section of all religious faiths in this country. This is in the truest sense a nonsectarian, nonpartisan movement inspired solely by the desire to rescue children—whoever they may be and wherever they may be—from disaster by all practicable means at our disposal."[23]

From USCOM's inception, the committee employed a nuanced public relations strategy to facilitate the consolidation of a range of privately initiated British child evacuation schemes under its umbrella, while simultaneously reframing them as a broadly conceived effort to rescue all endangered European children. This strategy quickly proved effective. On June 24, 1940, in a public gesture that recognized the now four-day-old committee as the leading national proponent of British child evacuation, the Child Welfare League voted its "full cooperation with the United States Committee" and offered "the services of the League" to support its work.[24] The public similarly signaled its support by flooding USCOM's headquarters with an "avalanche" of letters offering shelter and assistance for British children.[25]

USCOM turned next to the logistical challenges of bringing an undetermined number of British boys and girls to America. The situation looked promising; the United Kingdom's immigration quota of 6,500 per month was generous and largely unused, providing a surplus of available visas. Since they were intended for permanent residents, however, the corresponding application process was too lengthy and complex for an emergency evacuation program. Moreover, as USCOM's leaders had learned through previous Jewish child rescue efforts, U.S. law made no statutory provision for the immigration of unaccompanied minors.[26]

Following the precedent established by GJCA in 1934, USCOM's leaders approached the Departments of State and Justice to negotiate terms for expediting the issuance of visas to unaccompanied British children. Emboldened by the participation of the British embassy and First Lady Eleanor Roosevelt in the negotiations and banking on the leverage afforded by outpourings of public support for their proposed efforts, an USCOM spokesperson informed the *New York Times* of the committee's hope that "some restrictions may be relaxed a little."[27] On July 13, 1940, following swift but intensive consultations between USCOM, the British Foreign Office, and representatives of the Departments of State and Justice, the attorney general authorized the "adoption of simplified procedures which [would] make possible the admission of refugee children from the war zones."[28]

Adapting and expanding procedures developed through years of negotiation with the GJCA, the attorney general agreed to issue nonquota visitor's visas to an unspecified number of children selected by USCOM and pledged to cut "formalities in the issuance of visas and other travel papers . . . to the legal minimum." In return USCOM provided the U.S. government with a "greatly simplified" corporate affidavit guaranteeing the proper care of the children while in the United States and ensuring they would not become a public charge. To support the affidavit, USCOM established a "reserve fund" into which the organization would deposit fifty dollars per child to cover emergencies or contingencies arising while the child was under USCOM care.[29]

The attorney general's order authorizing USCOM to bring children to the United States made no reference to children's national origins or religious identities, stating only that the State Department would provide visitor's visas to refugee children in the war zone "upon a showing of intention that they shall return home upon the termination of hostilities." This nondiscriminatory language represented a limited strategic victory for USCOM's leaders, who needed to shape the terms of the new migration procedure as inclusively as possible. The provision requiring intent to return to the home country revealed a clear bias on the part of Departments of State and Justice officials *for* the admission of British children—and *against* the admission of their Jewish peers.

In July 1940 the State Department agreed to issue nonquota visitor's visas to USCOM-sponsored British children under sixteen years of age without requiring that they demonstrate the ability and intent to return home—an eventuality that, given Hitler's advance across the continent, was far from certain. At the same time, holding firm to restrictions imposed on GJCA efforts in the 1930s, the State Department declared that most European Jewish refugee children remained ineligible for visitor's visas, on the basis that *they* would likely be unable to return home at the end of hostilities. Further, whereas the GJCA's migration agreement required private individuals to fund children's travel to the United States, in order "to facilitate evacuation of children regardless of their financial circumstances," USCOM children's transportation costs could be covered by "a foreign government or non-profit corporation." Facilitating the British government's goal of creating a public evacuation program in order to ease class-based resentments sparked by the privately funded overseas relocation of elite children, this modification of U.S. immigration law reflected the official desire to maintain strong Anglo-American relations rather than concern for the best interests of endangered children.[30] It also speaks to the extent to which U.S. government officials were willing to bend existing immigration law to admit white Christian British children—while withholding similar accommodations for Jewish boys and girls.

USCOM's child evacuation plans must also be understood in relation to new executive branch foreign policy considerations emerging from the

United States' shifting position vis-à-vis the European war. Although FDR maintained an official policy of neutrality, after the stunning Nazi victories in Western Europe during spring 1940, he privately concluded U.S. military aid would be essential to save European democracy.[31] Not coincidentally, FDR simultaneously expressed support for the evacuation of British children to the United States.[32] In doing so, he strategically deployed the geopolitics of compassion in the service of his evolving foreign policy agenda. With U.S. direct military aid blocked by neutrality laws, a presidential endorsement for plans to bring British boys and girls to America—which required neither federal funding nor congressional approval—lent quasi-official character to USCOM and provided the U.S. government with a cost-free demonstration of solidarity with Britain. In addition, official support for the committee reinforced the United States' international reputation as a sanctuary for asylum seekers, while allowing the federal government a degree of control over the placement of foreign children with American foster families. Further, USCOM's efforts might have brought home to Americans the horrors of the war, fostering awareness of the urgent need for direct U.S. involvement in the fight against Nazism. Presidential support for USCOM thus sought to harness the political capital generated by Americans' concern for white Christian British children in the service of U.S. foreign policy objectives.

The modification of immigration procedures, FDR's endorsement of the committee, and the attorney general's order barring other organizations from using visitor's visas for endangered children without prior federal authorization, converted USCOM into a quasi-official government agency. The committee's status rose further with an attorney general order requiring local childcare agencies recruiting coreligionist foster homes to be licensed by the Children's Bureau and provide regular reports to USCOM.[33] To facilitate a close relationship between the two organizations, three Children's Bureau staff, including Delinquency Division director Elsa Castendyck, a strong proponent of international child evacuation efforts, were assigned to work directly with USCOM.[34]

Collaborating with USCOM provided the Children's Bureau with an unprecedented opportunity. The bureau was burdened by public perceptions of its mission as peripheral to the national interest and of "paraprofessional" social workers as unwarranted state appropriation of caretaking responsibilities rightfully belonging to women and private charities.[35] The USCOM-Children's Bureau partnership served to institutionalize the expectation of federal government oversight over the placement of foreign children in U.S. foster homes—a normative shift that laid the groundwork for a growing federal role in funding and regulating "modern" foster care programs.[36] After the United States entered the war, the Children's Bureau consciously drew upon the child-saving rhetoric popularized by USCOM in its own campaigns to secure foster homes for a growing number of needy U.S. children, framing them as the nation's own "war orphans" and the provision of foster care as essential wartime service.[37] By the end of the war, these conjoined USCOM and Children's Bureau public relations campaigns would also cement emerging understandings of foster care and social work projects in general as a sphere in which ordinary Americans could participate in promoting the nation's foreign policy objectives.

As terms for British child evacuation were being worked out with the federal government, USCOM began to set up the international and domestic infrastructure necessary for the reception of children in the United States. In late June, guided by the U.S. embassy in London, the committee contacted the American Committee for the Evacuation of British Children, a group of expatriate businessmen in the United Kingdom organized at the Ambassador's request to assist consular staff with processing British children. They quickly reached an agreement whereby the American Committee assumed responsibility for selecting children for USCOM sponsorship and helping to expedite their visa applications; in return, USCOM designated the American Committee as their official affiliate in London and provided partial funding for their activities. By mid-July the American Committee had begun processing evacuation applications.[38]

On the home front, USCOM took steps to establish its own nationwide fundraising and infrastructure. Maneuvering to get in front of grassroots efforts, the committee took steps to delegate programmatic aspects of a national child-saving program to local councils of social agencies and gave municipal community chests jurisdiction over the "money angle." In coordination with the Children's Bureau, American Red Cross, National Community Chests and Councils, Inc., and state public welfare departments, USCOM sent letters on July 5, 1940, to hundreds of civic, business, and religious leaders across the U.S., requesting they establish USCOM-affiliated local committees to coordinate all activities in their region related to the evacuation of British children.[39] When wary local leaders asked about the race and religion of the refugee minors being brought to the United States, USCOM directives clarified they were "interested in all European children;" citing, however, the imminent threat of invasion in Britain as well as "communication and transportation difficulties" that impeded continental child-saving activities, USCOM emphasized that "immediate provision" of U.S. foster homes would be limited to boys and girls from the United Kingdom.[40] Reassured, private citizens organized more than 175 USCOM-affiliated local committees by the end of July, absorbing the majority of grassroots-organized child evacuation groups. These newly formed committees immediately began seeking suitable foster homes for as many as 50,000 British children by Labor Day.[41] They also launched local drives to support USCOM's national fundraising campaign with the goal of raising $5 million.[42]

Shifting circumstances across the Atlantic undermined USCOM's plans. By the end of June, the exploding demand for overseas evacuation opportunities had exacerbated political leaders' fears that the CORB program would prove harmful for both national morale and Britain's international reputation. The precipitous increase in vessels sunk by German U-boats during the summer of 1940 made transatlantic travel more dangerous.[43] In addition prominent child welfare advocates, including Anna Freud, emphasized the psychological risks of separating children from their mothers, warning that these "artificial war orphans" might be prone to depression and "retardation," as well as antisocial tendencies later in life.[44] On July 1, with opposition mounting, Churchill's War Cabinet directed Geoffrey Shakespeare, MP, to issue a press release warning parents about the difficulties and dangers associated with overseas evacuation and to emphasize that "any idea of mass migration is absolutely contrary to the wishes of the Government."[45] Nine days later, after the British Admiralty withdrew naval protection for ships carrying children, the War Cabinet declared government-sponsored evacuation efforts suspended.[46]

Justin R. Weddell, executive chairman of the American Committee for the Evacuation of British Children, remained undeterred. On July 16, 1940, he cabled USCOM's leadership that "ample funds [could still] be obtained from private sources" to cover the cost of transporting "poor children and European refugee children" to the United States. The committee in London was "proceeding full speed" in processing children for evacuation.[47] The following day Marshall Field announced to the media that in the "absence of affirmative disapproval of the British government," USCOM was "prepared to receive children from the British Isles whose parents or guardians [were] willing to assume the responsibility of having such children cross the Atlantic Ocean on ships which may or may not be convoyed." USCOM remained poised to offer "the hospitality of this country to the children when they arrive here and is ready to give full assurance of their proper care while in the United States."[48]

Despite USCOM's resoluteness, newspapers around the country reported it was "generally agreed that a plan will have to be scrapped completely unless

Collateral Humanitarianism

American ships [were made] available."[49] Americans sprang into action. A Women's Mercy Ship Committee was formed, with Mrs. Harold T. Pulsifer of East Hartwell, Maine, as chair. Taking out full page ads in leading newspapers, they called on the government to immediately provide "mercy ships" to carry British children to safety in the United States.[50] Public demand for congressional action quickly escalated. FDR responded, expressing support for legislation authorizing U.S. ships to transport British children. Then on July 24, Congressman Thomas C. Hennings Jr. (D-Mo.) introduced a bill to amend the 1939 Neutrality Act to allow U.S. ships possessing safe-conduct guarantees to evacuate children from British ports.

The media offered its overwhelming support. In a July 24 op-ed that appeared in newspapers across the country, celebrated *Washington Post* columnist Raymond Clapper proposed that the newly built SS *America*, "the finest ocean liner ever built in the United States," be put to use transporting evacuees. Anticipating detractors' fears that the German sinking of a vessel carrying evacuated children would force the United States into declaring war, Clapper insisted—with a confidence as jarring as it was misplaced—"Hitler is no fool. He isn't dragging us into the war right now if he can help it."[51]

Representative John McDowell (R-Pa.) echoed these sentiments, arguing the Germans were "not interested in killing children." However, other legislators maintained that the evacuation scheme was a ruse designed to provoke a confrontation with Germany. Representative Samuel Dickstein (D-N.Y.) pointed out the selectivity of American concern for overseas children, arguing "we ought to take care of some of the children from Holland, Belgium, and Poland who are in the same condition." Others, including Representative John Charles Schafer (R-Wis.), framed their objections in domestic terms, reminding legislators of the pressing needs of vulnerable American children and suggesting that "people who really want to be helpful to children" might take in American orphans "who are now being cared for in institutions" paid for by "overburdened American taxpayers." Still others noted that if European parents did not survive the war or were unable to repatriate their sons and daughters, those children would become permanent immigrants to the United States.[52]

The British Home Office, USCOM, and a national media that overwhelmingly supported the Mercy Ships campaign, along with thousands of constituents eager to welcome child evacuees into their homes relentlessly pressured Congress to act. At the same time, growing domestic and international pressure for the United States to play a more active role defending European democracy motivated legislators, especially the frustrated

Dickstein who characterized American contributions to the war effort as "just talk" when it came to supporting the Hennings Mercy Ships legislation. Following a cursory voicing of reservations, the great majority of legislators ultimately voted in favor of the bill. Representative Dickstein summarized the legislative bodies' sentiment that the bill was simply "the right thing" to do.[53] On August 28, the Mercy Ships legislation—a vivid example of the geopolitics of compassion enacted—passed with overwhelming majorities and was quickly signed into law by FDR.

USCOM now anxiously awaited the arrival of its first children. In the interim private evacuations had continued. In late July 1940, 125 children of Oxford families (some accompanied by their mothers) reached Canada by ship before traveling by train to New Haven, Connecticut.[54] Galvanized by their arrival, USCOM continued to work through its London affiliates to secure space aboard British ships and coordinate with local branch committees to identify foster homes and financial sponsors for an untold number of children.[55]

In early August, USCOM secured passage aboard two British ships for 138 girls and boys, the first lot of a total of 861 children between ten and fourteen years old from the suburbs of London.[56] Selected as the most physically attractive, healthy, and intelligent among the aspiring evacuees, the excited and frightened children were met at the docks by CORB representatives, who exhorted them to think of themselves as emissaries of their besieged nation. Director Geoffrey Shakespeare urged the children to be obedient and well-mannered, saying: "If you behave well, people will say, 'What splendid children these are! We must do everything we can to help their parents win the war.'"[57] CORB representatives also instructed these and subsequent groups of children not to offend their American hosts by drawing unfavorable comparisons between the United States and Britain.[58] These pre-departure instructions communicated to children that the course of the war—and perhaps the United Kingdom's survival—rested upon their behavior away from home. For some boys and girls, the belief they could contribute to their nation's defense may have been a source of pride that gave meaning to their separation from their parents; it was, no less, a heavy psychological burden for children to bear.

The first USCOM children and their British escorts selected by the American Committee arrived in New York on August 21, 1940. They were taken to reception centers, which included the Gould Foundation for Underprivileged Children in the Bronx, the Seamen's Church hostel in Lower Manhattan, and the Guggenheim family estate on Long Island, New York.[59] After

Collateral Humanitarianism

undergoing a thorough medical checkup, the children were outfitted with clothing, toiletries, and medicines. Volunteer teachers offered lessons on U.S. history and culture; local residents hosted parties for the young evacuees, took them to movies and church services, and on sightseeing trips of the city. USCOM reception center staff and volunteers marveled at the children's reactions to meals served with milk and fresh fruit, both of which had become "a distinct luxury" in wartime Britain. They also noted the well-behaved children's expressions of "surprise and delight at many aspects of everyday life in the United States which seem commonplace to us: skyscrapers, the city noises, uncensored news, and lights." The younger children, accustomed to London's wartime blackouts, were especially "fascinated by New York after dark."[60]

After anything from a few days to several weeks of reception care, children were picked up by sponsors or traveled with escorts to their new foster homes, where they expected to remain throughout the war and for a "reasonable time thereafter."[61] They joined foster homes in 21 states and in Hawaii, with more than half in New York and Massachusetts; 105 children went to Connecticut, and 85 more to Ohio.[62] "Specified" children—known by name to their sponsors or traveling as part of a specifically requested group—made up the majority of the evacuees. In summer 1940, 84 children of employees of the Hoover Company in England were welcomed into the homes of Hoover employees in Canton, Ohio; 165 children of workers from the Kodak factory in Harrow, England, were placed with Kodak employees in Rochester, New York; and 47 children of employees of Warner Brothers' London offices joined the families of Warner Brothers employees in New York and California.[63]

USCOM placement officers matched "unspecified" children with host families, making assignments based on information provided on the affidavit and registration forms filled out by prospective sponsors. Reflecting the committee's normative assumptions about heterosexuality, class, and religion, the forms asked for husbands and wives' names, professions, and religious/denominational affiliations. Prospective host families could also record their preferences as to what kind(s) and how many children they were willing to host, specifying their gender, age range, religious affiliation, and nationality, as well as, in what was probably an oblique way of signaling racial, ethnic, and class identities, their "background."[64] USCOM's staff sought to adhere to "modern" social work practices that recommended placing foster children with parents of similar socio-economic backgrounds and "mental and personality levels," a broad category influenced by notions of race and ethnicity, class, gender, and sexuality, among other markers of identity.[65]

USCOM's placement model also prioritized placing children in families, rather than collective environments.[66] However, recognizing the long-standing middle-class British tradition of boarding school, the committee explained to local agents that "some school groups or refugee children [would] wish to keep their group entity." When feasible those wishes were respected, and especially when U.S. boarding schools offered free or highly reduced tuition for evacuee children.[67] Emphasizing the best interests of the individual child, the committee urged "particular attention . . . [when] selecting for each child the kind of home where he would be well cared for and content physically and spiritually."[68] This recognition of children's individual needs and wishes contrasted starkly with the GJCA policy of discouraging Jewish refugee children's desire for collective living arrangements. USCOM's distinct approach was based on the assumption that, unlike Jewish children, British child evacuees' stay in the United States would be temporary. But it may also be that the committee's staff implicitly understood white Anglo-Saxon Protestant children as less "foreign" and threatening than Jewish children—and, therefore, less in need of Americanization.

Most American foster families went to great lengths to welcome evacuated children. USCOM noted that "the American people want these guest children to have the protection they would hope for their own children in similar circumstances."[69] Communities took steps to ensure the inclusion of British children in local public schools. A number of state boards of education passed resolutions specifying that evacuees—though on visitor's visas—would be considered "legal residents of any district where the sponsors live." Public schooling could thus be provided to the guest children without charge "as for our own children."[70]

Moved by the plight of the "brave, well-mannered, disciplined refugees from unspeakable terror," many Americans felt deeply affirmed by the children's gratitude for their hospitality.[71] Others interpreted evacuees' excitement at the differences between the United Kingdom and the United States as proof of America's superior way of life. Jennie Haxton of the New York City Kindergarten Association noted approvingly that many USCOM children seemed "anxious to be and act like Americans." This inspired Ms. Haxton to ponder whether she and her fellow citizens "really appreciate this life that America offers us?"[72] Media accounts of USCOM children echoed this portrayal of evacuees' enthusiasm for all things American as both spontaneous and sincere. No public commentator appears to have contemplated that the children might have been warned to be on their best behavior—or urged to

Collateral Humanitarianism

ingratiate themselves with their host families and communities as a means of inspiring greater American support for the war effort.

Even when children tried to be on their best behavior, placements sometimes created confusion and even conflict in U.S. households. Many foster parents objected to the required home inspection to ensure compliance with the Children's Bureau standards. USCOM anticipated this potential point of conflict and advised local committees to explicitly address the details of home studies during preliminary interviews, but still many sponsors resisted what they considered an unwarranted violation of privacy.[73] Similarly, although USCOM policy made clear that evacuee children would be "subject to visitation and friendly supervision by the designated child welfare agency," some sponsors resented the committee's ongoing intrusion into their home life—especially those who viewed the new profession of social work and its almost-entirely female practitioners with suspicion.[74] Many host families were also unclear about the difference between foster care and adoption. Although USCOM informational materials emphasized the "adoption of British children outside the dominion of the British empire [was] forbidden by an Act of the British Parliament,"[75] this prohibition surprised and disappointed foster parents whose desire to grow their families played a role in the decision to take in a child evacuee.

As British children adjusted to life in U.S. families, USCOM encountered its first opportunities to assist endangered Jewish children. On August 19, 1940, the SS *Quanza* docked in New York, disembarking passengers with U.S. visas. The remaining eighty-six Jewish refugees, including five unaccompanied children, were turned away. After the group was denied entry in Mexico, American Jewish leaders—including GJCA founding members and USCOM affiliates Rabbi Stephen Wise and Cecilia Razovsky—lobbied First Lady Eleanor Roosevelt on their behalf. Their intercession proved successful when FDR, over Assistant Secretary of State Breckenridge Long's furious objections, instructed the State Department to issue visas to the refugees. The five unaccompanied children also received authorization to enter the United States under the USCOM affidavit. During the next several months, they collaborated with the Unitarian Service Committee (USC) to successfully petition the State Department for twenty-nine visas for children, mostly Polish and Jewish, in refugee camps in unoccupied France. These were among a small number of "continental" Jewish children entering the United States under committee sponsorship in 1940 and placed by the Hebrew Immigration Aid Society (HIAS) in foster homes.[76]

As the British evacuation scheme gained momentum, the Dutch ship *Volendam*, carrying 321 CORB-sponsored children as well as 20 others traveling under private arrangements, was torpedoed. The children were rescued and carried safely to shore in Scotland, but the incident provoked intense public reaction across the United Kingdom including calls to end overseas evacuation.[77] Then, on September 17, the SS *City of Benares*, carrying ninety CORB children bound for foster homes in Canada, was sunk by a German U-boat. Two hundred fifty-five crew members and passengers, including eighty-four children, drowned in the frigid Atlantic. Back in the United Kingdom, the Royal Air Force's recent victory over the Luftwaffe dramatically reduced fears of a German invasion. With public opinion turning definitively against overseas evacuation, Churchill called for the suspension of the CORB program.[78]

USCOM leaders attempted to downplay the tragedy of the *City of Benares*, arguing that overseas travel presented a much lower risk than remaining in Britain's besieged cities.[79] However, on October 3, 1940, publicly funded evacuations were suspended.[80] On the same day, more than 500 USCOM-sponsored children—the last large group of British evacuees to enter the United States—arrived in New York.[81] Two days later Marshall Field reluctantly announced USCOM was halting efforts to evacuate children from the British Isles. Their recently launched $5 million fundraising campaign was suspended, and 100 of 175 salaried employees were dismissed by the end of the week. The committee continued to operate on a much-reduced basis, overseeing the care of sponsored children and assisting the approximately 2,500 British children brought to the United States under private arrangements.[82]

USCOM's leaders remained unwilling to call it quits. Reviving the principled opportunism that inspired the committee's formation, they resolved to leverage their newfound political capital—a product of their national visibility and newly institutionalized relationship with the federal government—to rescue European children. Field reminded the media that USCOM's initial focus on British evacuees flowed from the committee's overarching mission to provide aid "in any way possible" to child evacuees "from the war-stricken countries." "Whether or not the war continues next year or thereafter," he maintained, "there will clearly be need for an indefinite period for an organization to handle the problems of children who are evacuees from Europe and the Committee will remain ready and willing to undertake that responsibility."[83] He encouraged disappointed local committees that had eagerly awaited the arrival of British children to "stand by" to assist other endangered boys and girls "as necessity arises."[84]

USCOM, in a strategic pivot, drew on ties with the American Friends Service Committee (USCOM cofounder Clarence Pickett was also the AFSC's executive secretary), which together with the Unitarian Service Committee was providing aid to Spanish Republican and European Jewish children in French refugee camps.[85] In February 1941, despite reservations about using its already limited resources, the AFSC agreed to work with USCOM "on a project basis" to evacuate one hundred children of Central European Jews deported to Nazi concentration camps, many of them living in homes operated by the Russian-French child welfare organization Oeuvre de Secours aux Enfants (OSE). The Quaker relief organization's local staff assumed responsibility for selecting candidates for evacuation and USCOM would secure visas for the children.[86]

This presented no small feat for the committee's dramatically reduced staff, especially since State Department officials remained resistant to offering accommodations to Jewish children.[87] Fortunately the government's approach to the refugee crisis had begun to shift—albeit slightly. In July 1940, as Nazi aggression were spreading across Western Europe, FDR had established the President's Advisory Committee on Political Refugees (PACPR), which had brought 2,000 "outstanding" Jewish scholars, artists, and scientists to the United States. The PACPR, despite its limited and elitist focus, represented the first official U.S. recognition of an obligation to give preferential admission to people fleeing persecution.[88] At the same time, the possibility that the war might displace tens of millions of people before its conclusion led the president and government leaders to acknowledge voluntary agencies' crucial role in mitigating the human costs of the conflict.[89] With its bargaining position thus enhanced and continued behind-the-scenes advocacy by the First Lady, USCOM successfully petitioned the State Department for quota visas for the first hundred children from unoccupied France in May 1941.[90]

USCOM's leadership also recognized the need for a communications strategy to maintain support for their efforts as they shifted their energies toward Jewish children. In a May 1941 bulletin *We Are Standing By*, the committee represented current efforts to rescue children from unoccupied France as a logical extension of British evacuation, encouraging their supporters to imagine the recent nationwide sympathy for white Anglo-Saxon Protestant boys and girls as reflective of a broader national concern for the well-being of all children. Acknowledging that more children coming from the United Kingdom to the United States was "unlikely in the near future," the bulletin affirmed there were still "thousands of parents abroad, both in England and on the Continent" who desired to "send their children to America for safety and protection." USCOM would thus "continue to explore the feasibility of the various plans suggested for bringing additional children to safety here."[91] The omission of further information about race, religion, or national origins strategically conflated future evacuees with the British boys and girls who preceded them. The text omitted mention of USCOM's collaboration with AFSC to resettle Jewish children in the United States and buried a brief note about the December 1940 arrival of a group of "children from unoccupied France" in the bulletin's appendix.[92] This deliberate vagueness about the scope and timing of USCOM's involvement with "continental" children further suggests the bulletin's authors wished to keep public attention on the committee's association with British children while framing Jewish child-saving efforts as a future possibility rather than an ongoing commitment.

When most USCOM's supporters received *We Are Standing By*, the committee's Jewish child-saving efforts were well underway. On May 31, 1941, the one hundred AFSC-selected children and their adult chaperones left Marseille on a train bound for Lisbon, where they boarded the SS *Mouzinho* on June 10. Arriving in New York eleven days later, they were quickly followed by a second group of forty-five children, who arrived on September 2. A third group of fifty-seven children disembarked the SS *Serpa Pinto* in New York harbor on September 24, 1941.[93] In June as the number of Jewish children under its care expanded, the committee established a new collaboration with the German Jewish Children's Aid. USCOM would handle visa applications and provide the required affidavit of financial support for all European children selected for evacuation to the United States by both organizations. The committee would also provide the perpetually cash-strapped GJCA with a $25,000 annual administrative stipend, in return for which the agency—still under the leadership of placement director Lotte Marcuse—would assume responsibility for the reception, care, and placement of all "U.S. Committee continental children, Jewish by faith."[94]

By the end of the year, USCOM and the GJCA had succeeded in settling approximately 200 additional children in American foster homes. After the United States declared war in December 1941, they secured quota visas for another 110 European Jewish and Spanish Republican refugee children. The first of these children disembarked from the *Serpa Pinto* in New York on June 25, 1942, followed by a second group on the SS *Nyassa*, which arrived in Baltimore on July 30, 1942.[95] USCOM's transition from a nonsectarian organization founded to oversee the evacuation of British children to a primarily Jewish child rescue organization was complete.

Although by 1943 USCOM resources were focused almost exclusively on rescuing "continental" children, posters and pamphlets like this one avoided signaling toward their Jewish identities.
Courtesy of the World War Poster collection (Mss036), Literary Manuscripts Collection, University of Minnesota Libraries, Minneapolis.

The committee deliberately continued to focus public attention on the white Anglo-Saxon Protestant children evacuated during the summer and fall of 1940. Representations of children in USCOM's public relations materials after the U.S. entry into the war reflect this determination to obscure the ethnic and religious identities of the children to whom they were now almost exclusively devoted.

The two European children featured in this 1942 USCOM poster could have been Jewish; however, all outward signs indicated otherwise. Everything about the children—their visible good health, clean, pristine clothing, and meticulous grooming, even the suitcases they carried—communicated origins in intact households where parents continued to be present, rather than impoverished refugee camps in France. These were not hungry, traumatized waifs with mothers and fathers deported to concentration camps; instead, the smiling children appeared vulnerable but admirable, brave, stoic, and self-assured. Descending a ship's steps with the Statue of Liberty in the background, the children invited Americans to imagine USCOM's work not as charity for Jewish refugees, but as an act of solidarity with white Anglo-Saxon Christian families like their own.[96]

By the summer of 1942, USCOM, due in part to its popular association with British child evacuations, consolidated its reputation as the nation's leading child-saving and resettlement organization. In recognition, the War Relief Control Board made the committee a licensed war relief agency in September of that year. Now with permission to solicit financial support from the nation's more than 400 war or community chests, the committee launched a new fundraising campaign.[97] Worsening conditions in France soon compelled the committee to intensify its activities.

In spring 1942, Nazi officers aided by French police began mass arrests of Jews in both occupied and unoccupied zones of France, followed by deportation to Eastern European concentration camps.[98] Over the next two years, these deportations sent thousands of children to their deaths. They also tore Jewish families apart, separating parents, grandparents, and elder siblings from younger children, sending thousands more unaccompanied minors flooding into refugee camps and homes run by the OSE and the Swiss Red Cross.[99] Jarred momentarily out of the global apathy for European Jews' desperate plight, a handful of nations, including Canada and the Dominican Republic, opened their doors to a limited number of child refugees. Cables from Europe poured into the United States, begging for assistance.[100] USCOM and the American Jewish Joint Distribution Committee (JDC), the preeminent Jewish humanitarian relief agency founded during World

Collateral Humanitarianism

War I, responded by launching an emergency program to rescue endangered children.

On September 18, 1942, disregarding Assistant Secretary of State Breckenridge Long's warning that the admission of "derelict" refugee minors would set a dangerous precedent, the U.S. Department of State bowed under pressure from the White House to authorize visas for 1,000 foreign-born Jewish children under the age of sixteen facing immediate deportation from unoccupied France.[101] That same day, Vichy Premier Laval, incensed by international condemnation of his government's recent actions, cancelled all exit visas for adult Jews and threatened to withhold exit visas for Jewish children.[102] Following a series of urgent consultations between USCOM and JDC representatives in the United States and Europe, committee leaders determined that a public offer by the United States to admit a larger number of children might induce Laval to authorize their departure. USCOM's leadership reapproached the State Department, requesting a public announcement offering to admit up to 5,000 Jewish children.

As negotiations to establish the final number of visas continued, other details of the migration agreement were worked out. The State Department agreed that German, Austrian, Czech, Polish, Russian, Belgian, Dutch, and stateless children were admissible to the United States, but still insisted they apply for quota visas.[103] JDC representatives in Europe pleaded for all children to receive temporary visitor's visas, as British children had. Permanent immigrant visas required consuls to cable the United States for quota numbers for each child, which would produce "interminable" delays in processing. And many refugee children lacked passports and other documents required in the standard visa application process. But the State Department held firm on requiring that children apply for quota visas. What's more, the State Department limited admission to alien children under the age of fourteen, and non-enemy alien children under sixteen, despite the fact that many of the refugee children in unoccupied France were in their late teens.[104]

Under these disappointing terms USCOM and the JDC pushed forward with plans for transporting the first 1,000 boys and girls to the United States. Once again, they sought help from the American Friends Service Committee who, despite misgivings about diverting resources from refugee camps to support evacuation of a limited number of children, agreed to assist OSE volunteers in selecting children and submitting visa applications to U.S. consuls in Marseille, Nice, and Lyon. Disagreements quickly arose within and between the voluntary agencies over which children to save. Deferring to State Department instructions, USCOM's leadership stressed to its partners in France that children certified by a U.S.-consul approved doctor as "of good mental and physical health" were eligible for evacuation; "no problem children, or children with behavior problems, should be chosen." Representatives of the JDC, AFSC, and OSE objected, arguing that children whose parents had already been deported should receive the first priority. Although agreeing in principle, USCOM's leaders nonetheless stressed the importance of deferring to the State Department which had final authority to grant or withhold visas; they also emphasized that admission of "undesirable" children might produce public backlash and end the evacuation efforts. Making the same "devil's bargain" as the GJCA during the mid-1930s, USCOM accepted the limitations of the current geopolitics of compassion, officially maintaining the policy of priority evacuation for the most healthy and attractive children.[105]

Disagreements also emerged over whether special priority should be granted to children with ties to the United States; thousands of calls and letters flooded into the committee's New York headquarters from Jewish Americans who, unable to secure visas for adult relatives, sought to prevent their children's deportation to Nazi camps. Ruth Larned of the International Migration Service wrote to USCOM on behalf of an American Jewish family from Wisconsin, begging that their five-year-old Austrian niece be selected for evacuation. Knowing the parents' failure to secure exit visas from France almost certainly represented a death sentence, the child's American aunt and uncle hoped "to offer a home to their niece and to bring her up like their own child" alongside their own eleven-year-old daughter.[106] Moved by innumerable requests like this, USCOM's leadership asked European partners to prioritize children named by guardians and close relatives in the United States for evacuation. The JDC, however, objected noting that doing so would slow down the process of saving as many children as possible.[107]

As planning continued USCOM's leaders stressed to their European partners, including the JDC, AFSC, and OSE, the importance of avoiding "premature publicity"—both to prevent re-inflaming American anti-Semitism and antagonizing occupied France's Premier Laval, who feared media coverage of the evacuation of refugee children would further damage the Vichy regime's international reputation.[108] For the same reasons, the State Department similarly sought to downplay its role in the evacuation of European refugee children. Undersecretary of State Sumner Welles, when pressed directly at an October 15 press conference, admitted that a number of "private organizations" were currently bringing "destitute children" of "no particular race or nationality" to the United States, stressing they were admitted strictly "under the terms of existing immigration laws" and refusing to confirm the exact number of visas granted.[109]

Sumner Welles' disavowal of any official U.S. involvement did little to avert Premier Laval's rage. Ordering a hold on the promised exit visas, he threatened to cancel the whole project, insisting it "was being used for the purpose of propagandizing against the French government."[110] USCOM and its partners scrambled to reinitiate stalled discussions with the Vichy regime.[111] With the lives of thousands of Jewish children hanging in the balance, FDR finally decided to intervene. Overriding the State Department, he personally ordered the attorney general to authorize the admission of 4,000 additional children.[112] Laval relented and granted exit visas for 500 children—half the number originally approved—and only for "bona fide orphans." In blatant denial of the accelerating genocide hailed by Nazis as the "Final Solution," Laval refused to include children with parents deported to Central European death camps.[113]

USCOM knew this might be the last chance for any refugee children trapped in Vichy France, so they set a hastily arranged evacuation plan in motion. Five hundred boys and girls were selected, exit visas secured, and affidavits in lieu of passports provided to U.S. consuls; with travel arrangements finalized, the children gathered in Marseille with their escorts, awaiting departure by train to Portugal on November 12, 1942. A group of USCOM-designated American escorts and AFSC relief workers set sail from Baltimore, with plans to return from Europe with the children by mid-December. In the end, however, their trip was in vain. On November 8, the Allied forces announced the joint Anglo-American invasion of French North Africa. Within days, the Nazi army occupied Vichy France and closed the borders.[114]

Aware that those remaining in French refugee camps faced almost-certain death, a handful of relief workers, including AFSC staff, fled the country with their youthful charges in tow, smuggling as many as 500 Jewish children into Spain and Portugal.[115] In the meantime, the USCOM and AFSC escorts arrived in Marseille. "Bitterly disappointed" by the collapse of the evacuation plans, they quickly regrouped. Beating a hasty exit from Nazi-occupied France, they made emergency plans to transfer now drastically reduced child-saving operations to Spain. On January 27, 1943, they returned to the United States via Lisbon with thirty-one boys and girls, including a handful of Spanish loyalist refugee youth as well as French and German Jewish and mixed-race "Non-Aryan" Christian children who had fled across the Pyrenees.[116] By May of that year, USCOM and its partner agencies managed to evacuate fifty-six more children to the United States.

After fall 1942, USCOM, the AFSC, and JDC continued to collaborate with the GJCA, recently renamed the European-Jewish Children's Aid (EJCA), to bring a small number of Jewish refugee children from Spain and Portugal to the United States.[117] The committee also continued to consolidate their position and broaden their mandate as the leading American child rescue agency. Earlier that year, USCOM voluntarily assumed responsibility for overseeing care of the approximately 3,000 privately evacuated British children in the United States. In a letter to their network of affiliated agencies, USCOM's directors stressed that sponsors who signed individual affidavits of support for privately evacuated British children would continue to be financially responsible for their charges "for so long as said children remain in this country." However, in a striking departure from their previous operational model—and in seeming contravention of the terms of the migration agreement—USCOM announced they would henceforth guarantee the provision of all necessary services to all evacuated children, even when their foster or birth parents were unable to pay for them. In a bold statement reflecting USCOM's incipient understanding of children as rights-bearing subjects rather than simply objects of humanitarian concern, the letter concluded that "a child in need is a child in need, regardless of its political or governmental status."[118]

To harmonize the committee's expanded mandate with the requirements of immigration law, USCOM sought and received authorization from the Departments of State and Justice to issue a new blanket corporate affidavit assuming ultimate financial responsibility for all British children in American foster care. Shortly after, the President's War Relief Control Board designated USCOM the only agency authorized to assist privately evacuated British minors—further consolidating its stature. As a result of its increased efforts, by May 1943, USCOM had placed 1,193 children in homes in 65 cities and 35 states across the country. Of these, 791 were English and the rest mostly European, although they also included 1 Turk and 16 children listed as "stateless." There were 735 Protestant Christians, 113 Catholics, and 320 Jewish children. The same month, the committee also assumed responsibility for 426 Jewish children brought to the United States by the EJCA. In June, they also agreed to underwrite some of the EJCA's administrative expenses and part of the cost of care for children brought in under EJCA affidavit, in return for which the EJCA would assist USCOM in securing foster homes for Jewish children brought to the United States in the future. Despite this significant expansion in activities, USCOM's leaders proudly reported that the committee continued to operate from "a position of financial security," attributing this to both continued public support and their status as a licensed War Relief agency, which guaranteed access to federally distributed war relief funds.[119]

During 1943 the shifting course of the war and changing perceptions of refugees drove further expansion of USCOM's mandate. By summer, a string of Anglo-American victories predicted Allied success while growing numbers of firsthand reports confirmed the mass murder of Jews in concentration camps. A deeply shaken Roosevelt took action, establishing the War Refugee Board in January of 1944 to support voluntary agencies engaged in rescue efforts and temper the State Department's continuing intransigence on refugee admissions.[120] Sensing the president's newly pro-refugee stance as an opportunity, USCOM's leaders tried to renegotiate the terms of their migration agreement. On July 25, the committee's acting director Ingeborg Olsen sent a letter to the Departments of State and Justice requesting they issue the remainder of the 5,000 visas previously designated for children in unoccupied France to endangered children "seeking to come to the United States from any European country, including enemy controlled countries."[121] Cognizant of growing public and congressional support for the president's refugee advocacy, the Departments of State and Justice granted USCOM's request. This concession further enlarged the scope of USCOM's activities while reinforcing its position among the nation's leading war relief agencies.

As the defeat of the Nazis appeared imminent, USCOM's forward-looking leadership began to consider its potential role in the postwar era. They expected all but a few of the British children to return home. The committee's legal responsibility to the almost 800 "continental" children still in its care—few of whom would be willing or able to return to Europe—continued until the youngest reached majority in 1958. Given that USCOM's founding mission had been the coordination of children's evacuation and foster home placement rather than direct oversight of their care, that responsibility might conceivably be transferred to local child welfare agencies. Executive board members were nonetheless reluctant to dissolve the committee. In a letter to affiliate agencies, Director Robert Lang predicted an important role for USCOM in responding to the ongoing humanitarian challenges of the times. "Who can tell what may yet be asked of any of the war relief organizations," he wrote, "I am inclined to believe that there is a pre-post war era which will require fast action, and the U.S. Committee program may be a logical answer."

In a subtle reference to the Holocaust—the extent of which had only recently begun to be reported in the U.S. media—Lang further speculated that in light of "certain deliberate brutalities of totalitarian war . . . the democratic peoples will be forced to outdo anything they now dream of doing in behalf of many nationality groups." Foreshadowing the evolution of American refugee policy over the next fifty years, he insisted that the U.S. government must affirm, for the first time, "a basic federal responsibility" to alleviate suffering for those fleeing persecution. He stressed that "the planning and staffing of the myriad necessary human reliefs" after the war would of necessity continue to "draw deeply on the experience and resources" of organizations like USCOM. Such organizations, therefore, had a fundamental obligation to stay the course until victory was won, as well as prepare for a leading role in the postwar world. "No war relief agency with integrity can fail to be on the alert and to be aggressive in its participation and thinking contribution toward what eventually will need to be done," he asserted. "I hope therefore, that the U.S. Committee will aggressively prosecute its present program for children, and that the future aspects of need will find the Committee aware and 'on the ready.'"[122] This assertion of a state obligation toward displaced persons in general and the young in particular signaled USCOM's ongoing evolution from a narrowly focused child-saving committee into an influential humanitarian organization willing to challenge—albeit obliquely—the U.S. government's geopolitics of compassion, by publicly asserting an incipient philosophical commitment to both refugees and children's rights.

Foster children receiving care also expressed notions of their identities and rights. Their experience in the United States was mixed. Many British evacuees later recalled their time in overseas foster homes as a positive experience, enjoying the freedom of expression and behavior permitted in American schools and establishing close emotional relationships with host families that endured for years.[123] Other children struggled to fit in and make friends. Many children felt uncomfortable living in foster families where marked differences in social class or temperament made them incompatible. And a small number of evacuees initially placed in unstable homes marred by poverty, marital discord, or alcoholism experienced mental or physical abuse at the hands of their foster parents. As a result of these and other factors, almost half of USCOM's British children were replaced at least once, and 135 children were moved between 2 and 5 times.[124]

As years passed, even the most successful placements could show signs of strain. Many foster parents lost their sympathy for the beleaguered British; by 1943, confronted with gasoline and food rationing and a skyrocketing cost of living, some came to see evacuees as a burden, increasingly resenting what they considered to be the exploitation of American generosity by British families.[125] These tensions also rose when foster parents took a child out of a sense of obligation toward friends or relatives, rather than because they were truly willing or able to provide care.[126] By early 1944, British ambassador Lord Halifax wrote the Home Office that enthusiasm for the foster program had "entirely vanished;" children once intended to serve as emissaries of good-will had become "unwelcome visitors" in American homes, and a source of "festering . . . anti-British feeling."[127]

The experience of European Jewish children was equally ambivalent. Some formed close relationships with their foster families and earned "brilliant educational records" in U.S. schools, even winning scholarships to Harvard, Princeton, and other universities.[128] But many children were lonely and uneasy in their foster homes. Middle-class Jewish youth frequently argued with American host parents about money, and many were bitterly disillusioned by educational opportunities far below their middle-class origins and career aspirations.[129] Even children who enjoyed happy placements confronted daunting cultural and linguistic challenges as they struggled to learn English and adapt to American ways of life.[130] For their part, even well-intended foster parents were alarmed when, instead of the well-behaved, happy, and grateful children they had been naïvely expecting, they were assigned preternaturally mature boys and girls who smashed norms of appropriate "childlike" behavior by swearing, smoking, and refusing to obey curfews and household rules. Other children asserted their autonomy by clinging to their cultural identity, home language, or traditional forms of religious observance, even when these clashed with those of the host families.[131] As with British children, these kinds of tensions were heightened when the children's families were known to their American surrogates.

The majority of European Jewish children also struggled to overcome the emotional trauma of wartime displacement as well as grief and guilt associated with their parents' death or disappearance.[132] More serious emotional and psychological problems, including anger, resistance to authority, food hoarding, sexual promiscuity, and stealing, were also common among Jewish unaccompanied refugee minors, especially older boys who spent time in Nazi labor or concentration camps.[133] Notwithstanding the committee's consistently upbeat reports to its supporters nationwide, the reality was that USCOM and its affiliate agencies—though founded and staffed by professional child advocates—were ill prepared to meet the extraordinary needs of displaced and traumatized Jewish children. Between one-half and two-thirds of Jewish children resettled in the United States eventually required replacement. Over time more "difficult" refugee youth, especially adolescent boys, were sheltered in group homes or boarding houses.[134]

USCOM's success was largely a product of the principled opportunism of its founders, veterans of the Non-Sectarian Committee for German Refugee Children who saw in the changing course of the war an opportunity to reposition themselves at the vanguard of a new American child evacuation project while quietly resurrecting stalled Jewish child-saving efforts. Joined in 1940 by an increasing number of powerful and well-known child advocates, committee founders who since the mid-1930s had advocated for the well-being of endangered European children represented an important thread of continuity between prewar and wartime child evacuation. USCOM, convinced that the international resettlement of endangered children represented an effective humanitarian response to the rise of fascism in Europe, built upon precedents established by the then-GJCA in order to seek federal sanction as it strategically shifted focus toward British children and temporarily away from—and then back toward—European Jewish children. In doing so, USCOM encountered a powerful ally in the women-headed Children's Bureau, whose partnership with the committee allowed it to similarly expand its authority over the nation's still largely unregulated child welfare system.

USCOM's leaders made several opportunistic choices to achieve their objectives. Drawing lessons from the failed Wagner-Rogers Bill campaign, USCOM's leaders decided against calling publicly for amendments to existing immigration law. Instead, they elected to work behind the scenes with the Departments of State and Justice to secure the admission of specific groups of children, remaining attentive to opportunities to seek additional administrative accommodations to progressively broaden the scope of their child-saving activities. They also opted not to confront Americans about the selectivity of their humanitarian sentiments; instead, they reinforced public association between the committee and their British children evacuees, downplaying the extent to which, by 1941, USCOM had become a Jewish child-saving organization.

By 1943 USCOM's leaders challenged the deeply discriminatory legal, political, and social norms that undergirded the FDR administration's geopolitics of compassion, declaring that their mission encompassed all children in the war zone and resolving to guarantee the care of all needy evacuee children. They also publicly asserted a heretofore-unrecognized "federal responsibility" to alleviate the suffering of refugees. However, despite this late-in-the-war foray into norms entrepreneurship, at no time did USCOM directly criticize the ethno-racial and religious boundaries of American humanitarian sentiment, the racialized logic of U.S. immigration law, nor the assumption that refugee admissions should continue to be extremely limited. In the end, USCOM's principled opportunism gave rise to a "collateral humanitarianism," through which the committee succeeded in resettling a small but relatively diverse group of endangered European children while simultaneously rendering themselves complicit with the discriminatory laws and policies that worked to actively exclude most Jewish children and their parents from the United States.

USCOM's successful negotiation of an ever-more inclusive series of migration agreements revealed the extent to which a famously restrictionist State Department could act without legislative sanction—when it served its own interests—to admit at-risk unaccompanied children to the United States. Thus, the committee's leaders helped establish a new precedent within U.S. immigration policy for the provision of special treatment to unaccompanied refugee minors, regardless of racial, ethnic, or religious background. Their willingness to work within the system laid the groundwork for future collaborations between the federal government and voluntary agencies to facilitate the admission and care of displaced and endangered children to the United States. This new public-private dynamic served as a catalyst to expand federal funding and regulation of the nation's domestic child welfare system and to institutionalize programs to care for unaccompanied refugee minors in the postwar era.

3

War Orphans and Children on Demand

Unaccompanied Refugee Minors and Intercountry Adoption, 1945–1956

After 1945, as the United States adjusted to its new role as a world leader, decisions about who to admit and who to exclude would become increasingly tied to the nation's Cold War foreign policy. As new understandings of U.S. responsibility toward people displaced by communist regimes began to emerge, evolving midcentury notions of race, religion, and family life renewed debates about Americans' humanitarian obligation to endangered foreign children. Which girls and boys, if any, were deserving of admission and care in the United States? For which of them should the state accept responsibility and on what basis? On whose behalf would different voluntary agencies and private citizens advocate—and why or why not?

In the decade following World War II, a growing number of private agencies and individuals offered their own answers to these questions. Beginning in 1946, the U.S. Committee for the Care of European Children (USCOM) collaborated with the Children's Bureau, the European Jewish Children's Aid (EJCA), and the American branch of the International Social Service (ISS) agency to bring a small number of European "war orphans" to the United States. Empowered by new laws that for the first time explicitly provided for the admission of unaccompanied refugee minors—albeit of narrowly defined ethno-racial and national origins—these agencies sought to provide homes to unaccompanied and destitute children. Even as leaders of USCOM and its affiliated agencies began to express their first doubts about the ethics of separating vulnerable children from their families and nations of origin, they found themselves competing with new agencies and individuals seeking to bring children to the United States after the war. At the same time, leaders of the most established voluntary agencies were confronted by the growing popularity of private intercountry adoptions, which many Americans saw as an effective means of assisting war-afflicted children, participating in the struggle against communism, and growing their own families. Beginning in 1950 new challenges also came from a Congress that was eager to reassert control of the nation's immigration laws. Over the next several years, legislators offered strategic support toward making private intercountry adoption quicker and easier while simultaneously limiting the admission of unaccompanied children to the United States. The combined efforts of restrictionist lawmakers and intercountry adoption advocates reinforced prewar tendencies to evaluate refugees of all ages for admission based on geopolitical and domestic political considerations rather than their demonstrated need for protection, while also reinscribing notions of unaccompanied children as objects of charity rather than autonomous rights-bearing subjects.

By Victory in Europe Day (V-E Day) on May 8, 1945, the European continent had been transformed into a wasteland of suffering. Thirty million people died as a result of Nazi aggression and, among those who survived, 6.5 million people had become refugees or displaced persons (DP). This included untold numbers of children liberated from concentration camps as well as those separated from deported or deceased parents.[1] As many as a million children lived in orphanages and other hastily established institutions across the western part of the continent; other less fortunate "street urchins" roamed the streets of European towns and cities, scavenging for food and sleeping in abandoned buildings.[2] Others languished in makeshift and horrifically overcrowded DP camps, awaiting relief, resettlement, or repatriation by the United Nations Relief and Rehabilitation Administration (UNRRA).

UNRRA worked under Allied military supervision and alongside a multitude of voluntary agencies to return more than 4 million people to their home countries during the first several months after the war's end.[3] By the summer of 1945, there were still at least 1.65 million refugees and displaced people unable or unwilling to return to their homelands.[4] Approximately 153,000 children under the age of fourteen remained in German and Austrian camps. In the U.S. occupied zone alone, displaced minors without legal guardians, ranging in age from babies to teenagers, numbered between 30,000 and 40,000.[5] During the initial chaos after V-E Day, little attention had been paid to any of those children; although some were taken in by informal foster families, most were left to fend for themselves in DP camps.

This all began to change in June 1945, when the UNRRA created a Child Welfare Division to deal with the special needs of homeless and separated children within the Allied zones (children in the Soviet zones were outside their mandate). Developing hasty procedures for tracing and documenting children, the new agency quickly established the first internationally coordinated family unification and repatriation programs.[6] UNRRA-supported children's homes were also set up in a number of European countries.[7] By summer 1947 UNRRA handled the cases of more than 22,000 unaccompanied children in Germany and Austria.[8]

UNRRA, short on resources and already caring for more than 1 million displaced people in the Allied zones, was woefully unprepared for the scope and complexity of the children's crisis in Europe. While the agency struggled to get programs for refugee minors up and running, criticisms quickly began to mount. News media drew worldwide attention to the desperate plight of child victims of the war; U.S. newspapers and magazines printed emotional stories about army "mascots"—displaced adolescent boys who attached themselves to military units that provided them with food, clothing, and shelter—that were abandoned when troops left Europe.[9] In response a number of nations offered temporary asylum to orphans and unaccompanied children.[10] Jewish voluntary agencies, including the American Jewish Joint Distribution Committee (JDC), organized private efforts to move some children out of Germany. As early as December 1945, Zionist organizations like the Youth Aliyah began transporting Jewish youth—many of them older adolescents who had been in camps, in hiding, or had fought with partisans—on unauthorized ships departing Marseille for Palestine.[11]

Representatives of the U.S. Children's Bureau, USCOM, and other American voluntary agencies visited the Allied zones to assess the conditions of unaccompanied children in DP camps. Concerned with the spartan conditions, lack of adult supervision and educational opportunities they observed there, the AFSC, JDC, the Unitarian Service Committee (USC), Church World Service, Lutheran World Relief, and the Catholic War Relief Services (WRS) quickly launched domestic fundraising appeals and expanded their European field operations to provide relief to children.[12] At the same time, working with USCOM and the EJCA (whose current operations had been reduced to overseeing the care of the small numbers of British and European

Jewish children still in foster care), the Children's Bureau began studying the feasibility of bringing additional unaccompanied children to the United States.[13]

By July 1945, the Children's Bureau, USCOM, and the EJCA concluded that resettlement in the United States, rather than the provision of funds for continued care in Europe, was the best option for some unaccompanied children. Believing all resettlement efforts had to be overseen, as during the war, by professional child welfare organizations, they were deeply troubled by reports that some Americans had already taken individual action to bring European "war orphans" to the United States, and they were worried about a possible influx of unaccompanied children into privately arranged and potentially unsuitable foster or adoptive homes.[14]

To ensure traumatized child survivors of the war made a "sound and satisfactory adjustment to life in the United States," the Children's Bureau called for all agencies seeking to place unaccompanied refugee minors to employ a rigorous case study method, in accordance with best practices for "modern child-welfare programs," when matching children to their new host families.[15] This included gathering detailed information on each child's family background, the circumstances of their separation from their parents or siblings, and the conditions under which the child had lived since displacement. Information about children's previous educational achievements, interests, vocational aptitudes, religious identification and practices, and English ability, as well other aspects of their personality and "character traits," including eating, sleeping, work and "personal hygiene" habits, relationships with peers and adults, and "sex awareness and interest" were also part of the package. This case study approach, the Children's Bureau argued, guaranteed, to the extent possible, home, school, and vocational arrangements in line with each "child's plans and wishes."[16]

The Children's Bureau, USCOM, and the EJCA recommended the attorney general extend the 1940 order requiring unaccompanied children to enter under corporate affidavits "for a period of sufficient duration to assume orderly migration of children to the United States from war-affected countries." They noted that agencies using corporate affidavits to bring children to the United States before and during the war were "unanimous in their opinion that these procedures [had] provided protection and services needed."[17] Strong ethical arguments supported continuing to regulate the migration of postwar unaccompanied children under the corporate affidavit. The order's requirement for voluntary agencies to provide financial guarantees for each child, together with placement in Children's Bureau approved homes, and ongoing supervision by Bureau-licensed child welfare agencies, ensured that responsibility for children's safety and well-being belonged to an "officially recognized organization." Considering the significant variations in state-run child welfare, residency, and adoption laws during the 1940s, the oversight of a designated federal agency was the only way to guarantee a minimum standard of protection to international children placed with families across the nation.

There were also pragmatic considerations involved. Since the 1940 attorney general's order granted broad new powers of oversight to the Children's Bureau, its extension would safeguard its new prominence in national child welfare. As for USCOM, at the end of the war it was the only agency authorized to use the corporate affidavit. Maintaining the 1940 migration agreement thus preserved its privileged relationship with the federal government and allowed it to protect professional turf carved out through its child-saving efforts over the past decade. Once again USCOM's principled opportunism seems to have been at work.

Other long-term objectives also motivated the committee's continued support for the attorney general's order. Children's Bureau officer Elsa Castendyck wrote in an exceptionally forward-looking July 1945 memo to bureau chief Katharine Lenroot that encouraging the widest possible use of the corporate affidavit in the postwar period would begin to decouple decisions about children's admission from the requirement of individual sponsorship. If all unaccompanied refugee minors were admitted under corporate affidavits, "not only [would] these children be assured protection and supervision, but these provisions [would] be available in those instances for a child who for adequate social reasons should be admitted to the United States and where there is difficulty in securing satisfactory private affidavits."[18]

Castendyck's memo clearly recommended an expanded federal government role in regulating unaccompanied refugee minors' care in the United States. However, in the immediate postwar moment, her belief that "adequate social reasons" justified children's admission was not widely held. Nor was it reflected in U.S. law, which still in 1945 required both immigrants and refugees, regardless of age, to meet the same stringent requirements for admission. Castendyck appears to intimate that a significant number of unaccompanied European minors admitted to the United States under corporate affidavits after the war would strengthen precedent for this novel practice. It would also reinforce the idea that children alone and in need of protection had a unique claim on admission to the United States. Challenging prewar notions of refugee resettlement as a "private" matter, Castendyck's memo takes for granted that the federal government should in the future continue to open its doors not only to those fortunate enough to be privately sponsored, but also to children whose circumstances made them deserving of admission—even if individual financial guarantees had yet to be secured. As such, the memo reflects both the incipient commitment to children's and refugee rights toward which USCOM and other voluntary organizations began to move by 1943, as well as the emerging understanding that refugee resettlement could best be managed through a partnership between the state and nongovernmental actors.

Some private citizens disagreed, however, seeing individual acts of charity as the quickest and most effective way to ease the suffering of Europe's orphaned and displaced boys and girls. Despite objections from the Children's Bureau and its partners agencies as well as the UNRRA, all of which emphasized the importance of recently initiated family reunification and repatriation programs, a growing number of American couples traveled to Germany in the last months of 1945 and into 1946 to search for children in need of homes. Taking advantage of the chaotic situation in the Allied zone and a fortuitous loophole in U.S. law that allowed Americans living or traveling abroad to petition for adoption in foreign courts, hundreds of couples negotiated ad hoc adoptive arrangements with local German officials that bypassed the military command and United Nations authorities.[19]

In many cases these private adoptions stemmed from sincere concern for the youngest victims of the war. They also reflected changing postwar social norms in the United States, where more childless couples had begun to consider adoptions as a viable path to creating a family.[20] However, they were also motivated by the extreme scarcity of adoptable white children in the United States and by the mounting impatience of aspiring parents, an increasing number of whom had already begun to turn to "gray market" adoptions in order to avoid the red tape and costly processes of dealing with a professional agency. By 1946 some frustrated couples concluded that privately arranged overseas adoption presented both an expedient solution to Europe's unaccompanied child crisis *and* a way of growing their families.[21]

Many of these first Americans to adopt European "war orphans" shared voluntary agencies' deep concern for the plight of orphaned and displaced European children. But their sympathies did not necessarily extend to adult refugees. Despite Americans' shock upon realizing the full extent of the Holocaust, a majority still opposed the admission of large numbers of Jewish survivors or other displaced persons. As many as 50 percent felt that the United States should not take in *any* DPs.[22] Sensitive to public opinion,

Congress was reluctant to amend the nation's immigration laws to provide sanctuary for victims of the war. But the swearing in of new president Harry S. Truman in April 1945 reshaped the context in which U.S. immigration policy was fashioned. Confronted with the need to respond immediately to the devastation on the European continent and under pressure from American Jewish leaders outraged by the intolerable conditions in U.S. Army–administered DP camps, the deeply religious Truman quickly called for the admission of refugees. However, Truman also understood the European DP crisis through a geopolitics of compassion.[23] The new president saw Western Europe's rapid reconstruction as essential to countering recent Soviet expansion. Since the continued presence of a large refugee population in the Allied zones threatened the economic and social stability of United States' allies in the region, Truman concluded the American public would have to be persuaded to accept a significant number of displaced persons.[24]

Truman's hopes that Americans might be convinced to abandon their restrictionist views were not entirely unfounded. During the war propaganda denouncing Nazi racialism, the near-universal experience of male military service, and nonsectarian campaigns against anti-Semitism and racism had facilitated the increasing incorporation of southern and eastern European "ethnics" (though not Black, Latinx, or Asian Americans) into the social mainstream.[25] At the same time, progressive Americans had grown more uncomfortable about racial and national origin restrictions on immigration that clashed with the nation's (imagined) cultural pluralism. However, anti-Semitism and xenophobia remained prevalent, and despite the burgeoning power of "ethnic" urban voters, powerful legislators' commitment to the quota system and fears of postwar economic contraction reinforced a bipartisan consensus that admissions to the country be strictly curtailed.[26] As winter fell over Europe in the last months of 1945, a frustrated President Truman thus began to seek ways of opening an emergency "side entrance" to some of the millions of displaced persons of all ages now facing imminent death by starvation or exposure.[27]

Bypassing Congress and the State Department, President Truman issued an executive order on December 22, 1945, reserving half of the unused annual visas allotted to European nations for displaced persons. The president's directive also ordered the State Department to immediately resume immigration from Europe and committed the United States to admitting approximately 40,000 DPs per year.[28] In addition it authorized licensed welfare agencies to provide corporate affidavits of support—to date, only used to guarantee the admission of unaccompanied minors—to cover people

War Orphans and Children on Demand

who might otherwise become public charges.[29] Deliberately leveraging the power of an expanded wartime presidency on behalf of refugees, Truman sought to minimize anti-Semitic backlash by stressing that his directive did not give priority to Jews. Rather, it would allot visas equally to displaced "natives of central and eastern Europe and the Balkans," including victims of Nazi aggression and terror as well as those who feared returning to Soviet-dominated nations.[30] But the Truman Directive *did* stipulate that preferential consideration for visas would be given to "orphan children" in the Allied territories.[31]

Truman's order also designated the U.S. Committee for the Care of European Children as the sole agency authorized to select children for the "orphan program."[32] As during the war, USCOM would ensure all unaccompanied refugee minors' placement in Children's Bureau–approved homes and their supervision by an approved social welfare agency until they turned twenty-one, or eighteen if they became self-supporting, joined the army (in the case of boys) or married (in the case of girls).[33] The government also authorized the committee to submit a one-time "blanket" affidavit to the government on behalf of *all* children admitted to the United States under its auspices—to be replaced later by individual affidavits of support if they became available—to meet the public charge requirement.[34] The new blanket affidavit for unaccompanied minors—and the use of corporate affidavits on behalf of displaced persons of all ages—affirmed for the first time that "adequate social reasons" justified some refugees' admission to the United States even when they were otherwise unable to satisfy legal requirements. These provisions implicitly legitimized incipient norms of children's and refugees' rights emerging from the experiences of voluntary agency personnel during the war. They also reinforced the relationship established between the federal government and USCOM in 1940, enhancing the committee's authority, status, and other operational advantages vis-à-vis other child-serving agencies.

Following the president's directive, USCOM sprang back into action, establishing overseas headquarters in April 1946 in Frankfurt, with district offices in Wiesbaden, Bremen, Munich, and Salzburg.[35] They also established an embarkation camp at Bremen, where children cleared for resettlement waited for space on U.S. planes or ships. The committee quickly hashed out a new working arrangement with UNRRA, who agreed to refer minors whose parents had been confirmed dead or disappeared. UNRRA officers also handled the process of securing written releases from any living relatives, consenting to the children's emigration and relinquishing any rights or benefits connected to their relationship with the child, and obtaining releases from the national liaison officer of the child's country of origin and from Allied military authorities, both of which were required before resettlement was authorized.[36] For its part, a staff of six USCOM officers was responsible for selecting and processing children from among those referred by UNRRA and other voluntary agencies; registering them with the U.S. government Displaced Persons Commission; collecting birth certificates or affidavits of identity, health certificates, and other documents demonstrating their eligibility for immigration; and applying for quota visas on their behalf.[37]

USCOM's leadership sought to establish mutually beneficial relationships with other voluntary organizations assisting refugee children. Prominent among these was the ISS agency, originally established in Geneva in 1922 to assist families separated across national borders and now tasked by UNRRA with delivering casework services to separated refugee families in the Allied zones.[38] The Catholic War Relief Services (WRS), founded in 1943 as the predecessor to the Catholic Relief Services (CRS) agency, was also expanding work with displaced and "war-afflicted people" of all races and creeds, especially children.[39] By early 1946 the WRS had placed 250 exiled Polish boys and girls in a U.S.-funded colony in Santa Rosa, Mexico, and in Catholic schools and orphanages in the United States.[40]

Taking advantage of their exclusive authorization to grant blanket affidavits to gain the lead in U.S. child resettlement activities, USCOM kicked off European operations as quickly as possible. On May 16, 1946—approximately a month after opening its Frankfurt office—the committee dispatched its first transport, embarking sixty-seven children from Bremerhaven aboard the SS *Marine Flasher*. Over the next two years a steady trickle of small groups of children followed. Approximately three-quarters were adolescent Jewish boys from Soviet-controlled areas, especially Poland, Czechoslovakia, and Hungary, although the committee also resettled smaller numbers from Germany, Lithuania, and Estonia.[41] Upon arrival the children were transported to one of USCOM's two reception centers in the Bronx, where they were fed, issued new clothes, and assigned a bed. They then underwent thorough physical examinations and any immediately necessary medical and dental treatment before meeting with caseworkers tasked with gathering information to facilitate their placement in a suitable U.S. home. During the several weeks they spent in reception care, children also resumed their education, many after several years' absence from school, receiving initial lessons in English and U.S. history, geography, and culture.[42]

Sensitive to the fact that many of the adolescent refugee minors were accustomed to independent living, USCOM caseworkers placed children as quickly as possible.[43] They allowed older unaccompanied children to choose between foster families and collective living arrangements, a departure from their earlier model.[44] However, children's religious background remained the primary determinant of placement. Since most refugee minors admitted under the Truman Directive were Jewish, they were assigned to the European Jewish Children's Aid, which matched them with host families. To place Catholic and Lutheran girls and boys, USCOM depended on new relationships with the Catholic Committee for Refugees and the National Lutheran Council, who agreed to identify homes for coreligionist children. Other Protestant and Eastern Orthodox children, as well as a "scattered few" Muslim and Buddhist boys and girls, were placed directly by USCOM, who also retained financial responsibility for their care. This placement procedure continued until 1948 when the interdenominational Church World Service agreed to assume responsibility for all children not assigned to a national sectarian agency.[45]

Initial appeals from USCOM and the Children's Bureau, along with campaigns by national sectarian agencies and a sympathetic media, inspired American families to welcome unaccompanied children into their homes. Although some parents rescinded offers when they learned most refugee minors were boys fifteen and older, the committee and its partners had placed approximately 400 children in homes across the nation by June 1947.[46] Many placements turned out to be successful; however even the most well-intended host parents were often ill prepared for the challenges of incorporating unaccompanied children into their families. Seeking to inspire public participation in the resettlement efforts, media stories featuring poignant photographs of young European children adjusting easily to their new American homes obscured the fact that most of those in need of homes were traumatized and preternaturally mature teenagers. Wary of adults and resistant to authority, many of these youth struggled to adjust to their new lives and roles within American families.[47]

The distinction between fostering and adopting also continued to confuse many host parents. While the media reported on suffering war orphans, intercountry adoption was becoming increasingly appealing to American couples frustrated by the scarcity of healthy white adoptable children.[48] As a result, many potential foster parents who wrote to USCOM and the Children's Bureau offered homes only to young (and adoptable) refugee minors. Some even described in careful detail the age, gender, and physical appearance of the children they considered acceptable members of their families.[49] These requests reveal an early disconnect between the goals of child welfare workers who saw the resettlement of children as a response to a humanitarian crisis, and the desires of private citizens who hoped to grow their families by taking in racially, religiously, and culturally desirable "war orphans."[50] Well aware, however, that the aspirations of prospective adoptive parents provided crucial impetus for their efforts—and equally experienced in turning peoples' assumptions about their work to their advantage—USCOM and its partner agencies publicly downplayed the fact that few unaccompanied European minors were under the age of twelve, while at the same time instructing caseworkers to manage potential host families' expectations about the kinds of children actually needing homes.

However, domestic placement difficulties paled in comparison to the logistical challenges confronted by USCOM and other refugee-serving agencies overseas. UNRRA was allowed to expire on June 30, 1947, before plans for its successor the International Refugee Organization (IRO) had been completed, compounding the practical difficulties of moving unaccompanied European children to new homes. Similar to UNRRA, the IRO Constitution mandated special "priority assistance" for unaccompanied or orphaned children under the age of sixteen outside their country of origin.[51] However, the IRO lacked adequate staff, budget, and authority to effectively care for the more than 1 million DPs of all ages remaining in camps. USCOM and other U.S. voluntary agencies, including the AFSC and the USC, were thus forced to dedicate resources toward raising the standard of care for unaccompanied children in DP camps and children's homes in the Allied zones, and away from their own resettlement efforts.[52]

The most critical obstacle to USCOM's work, however, remained U.S. immigration law. Despite President Truman's efforts to expedite the resettlement of displaced people, the limitations of his 1945 directive became almost immediately apparent to refugee advocates. Under the United States' racially selective national origins quota system, less than one-sixth of the 150,000 visas allotted to all European countries were reserved for the eastern and southern European nations from which most refugees originated. Protracted visa processing delays were also common; since rates of visa issuance had been mostly below quota since 1924, understaffed European consuls accustomed to a slower operational pace were ill equipped to handle the sudden expansion of demand for services.[53] As a result, and alongside constant pressure from German authorities who viewed unaccompanied minors as an economic burden and social problem, thousands of confused and restless boys and girls continued to languish in camps and children's homes.[54] In some cases children waited up to six years for heavily over-subscribed quota numbers to become available. Many more times, despite USCOM's success in lobbying the U.S. government for authorization to use its corporate affidavit to admit children under eighteen (sixteen was the age specified in the president's directive), adolescents would "age out" of eligibility for USCOM sponsorship before visas became available.[55] Others in urgent need of resettlement were rejected because they failed to meet the stringent health requirements of U.S. immigration law. As time passed USCOM's frustrated overseas staff became increasingly disheartened by its inability to resettle more needy children.[56]

Despite formidable logistical and legal obstacles, USCOM managed to bring 1,387 children to the United States under the terms of the Truman Directive.[57] But more needed to be done. Even after Canada, Australia, New Zealand, Sweden, and Belgium launched their own limited programs for refugee minors, as late as June 1948 there were still approximately 2,000 unaccompanied children living in IRO camps in the U.S. zones of Austria and Germany. And their numbers were on the rise, as those who had been in the U.S. zones lost parents who died from hunger, illness, or exposure in DP camps and were joined by thousands more children fleeing political upheaval in Eastern Europe.[58] Others were dropped off at children's centers by informal foster parents or relatives who, struggling to survive in economically devastated postwar Germany and Austria, were no longer willing or able to provide care. Other surrogates, upon learning immigration requirements allowed only "bona fide" families to apply for visas together, came to view informal foster children as an impediment to their own resettlement.[59] Thousands of orphaned German children, as well as the sons and daughters of white and Black Allied soldiers whose destitute German and Polish mothers left them in orphanages, also needed care and protection. However, since most of these endangered children did not qualify under UN/IRO terms as persons displaced across international borders, they were ineligible under the president's directive for resettlement in the United States.[60]

At the same time, encouraged by ongoing media attention to the suffering of "war orphans"—not all of whom were technically orphans—individual Americans continued to make private arrangements to bring European children to the United States. Between 1946 and 1947, the Children's Bureau received a steady flow of inquiries about how to arrange visas and foster or adoptive homes for overseas children, as well as requests for casework services involving "problems growing out of the presence of our troops in foreign countries."[61] Several thousand unaccompanied children, most with American relatives, were admitted to the United States during this period, under individual affidavits of support. A smaller number were adopted by military or civilian personnel living in Europe, or by American couples who traveled to Allied occupation zones to search out children in orphanages.[62]

But parents quickly discovered that bringing a child adopted overseas home was almost as difficult as sponsoring an unaccompanied minor. Under existing law, adoption did not confer citizenship nor guarantee a child's admission to the country; like all other immigrants, adoptees were required to secure the appropriate visa before entering the United States. Nor did adoptive children enjoy any priority within their national origins quota.[63] Working around these restrictions, hundreds of American families nonetheless succeeded in returning home with privately adopted European children, including a growing number of mixed-race German "brown babies," almost 7,000 of whom were taken in by mostly African American families during the next two decades.[64]

By 1947, however, USCOM and other voluntary agencies saw the expansion of private intercountry adoption as a threat to both children's welfare and their own leading role in overseas child-saving efforts. Joining forces with a coalition of domestic pressure groups, including religious and ethnic community organizations that were key supporters of the Democratic Party, they pressed Congress to admit more refugees of all ages—including unaccompanied refugee minors—to the United States.[65] President Truman also lent support for legislative action, calling on Congress in his 1947 State of the Union address to grant asylum to a much greater number of displaced persons.[66] Stressing that the United States admitted only 5,000 refugees since May 1946, the president argued congressional action was required for the United States to fulfill its responsibilities to the "thousands of homeless and suffering refugees of all faiths."[67] Truman also linked refugee legislation to the United States' shifting geopolitical objectives in the postwar period, repeatedly insisting that the United States had a moral obligation to assist freedom-loving people fleeing Soviet-dominated nations and that a robust DP resettlement program helped U.S. foreign policy goals vis-à-vis the Soviet Union.[68]

Linking the refugee crisis to the emerging Cold War, Truman and his supporters convinced a handful of lawmakers to take action. In April 1947, Representative William Stratton (R-Ill.) introduced a bill proposing resettlement of 400,000 displaced persons in the United States over a four-year period.[69] The proposed legislation expedited the number of refugees admitted by "mortgaging" up to 50 percent of any country's future annual visa allotment.[70] Despite supporters' insistence that the Stratton Bill was a limited and

War Orphans and Children on Demand

temporary response to an emergency situation, it met immediate opposition from conservative Republicans and southern Democrats who maintained the bill was a "wedge" to breach the nation's national origins quota system.[71] Led by powerful lawmakers Senator Pat McCarran (R-Nev.) and Representative Francis Walter (D-Pa.), legislators from both parties declared their opposition to liberalizing immigration law to allow admission of more refugees.[72]

Most Americans also remained hostile to the relaxation of the nation's immigration law.[73] Patriotic organizations like the American Legion and the Veterans of Foreign Wars argued that DPs would take jobs away from returning service members. They also questioned many DPs' ability to assimilate. Reflecting growing alarm about the expansion of communism, opponents also warned that displaced populations were "rife with communist sympathizers."[74] Countering these objections, secular and religious voluntary agencies offered vocal support for the president's efforts to "assume . . . world leadership" of the refugee crisis. Stressing that it wasn't just a "Jewish" problem, they urged Americans to fulfill the nation's "Christian" obligation to welcome its "fair share" of refugees.[75] Organized labor and Central and Eastern European community organizations similarly offered support for the displaced person's bill.[76] The national media entered the debate, focusing coverage of the DP crisis on children, who they portrayed as uniquely vulnerable and symbolic of the suffering of displaced persons of all ages.[77]

As debate dragged on into 1948, coverage of the "war orphan" crisis and the efforts of humanitarian organizations like USCOM, Save the Children, and the newly established United Nations Children's Fund (UNICEF) ensured that the suffering of unaccompanied refugee minors continued to haunt Americans' imagination. While many continued to resist the admission of more DPs, other Americans were coming to believe that displaced youth represented an exceptional case. Taking place at the same time as public confidence in the United States' economic, political, and cultural superiority reached new heights, this normative shift reflected the postwar consolidation of a new understanding of childhood as a time of unique vulnerability and dependence. Together these increasingly common beliefs would convince a growing number of Americans that their nation had a special responsibility to save the world's children.[78] This sense of obligation, however, remained limited and highly selective: although growing numbers of Americans participated in supporting war-afflicted children in Japan and China through new organizations like the Foster Parents' Plan, no organization to date had lobbied for the liberalization of U.S. immigration law to allow for the resettlement of Asian war orphans in the United States.

Moreover, advocates for admitting European unaccompanied minors did not necessarily support expansion of state-sponsored resettlement. Many Americans believed privately arranged adoption was the best choice for the continent's children—*and* an opportunity to fulfill the desires of couples seeking to grow their families. As the number of adoption inquiries received by the Children's Bureau and USCOM steadily mounted, so too did the frustration of prospective parents facing an interminable visa application process as well as strict age and national origin limitations on children considered adoptable.[79] In response to pressure from well-connected constituents, on March 10, 1947, Senator Irving Ives (R-N.Y.) and Representative Jacob Javits (R-N.Y.) introduced legislation to permit nonquota admission of European war orphans under the age of fourteen for the purposes of adoption.

Although it predated and was deliberately proposed separately from refugee legislation, the adoption bill was intertwined from the beginning with the broader displaced persons question. Ives and Javits insisted that theirs was "not an immigration bill," but rather a humanitarian act on behalf of the approximately 6,000 unaccompanied European minors still awaiting resettlement.[80] Aware that the continued association of DPs as Jewish worked against them, Representative Javits also stressed the bill did not discriminate "on the basis of religion or race," encompassing "all children who are the victims of the war's holocaust."[81] Media coverage declaring the Javits Bill an act of mercy toward the "most desperate" of those remaining in the DP camps further reinforced the legislation's humanitarian objectives, overlooking the role of individual self-interest in overseas adoption.[82]

However, congressional debate suggested that politicians understood the legislation mostly as a way of satisfying U.S. citizens' growing demands for adoptable European children. While praising its humanitarian intentions, pragmatic lawmakers still demanded evidence of a sufficient number of people seeking to grow their families through adoption. Making clear the bill's viability depended on the initiative and resources of prospective adoptive parents, legislators continued to confine the federal government's role in the resettlement of unaccompanied children to regulating admission or exclusion.[83] Congressional support for private adoption nonetheless alarmed voluntary agency personnel who increasingly advanced a rights-based argument for expanding government involvement in meeting the needs of unaccompanied minors. Accordingly, they redoubled their efforts in support of broadly based refugee legislation. By spring 1948, public discussion of the UN's proposed Universal Declaration of Human Rights—which formally recognized children as rights-bearing individuals and asserted all people's right to seek

War Orphans and Children on Demand

asylum from persecution—had nudged Americans toward greater support for refugee admissions.[84] Advocates also took advantage of rising Cold War tensions, pushing restrictionist politicians to concede that the nation's refugee policy was inextricably linked to the anti-communist struggle.

After two years of dedicated lobbying by the president and refugee advocates, the Displaced Persons Act passed on June 25, 1948.[85] Defining "displaced persons" as those who were deported or compelled to leave because of "reasons of race, religion, nationality or political opinion," the act was a first step forward for the United States in granting formal refugee status to victims of persecution. However, it limited that status to those fleeing "fascist regimes" or the "foreign power" now dominating Eastern Europe and the Baltic nations. In doing so, the legislation continued the tradition of identifying refugees as victims of particular nation-states, while refusing to acknowledge any responsibility to open the nation's doors to displaced persons outside of Europe.[86] The amended legislation also admitted only 202,000 displaced persons, approximately half the number originally proposed, and contained measures limiting the admission of Jewish and other "undesirable" DPs.[87] The act further required that visas granted to displaced persons be "mortgaged" against the annual quotas of their nations of birth—even though most DPs came from countries with visa allotments so small that admissions in any significant number would lead to the mortgaging of their quotas for hundreds of years into the future.[88] Decrying the Displaced Persons Act as "flagrantly discriminatory," the president reluctantly signed it into law.

The Displaced Persons Act provided a number of concessions to both child welfare agencies and the emerging intercountry adoption lobby.[89] It authorized the admission as nonquota immigrants of 3,000 "orphans," defined as those who experienced the "death or disappearance of both parents" and were present in the Allied zones before June 25, 1948, a provision which provided relief to unaccompanied refugee minors from nations with heavily over-subscribed quotas.[90] It also meant children would no longer be in competition with adults for the limited number of immigrant visas. The legislation thus simultaneously expedited the visa application process for USCOM children while making it quicker and easier for Americans to bring adopted European children home to the United States.

But the legislation also required "orphans" to be under the age of sixteen at the date of its passage, excluding the majority of the refugee minors remaining in children's centers, who were between the ages of sixteen and eighteen. For them, the only option was applying for resettlement under the general provisions of the Displaced Persons Act, which meant continuing to wait for quota visas. USCOM and Children's Bureau officials criticized these strict age limits as well as the law's failure to provide "for the large number of half-orphaned children living in children's centers," because their surviving parent was "incapable of caring for them."[91] Among these were the mixed-race sons and daughters of African American military fathers and destitute German or Polish mothers who, on their own and in the face of antiblack racism and cultural prejudices against "occupation children," were unable to provide for their care.[92]

Despite its limitations, the DP Act represented a victory for advocates of children's admission as refugees rather than adoptees. Containing the first-ever congressional authorization for the admission of unaccompanied refugee minors, the law articulated an obligation to open the nation's doors to endangered overseas children. Although it categorized them as "orphans" rather than unaccompanied refugee minors, the law made clear children need *not* be preselected by adoptive parents to be eligible for admission. The act also designated USCOM the sole agency from whom a new Displaced Persons Commission would accept resettlement applications, suggesting Congress expected USCOM and Children's Bureau–supervised agencies to continue placing most children in foster homes. It also granted the committee a new power to issue "block assurances" guaranteeing the care and supervision of all sponsored children until they were adopted or reached the age of eighteen.[93]

At the same time the Displaced Persons Act required strict oversight of all overseas adoptions by the commission, imposed a year-long waiting period on the adoption of resettled children in U.S. foster homes, and blocked most independent adoption agencies from sponsoring children's resettlement or arranging their placement with new families. Even though the act conflated the categories of orphan and unaccompanied refugee minor—perhaps in a deliberate attempt to satisfy the entangled interests of early proponents of transnational adoption and advocates for the resettlement of all endangered children—the legislation made clear that children's eligibility for visas rested upon their needs rather than the desires of prospective U.S. citizen parents. In line with incipient understandings of refugees of all ages as rights-bearing subjects, children's "adequate social reasons" for admission qualified them to come to the United States, not their adoptability.

With their leadership of refugee minors' resettlement consolidated by the Displaced Persons Act, USCOM and its partner agencies in Germany intensified their efforts. The refugee legislation was set to expire in June 1950, at which time the International Refugee Organization would also cease operations. Adding to the urgency, many boys and girls in the camps were only months away from the new cut-off age of sixteen.[94] After delays lasting several months, "interminable to the Committee's staff and to the children, who knew that the time . . . was running out," the first Europeans admitted under the DP Act departed Bremerhaven aboard the army transport ship the *General Black*. Among the first to disembark in New York were sixty "war orphans," who were transferred to USCOM reception centers to await placement with U.S. foster families.[95]

As the committee worked feverishly to send as many children as possible to the United States, the expansion of USCOM's mandate sparked confusion and tensions with the IRO and other voluntary agencies operating in Europe. Unfamiliar with both U.S. immigration law and the "protective purpose of the Committee's program," IRO officers found it difficult to understand why they could not refer children in need of resettlement directly to American sectarian agencies.[96] IRO attempts to streamline the resettlement process by working directly with sectarian agencies also created territorial disputes between USCOM and those organizations. A particularly serious rift emerged between USCOM and Catholic agencies who felt the committee prevented them from working directly to resettle coreligionist refugee minors. They also resented the Children's Bureau oversight of children placed by Catholic childcare agencies, seeing this as an unwarranted interference in their affairs.[97] Although USCOM would work closely with Protestant agencies in the coming years, its relationship with Catholic agencies remained tense. Finally, in February 1949, USCOM and the IRO agreed to clear procedures for working together in the committee's expanded zone of operations.

Mounting Cold War tensions further complicated children's resettlement.[98] Viewing emigration as a last resort, IRO policy dictated all possible efforts be made to reunite separated children with living relatives; when this wasn't possible, they were referred to representatives of their nation of origin (if it could be determined) who decided whether to release them for resettlement.[99] Eastern European nations mostly assented to resettlement of Jewish unaccompanied minors, many of whom wanted to start new lives in Palestine.[100] Concerned with the long-term impact of population decrease on rebuilding national economies and militaries, Soviet-aligned states increasingly called for the return of (non-Jewish) children. The USSR also began to demand the return of displaced Estonian, Latvian, and Lithuanian youth whose nations were absorbed by the Soviets in 1940. Baltic peoples were granted Soviet citizenship, and the USSR insisted on their repatriation.

The United Nations and United States did not acknowledge the absorption of the Baltic republics, and they initially refused to return anyone against their wishes. Nor did they recognize Baltic states' authority over unaccompanied children originating in the region—most of whom were adolescents and avowedly anti-communist and didn't want to be returned.[101] The resulting stalemate meant that few Baltic children were approved for resettlement until 1948, when the IRO responded to complaints from voluntary agencies and pressure from American and British authorities by declaring that "the best interests of the child" superseded the claims of Soviet authorities.[102] As a result of this policy shift, most of the children who fell under IRO mandate were resettled in the United States.[103] These geopolitically motivated struggles contributed to Cold War tensions while also slowing the efforts of USCOM and its partner agencies to assist displaced children.

By June 1949 only 175 unaccompanied refugee minors had come to the United States under the Displaced Persons Act—a far cry from the 3,000 authorized by Congress. Once they were in the country, USCOM staff confronted further challenges placing them in suitable homes. The few small children sponsored by the committee moved quickly out of reception care; among these "attractive youngsters" were a group of sixty-seven Latvian orphans who, after arriving in the United States in March 1949, were escorted to their new homes with great fanfare and attention from the media.[104] However, as one exasperated Children's Bureau officer noted, it was simply "not possible to meet [the] requests for young children."[105] The bureau also received constant complaints about USCOM's rule that adoptable children spend a year in foster care in an agency-approved home before adoption proceedings could be initiated—and only if this was determined to be in the child's best interest.[106]

Of course, most refugee youth—adolescent boys, sibling groups, and older children of both sexes with behavioral problems or disabilities—were unadoptable.[107] After child welfare staff disregarded inquiries from people seeking free domestic labor from a "strong . . . presentable young girl" or boy, suitable homes were in short supply for these children.[108] And even when foster families were available, older children often resisted resettlement outside New York City. Determined to remain close to friends from the DP camps who were placed nearby, some of these youth ran away from foster homes in other states to return to the city.[109] By summer 1949 ongoing struggles to place children compelled USCOM partner agencies to reconsider long-held assumptions about acceptable foster parents. With the impending expiration of the DP legislation the following year adding new urgency to resettlement

War Orphans and Children on Demand

efforts, the Children's Bureau agreed to allow the placement of children with middle-aged couples whose own children were grown.[110]

Resettlement still proceeded far more slowly than children's advocates had hoped. By June 1950, with the IRO set to suspend operations, at least 1,000 registered unaccompanied children remained in the Allied zones, and thousands of additional separated or abandoned boys and girls who had never been registered with the UNRRA or IRO still roamed the streets of European cities alone.[111] Although homes would be found for some of these children in Canada, Australia, New Zealand, and a handful of European and Latin American countries, opportunities for resettlement in the United States were declining.[112] By the beginning of the new decade, most Americans had lost interest in European DPs; distracted by the victory of Communist forces in China in 1949 and the deployment of U.S. troops to the Korean peninsula the next year, both political leaders and the public were increasingly focused on the expanding global struggle between capitalism and communism.[113]

As the nation's geopolitical priorities shifted, so did the impetus behind its refugee policy, away from resettling those displaced by World War II toward those fleeing the threat of communism in Eastern Europe, Italy, and Greece.[114] Sensing their opportunity, longtime restrictionist congressmen Pat McCarran and Francis Walter organized conservative Republicans and southern Democrats to oppose passage of a proposed expansion of the DP Act. On June 16, 1950—nine days before all remaining visas for displaced persons were set to expire—Congress voted to extend the legislation for a year and to increase the number of visas allotted from 205,000 to 339,000, but only after restrictionists secured amendments returning control over refugee admissions to the State Department and the Immigration and Naturalization Service (INS) (part of the Justice Department since 1940), which ensured stricter enforcement of the law's screening and security provisions.[115]

The amended act was a partial victory for advocates of refugee minors. It allotted an additional 2,000 visas for "eligible displaced orphans," bringing the total to 5,000.[116] Eligibility expanded to those sixteen or under on June 16, 1950, children from Soviet-dominated nations who entered the Allied zones after the war, and displaced and abandoned or "half-orphan" children whose parents could not care for them because of "mental or physical illness or incompetency."[117] In a concession to insistent proponents of overseas adoption, legislators also created a new category of nonquota visa for adoptable European children under ten years of age who previously were ineligible under the displacement provisions of the DP Act.[118]

However, Congress also responded to increasingly vocal demands from the Catholic Committee for Refugees by removing Children's Bureau oversight as a precondition of children's resettlement. Beginning in 1950 standards for foster home placements could be set by any "appropriate agency" in the unaccompanied refugee minors' new state of residence.[119] Since states had markedly different standards of care—and equally inconsistent child welfare services—national sectarian agencies became in most cases the sole guarantors of children's welfare. A vindicated National Catholic Welfare Conference subsequently withdrew from cooperation with USCOM and the Children's Bureau. Negotiating an agreement with the IRO to expand their own direct resettlement efforts, they deliberately circumvented USCOM's authority to clear European "orphans" for emigration by applying for visas on children's behalf under the general DP allotment.[120]

While the amended DP Act undercut USCOM's leadership of American child-saving efforts overseas, its revisions opened up new opportunities for the committee to bring children to the United States. In particular, it opened the way for the immigration of unaccompanied children from Greece where long-standing ideological differences exacerbated by the German occupation and deprivations of the postwar period had erupted into armed conflict in 1946. The brutal civil war, the first proxy Cold War confrontation between the United States and the USSR, left more than 1 million Greek people, including as many as 50,000 "unprotected children," as refugees or internally displaced persons by its end in 1949.[121] By then, Greek children had captured the world's attention after the government charged Communist guerillas of forcibly removing as many as 28,000 children to Albania, Yugoslavia, and other Soviet-dominated countries for indoctrination as "enemies of their country, religion and parents."[122] By the time of the DP Act's extension, media coverage of struggles to reunite evacuated boys and girls with their parents had inscribed Greek children in Americans' imaginations as the latest youthful victims of communism, prompting Greek Americans to take action on their behalf.

On May 11, 1951, the leaders of the American Hellenic Educational Progressive Association (AHEPA), a Greek fraternal organization founded in 1922 to combat anti-Greek discrimination spearheaded by the Ku Klux Klan, met in Washington, D.C., with representatives from the State Department, the Displaced Persons Commission, and USCOM. They agreed to collaborate on a program to bring Greek "war orphans" to the United States. AHEPA would solicit sponsors from among its national membership to cover USCOM's administrative costs as well as transportation, clothing, food, and medical examinations for each child selected for resettlement. In return USCOM affiliates in Athens would select and process children for emigration.[123] The U.S.-based committee would handle the visa application process, plus corporate affidavits (countersigned by AHEPA) on behalf of each child, and reception care in New York.[124] They would also coordinate home studies, arrange children's transportation to their new homes, and provide local welfare agencies with advice on "child care problems; breakdowns; and replacements," as well as matters related to naturalization and citizenship, adoption and guardianship.[125]

By September 1952, USCOM had overseen the placement of 200 Greek children, two thirds of whom were teenaged boys, in foster care with relatives or other Greek Americans known to their families.[126] Most were not actually orphans, but rather were children of widowed and impoverished mothers, many of whom may have understood sending their adolescent sons and daughters overseas as an extension of Greek's historic patterns of kinship-based economic migration to the United States rather than as a relinquishment of parental rights.[127] Surviving parents were nonetheless required to sign a "certificate of abandonment" revoking any rights associated with their relationship with the child—a provision likely inserted in the legislation by restrictionists seeking to prevent unaccompanied refugee minors from sponsoring their family's immigration in the future.[128] While many adapted well to their new living arrangements, other children's experiences of trauma and separation or incompatibility led to conflicts between unaccompanied Greek minors and their foster families. This sometimes led to separation from relatives and replacement with non-Greek American foster families. In at least one case, a Greek American family sought to return a child to Greece "before sufficient time was given for the child to adjust," and was only dissuaded after a local AHEPA member was called in to provide "support and strength."[129]

Increasingly uncomfortable with the Hellenic society's haphazard approach to resettlement, USCOM severed its agreement with AHEPA in fall 1952. However, their initial logistical support allowed AHEPA to take advantage of the amended DP Act's broader eligibility standards to secure foster homes for a first wave of impoverished Greek youth in the United States. By the midfifties, these initial efforts would balloon into a politically popular but legally questionable "crusade" to find (white) Greek babies for American adoptive parents, as a result of which approximately 3,200 Greek children would be adopted by American parents by the early 1960s.[130]

AHEPA's adoption program, which initially attracted both positive media attention and congressional support, would eventually fall into disrepute in both Greece and the United States, as critics accused the organization of profiting from a gray-market baby trade that coerced impoverished Greek mothers into giving up their children. However, other voluntary organizations also struggled to balance the possibilities and perils embedded in the amended DP Act's new provisions for the admission of European "half-orphans." The revised legislation imposed an unprecedented moral obligation on voluntary agency staff overseas: determining when to authorize children's separation from impoverished mothers who were unable or unwilling to emigrate. Continued economic devastation in Europe and the looming closure of the IRO put pressure on ill and destitute parents to make a decision; so too did U.S. social workers who believed in the benefits of resettlement and the "great abundance of America" despite the increasingly recognized psychological importance of keeping families together.[131]

AHEPA was not the only agency to sometimes cut corners in making these assessments. While instructing overseas staff to guide parents in considering "all the implications of releasing their children for resettlement with strangers in a strange land," USCOM's leadership conceded that time constraints often prevented staff from providing "the lengthy casework sessions such a serious decision demanded." What's more, although it insisted that "in most cases, the possibility of adoption plans was discussed," the committee admitted that explicit approval for children's adoption was not always included in consent forms.[132] It's unclear why language granting explicit consent wasn't included in every certificate of abandonment—especially since some American foster parents would later seek permission from U.S. courts to adopt children with one or more living parent in Europe.[133]

Moreover, the application of the amended DP Act continued to restrict resettlement to white European children. When German officials approached the DP Commission for support for an intercountry adoption program for mixed-race "GI babies"—their request was summarily denied.[134] Instead the commission recommended resettling Afro-European children in Central and South America where, they claimed, "issues of race" held less significance. At the same time, DP Commission representatives inquired about the availability of white ethnic German orphans, who were in high demand with prospective American adoptive parents.

Official indifference to the plight of German "brown babies" generated a storm of protest from African American civic organizations, who argued that the children were a "political problem" created by the military's discriminatory policy allowing white service members to marry European women while denying Black soldiers permission to marry the white mothers of their children.[135] The federal government continued to refuse any obligation toward the sons and daughters of Black service members overseas. Federal adherence to this policy suggests that prejudices that had excluded African Americans from New Deal benefits continued to shape official understandings of Black women and children as undeserving of public support into the 1950s—while revealing the racialized limits on which overseas children were imagined as deserving of U.S. protection.[136]

Neither the Children's Bureau nor USCOM—both of which served an almost exclusively white clientele and perceived Black foster children as extremely "difficult to place"—ever stepped forward to champion the cause of needy Afro-European boys and girls.[137] Black American leaders and organizations ultimately initiated their own fundraising campaigns to assist mixed-race children in German orphanages while facilitating private intercountry adoptions for those select few who could afford them. Notable among these was Mabel Grammer, a correspondent for the African American Baltimore newspaper *Afro-American* living in Mannheim, Germany, with her service member husband, who beginning in 1951 personally oversaw the adoption of as many as 700 Black German children by African American families. This remarkable effort earned her the enmity of the American child resettlement agencies she bypassed in the process.[138]

By 1951, millions of people had been displaced by new conflicts in India, China, Indonesia, and the Middle East, and millions more rendered homeless by the civil war in Korea. It became clear to President Truman that the postwar refugee crisis was not a limited or strictly European phenomenon, and U.S. involvement in the rapidly decolonizing "third world" might lead unprecedented numbers of displaced nonwhite people to seek asylum in the United States. Rethinking his commitment to refugees, Truman declined to submit the newly promulgated United Nations Convention Relating to the Status of Refugees to Congress for ratification. He justified this decision on the basis that the treaty applied primarily to refugees displaced by the Second World War, and the United States had already done its part to resolve the DP crisis. Ratification, therefore, had no "added value," while unnecessarily constraining U.S. sovereignty over its own immigration policy.[139]

At the same time, congressional restrictionists launched a complete overhaul of the nation's immigration law. This culminated with the passage in June 1952 of the McCarran-Walter Act that, despite granting symbolic quotas for previously excluded Asian nations, otherwise reaffirmed the national origins quota system. It also imposed new security screening requirements making immigration more difficult for all applicants.[140] Since legislators had no interest in continuing "anything like the post-war displaced persons program," the act provided no additional visas for refugees of any age.[141] Passed over the president's objections, the new immigration law was a victory for restrictionists determined to end the relatively generous refugee admissions of the past four years. It also reinforced prewar understandings of refugees as an exception to be addressed through emergency legislation, rather than as a recognized category of migrants with a right for admission within permanent U.S. law.

In spring 1951, with the extended Displaced Persons Act about to expire, the IRO began the process of delegating the care of their approximately 1,400 remaining unaccompanied minors to local German and Austrian authorities.[142] On June 28, however, the Displaced Persons Act was extended at the last minute, allowing resettlement efforts to continue for another year.[143] Confronting the final end of refugee admissions in June 1952, USCOM began to finally wind down operations in Europe. In January 1953, Theodora Allen, an USCOM representative in Europe, approached the directors of the International Social Service (ISS) branch in Munich—to date not involved in resettling unaccompanied refugee minors overseas—to propose that they assume responsibility for embarking the small number of unaccompanied children still awaiting visas for the United States. The American branch of ISS initially declined, since USCOM's terms bypassed its U.S. office; ISS also feared expanded activities in the United States might engender conflict with "touchy" sectarian—especially Catholic—organizations.[144] However, reluctant to turn down the "golden opportunity" to gain access to USCOM's ample reserve funds as well as "a larger place in the U.S. Welfare field as far as . . . foreign children are concerned," ISS agreed to take charge of USCOM's few remaining European cases.[145]

With the chances of refugee admissions reduced almost to nil under the McCarran-Walter Act and calls for new refugee legislation resoundingly rebuffed, USCOM's leaders concluded that opportunities for relocating unaccompanied European children to the United States had been exhausted. In April 1953, USCOM executive director Ingeborg Olsen wrote to her counterpart at ISS in New York that "no other mass immigration of children was planned."[146] That same month, USCOM concluded operations, turning over the 748 children—the rest aged out of the program, including 208 who enlisted in the U.S. military—still under their care to ISS's American branch.[147]

Signaling the end of an era in the history of unaccompanied child migration to the United States, ISS's assumption of responsibility for the nation's stalled refugee minor resettlement program followed closely on the heels of

Republican Dwight D. Eisenhower's inauguration as the nation's thirty-fourth president in January 1953. Convinced that the United States' anti-communist foreign policy required admission of more European refugees and immigrants, and seeking the support of Catholics and Eastern European Americans who traditionally voted Democratic, the celebrated U.S. Army general repeated his opposition to the McCarran-Walter Act throughout his 1952 campaign.[148] Once elected, however, the popular new president opted not to expend political capital by demanding immediate immigration reform, choosing instead to work behind the scenes to generate support for another emergency refugee bill.[149] Passing Congress on July 28, the same month as the cease-fire ending the Korean War, the Refugee Relief Act (RRA) of 1953 authorized the entry into the United States of an additional 214,000 DPs and "victims of natural disaster, oppression and persecution."[150]

But the legislation was less a testament to U.S. concern for victims of persecution than to congressional restrictionists' determination to continue cherry-picking refugees whose admission advanced the nation's foreign policy objectives—and preserved its white-majority identity. Although the RRA granted refugees access to nonquota visas, it limited eligibility primarily to asylum seekers from current or emerging Cold War conflict zones and allotted visas according to a formula that reinforced the racial priorities of the national origins system. Despite the dramatic expansion of U.S. involvement in Japan, Taiwan, Korea, and Vietnam during the postwar period, the legislation prioritized the admission of Soviet-bloc "escapees" over the millions of Asian victims and opponents of communism.[151]

In another concession to defenders of the prewar immigration restrictions, the RRA also overturned the Displaced Persons Act's provision allowing voluntary agencies to issue corporate affidavits guaranteeing refugees would not become a public charge, reinstating previous requirements that each visa applicant secure an affidavit from an individual sponsor promising them employment, housing, and other necessary support.[152] State Department officials tasked with overseeing the RRA also revived administrative techniques from the 1930s to slow the issuance of visas, including exhaustive security pre-clearances and ideological screenings.[153] During the legislation's three-year term, these provisions of the Refugee Relief Act provided a stark counterpoint to the growing international recognition of refugees' right to seek asylum contained in the 1948 Universal Declaration of Human Rights—of which the United States was a signatory—as well as emerging notions of refugees as entitled to admission under different rules than voluntary immigrants that had been reflected in the DP Act.

The RRA similarly quashed hopes for resuming efforts to resettle unaccompanied refugee minors in the United States. At first glance, the new law appeared to expand upon the children's provision of previous legislation. Setting aside 4,000 visas for "eligible orphans" under the age of ten who experienced the death, disappearance, or abandonment of both parents, or "half-orphans" whose sole responsible parent had released them for emigration and adoption, it also opened the doors for the first time to children without respect to their national origin.[154] But in a striking departure from the DP Act, RRA visas would *only* be granted to children adopted abroad by an American citizen and their spouse, or when consular officers received adequate assurances they would be adopted immediately upon arrival in the United States.[155] The act also established new procedures for adoption by "proxy," authorizing prospective parents to designate an overseas representative to take custody of their child on their behalf. Ignoring child welfare professionals' repeated calls for the restoration of the Children's Bureau's role overseeing the placement of all unaccompanied children admitted to the United States, the RRA left the regulation of overseas adoption in the hands of state and local authorities. Conditioning eligibility for the first time upon unaccompanied minors' status as adoptees, the RRA's orphan provisions categorically excluded their admission *as refugees*. In doing so, it overruled the DP Act's framing of children as autonomous rights-bearing subjects whose resettlement depended upon the existence of "adequate social reasons" rather than the desires of U.S. citizen adoptive parents.

More than just a convenient means of providing concessions to a well-organized coalition of adoptive parents, the inclusion of what was effectively the nation's first intercountry adoption bill within refugee relief legislation deliberately blurred the lines between state-sponsored humanitarianism and private charity. The RRA allowed lawmakers to claim they were once again extending "America's helping hand" toward needy youth overseas, enhancing the nation's international reputation while simultaneously putting a halt to almost two decades of steadily developing federal involvement in the resettlement of unaccompanied refugee minors.[156] In a political sleight of hand as brilliant as it was cynical, the RRA's supporters took advantage of ongoing public confusion about the distinction between refugee children destined for foster homes and "war orphans" preselected for adoption, preserving the appearance of a humanitarian policy toward unaccompanied refugee minors as they effectively barred them from the country.

The difference between unaccompanied refugee minors and intercountry adoptees was glaringly apparent to established child welfare professionals

War Orphans and Children on Demand

who objected to the legislation's emphasis on adoption at the expense of refugee relief. Alarmed children's advocates, including ISS officers in the United States and the Allied occupation zones, warned that allowing small and sparsely regulated private adoption agencies to bypass the Children's Bureau's thorough procedures gravely threatened children's safety and well-being.[157] They also criticized the RRA for restricting visas to children under ten, which excluded many of those most in need of new homes. Their complaints only underscored that the purpose of the act's orphan provisions was *not* to provide care and protection to endangered youth—but rather to increase American citizens' access to adoptable children.

Objections to the RRA also revealed how notions of children's best interests had evolved since the war years, leading at least some child welfare workers to question the efficacy of overseas evacuation. Some leaders and staff involved since the 1930s in resettling refugee minors had become increasingly attentive to psychologists' warnings about the negative consequences of removing young boys and girls from their families and nations of origin.[158] Many were especially troubled by the growing placements of children in foster or adoptive homes when one or both of their parents was still alive— something they had contributed to by lobbying for "half-orphans" eligibility for resettlement. In a 1953 retrospective of USCOM's child-saving efforts, written while debates over the RRA were still ongoing, committee historian Kathryn Close admitted that:

> Doubts have also arisen about the advisability of encouraging parent-child separation under the DP program. . . . In a comfortable and vigorous America, it can be difficult to understand the despair for a child's future that both parents and selection agent can feel in an environment which promises only degrading poverty. Nevertheless, the fact is inescapable that some children came to this country with feelings of rejection or guilt standing in the way of their happy adjustment. Since it was not always possible to offer hospitality to their surviving parents too, would it have been better to look for ways of improving their opportunities in Europe?[159]

Echoing still-nascent norms articulated in the 1951 UN Convention Relating to the Status of Refugees, which defined family unity as "an essential right of the refugee," Close stopped short of explicitly acknowledging that her nation's restrictive national origins quotas played a role breaking up families by preventing many war-afflicted parents from seeking asylum in the United States with their children. Her words suggest that by the time of the RRA's passage, at least some professionals involved in children's resettlement had begun to take seriously the negative consequences of family separation—and even to reflect upon the role of both U.S. immigration law and voluntary agency personnel in encouraging it.

At the same time, a growing number of organizations and individuals seized the opportunity presented by lax state laws to enter the overseas adoption business. Newly exempt from national origins quotas that restricted admission to the country almost exclusively to European boys and girls, these proponents of intercountry adoption began to look further afield—both geographically and racially—for new sources of adoptable "war orphans." Between 1953 and 1956, 4,000 adopted children under the age of ten from Greece, Italy, Austria, Japan, and Korea started new lives in the United States.[160] During this period, following the 1950 U.S. military intervention in what would grow into a devastating civil war between Korea's capitalist south and its communist north, the RRA's proxy adoption statute and a tentative new openness to interracial family formation (though it rarely crossed the midcentury United States' rigid Black-white divide) fueled the rapidly accelerating transfer of Korean adoptees, including the mixed-race children of U.S. service members and Korean mothers, to the United States.[161]

During this time, human interest features in newspapers and magazines celebrated intercountry adoptions as a way for Americans to demonstrate racial tolerance and embrace the nation's new role as the benevolent paternal savior of children victimized by communism.[162] In 1955, the story of Harry and Bertha Holt—an evangelical couple from Oregon who adopted eight Korean children before founding what would become one of the United States' largest intercountry adoption agencies—sparked a media frenzy, with women's magazines leading the charge in encouraging families hungry for children to look for them in Asia.[163] The insistence by both the American media and adoptive parents on their humanitarian motives hid the fact that their government provided no financial support to war-afflicted families in Korea or admitted a significant number of Korean refugees, actions which might have allowed some mothers to keep their children instead of surrendering them to adoptive parents. To be fair, despite their criticisms of proxy adoptions, U.S. child welfare professionals similarly declined to propose programs for unaccompanied Korean refugee minors who might have benefited from resettlement.[164]

Intercountry adoption advocates' insistence on their humanitarian motives represented a particularly jarring example of the willingness of some

Americans to disregard the coercion and exploitation involved in separating children from their families and nations of origin, in order to grow their own families as quickly, easily, and with as little state interference as possible.[165] That a public who broadly supported admission of British and European minors to the United States (as both refugees *and* adoptees) only took action on behalf of Korean "war orphans" when they were reframed as the children of white parents speaks cuttingly to the persistent racial limitations on mid-century American concern for endangered overseas children.

By the time the DP program concluded in August 1952, more than 400,000 Europeans had been resettled in the United States, including 3,037 unaccompanied refugee minors under the age of sixteen. Of these, 1,462 had been admitted under USCOM's blanket affidavit.[166] They owed their new lives in America to President Truman and a diverse coalition of American refugee advocates, whose tireless work pushed Congress and the public to accept a new responsibility toward displaced persons of all ages.[167]

Convinced that the carefully regulated resettlement of endangered overseas children remained a legitimate humanitarian strategy, USCOM and its allies played an active role in lobbying efforts leading to the passage of the 1948 Displaced Persons Act. This unprecedented legislation and subsequent amendments gave official form for the first time to the incipient wartime notion of a state responsibility toward unaccompanied refugee minors, while creating new opportunities for the placement of a broader range of needy foreign children in American homes. Using the DP Act's provisions, the committee and its partners succeeded in placing thousands of unaccompanied European refugee minors in safe homes while strengthening their privileged relationship with the federal government and garnering distinct advantages over other U.S. child welfare organizations.

But USCOM's preeminence was soon challenged by a growing number of agencies that launched competing programs to bring unaccompanied European children to the United States. Congressional defenders of the nation's prewar immigration laws also worked to counter attempts by the committee and its allies to define refugees and children's rights more broadly by imposing new restrictions on the admission of unaccompanied minors. By then, however, leaders of USCOM and other established voluntary agencies harbored quiet doubts about the efficacy and ethics of resettling endangered overseas children in the United States—especially when this meant separating them from living parents or relatives.

Others, including some who argued taking in children from nations threatened by communism was both the most effective humanitarian response to their suffering *and* a way to advance the nation's Cold War foreign policy interests, had no such doubts. Reflecting distinct but intertwined responses to the emergence in the American mind of the "war orphan," efforts to resettle unaccompanied refugee minors and intercountry adoption schemes operated at cross purposes until the passage of the 1953 Refugee Relief Act, which set off a sudden upsurge in adoptions from war-devastated South Korea while effectively barring the resettlement of additional unaccompanied refugee minors in the United States. At the same time, official and media discourses celebrating intercountry adoption as a way to "rescue" needy foreign boys and girls obscured the racialized limits of American humanitarian sympathies, reinscribing both understandings of childlike nonwhite nations as dependent upon paternal U.S. benevolence and prewar notions of displaced boys and girls as objects of charity.[168]

Following the passage of the DP Act, more than two decades would pass before the United States amended its refugee laws to explicitly recognize unaccompanied refugee minors' unique claims on asylum. In the meantime, decisions about the admission and care of unaccompanied children would remain subject to the nation's ever-evolving geopolitics of compassion. As the Cold War reached new heights, the racial, national origins, and age-based divides between children admitted for resettlement, those who were adopted, and those who were excluded continued to harden. The popularity of intercountry adoption also continued to grow, encouraging more Americans to think of crisis-stricken developing nations as a source of "children on demand" while distracting them from ever-more critical debates about their nation's obligation toward refugees of all ages.

War Orphans and Children on Demand

4

Cold War Kids

Hungarian Unattached Youth and Refugee Resettlement in the Eisenhower Era, 1956–1958

In November 1956 as Hungarians fleeing Soviet repression streamed across the borders into Austria and Yugoslavia, the United Nations initiated an unprecedented effort to relocate escapees to new homes across Western Europe and in Canada and the United States. President Dwight D. Eisenhower, determined to demonstrate U.S. leadership in response to the crisis and reinforce the nation's commitment to anti-communist allies, launched the first federally driven resettlement effort in U.S. history. More than 38,000 Hungarians were admitted to the United States between November 1956 and March 1958, including approximately 800 unaccompanied refugee minors placed in American foster homes. An unprecedented state intervention in refugee resettlement, this first quasi-official program for Cold War kids represented a logical extension of postwar notions of the United States' responsibility to protect endangered overseas children and a response to emerging understandings of communism as a threat to young people's ideological and spiritual formation. Americans eagerly opened their homes to young white Christian Hungarian children—and less so to the adolescent boys making up the majority of unattached youth—reflecting the ways that race, gender, religion, and age continued to circumscribe U.S. concerns for vulnerable foreign children as well as the mixed motives of couples who hoped fostering might lead to adoption.

The resettlement of Hungarian youth constituted a radical departure from the ways voluntary agencies, which bore the brunt of implementing refugee policy, had worked with displaced children before. Operating under extreme pressure to move refugees of all ages as quickly as possible into new homes, agency leaders and staff found themselves compelled to subsume the unique needs of unattached Hungarian youth into the broader Cold War objectives of Eisenhower's resettlement program. The negative consequences of these rushed placements reignited latent tensions between sectarian and nonsectarian voluntary agencies, the U.S. federal government, and the United Nations over who was best qualified to make decisions on unaccompanied refugee minors' behalf—and whether resettlement in the United States served their best interests.

Driven more by a growing belief in refugees' importance to the United States' position in the Cold War than by humanitarian conditions, changing ideas about the appropriate role of the federal government in refugee resettlement only exacerbated these tensions, blossoming by 1957 into open conflict over who held ultimate responsibility for children arriving alone to the United States. By the time the nation's doors finally closed to Hungarian youth in March 1958, these debates led to a radical renegotiation of the public-private partnership which structured previous child evacuation schemes, changing forever the terms under which unaccompanied minors were brought to the United States. But one constant remained, linking the stories of resettled Hungarian youth to those of other displaced children who preceded or followed them: the extent to which the best interests of this latest generation of unaccompanied refugee minors was subordinated to the nation's more pressing geopolitical and domestic political priorities.

On October 23, 1956, the eyes of the world were fixed on the dramatic anti-Soviet uprising in Hungary. Nightly television news broadcasts beamed images of adolescent boys armed with Molotov cocktails waging a doomed battle against Red Army tanks in Budapest, while newspapers featured stark photographs of city streets filled with corpses. As refugees flooded into makeshift camps in tiny neighboring Austria, the United States' Western European allies, Eastern European émigrés around the world, and anti-communist Americans at home raised their voices to blame the CIA-sponsored Radio Free Europe of inciting the Hungarians and accuse President Dwight D. Eisenhower of failing to provide support for the uprising.[1]

Seeking to redirect attention away from the question of U.S. culpability and toward U.S. benevolence, Eisenhower announced he was allocating $20 million to the United Nations to provide emergency food and relief supplies to Hungarian refugees in Austria.[2] In early December—when it was clear initial European offers of asylum were insufficient to contain the refugee crisis—Eisenhower called on representatives from the State Department and Departments of Justice and Defense to discuss launching a "Hungarian Refugee Project." At that meeting the president expressed his opinion that, in the interest of regional stability, escapees must be moved out of Austria as fast as possible.[3] A quick offer by the United States to take in displaced Hungarians was needed to encourage other nations to continue admitting refugees—and to maintain the appearance of U.S. leadership in responding to the crisis. The president also hoped a robust resettlement effort would deflect hawkish critiques of his failed policy to "roll back" communism in Eastern Europe and mollify ethnic voters with origins in the region.[4]

The leadership of the Departments of State, Justice, and Defense agreed that a Hungarian refugee program should be "initiated by our government in service of its own national interests."[5] Initial plans were made to admit up to 5,000 escapees, who could be brought into the United States on some of the remaining 10,000 visas available under the 1953 Refugee Relief Act (RRA) which was set to expire at the end of 1956. The Departments of State and Justice agreed to expedite admissions by waiving current requirements that all foreigners undergo a thorough security screening before admission to the United States. To further facilitate quick resettlement, $1.5 million was appropriated from the president's discretionary Mutual Security Act fund to establish a reception center at Camp Kilmer, a decommissioned army barracks in New Jersey.[6]

Before the U.S. plans could be set in motion, the crisis in Central Europe expanded precipitously; by the end of November more than 100,000 escapees were crowded in Austrian camps. Members of the overseas diplomatic community, the State Department, the U.S. media, and civic, ethnic, and religious organizations united to pressure the president to scale up resettlement efforts, warning that America's humanitarian credentials were being undercut by more generous refugee policies adopted in Western Europe and Canada.[7] If the United States was going to reassure its allies of its commitment to freedom-loving people around the world, it would have to accept a greater share of the refugees—and fast. But how? The small number of visas still available under the Refugee Relief Act would expire in a few weeks. And the tiny Hungarian quota had been heavily mortgaged to admit refugees from the nation under the Displaced Persons Act, which made their entrance as quota immigrants virtually impossible.

Undeterred, on December 1, 1956, the president announced he was directing the Departments of State and Justice to admit an additional 21,500 Hungarian refugees "with the utmost practical speed." The first 6,500 received the remaining Refugee Relief Act visas; the additional 15,000 would enter under a provision of the 1952 McCarran-Walter Act authorizing the attorney general to "parole" into the country on a case-by-case basis a limited number of individuals whose admission served the national interest. Stressing that parolees would have "no permanent status in the United States," the president said he would ask lawmakers in January "for emergency legislation which will . . . permit qualified escapees who accept asylum in the United States to obtain permanent residence."[8]

A skilled political strategist, Eisenhower understood that the consent of a deeply restrictionist Congress to his unprecedented use of the parole statute depended on maintaining widespread sympathy for the anti-communist escapees.[9] Fortunately, for the moment it was high; by November 19, the State Department had received over 1,500 citizen inquiries offering assistance to refugees.[10] But favorable public sentiment wasn't something that the president could take for granted. Even in November and December 1956, when sympathy for the Hungarians was at its highest, as many as a third of Americans objected to any liberalization of immigration policy, and the White House had already received a considerable number of letters opposing the admission of further refugees.[11] Leaving nothing to chance, the president asked his close friend and former undersecretary of the Army Tracy S. Voorhees to convene a President's Committee for Hungarian Refugee Relief (PCHRR).

Ostensibly private but funded through the Mutual Security Act and administered according to Eisenhower's directives, the PCHRR would oversee the resettlement of Hungarians across the nation. Expecting voluntary agencies to continue handling the logistics of resettlement, Voorhees understood the committee's primary task as maintaining public support for the president's geopolitically driven "crash" program. He contacted the public relations branch of the prestigious McCann Erickson Advertising Agency that had helped win Eisenhower's recent reelection to develop a media campaign for the hearts and minds of everyday Americans on behalf of the Hungarian refugees.[12] Only once this public relations strategy was in place did Voorhees reach out to voluntary agencies to ask for their assistance in putting Eisenhower's program into motion.

Voorhees met with representatives of major voluntary agencies to lay out the terms of the public-private partnership for Hungarian resettlement in the

United States. In the interests of speed, agency personnel in Austria (rather than consular or Immigration Service officials) would select those to be resettled. After a cursory screening, they embarked to the United States, where they were transferred to the newly christened Joyce Kilmer Reception Center for a few days of reception care. Sensitive to the optics of displaced Europeans spending their first days in America in a military camp, Voorhees rebranded the barracks with a civilian name. The federal government provided voluntary agencies with a stipend of fifty dollars per refugee and reimbursed the cost of transportation to their new homes. Ever attentive to the resettlement program's geopolitical objectives, Voorhees repeatedly stressed that new arrivals should move through Kilmer as fast as possible; any suggestion by the media that refugees were being held in a space he admitted resembled "a big concentration camp" would be a public relations "nightmare."[13]

Eisenhower's program represented an unprecedented departure from the past, when the initiative, responsibility, and funding for resettlement had come primarily from private sectarian agencies. Moreover, previous programs had required extensive preplanning and overseas screening to ensure refugees wouldn't become a public charge in the United States. As a result of these stringent requirements, European displaced persons (DPs) had often waited several years before receiving visas; even "fast-tracked" communist escapees admitted under the 1953 RRA waited an average of one year for their admission to be approved.[14] Understandably, then, voluntary agencies expressed deep reservations about the ways the PCHRR plan departed from previous practices. Already concerned about the uncertain legal status of Hungarian "parolees," they were equally distressed by the "unheard-of speed" of the resettlement process. With parole status granted on a first-come, first-served basis by voluntary agency personnel, sectarian leaders and staff faced a stark choice. If they delayed participation in Eisenhower's "crash" resettlement program to negotiate terms, they risked surrendering operational terrain to agencies willing to accept the PCHRR's terms and begin immediately embarking refugees to Kilmer. As a result, fewer of their own coreligionists would be admitted to the United States.[15]

Sixteen voluntary agencies pragmatically chose to respond to Voorhees' call. Pitted against one another in the competition for a limited number of resettlement opportunities, these agencies, along with a handful of smaller newly formed Hungarian relief committees, descended upon Kilmer jockeying for physical space in the crowded reception center. Lacking clear direction from the PCHRR, agency staff scrambled in a haphazard and uncoordinated manner to prepare for the impending arrival of tens of thousands of refugees.[16]

Voorhees announced to the media on December 5, 1956, that "Operation Mercy" was now underway. The first 9,500 Hungarians were airlifted to the United States from Bremerhaven, Germany, in early December; an additional 7,000 departed the coastal city by midmonth on American naval ships.[17]

Conspicuously absent among the participants in the crash program was the American Branch of the International Social Service (ISS)—the Geneva-based agency selected by USCOM in 1952 to assume responsibility for its remaining European minors awaiting resettlement in the United States. The agency instead reached out to the Department of State to urge it to plan for any unaccompanied children among those dispatched to the United States. ISS's European branches were already collaborating with the UN High Commissioner for Refugees (UNHCR) in Austria. While the ISS's position was that unaccompanied Hungarian children were best cared for temporarily in neighboring countries until their parents and relatives could be traced, American Branch director William T. Kirk emphasized that his staff was prepared to assist the U.S. government in planning for any that made their way to the country.[18] Urging "early and special attention" to these Cold War kids, Kirk suggested that those under eighteen unaccompanied by a close family member be registered on a special list "carefully kept for future use in searching for families." He also recommended that all relief organizations operating in the Austrian camps collaborate with a major national voluntary agency to make "the best plan possible" for children selected for resettlement.[19]

The ISS's principled calls for a federally coordinated plan to oversee minors' resettlement reflected the growing consensus among midcentury child welfare professionals about the need for age-specific refugee policies. However, accompanied as it was by an assertion of their unique qualifications to oversee other voluntary agencies, it may also have been partially motivated by the ISS's determination to assert a leading role in responding to the Hungarian crisis. Either way, it put the agency at odds with the White House, the PCHRR, and the State Department, all of whom were focused almost exclusively on the geopolitically motivated goal of a quick refugee resettlement effort. A week after registering the agency's concerns with Pierce J. Gerety, the Refugee Relief Program deputy administrator, Kirk received a terse note from Gerety declining to implement any of its suggestions.[20] The short letter made the government's position on Hungarian unaccompanied minors abundantly clear: if they were admitted to the United States, it would *not* be because they merited special consideration as endangered children—but rather because of their designation as anti-communist refugees. Nor would attempts be made to provide specialized services to minors, since this would inevitably slow down efforts to quickly move as many Hungarians as possible out of Austria. In this latest articulation of the geopolitics of compassion, age-based needs would take a back seat to the nation's Cold War foreign policy objectives.

Press dispatches from Austrian camps had raised public expectation that unaccompanied children would be coming to the United States. On December 3, an image of nine-year old Nicholas Szilagyi, photographed at the Red Cross Center in Andau, Austria, appeared in newspapers across the country. Accompanied by a caption saying "the boy's foster parents were killed early in the Hungarian revolt," the poignant photo of a thin, knock-kneed, rucksack-toting refugee youth reactivated American memories of the "war orphans" from the Second World War.[21] Journalists proclaimed Operation Mercy a "great humanitarian venture" in the tradition of the Berlin Airlift, and media coverage emphasized that "women and children would have priority on the planes" leaving Germany.[22] On December 13, a *New York Times* correspondent commented on the "many children" among the "fugitives of despotic communism" departing on one flight from Munich.[23] Another correspondent counted at least nine children, "dressed in tattered clothing," aboard another refugee flight, the youngest of whom was "just one year old."[24] Neither story mentioned the presence (or absence) of the children's parents.

U.S. journalists continued to pay disproportionate attention to the relatively small numbers of young children arriving via Operation Mercy. On December 13, the *New York Herald Tribune* accompanied a story on the arrival the previous day of 199 refugees with a photograph of a smiling Women's Auxiliary Air Force officer holding a cozily bundled "infant refugee" in her arms, and no parents in sight.[25]

Newspapers across the country featured equally evocative photos of tired refugee children, huddling against the cold and sipping warm drinks or munching on donuts. In most cases, no family appeared with them.[26] Perhaps the media crafted stories in this way to elicit sympathy from a public historically opposed to generous refugee policies. Whatever the motivation, they joined an international brigade of journalists, politicians, and activists who sought to advance political and social objectives by making use of sentimentalized discourses and images of children in need of rescue.[27] By focusing on Hungarian children without reference to parents, these representations also reinforced postwar conceptions of unaccompanied refugee minors and "war orphans" as alone and isolated, with neither families or communities capable of protecting them.[28] These representations emphasized the vulnerability of Hungarian refugee youth—indeed, of refugees of all ages—to communist

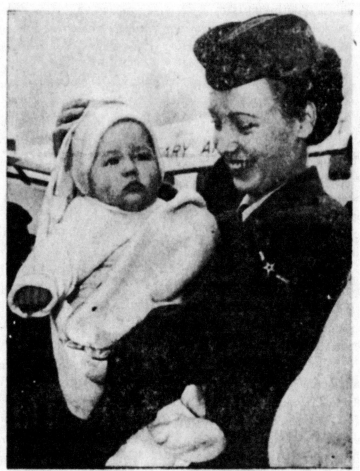

SAFE FROM TERROR OF HUNGARY—An infant refugee being held by a WAF at McGuire Air Force Base yesterday.

Newspaper photographs of Hungarian refugee children without their parents emphasized notions of refugees of all ages as passive and dependent, while creating the misperception that large numbers of adoptable "war orphans" would be coming to the United States. *Courtesy of Rutgers University Special Collections and University Archives, Tracy S. Voorhees Papers, MC 1407.*

abuses and deprivations and their dependence on the protection of a benevolent United States. They also helped create a widespread belief that thousands of young unaccompanied children were streaming across the border into Austria and might be brought to the United States by Operation Mercy.

Civic and religious leaders similarly sought to raise public sympathy for refugees by urging Americans to provide shelter to Hungarian children and "war orphans." A number of voluntary agencies launched fundraising campaigns prominently featuring young refugees, including newspaper ads stating donations provided resettlement opportunities for unaccompanied minors.[29] Among the most misleading of these, on December 10, the Save the Children Federation sent an emotional plea to donors asking them to contribute a "Christmas gift" in the form of aid to the "thousands of little Hungarian children whose parents sent them across the Austrian-Hungarian border before the Iron Curtain of death and terror clanged down between them."[30] The ISS-American Branch attempted to clarify that rumors about Hungarian children being sent to Austria alone had "not been substantiated."[31] But with the demand for adoptable white children reaching a new high midcentury, ISS's warnings fell on deaf ears. Beginning in mid-November, thousands of prospective adoptive parents wrote to U.S. voluntary agencies, religious leaders, congressional representatives, the State Department and the Immigration and Naturalization Service (INS), and even to the president and Mrs. Eisenhower, offering "forever homes" to displaced Hungarian boys and girls. Many enclosed newspaper clippings of the Associated Press photograph of Nicholas Szilagyi, along with requests for information on how they might adopt him, attesting to the power of child-centered media images as well as ongoing confusion over the distinction between unaccompanied refugee minors and adoptable overseas children.[32]

Like early advocates of intercountry adoption, many Americans offering to take in a Hungarian child expressed their motivation in ideological terms. Mrs. Lillian Mazzetta's letter to the president framed her desire to grow her family as an extension of the nation's foreign policy, describing adopting a "war orphan" as a "truly democratic act." Others spoke more broadly of their "spiritually inspired desire" to "be of service to those less fortunate than ourselves."[33] The overwhelming majority of letters, however, were motivated by prospective parents' frustrated desires to expand their families. Letters came from couples who already had several children, reflecting personal and midcentury cultural preference for larger families; in other cases, parents wished to provide an only child with a sibling. Many especially poignant pleas were penned by childless couples or those who had experienced the death of a son or daughter, who poured out their pain and longing to the unknown government officials and voluntary agency personnel who read the letters.

Most prospective parents followed the lead of postwar intercountry adoption proponents in imagining the Hungarian crisis as an opportunity to grow their families while doing something politically and morally virtuous. This sentiment was expressed concisely by Mr. C. E. Olds, who observed in a letter to Tracy Voorhees that "the humanitarian aspects of caring for the unfortunate from Hungary might fulfill their desire to provide their daughter with a sibling."[34] However, the disturbingly transactional nature of many adoption inquiries was revealed in letters openly expressing prospective parents' hopes that the refugee crisis might provide them with a quick and easy alternative to domestic adoption. Mrs. William Dominish of Painesville, Ohio, succinctly articulated this naïve opportunism in a letter to the president. "Surely there must be hundreds and hundreds of homeless children," she wrote. "It seems like we should have no trouble at all."[35]

Complaints about how difficult the domestic adoption process was in the midcentury United States were common. Expressing her resentment of welfare workers' perceived class biases, Mrs. John Wilson of Kinney, Minnesota, lamented in a letter to President Eisenhower that she and her husband had tried "a number of times to adopt," but that "it seems you have to be practically a millionaire . . . before they'd even consider it."[36] Mrs. W. Jack Hunsucker of Birmingham, Alabama, similarly confided to the president that she and her husband had found it "almost impossible" to adopt a child under six years of age. In a particularly heartrending letter, Mrs. Albert Hester of Winchester, Illinois, also asked Eisenhower for help finding a Hungarian child for her son John, a disabled World War II veteran. Unable to adopt locally, the Hester family had already started looking for overseas alternatives; John's sister, who was stationed in Germany with her husband, tried unsuccessfully "to get a baby for him" there. "What a wonderful Christmas it would be for all of us if they could have a child!" she exclaimed. "Won't you please see what you can do?"[37]

Notwithstanding the deep affection for children contained in many letters, they also reveal in startling ways the extent to which increasingly consumer-oriented midcentury Americans had come to think of foreign crises as an opportunity to grow their families. That many understood overseas adoption primarily as a source of "children on demand" was laid bare by letter writers who prefaced requests for information about children by stating they were unable (or unwilling) to provide relief to adult Hungarian refugees.[38] Most letters were also highly specific about which children Americans were

Cold War Kids

willing to open their homes to. In addition to gender preferences, many prospective parents were only interested in adopting children under the age of four. Most also requested children who were "normal mentally" and "free from contagious diseases."[39] Others said they wished to adopt Catholic or Protestant children.[40] A small minority, including Mrs. Faye Blumberg and her husband, wished to offer a "respectable [sic] upbringing" to "a Jewish child" or "a child of mixed parentage with some Jewish background."[41]

Many prospective parents—themselves mostly white—emphasized the importance of the children's European origins, asking for boys or girls whose hair, eye color, and skin tone were similar to their own. Others made racial requirements explicit, like Mr. and Mrs. Allen Norris of Nashville, Tennessee, who asked President Eisenhower for his help in "securing a little white girl between the ages of 3 and 6." Others made clear that despite Hungarians' whiteness, they presumed the children to be culturally inferior to U.S. children, as did Mrs. Robert Schuerger of Saint Louis, Missouri, who informed the president that after several years of failed attempts to adopt domestically, she was now so desperate to be a mother that she would "even take one of them" if she "couldn't get an American."[42]

By mid-December 1956, the International Social Service-American Branch's New York office was swamped with more than 3,000 requests to adopt Hungarian children. An alarmed spokesperson stressed to the *New York Times* that "virtually no orphans were arriving from Hungary, and that other children could not be given for adoption." But the ISS also recognized that Americans' desire for white Hungarian refugee children played a crucial role in sustaining public support for their adult countrymen and women's resettlement. In a private letter to ISS-Austria director Hildegard M. Luft, Susan Pettiss of the American Branch reflected with exasperation on "the emotional appeal that unaccompanied and orphaned children [had] in this country," which put the agency "in a rather difficult spot publication relation-wise as we do not want to appear negative about giving help to children needing to come in. At the same time, it does seem a shame to have individuals raise their hopes . . . in looking forward to taking in the children." She nonetheless acknowledged that the current geopolitics of compassion demanded a "sympathetic interpretation" of these offers, with a "view to directing such well-meant interest toward other areas of the refuge problem in which help is acutely needed."[43] To strategically navigate this bind, the agency brought in a public relations consultant to help them draft press releases on the topic of unaccompanied refugee minors.[44] The following day, ISS-American Branch director William T. Kirk explained to the media that some Hungarian children had indeed become temporarily separated from parents while crossing the border; however, most were quickly reunited with their families. Reassuring the public that the agency had "plans to care for any child whose parents have been killed or deported and whose relatives are unable or unwilling to offer aid," Kirk also gently reiterated that few young children were expected to be available for foster care or adoption.[45] Careful to avoid offending everyday citizens upon whose support Eisenhower's resettlement program depended, the PCHRR prepared several drafts of a form letter responding to adoption inquiries. They first thanked prospective parents for their "heartwarming interest" in a Hungarian refugee child, before delicately pointing out that since "small children fleeing their homeland would ordinarily be accompanied by their parents or relatives," few adoptable boys and girls were expected to come to the United States.[46]

The scarcity of "war orphans," of course, didn't mean there were no unaccompanied children among the refugees. The ISS accurately predicted that as many as 3,000 minors were among the 200,000 people fleeing Hungary after the uprising. These included young people who initially crossed into Austria with relatives or other adults as well as some who left alone. Others were youth who had participated in the anti-Soviet rebellion and feared to return; and some came across in class groups directly from their schools, under the care of teachers. Still others, who were unhappy at home, frustrated by the lack of economic and social freedom in Communist Hungary, or frightened by rumors of mass deportations to the Soviet Union, also joined the human current flowing across the border into Austria or Yugoslavia.[47] During the chaotic first weeks of the exodus, many of these youth—approximately three-quarters of whom were boys between the ages of fourteen and seventeen—began to congregate in Austrian refugee camps, where they were initially housed with the general population.

The unaccompanied refugee minors sparked new tensions between the Austrian government and Hungary, which demanded the immediate return of all escapees under the age of eighteen. New divisions also emerged among voluntary agencies about the best way to handle them. Sensitive to the ways postwar resettlement efforts sometimes produced (rather than remediated) family separation, veteran agencies including the HIAS (founded as the Hebrew Immigrant Aid Society) and the Lutheran Refugee Service (LRS) concurred with the ISS that migration of unaccompanied minors to the United States should be discouraged. The Church World Service, although agreeing about the need to proceed carefully, was more open to youth resettlement. Alone among the sectarian organizations, the militantly anti-communist Catholic agencies were determined to resettle as many escapees as possible—regardless of age.[48] They concluded that the unwholesome environment in Austrian camps and threat of repatriation to young people's spiritual and moral well-being made quick emigration the best option for young escapees. By early December 1956, the U.S. National Catholic Welfare Conference (NCWC) had already petitioned the Austrian Refugee Relief Program administrator for permission to bring a group of 150 Hungarian children to the United States, for resettlement at a Catholic boarding school where they could continue their education under the supervision of Hungarian refugee teachers.[49]

Despite other major agencies' reticence to resettle unaccompanied children, unrelenting pressure to move escapees out of Austria as quickly as possible led to some boys and girls being sent alone to the United States. Streamlined screening procedures directed agency personnel to only interview the male head of households seeking refuge together. Since few caseworkers spoke Hungarian, a number of younger children who attached themselves to unrelated adults in the camps were miscategorized as members of other family units.[50] An undetermined number of youth also lied about their age, claiming to be over eighteen in hopes of more quickly receiving permission to emigrate.[51]

Alarmed by the "too speedy immigration of . . . young people to overseas countries," ISS-Geneva director Dicey Dodds met directly with Warren A. Pinegar of the UN High Commissioner for Refugees to warn against the grave "social, legal, and psychological" consequences—and the political perils—of hastily conceived child evacuations.[52] Dodds urged the United Nations to protect the best interests of children by barring emigration of Hungarian escapees under the age of sixteen and to ensure legal and social protections for youth who had already migrated alone. Her subsequent correspondence with Pinegar also suggest that the ISS's activism in this arena also reflected its desire to assert a leadership role in responding to the refugee crisis. Pointing out that the ISS was given "responsibility for all IRO [International Refugee Organization] unfinished work on unaccompanied children" after World War II, Dodds offered the agency's services to the UNHCR in handling this "special problem." She further asserted that the ISS's nonsectarian identity and decades of specialized experience in international casework made it the only agency qualified to oversee the migration of unaccompanied children.[53]

ISS leadership in Austria and New York similarly attempted to establish control over the resettlement of Hungarian youth. At a series of December 1956 meetings with U.S. Ambassador Llewellyn E. Thompson and representatives of the major American voluntary agencies in Vienna, they urged that "no Hungarian minor . . . be sent abroad unless the tragic fact, that he or she will *remain* [underlined in original] unaccompanied, has been established." Even then, they emphasized, placements should be "planned individually and with greatest care." Lest another agency be made responsible for this function, ISS-Austria director Hildegard M. Luft reminded the ambassador in a follow-up letter that her agency was "eager to assume responsibility."[54] At the same time in the United States, ISS-American Branch directors Susan Pettiss and William T. Kirk visited Camp Kilmer where they met with representatives of the President's Committee for Hungarian Refugee Relief and the Department of Health, Education, and Welfare (HEW) to advocate for a more cautious approach to the resettlement of unaccompanied Hungarian minors.[55] As in the past, though, their warnings—and their offers of help—went conspicuously unacknowledged.

As a result, hundreds of unaccompanied minors were among the first planeloads of refugees and parolees arriving in the United States in December 1956. Exactly how many is uncertain, since the Joyce Kilmer Reception Center record-keeping procedures did not distinguish between children who arrived with or without adults; in many cases, the fact that a child was unaccompanied wasn't discovered until weeks later. In a notable departure from U.S. law, which considered eighteen as the age of majority, Hungarian escapees sixteen years and older were registered by Kilmer staff as adults. Camp records further classified the two-thirds of the refugees who were employable "adults" over the age of sixteen by sex, height, weight, marital status, language ability, educational level, and occupational experience, noting of "the remaining third" only that they were "children . . . or housewives."[56]

Children and youth arriving alone were housed among the general refugee population with no supervision or age-appropriate recreational activities, a reflection of the PCHRR's lack of concern for refugees' age-specific needs.[57] The camp's 200 page operations manual—which established policy and procedures for everything from intelligence screenings to barracks operations, food, post exchange, and diaper service, as well as health, interpretation, educational, and mail services—included only one reference to unattached minors. The brief entry noted that a (single) representative of the federal Department of Health, Education, and Welfare "was working out plans to identify individuals with special health and welfare problems," including unaccompanied children, in order to provide services to them *after* resettlement. Despite repeated offers by HEW to assume a more active role caring for unaccompanied minors, the PCHRR chose to limit the department's role in the crash resettlement program to coordinating care for active tuberculosis patients.[58] HEW's circumscribed responsibilities were even more striking when compared to the State Department's robust presence at Kilmer, where they posted several officials to ensure resettlement efforts were carried out in ways consistent with "the foreign policy and foreign relations of the United States."[59] These deliberate omissions attest to the Eisenhower administration's view of Hungarian youth as first and foremost anti-communist refugees, and only peripherally as children.

Deliberate inattention to these Cold War kids age-specific needs also impacted placement procedures. Unlike previous programs, the president's crash resettlement scheme did not involve the Children's Bureau in establishing specific guidelines for processing unaccompanied refugee minors.[60] In the absence of federal guidelines or oversight, agency personnel under extreme pressure to move refugees of all ages out of reception care as fast as possible sometimes processed children under the age of sixteen as adults. This was common for youth who left school in Hungary at age fourteen for industrial jobs and self-identified as "workers." Other youth lied about their age, claiming to be sixteen or older, in order to be resettled independently. In the absence of birth certificates or other documents, overtaxed agency staff sometimes chose to take unaccompanied youth's statements at face value, since processing them as adults was quicker and easier. Employment opportunities thus became the primary—sometimes only—criteria for many unaccompanied refugee minors' placements.[61] Some voluntary agencies, notably the HIAS and the Lutheran Refugee Service, made a greater effort to secure appropriate placements for younger children in boarding schools, group homes and institutions, and with foster families. But these agencies handled very few unaccompanied minors. In most cases, since little to no advance casework was conducted before minors were sent to Kilmer, agency personnel tasked with resettling young people—few of whom were trained social workers or spoke Hungarian—grappled to make decisions without access to crucial information about family background, educational history, psychological needs, or future aspirations.[62]

The PCHRR's demand that refugees flow out of Kilmer as quickly as they arrived was unrelenting. As the need to secure suitable placements for young people grew more urgent, Hungarian-speaking persons and industrial recruiters began appearing at the camp to collect promising young workers and purported relatives—claims that overwhelmed agency personnel had neither the time nor capacity to verify. Other youth, resentful at being held in a military facility and impatient to begin their lives in the United States, simply climbed the fences and set off on their own.[63] Responding to multiple pressures, the NCWC, upon whose caseload most unattached youth fell, relaxed its usual placement procedures and standards. By the end of the year, the Catholic agency had resorted to assigning "quotas" to communities, dispatching groups of Hungarians of all ages—sometimes with less than a day's notice—to local parish priests and Catholic welfare agencies tasked with finding homes for them.[64]

The NCWC wasn't the only agency guilty of compromising its standards to expedite the relocation of unaccompanied minors. Responding to ongoing pressure from the ISS and troubled by Children's Bureau reports about the consequences of hasty placement, on February 27, 1957, assistant to the secretary of Health, Education, and Welfare Willis D. Gradison Jr. wrote to PCHRR chair General J. Lawton Collins (retired) about the need for HEW intervention to more adequately meet the needs of refugees at Kilmer. Singling out the unique vulnerability of unaccompanied refugee minors, Gradison noted the obligation to ensure that state-level standards for non-resident children's foster placements were consistently observed and appropriate supervision provided to all unattached Hungarian youth. Affirming the PCHRR's position that Hungarian resettlement should be "primarily a job for the American people acting through their voluntary organizations," the letter also emphasized that "these problems must be dealt with by private *or* [emphasis mine] public agencies when individual . . . resources are insufficient."[65]

Ignoring these warnings, the PCHRR continued to leave young peoples' living arrangements entirely at the voluntary agencies' discretion. By the end of December 1956, the constant pressure to process refugees led most agencies to follow the NCWC's lead in relaxing standards for unaccompanied minors' placements. At the extreme, agency staff who operated exclusively through their own social welfare networks sometimes failed to inform state or local welfare departments that they had placed unaccompanied Hungarian youth in their jurisdictions.[66] With the exception, perhaps, of the HIAS and the Lutheran Refugee Service, voluntary agencies opted to implement the unspoken policy directive emanating from the White House: namely, that unaccompanied children be treated as though they were adults.[67]

Inattention to age-specific needs, compounded by the failure of voluntary agencies to provide local communities and foster families with information, training, and ongoing support, meant that many placements quickly foundered. Although some families formed warm and respectful relationships with their new foster children, others quickly complained to agency personnel about willful teenaged boys who "talked back" and refused to adhere to household rules. Others were distressed by the compulsive behaviors of youth who sought to overcome the traumas of state-sponsored repression and violence, forced migration, and family separation by hoarding food or working long hours to send money to relatives still in Hungary.[68] Other foster parents were embarrassed by the unseemly conduct of youth who smoked, drank, engaged in "raucous" behavior in public spaces, spent money foolishly, or bought cars and "drove them without adequate skill."[69] Many were also offended by Hungarian youth who expressed anger at the United States' failure to support the uprising, refused to demonstrate "gratitude" to host families, or insisted on maintaining their self-identification as Hungarians "rather than as immigrants or newcomers to the United States." Still others, once the effusive displays of public support that accompanied youth's arrival in host communities had faded, were dismayed to realize that they were "stuck" with long-term responsibilities for children they had imagined as temporary guests in their homes.[70]

In the absence of support from national resettlement agencies, foster families sought help from community welfare agencies and from one another. Women organized "mother's clubs" to share ideas on how to plan for refugee minors' future education, vocational training, or employment. Others pooled resources and hired social workers to meet with them monthly. When these efforts failed, some host parents made private arrangements for youth to be taken in by another family. Others simply "washed their hands" of their wards, returning them to local sponsoring agencies.[71]

Unaccompanied Hungarian youth also struggled to adjust to their new American lives. Since most had not received English or cultural orientation classes during their brief stay at Kilmer, they found it extremely difficult to communicate with foster parents, few of whom were of Hungarian ethnicity or spoke the Magyar language. The youth's limited English skills further compounded the extraordinary academic and social challenges that accompanied transition into local schools. Many adolescents over the age of fourteen who worked full time in Hungary resisted foster parents' attempts to force them to go to school, even though the United States required attendance for children under sixteen. Even for those who left Hungary with hopes of continuing their education, poor high school grades were a source of constant anxiety and frustration. Others were heartbroken when foster families of modest means could not provide them with support for college.[72] Isolated and alone, grappling with the confusion and loneliness produced by abrupt resettlement, and burdened with anxiety and guilt about family members trapped behind the Iron Curtain, many youth got into trouble at school or with local police. Others ran away. On January 3, 1957, the *Miami Herald* reported one case of a thirteen-year-old Hungarian boy picked up by the police after running away from his Coral Gables, Florida, foster family. When questioned through a translator, the weeping boy confessed that he'd set out in search of a local Hungarian American club he found in the Yellow Pages, and that he "just wanted to talk to someone in Hungarian."[73]

Placement experiences also raised unanswered questions about the children's care. Issues of custody were a recurring problem, since minors could not receive emergency medical treatment without the consent of a legal guardian—and securing written permission from parents in Hungary was a slow and uncertain process.[74] Since voluntary agencies participating in the crash program did not provide parolees with affidavits of support, neither were they granted the provisional legal guardianship that had allowed them to provide follow-up care and supervision to previous generations of unaccompanied refugee minors.[75] This sometimes led to conflict between foster youth, parents, and agencies over who had final say over a minor's living arrangements.[76] Even more troubling were questions about youth's status as parolees. Could they be deported if they were arrested for a minor legal infraction or contracted a contagious illness? Would boys be drafted when they turned eighteen—and if so, would serving in the American forces strip them of Hungarian citizenship, rendering them stateless? If a child became homesick and requested to be returned to their parents, would the government pay for their travel? If so, would this disqualify them from immigrating to the United States at a later date?[77]

Concerns about underage parolees' precarious legal status were exacerbated by uncertainty about who bore ultimate financial responsibility for unaccompanied youth. Some families were willing and able to fully support foster children; others felt a keen "moral" obligation toward their wards but could not afford the ongoing cost of care. Other host families demanded that sponsoring agencies or private refugee assistance committees meet all expenses beyond basic room and board. Determining who was responsible for funding children's healthcare was equally complicated. In some cases, when extraordinary medical expenses were incurred, local doctors and hospitals provided free services; in other cases, religious congregations covered urgently needed treatment. However, other than the HIAS which had established a consistent policy of providing refugees with healthcare, none of the voluntary agencies was prepared to assume blanket responsibility for children's medical expenses. According to a May 1957 statement by the American

Council of Voluntary Agencies for Foreign Service Fact Finding Committee on unaccompanied Hungarian youth, "it should be remembered . . . that the United States Government brought the people here;" therefore, it was "the United States Government who [was] responsible." In practice, however, no mechanisms existed by which agencies could apply to the federal government for reimbursement of refugee youth's medical bills.[78]

Struggles to meet the needs of unattached Hungarian youth stemmed directly from the federal government's refusal to guarantee the minimum standard of care which it had dictated for previous groups of children arriving alone in the United States. Seen in this light, the decision of the nation's leading sectarian agencies to participate in the crash resettlement program—which clearly prioritized Cold War geopolitical objectives over the best interests of unaccompanied refugee minors—appears to fly in the face of their humanitarian values. But agencies that accepted the PCHRR's resettlement model did so because it was the only way displaced Hungarians could be brought to the United States.

By the end of December 1956, with almost all of the 15,000 parole slots filled up, the limited window of opportunity for Hungarian refugee resettlement to the United States appeared on the verge of closing. A brief reprieve came January 1, 1957, when Eisenhower directed the attorney general to continue paroling 200 more Hungarians into the country per day, "until the Congress could consider all aspects of the problem;" but by the end of the month legislators had yet to take action to authorize additional admissions.[79] Nor had they responded to Eisenhower's requests to pass a bill permitting those already paroled into the country to remain as permanent residents.[80] Instead, on February 14, Congressman Francis Walter dispatched a furious letter to the attorney general, claiming the United States had already taken its "fair share" of escapees and demanding that he "discontinue forthwith the exercise of the discretionary power . . . on behalf of Hungarian refugees."[81]

By the new year, with congressional restrictionists again up in arms over refugee admissions, the future of Eisenhower's resettlement efforts looked uncertain. At the same time, the situation of unattached youth still in Austrian camps was becoming increasingly precarious; debates over the legality of their emigration threatened to provoke another international crisis. In January 1957, responding to demands from Budapest for the repatriation of all escapees under the age of eighteen, the Austrian government declared it would consider returning children under fourteen if the child could not demonstrate a credible individual claim on refugee status and their return reflected the "freely expressed wishes" of both parents. But Austria maintained that minors over the age of fourteen were considered "prima facie" refugees; therefore, under the terms of the 1951 UN Convention Relating to the Status of Refugees, they were protected by the principle of *non-refoulement*, which dictated that refugees should not be repatriated against their wishes.[82]

Drawn in to adjudicate the debate, the UNHCR attempted to walk a middle road between affirming the principle of family unity and supporting young Hungarians' right to flee oppression. The high commissioner's January 31, 1957, statement stipulated that "whenever possible," children should be reunited with parents or returned to their nation of origin. It also disagreed with older youth's designation as "prima facie" refugees, insisting that each minor's status be determined through individual consideration of the reasons for flight, family circumstances, and the extent to which each child was able "to express a will of [their] own." Effectively immediately, the resettlement of "unattached youth"—the UNHCR term used to distinguish adolescent Hungarian escapees, most of whom had living parents, from the postwar displaced and orphaned or abandoned children previously under IRO mandate—required approval from the Austrian courts.[83] To ensure the "especially difficult" work of determining unattached youth's eligibility for resettlement was performed "by persons specially qualified to deal with minors," the UNHCR also tasked the International Social Service with establishing a new office in Vienna.[84] Beginning in spring 1957, nine ISS caseworkers and six secretary-interpreters assumed responsibility for assembling data on unattached Hungarian youth, providing counselling and casework services, and making recommendations to the UNHCR and the Austrian courts on individual youth's refugee status and the advisability of their emigration.[85]

The United Nations' determination to slow the resettlement of unaccompanied Hungarian youth presented agency personnel with a series of new bureaucratic obstacles. At the same time, waning public sympathy for Hungarian refugees and a deepening congressional divide threatened to derail the president's resettlement program. As refugee advocates argued the United States had yet to admit its "fair share" of the escapees, an emboldened restrictionist coalition led by the indefatigable Congressman Walter argued the continued use of the parole statute to admit Hungarians constituted presidential overreach and threatened the integrity of the nation's immigration law. Journalists and agency leaders waded into the fray, reminding lawmakers of the geopolitical stakes of the nation's refugee policy. On February 20, 1957, the *New York Times* condemned conditions in the camps; quoting Reverend Fabian Flynn, field director of Catholic Relief Services in Austria, the newspaper warned that if decisive action wasn't taken soon, "hundreds of Hungarians" would redefect to their communist homeland.[86] But the political tide had turned against refugees. On April 5, giving into pressure from restrictionists, the attorney general informed the president that his authority to admit Hungarian escapees under the parole statute had expired. In the future, he stressed, "the extraordinary parole provision [could] not be used as a substitute for . . . legislation."[87]

Eisenhower's crash program ended ten days later. By then, the United States had admitted 31,083 Hungarian refugees through Camp Kilmer, including between 600 and 700 unaccompanied minors. The NCWC placed approximately 300 unaccompanied Catholic youth, most of them between fifteen and seventeen years old, in foster care, and the Church World Service resettled 331 mostly Protestant youth between fourteen and eighteen. According to a gendered policy reflecting midcentury assumptions about female vulnerability, the agency also made special living arrangements for a number of "girls" with "special problems" up to the age of twenty. The HIAS placed thirty minors in Jewish foster homes, the LRS another three in Lutheran homes, and the nonsectarian International Rescue Committee placed twenty children between the ages of fourteen and seventeen. A Hungarian American "Connecticut Committee" found homes for another seventy youth under eighteen.[88] However, on May 31, 1957, more than 30,000 Hungarian escapees remained in Austria and Yugoslavia, including 2,900 adolescents and several hundred younger children.[89]

Other countries followed the United States' lead by closing their doors to further refugees. Morale in the Austrian camps plummeted, leading to a rash of suicide attempts linked to escapees' despair over lost emigration hopes. In March and April, the U.S. Embassy in Vienna repeatedly cabled the State Department, warning "distorted reports of United States immigration policy have further depressed the morale of Hungarian refugees."[90] In May 1957, in Camp Roeder in Salzburg, as 1,800 people were still waiting for resettlement, escapees launched a three-day hunger strike to protest closure of the U.S. resettlement program. They declared themselves "prepared sooner to die of hunger than to continue to live in the uncertain conditions forced on us by the Americans."[91]

As the frustrations of escapees in Austria mounted, the situation was also worsening for unaccompanied youth. On May 10, the *New York Times* reported that efforts to repatriate minors under the age of fourteen from

Austria and Yugoslavia had intensified.[92] Under pressure from the Hungarian government, a growing number of parents wrote to their children, directing them to come home—in many cases, directly contradicting previous letters granting consent for their emigration. Austrian authorities challenged the letters' veracity, claiming they were written under duress, and maintained that youth over the age of fourteen could not be forced to return to Hungary.[93] Privately, however, they informed the State Department that they were "most anxious" for minors to leave the country.[94]

As the escalating struggle for custody of Hungarian unaccompanied minors threatened to transform Austria into a Cold War flash point, alarmed Hungarians flooded the Vienna consulate with requests for assistance applying for last-minute visas for minors still stuck in the camps. The growing number of cases were referred to ISS-Austria, which worked in tandem with the ISS-American Branch—mostly in vain—to secure authorization for the children's placement with relatives in the United States.[95] Rumors circulated that repatriated youth were deported to the Soviet Union instead of being reunited with their families as promised, reigniting American concern for the welfare of unattached minors.[96] On June 26, a *New York Times* op-ed condemned the ongoing "savage repression" in Hungary:

> Instead of congratulating ourselves . . . on the admission of a mere
> 32,000 refugees . . . we ought to be searching out new ways to
> help. . . . One way would be to relieve the increasingly desperate
> conditions of a few thousand Hungarian teenagers who fled their
> country last fall and are now stuck in Austrian camps where they
> are fast losing their future. A few hundred of these "unaccompanied
> minors" have relatives in the U.S. who would like to take them
> in—but who are stopped . . . by our immigration laws. . . . Fourteen
> hundred of these Hungarian children are already reported to have
> gone back or to have disappeared. Will official indifference . . . kill all
> hope for those who remain?[97]

In a July 30 letter to the editor of the *New York Times*, executive secretary of the U.S.-based Hungarian National Council Béla Fabian also advocated on behalf of Hungarian minors. Making a conspicuously geopolitical argument, he called for the admission via a "special act of legislation" of the estimated 500 unattached youth—some of whom he claimed "were themselves freedom fighters"—with relatives in the United States. The anti-communist youth, with their "faith in the ideals of Western democracy," would become "useful citizens of this country, to which they have already proved their faithful attachment."[98]

On June 19 President Eisenhower, responding to demands for the United States to demonstrate its commitment to anti-communist Hungarians, directed representatives from the Departments of State and Justice to meet at the White House. Following a contentious discussion, Commissioner Joseph Swing of the Immigration and Naturalization Service reluctantly agreed to authorize parole into the United States of an additional 150 Hungarians per week until the end of August. For the first time those in Yugoslavia were eligible, but only if they were spouses, children, or parents of refugees already in the country. Reminding the meeting's attendees of the ongoing problem of the unattached Hungarian youth, deputy administrator of the Office of Refugee and Migration Affairs Robert S. McCollum argued that unaccompanied children under sixteen years of age with relatives in the United States should also be eligible for parole. With "extreme difficulty," he eventually persuaded Department of Justice officials that minors should be included.[99]

The following day, McCollum met with the Committee on Migration and Refugee Problems of the American Council of Voluntary Agencies for Foreign Service (ACVAFS), a national coalition of voluntary agencies formed in 1943 to coordinate emergency postwar humanitarian relief activities among agencies as well as with the federal government.[100] He asked them to oversee a new effort to resettle unattached Hungarian youth in the United States. This more limited program—McCollum estimated only about 500 of the approximately 1,500 minors still in Austria had U.S. relatives—would end by August 31, 1957.[101] ACVAFS members peppered McCollum with a volley of questions that had arisen during the recently concluded crash program: How would children be selected? Who would oversee their placement? Who would bear ultimate legal and financial responsibility for the underage parolees? Visibly unprepared, McCollum reassured committee members that voluntary agencies had authority to make decisions on minors' behalf and remove them from unsuitable homes, but otherwise offered few details. When HIAS and ISS-American Branch representatives asked why opportunities for resettlement couldn't also be extended to children without family in the United States, McCollum declined to open the matter for discussion. Explaining it had been "extremely difficult" to secure support for the inclusion of any unaccompanied youth in the resumed parole, he warned that an effort to expand eligibility requirements would jeopardize the admission of even those minors with U.S. relatives.[102]

Following this contentious meeting, troubled committee members debated the ethics of participating in this second wave of youth resettlement. Concerned about the fate of increasingly restless youth trapped in "unwholesome" Austrian and Yugoslavian camps, they nonetheless objected to the new program's "youth to relatives" focus and the legal and financial risks of bringing additional minors to the United States under its yet-to-be-clarified terms. Committee chair and HIAS representative Ann Petluck warned that participating agencies needed to be extremely careful about language contained in their affidavits of sponsorship, since the word "support" might be taken as evidence of a legally binding commitment to prevent children from becoming a public charge.[103] Agencies also argued among themselves, to no avail, over the advantages of government funding versus the loss of autonomy that might come from "official" oversight, with the NCWC maintaining its steadfast objection to any external oversight of its activities.[104] Unable to reach consensus, in a June 10 report to HEW, the ACVAFS fact-finding committee concluded "certain critical problems facing the agencies in connection with the arrival of unaccompanied youth," including the establishment of proper placement standards, the provision of adequate supervision and other necessary services, the resolution of guardianship issues, and the "cost of foster care on a long-time basis" could be "more adequately dealt with" by a "centrally established government agency."[105] However, the proposed "youth to relatives" scheme provided none of these things.

More than a week after meeting with Deputy Administrator McCollum, voluntary agencies thus remained reluctant to commit. Then on June 27, 1957, they learned the Immigration and Naturalization Service had bypassed them by contacting unaccompanied minors' relatives directly to request they serve as sponsors. ACVAFS called an urgent meeting to "try to formulate [its] thinking with regard to the Government's proposal." Fearing a government-administered program would compromise their leading role in the care of unaccompanied refugee minors, several agencies argued in favor of participation. Committee chair Ann Petluck ruefully concurred the government had "really put the agencies in a box," and "the only possibility was to cooperate."[106] She appointed an Ad Hoc Committee on Children with representatives from the HIAS, NCWC, Church World Service, the International Rescue Committee, and the ISS-American Branch, and she tasked them with coordinating the new resettlement effort.[107]

On July 9 ACVAFS representatives attended an INS briefing on the "youth to relatives" program. In accordance with new UNHCR guidelines, children under the age of seventeen would be selected from the approximately 600 minors currently on the ISS-Austria caseload; the ISS was responsible for all casework required by the United Nations to authorize their emigration.[108] Agencies' questions about who bore ultimate legal and financial responsibility for children revealed a major problem with the plan. Since most of the youth had living parents, the INS's assumption that the United Nations could designate alternative legal guardians for the children was incorrect; voluntary agencies could not, therefore, assume custody for children they sponsored. Custody of the underage parolees remained with the INS district director, but only as a legal formality. As for financial responsibility, Deputy Administrator McCollum stressed "at no time would be the government consider expending money" for children's care.[109] The INS similarly declined to assume financial responsibility. Voluntary agencies and the children's relatives were told their commitment to unaccompanied minors should be considered "a strong moral . . . but not a legal obligation." On these dubious foundations, the U.S. Escapee Program of the Department of State and the American Council of Voluntary Agencies for Foreign Service executed a contract to launch the "youth to relatives" program on August 26.[110] Although the program remained solely under the jurisdiction of the INS, ACVAFS agreed to coordinate voluntary agency resettlement activities, liaise with the appropriate Government offices, and otherwise facilitate the admission of youth parolees. In return the Department of State would reimburse ACVAFS for all expenses incurred.[111]

In September 1957, ACVAFS-affiliated agencies turned to the task of resettling 500 Hungarian refugee minors whose relatives awaited them in the United States. Their efforts were plagued by frequent misunderstandings about basic operations, record-keeping and communications procedures, and ever-changing instructions from the INS officials ostensibly in charge. For example, on September 27 the INS informed the committee that the age limit had been raised from seventeen to eighteen years. Then, on October 9, they said the program was extending to include Hungarian unaccompanied minors in Yugoslavia. Throughout the fall, agency personnel, facing growing pressure to effect children's resettlement within a closing three-month window, lost irreplaceable time drafting letters, making repeated phone calls, and attending in-person briefings at the State Department and INS headquarters, desperately trying to stay abreast of the program's changing parameters and procedures.[112]

At the same time, attempts to maintain a centralized record of information about "youth to relatives" placements foundered. Although all agencies were asked to submit to the ACVAFS project secretary lists of children on whose behalf parole permits were being sought as well as updated information on the outcome of home studies, not all did so consistently; nor did the INS in Washington consistently share its action lists, detailing relatives accepted or rejected as sponsors and minors approved or disapproved for admission. As a result, by the end of September, sixty-nine children referred to U.S. voluntary agencies for resettlement had failed to appear on INS lists; thirty-nine children on INS lists hadn't been recorded on the ACVAFS central index.[113] Once again, the need for repeated phone calls and letters to locate the missing information and ensure it was disseminated to all concerned parties proved "disastrously time consuming."[114]

Tensions between agencies overseas and ISS-Austria further hampered the efficient dissemination of information. Although U.S. voluntary agencies recognized (if only among themselves) the deficiencies of the previous crash program, many objected to the ISS's United Nations–assigned intermediary role, arguing that they should deal directly with the UNHCR.[115] Sectarian agencies also resented the ISS's policy of accepting direct responsibility for cases when an applicant requested assistance from a nonsectarian agency or when they judged that other agencies were unqualified to meet a "special need," seeing ISS claims of "special competence" as an affront to their own expertise and a justification for "poaching" cases.[116] The NCWC was especially outraged by claims that the ISS's nonsectarian character enabled it to provide a more consistent quality of care than religious organizations and accused the ISS of seeking to displace sectarian voluntary agencies that had long "operated effectively each within its own sphere yet respecting the character and competence of each other."[117] Affronted Catholic personnel thus made every effort to avoid working with the ISS.

Tensions also rose between U.S. voluntary agencies and the federal government. In September, the INS informed ACVAFS that it would begin conducting its own home studies—in addition to those already required by individual agencies—as a prerequisite to approving relatives as sponsors. This state incursion into the agency's previously respected sphere of authority sparked ongoing struggle over who had the final say about the suitability of relatives' homes.[118] As the number of sponsors rejected by the INS grew, ACVAFS repeatedly requested clarification of its criteria for evaluating sponsors and their homes.[119] In some cases, INS decisions were uncontroversial: a seventeen year old female parolee planning to join an aunt in Canada was turned down, as was a sixty-nine year old widower residing in a studio and dependent on Social Security. A "single, unemployed" male living with two other single males was similarly rejected as a sponsor for a young girl.[120]

However, in a growing number of cases, homes found acceptable by voluntary agencies were rejected by the INS—even when the relatives expressed a strong desire to take in the child. Even more distressingly, the INS also rejected many sponsors solely because they were parolees.

As overseas efforts to prepare minors for emigration limped forward into October, ACVAFS sent multiple letters to the State Department and INS requesting explanations for unfavorable home studies and sponsor investigations, stressing the need for improved communication and "greater transparency and accountability" within the program. With one eye on the clock—the original ninety-day resettlement period was quickly passing—ACVAFS also urged federal officials to waive the requirement that minors be placed only with family members, especially when the agency could provide a suitable home close to their relatives, and asked for the category of "relative" to include close family friends whose homes were judged adequate by voluntary agencies. Barring these changes, ACVAFS personnel requested an extension beyond the original program termination date at the end of November.[121] But their increasingly anxious letters received only the most cursory replies.

Finally, in late November, frustrations boiled over. In a letter to James Hennessy at the INS, Ann Petluck asked on behalf of the agencies, "What does a 'suitable home' mean? What standard is the Service using that is particularly relevant when a trained child welfare worker finds that the home is suitable and the INS inspector rules otherwise?" She again raised the rejection of relative sponsors who were parolees and then demanded clarification of a report from Austria that the INS considered refugee children in the presence of an older sibling to be "unaccompanied" only when willing to be separated. "We have never heard of this ruling," she stated flatly. "If it exists, we urge that it be countermanded, and that the earlier position be maintained." In closing, she reiterated agencies' plea for an extension of the program's terminal date so that children with U.S. relatives still awaiting resettlement were "not left stranded."[122]

Hennessy's terse reply on December 2 reminded Petluck that the INS retained "primary responsibility to decide whether parole should be authorized." As for the report that siblings were being forced to separate or remain in Austria, the letter confirmed that, indeed, "children who are with any relatives [were] not considered to be unaccompanied." Hennessy followed with an even more shocking announcement, stating—for the first time since the program's inception—that the "youth to relatives" program was "intended to apply to United States citizens and permanent resident sponsors;" except in the most exceptional circumstances, parolees were ineligible to serve as foster parents. ACVAFS's request for an extension of the program's terminal date was approved—though only until December 31, 1957, when all Hungarian refugee resettlement would come to a definitive end.[123]

Discerning that the U.S. government's only remaining "interest was to finish this program," agencies scrambled to submit the names of all youth claiming American citizen or permanent resident family members.[124] After several months of feverish effort, the last "youth to relatives" program flight departed Austria on March 21, 1958. The program brought only 136 of the 351 children on whose behalf agencies requested parole permits to the United States. More than 1,100 youth left behind had to choose between making a life alone in Austria and Yugoslavia or accepting repatriation to their communist-controlled homeland.[125]

Dispirited and divided agency leaders came together to evaluate the outcome of their postwar efforts on behalf of Hungarian refugee youth. Their conclusions were sobering. In a February 1958 retrospective, ACVAFS acknowledged that agencies operating "under extreme pressure" consciously chose to participate in a program that prioritized speed over the well-being of refugees. Further, to the extent that agencies succumbed to sectarian rivalries and failed to hold out for a resettlement model that accounted for the specific needs of unaccompanied youth, they "must accept responsibility for some of the situations which arose in the Kilmer operation." This included recognition that placement procedures treating unaccompanied minors as adults were "contrary to sound child or youth placement standards."[126] However, ACVAFS's internal memos during summer and fall 1958 repeatedly attributed these failures to the government's geopolitically motivated demands for speedy resettlement; "general confusion and uncertainty" surrounding the program hampered efforts to make suitable living arrangements for minors, "even though the agencies were adequately equipped . . . for such planning (if time had allowed)."[127] Most importantly, though, ACVAFS argued that the PCHRR's disregard for the "traditional role of the voluntary agencies," particularly the refusal to allow agencies to work according to their own methods and set appropriate standards for care, was primarily to blame for the crash program's negative outcomes. ACVAFS alleged the "youth to relatives" program was similarly cursed by the government's intransigent demands for speed, its failure to provide necessary logistical and financial support, and shifting eligibility requirements.

As a result of these persistent shortcomings, children and youth who made it to the United States during fall 1957 and winter 1958 confronted the same struggles to adapt to new lives as those admitted via the crash program. Cultural differences between previous generations of Hungarian immigrants and those who came of age in postwar Hungary sometimes produced greater difficulties for youth placed with relatives than for first-wave unaccompanied minors. Issues of underage parolees' guardianship that had emerged during the crash migration also remained "an unresolved problem" as was the question of who bore ultimate financial responsibility for the young parolees. Well into summer 1958, voluntary agencies' repeated inquiries about the "provision by appropriate Government sources" for minors' support had "only yielded negative responses."[128]

In a final report to the Departments of State, Justice, and Health, Education, and Welfare, ACVAFS offered a somewhat more circumspect assessment of Hungarian youth resettlement efforts. Beginning by reassuring its official audience that nothing contained in it was "intended to imply that these young people should not have been brought . . . to the United States," the report asserted the two programs had done "a tremendous amount of good," "not only on the humanitarian level . . . but for foreign policy prestige around the world."[129] To meet those objectives, the report further allowed, it had perhaps been necessary to initially "overlook certain questionable policies and procedures" imposed by the PCHRR. But by the time the "youth to relatives" scheme began, "the Government might have taken stock of its activities" and returned control of the resettlement efforts to voluntary agencies. Instead, by maintaining the PCHRR's top-down approach, a crucial opportunity to remedy many of the crash program's errors had been missed.[130] This failure contributed to a high rate of unsuccessful placements as well as "hundreds of tragic cases involving separation of one or more members of a family from another."[131] In the future, ACVAFS concluded, to ensure that programs for unaccompanied refugee minors more effectively safeguarded their best interests, "policies, plans and procedures should be clearly and thoroughly spelled out and approved by all agencies involved."[132] And above all, geopolitical and logistical interests should "not be allowed to jeopardize other humanitarian considerations in the movement of people."[133]

The ACVAFS report acknowledged the growing scale of refugee movements and their importance to the nation's foreign policy pointed toward an expanded federal government role in resettlement. But divided voluntary agencies remained miles away from "any consensus as to the principle of a central control or the form it should take."[134] Similar debates emerged within and between government agencies as early as April 1957, when Tracy Voorhees recommended HEW be tasked with providing follow-up services to refugees after the PCHRR ceased operations. In June, following a call from a *New York Times* reporter informing him of the imminent publication of a story on the hardships faced by unemployed Hungarians, Voorhees again reminded the White House and State Department about the nation's "special responsibility" toward the refugees, who had been brought in "as a matter of government policy." "Aside from the humanitarian aspect," he warned, "there is a real danger of the Russians utilizing the situation . . . for propaganda purposes." To prevent refugees from becoming "a source of very bad publicity for the U.S.," he suggested that $500,000 be appropriated from the president's discretionary Mutual Security Act fund to provide emergency assistance to "hardship cases" whose parole status made them ineligible for state or local relief.[135] The stalwart Republican admitted that the use of federal money for refugee assistance was "quite a radical step." However, given the geopolitical stakes involved, it was "perhaps not impossible."[136]

Sensing a long-awaited opportunity to redefine the department's role in this area, HEW secretary Marion B. Folsom convened a special Task Force on the Health, Education, and Welfare of Refugees and Immigrants. In a June 1958 report, the task force concluded that the federal government had been ill prepared for the Hungarian refugee crisis and offered recommendations for improving its response to similar events in the future. Since the nation's Cold War foreign policy would likely continue to support admission of "groups subjected to external and internal totalitarian political forces," it was expected that "older administrative patterns and procedures [would] not meet the needs of the changed nature of immigration."[137] Moving forward, HEW should be involved alongside the Departments of State and Justice in formulating policy related to the health, education, and welfare of refugees and immigrants. They should also play a direct role in reception services and in overseeing all public and private agencies working with refugees and immigrants. Although the report anticipated volunteer agencies would continue to play a leading role welcoming refugees, it stressed the "proper balance between tax-supported and voluntarily financed activities" needed to be rethought. In the future, HEW should receive a new mandate to provide "financing of such additional health, welfare, and educational services as may be necessary to assist refugees and immigrants in their successful resettlement and integration into American life."[138]

The report also touched directly on HEW's role in resettling unaccompanied minors. Arguing that the nation's foreign policy objectives required abandoning its previous policy of "skimming the cream" of elite, highly skilled refugees to allow for the admission of a "fair share" of hard-core

cases—including the "sick, aged, handicapped and unaccompanied youth"—
the report asserted HEW's specialized knowledge would be even more crucial in the future.[139] To that end, the Children's Bureau should be restored to
its leading role in developing and overseeing standards for the protection
and care of children being brought to the United States, particularly when
unaccompanied.[140]

On July 25, 1958, Congress passed Public Law 85–559 allowing Hungarians
admitted to the country after October 23, 1956, to adjust their immigration
status from parolee to permanent resident.[141] Since the refugees were now
eligible for municipal and state relief, no action was ultimately taken on Tracy
Voorhees' recommendations. Instead, the welfare of Hungarian refugees—
including the approximately 800 unaccompanied minors whose admission
had depended more on their status as anti-communist refugees than any age-
based claim on the U.S. government's protection—remained in the hands of
voluntary agencies.

In years to come, a growing number of federal officials and refugee and
children's advocates would begin to question the efficacy of a refugee policy
that effectively transferred the burden of implementing the nation's foreign
policy onto the shoulders of private organizations and individuals. These
debates reflected and reinforced a growing belief that the state's responsibility
to displaced persons—and especially to unaccompanied minors—did not
end with their admission to the United States. First articulated by wartime
child-saving activists, this tentative new notion was inadvertently strengthened by President Eisenhower in December 1956, when he reversed the traditional relationship between the government and voluntary agencies by
initiating the nation's first federally sponsored resettlement program. Whether
couched in humanitarian or geopolitical terms, new Cold War understandings of the relationship between refugees and the state continued to grow
after the Hungarian Uprising, destabilizing the public-private dynamic that
long defined resettlement efforts in the United States. It also created space
for the unprecedented federal welcome provided to anti-communist Cubans
who began to flee their island three years later. And it would lay the groundwork, beginning in 1960, for the first-ever government-funded program for
unaccompanied refugee minors in the United States.

Building on lessons learned in 1956, the public officials and voluntary
agencies who worked together to bring Cuban children to the United States
would inherit the unresolved problems that handicapped the resettlement of

Hungarian youth. Struggling to resolve these issues in real time, they would attempt to create a new and more developmentally sensitive model for the care of children arriving alone in the United States. This deeply fraught process of improvisation would foster new collaborations and alliances between governmental and nongovernmental actors and sectarian and nonsectarian agencies. It also reignited latent conflicts over which young people were considered deserving of asylum in the United States, who was responsible for them once admitted—and whether resettlement in the United States in fact served their best interests.

5

An Exception within an Exception

The Cuban Children's Program, 1960–1966

In 1959, Fidel Castro's rise to power in Cuba accelerated the Cold War's expansion into Latin America. As the revolutionary government established new ties with the Soviet Union and U.S.-Cuban relations deteriorated, tens of thousands of Cubans would flee the island, including more than 14,000 boys and girls whose parents sent them to the United States alone. Approximately half of these children would be placed in government-funded foster care provided by the nation's first federally directed refugee resettlement program created in January 1961. Reflecting a growing recognition of the importance of both refugees and young people to U.S. Cold War foreign policy goals, the convergence of multiple child evacuation efforts under the umbrella of the Cuban Children's Program represented the beginning of a new public-private partnership in the care of unaccompanied refugee minors.

However, the hastily conceived program swiftly evolved into something none of its early proponents had envisioned. Beginning as a temporary child evacuation scheme to demonstrate U.S. support for Cuban parents in the anti-Castro underground and to safeguard the ideological and spiritual purity of the island's elite future leaders, it quickly ballooned into a comprehensive child welfare program struggling to provide long-term care for thousands of unaccompanied minors. Impeded by a lack of advance planning, precarious funding, and persistent congressional opposition, leaders at the Department of Health, Education, and Welfare and the Florida State Department of Welfare quickly became mired in an endless cycle of policy improvisation as they responded to the changing needs of diverse Cuban children arriving alone in the United States. At the same time overburdened voluntary agencies under constant pressure to find homes for children grew progressively more resentful of federal interference into their activities.

Well before it began to wind down in 1966, public officials, the mainstream media, and the exile community had declared the Cuban Children's Program an unqualified success, lauding it as an example of Americans' humanitarian concern for children and upholding it as a model for future child welfare initiatives. Privately, however, its exhausted and demoralized directors struggled to reconcile the program's positive geopolitical outcomes with the negative consequences of children's unexpectedly prolonged stay in foster care. Many quietly asked themselves, as postwar child-saving advocates had done, if separating children from their families had really been in the minors' best interests. These questions would linger in many participants' minds, including those of the thousands of youth whose lives were forever transformed by the decision to send them alone to the United States.

On January 1, 1959, Cubans of all races, classes, and political affiliations joined in an almost-unanimous celebration of the revolution that drove the hated U.S.-backed dictator Fulgencio Batista from their island. Confident that Fidel Castro's ascension to power would restore democracy and remake their society according to José Martí's egalitarian vision, Cubans' hopes quickly foundered in the face of bitter disagreements over the revolution's policies and mounting opposition to Castro's increasingly authoritarian leadership. At the same time, the revolution's attacks on the Catholic church and private education, the increasingly ideological content of public-school curricula, and growing pressure on children to join Soviet-inspired youth militias and mass organizations like the Pioneers and Rebel Youth, boosted fears about the revolutionary state's interventions in family life. By autumn 1960 these fears were stirred into frenzy by CIA-sponsored counterrevolutionary propaganda designed to convince Cubans that the revolution intended to deprive parents of legal custody, *patria potestad*, place children over the age of three in state-run boarding schools, and send older boys and girls to Russia for communist indoctrination.[1] Terrifying tales of forced family separations and brainwashed children betraying their parents to watchdog Committees for the Defense of the Revolution (CDRs) spread like wildfire.[2]

An Exception within an Exception

Child-centered propaganda was one of Eisenhower's deliberate efforts to destabilize and delegitimize the Cuban Revolution by encouraging an exodus of "refugees" from the island.[3] By June of 1960, as U.S.-Cuba relations deteriorated from distrust into hostility, the number of Cubans in Miami rose to more than 60,000.[4] By November, although the Immigration and Naturalization Service (INS) reported at least 8,500 "technically deportable" anti-Castro exiles in South Florida as well as another 30,000 on tourist visas soon to expire, the INS automatically extended limited voluntary departure status to all Cubans admitted on tourist visas and granted them the exceptional permission to seek employment.[5]

Miami residents, despite repeated statements by South Florida political leaders about the importance of extending a "good neighbor" welcome to anti-Castro exiles, were less enthusiastic about the federal government's laissez-faire policy toward Cuban admissions. Mired in a serious economic recession and struggling to keep a lid on civil rights–era racial troubles, Miami-Dade County was ill equipped to absorb a sudden influx of refugees. Miami's white majority was also prone to anti-Cuban prejudices, exacerbated by associations of Cubanness with Blackness in U.S. popular culture that predisposed them to see light-skinned, educated Cubans as sharing more with African Americans, Puerto Ricans, and Mexican immigrants than with middle-class Anglo-Americans.[6] Cuban's Catholic religion further contributed to an initially lukewarm reception by the city's Protestant majority, many of whom still viewed Catholicism as "alien" and antithetical to American democratic values.[7] After mid-1960, when Castro imposed harsh restrictions on émigrés' ability to take money off the island, the growing destitution of each group of new arrivals further reinforced associations between Cubans and other poor immigrants and people of color, deepening Miami residents' fears about their negative impact on municipal infrastructure, local schools, and public services.[8]

Amid growing controversy Eisenhower directed Undersecretary of State Douglas Dillon to meet with Tracy Voorhees to develop a coordinated response to the crisis in Florida.[9] State Department representatives agreed with Voorhees that anti-Castro Cubans must be welcomed and helped to prosper in the United States, since this provided concrete evidence of U.S. support for Latin American democracies and demonstrated the superiority of capitalism over communism. On November 9, representatives of the Department of Health, Education, and Welfare (HEW) drew upon similar foreign policy justifications to proactively assert a leading role for themselves in planning for Cuban refugees. Because of the "significant implications our treatment of the Cuban refugees may have for Latin American relationships," HEW recommended the response should be "primarily a government effort." And unlike the Hungarian program, from which they were largely excluded, "state agencies . . . must be drawn into the planning at the earliest moment."[10]

Eisenhower, following the recommendation of the State Department, on December 2, 1960, issued a statement declaring he was appropriating $1 million from the Mutual Security Program budget to assist newly arrived Cubans. Disregarding HEW advice, he once again tasked his close friend Tracy Voorhees with creating a federally funded but privately administered refugee program. Voorhees immediately set off for Miami where he went to work establishing a Cuban refugee center to provide initial reception and placement services. Voluntary agencies were expected to assume responsibility, as they had in the Hungarian program, for securing sponsors, homes, and employment for refugees.

Federal officials as well as local welfare agencies recognized that unaccompanied children would arrive among the new Cuban exiles. On November 8, James Hennessy of the Immigration and Naturalization Service met with Al McDermitt, Department of Labor in Miami, noting the "many unattached children" in the city and Key West. Although most had been sent to stay with relatives or family friends, a number of teenage boys were reported to be "roaming the streets" or depending on strangers for food and shelter.[11] Father Bryan O. Walsh, a young Irish American priest recently appointed director of Miami's small Catholic Welfare Bureau (CWB), was already making temporary arrangements to house and feed a small number of children for whom hastily made living arrangements broke down. Assuming that the number of unaccompanied children in Miami would grow as turmoil increased in Cuba, Walsh brought the problem before the city's Welfare Planning Council. On November 22, the council adopted a resolution calling on the federal government to provide funding to care for Cuban children sent to the United States to avert communist indoctrination.[12]

State officials also communicated with their federal counterparts about planning for the needs of children arriving alone in Miami. In early December 1960, Frances Davis, director of the Division of Child Welfare of the Florida State Department of Public Welfare (FSDPW), requested assistance from the U.S. Children's Bureau to develop policies for unattached Cuban children who came to the attention of child welfare agencies or juvenile courts. Determined not to be sidelined as it had been during the Hungarian refugee crisis, the Children's Bureau was already developing its own plans. On December 15, Katherine Oetinger, chief of the Children's Bureau, convened a meeting with

An Exception within an Exception

Frances Davis and representatives of the Social Security Administration to discuss establishing a short-term program to place a small number of Cuban refugee children in federally funded group homes. Such a program, they felt, would preserve the children's language and culture while they awaited a quick return home. However, they ultimately concluded that the model of previous child evacuation schemes in which voluntary agencies made individual placement decisions was more immediately feasible.

On December 19, after receiving reassurances from Voorhees of limited financial assistance if HEW deemed it necessary for unaccompanied children's care, FSDPW representatives met with the leadership of Miami's Catholic Welfare Bureau and the Jewish Family and Children Services (JFCS) agency. Father Walsh, already caring for fifteen boys and girls, agreed to accept responsibility for additional unaccompanied Catholic Cuban children in need.[13] The JFCS agency agreed to provide placement services for any unaccompanied coreligionist children arriving from Cuba. FSDPW representatives emphasized they expected most children to remain with relatives or family friends; placement with strangers was a last resort. State and federal officials also hoped voluntary agencies could absorb the cost of resettling those children, as during the Hungarian program. If this proved unsustainable Frances Davis would inform HEW of their need for federal assistance.[14]

Local, state, and federal officials worked feverishly finalizing plans for assisting Cuban refugees of all ages while the exodus of families from the island, still largely from the middle and upper classes, steadily grew. Parents unwilling to emigrate either because they were active in the anti-Castro opposition or because they feared their homes and properties would be confiscated, increasingly sent their children to stay with American relatives or friends. Catholic families could also turn to the church for assistance in placing their children in American boarding schools; among these were a group of fifty Cuban girls who left Havana in October for an Ursuline convent school in New Orleans.[15] As word of Father Walsh's activities spread through the island's Catholic parish and school networks, parents without personal contacts in Miami began to call the diocesan Centro Hispano Católico seeking assistance in securing placements for their sons and daughters.[16] It had long been tradition among Cuba's more privileged classes for children to attend high school or university in the United States, so few families initially saw these arrangements as particularly out of the ordinary; moreover, since few expected Castro's increasingly radical revolution to survive for more than a few months, most parents believed the separation from their children would be brief.

Following the lead of these first families, a group of parents from Ruston Academy, an elite American school in Havana that prepared students for admission to U.S. universities, approached headmaster James Baker for help sending their own children to study in the United States. Baker was a longtime resident of Cuba whose sympathy for the counterrevolution was well known. The headmaster understood some parents wanted to get children off the island so they could dedicate themselves fully to the anti-Castro struggle; he also empathized with fears that politically active adolescent sons and daughters might be arrested and imprisoned. For his own part, Baker was concerned about the long-term political consequences of communist indoctrination on Cuba's elite youth, from whom the nation's future leaders would almost certainly be drawn. He quickly agreed to help.[17]

Baker traveled to the United States to organize support for a private program to evacuate approximately 200 children from among the Ruston families' network.[18] Through contacts at the American embassy in Havana and the International Rescue Committee, a nonsectarian refugee resettlement agency collaborating with the CIA since October to facilitate relocation of Cuban exiles to the United States, he requested financial assistance from the Havana-American Chamber of Commerce, recently relocated to Miami. No fans of the Castro regime, the chamber quickly agreed to purchase airfare for the children.[19] Now it fell to Baker to arrange their placement, ideally in a boarding school established especially for Cuban youth or in leading American schools. Aware of Father Walsh's early efforts on behalf of unaccompanied Cuban children in Miami, Baker's Chamber of Commerce connections introduced the two men.[20]

Father Walsh readily agreed to place children sent to the United States by Baker's network, although his motives diverged somewhat from the headmaster's. Both men were committed anti-communists who wanted to rescue children from Marxist indoctrination, but Baker's concerns were primarily political; he saw spiriting children out of Cuba as a way to ensure the democratic education of Cuba's elite youth and support parents involved in the anti-Castro underground. In contrast Walsh, as a Catholic priest, embraced the Vatican's long-standing position that communism represented an existential threat to the church and to Christian family life and morals.[21] The young priest's primary goal was thus to help Cuban Catholic parents preserve their children's religious identity by protecting them from exposure to an atheistic and materialistic ideology.

As the administrator of a welfare agency, Walsh was also deeply concerned with the overall well-being of unaccompanied children. Having participated

An Exception within an Exception

at the parish level in the resettlement of Hungarian youth in 1957, he believed simply placing children in boarding schools, as Baker advocated, would be insufficient. Instead, Walsh insisted on a comprehensive program in which licensed child welfare agencies managed and supervised the children's care. Finally, because of his long-standing interest in Latin America and commitment to migrant advocacy work (he studied in Puerto Rico and helped establish the city's Centro Hispano Católico), Walsh was eager to assert a leading role for the Catholic Welfare Bureau in caring for Cuban refugee children.[22] Doing so promised visibility and prestige to his small agency—and, as Walsh knew through conversations with Tracy Voorhees and the FSDPW's Frances Davis, it could lead to an injection of federal funds.[23]

Under pressure to arrange the children's evacuation as quickly as possible, Baker agreed to leave placement details in the hands of the Catholic Welfare Bureau. Then, before returning to Cuba on December 13, he met with State Department officials in Washington, D.C., to request assistance facilitating the children's admission to the United States. The State Department, eager to support the anti-Castro underground, believed a privately organized scheme to bring a small number of elite Cuban boys and girls to the United States for a few months—like the 1940 USCOM program for British children that Baker's proposal resembled—would provide the federal government with a low-cost, high-impact opportunity to demonstrate tangible support for anticommunist Cubans on the island. Agreeing to authorize student visas for 250 Cuban youth, the State Department also accepted Baker and Walsh's request that the program be kept secret to protect children's parents against reprisals.

To proceed, however, they needed to relax a number of visa requirements and procedures that otherwise made the children ineligible. According to Baker's plan, the Catholic Welfare Bureau arranged for Coral Gables High School, Florida, to complete immigration form I-20 on the children's behalf, certifying their acceptance as students. And since the law barred entrance to aliens with travel funded by a corporation or association, monies from the American Chamber of Commerce went to the Catholic Welfare Bureau, which then disbursed checks to a handful of individuals who purchased air tickets in the children's names from a U.S.-owned travel agency in Havana.[24] The State Department also agreed to instruct the Havana embassy to waive the requirement that international students provide evidence of sufficient funds to support themselves for the duration of their studies.

The INS's preexisting policy admitting all Cubans arriving at a U.S. port of entry made obvious that the children's status as "students" was a formality—just as British children were designated "tourists" in the summer of 1940 as a means of working within and around immigration law to get them into the country. While federal support for both programs was motivated in part by a desire to reap foreign policy benefits from a private initiative, James Baker's child evacuation scheme also fit into a tradition in U.S.-Cuba foreign policy dating back to the founding of the island republic, whereby successive administrations promoted training Cuban teachers in the United States as a means of encouraging American-style democracy. Generations of U.S. political, civic, and religious leaders before Baker similarly promoted educational exchange programs intended to cement links between the U.S. and Cuban elites by training the island's future leaders.[25] A U.S. public affairs officer stationed in Havana in 1952 clearly articulated the enduring belief in the importance of young people and education to U.S. interests in Cuba when he described the "indoctrination of Cuban children in the principles of democracy" at American schools like Ruston Academy as "perhaps the most effective means of shaping Cuban opinion in the future."[26] This belief was echoed by Tracy Voorhees a few weeks after Baker's visit to the United States, when he observed in a January 1961 report to Eisenhower that Cuban refugee children educated in U.S. schools could be "fine ambassadors for us, if they return sometime to Cuba."[27]

On December 15, 1960, after receiving a list of the first 125 students to be embarked to the United States, Walsh set to work arranging temporary housing at a local Catholic girls school and a diocesan children's home. But the decision to bend the rules for Cuban children raised objections from visa section staff in Havana; Walsh received an urgent phone call from Baker in Havana on the 24, advising him that the embassy was refusing to issue their visas.[28] When an agitated Walsh asked the State Department to intervene, deputy director of the Bureau of Security and Consular Affairs Frank Auerbach informed him that the department had changed its position: visas would only be authorized if a voluntary agency assumed legal and financial responsibility for the children, as in previous child evacuation schemes.

Father Walsh was concerned by rumors that young people would not be allowed to leave the island after January 1, 1961, and confident the federal funding promised for the unaccompanied Cuban children's care would materialize. Therefore, without first seeking his bishop's authorization, Walsh agreed to the State Department's terms.[29] His word was sufficient to break the deadlock. The first of what would become known as "Operation Pedro Pan" children arrived in Miami on December 26, 1960. Twenty more followed by the end of the month.[30] They joined an undetermined number of children whose parents had already made private arrangements to send their children to boarding schools, relatives, or family friends in the United States. Then, less than a week later, a series of dramatic changes in Cuba and the United States rapidly remade the operation, originally intended as a small, elite-centered child evacuation scheme, into a much broader program.

In Havana political and economic conditions worsened during the last months of 1960. At the same time, rumors of an impending U.S.-backed exile invasion and Fidel Castro's December 31 announcement that the 1961 school year would end early so that students could be mobilized as an "army" of volunteer literacy instructors sent a new wave of parents scrambling to get their kids off the island.[31] On January 1, deteriorating U.S.-Cuba relations reached the point of no return when President Eisenhower ordered the Havana embassy closed. Because the suspension of consular services meant Cubans could no longer apply for visas, on January 3, Attorney General William Pierce Rogers announced he would begin paroling anti-Castro "refugees" into the United States. Unlike the Hungarians who preceded them, Cuban parolees did not need advance sponsorship from a voluntary agency to guarantee they wouldn't become a public charge. However, both Cuban law and airline regulations required anyone leaving the island to possess a valid visa. By January 3, only 22 of the 250 preauthorized visas had been issued to children from the Ruston Academy network, and there were then 510 students on Baker's list.[32]

On January 4, Baker returned to the United States, leaving plans to evacuate Ruston Academy network children in the hands of a former employee, Penny Powers, who worked for the British embassy's intelligence division and had links to the International Rescue Committee. Baker and Father Walsh traveled to Washington, D.C., to renegotiate the terms of the program with the Departments of State and Justice. At a meeting four days later with Frank Auerbach and head of the Visa Office Robert Hale, the men reported that Penny Powers was arranging student visas to allow some children to travel to the British possessions of Jamaica and Bahamas; they agreed those students could be granted U.S. student visas in Kingston, and then continue on to Miami. More importantly, Auerbach authorized Father Walsh to provide emergency visa waivers—a State Department affidavit certifying the recipient was pre-authorized to enter the United States—to children in "imminent danger" of communist brainwashing.[33] INS officials would then grant student visas to the children at the U.S. point of entry.

Walsh and Baker received initial approval to issue visa waivers to the remaining 228 children on the original list of 250, with the understanding that more could be requested if needed.[34] The International Rescue Committee and the exile Cuban Revolutionary Council, both of which had links to the CIA, were similarly authorized to provide visa waivers to Cuban adults whose admission to the United States was judged particularly pressing; these had to be requested by a U.S. relative, usually one connected to an exile organization, and were only granted after a lengthy security screening. Because the State Department had authorized Walsh to issue immediate waivers to any boy or girl between the ages of six and sixteen (as well as to seventeen and eighteen-year-old youth, after FBI clearance), it was now much quicker and easier to secure travel documents for children traveling alone.[35] These unique age-based administrative accommodations meant unaccompanied children whose admission had previously been facilitated by a general relaxation of immigration requirements for all anti-Castro Cubans were redefined after January 8 as "an exception within an exception."

Granting expedited visa waivers to children traveling alone did much more than ensure the evacuation of Ruston-affiliated youth from the island because it coincided with a rupture in diplomatic relations that foreclosed the possibility of emigration for Cuban adults without U.S. resident relatives. Unaccompanied children's exceptional new status meant that sending them to Miami, where they could request visa waivers for other family members, now represented the only legal way for many Cubans to get to the United States. The State Department's age-based visa waiver policy thus served as a catalyst for the rapid transformation of the Walsh-Baker program, initially designed to protect a few hundred elite teenagers from the hazards of revolutionary life, into a broadly based operation in which thousands of boys and girls of all ages left home in a new chain migration process.

John F. Kennedy's presidential inauguration on January 20, 1961, led to a dramatic expansion and restructuring of the refugee response launched the previous December, further accelerating the flow of unaccompanied children from Cuba. Like Eisenhower, Kennedy was a committed anti-communist who saw the exodus of anti-Castro Cubans from the island as fundamental to the demise of the revolution. However, unlike his Republican predecessor who adhered to traditional understandings of refugee resettlement as the prerogative of private and primarily sectarian organizations, the new Democratic leader had a more expansive vision of the government's role. As the increasingly destitute Cuban population in Miami continued to grow and with Americans slow to step up as they had during the Hungarian crisis to fund voluntary agency efforts or provide exiles with jobs and sponsorships, Kennedy decided it was time for decisive federal intervention. On February 3, avowing that the nation's support for anti-Castro Cubans was "important to the security of the United States," the president announced a $4 million allocation from the Mutual Security Act contingency fund for refugee relief and resettlement during fiscal year 1960–61.[36] He charged secretary of Health, Education, and Welfare Abraham Ribicoff with establishing a comprehensive program to provide monthly welfare payments, healthcare, education, and vocational training, as well as resettlement assistance for exiles and their families.[37] Kennedy also instructed the secretary to develop a special program for unaccompanied children, whom the president described as the "most defenseless and troubled group among the refugee population."[38]

Ribicoff tasked the Children's Bureau with negotiating and supervising a contract with the Florida State Department of Public Welfare to provide care in foster homes or institutions to Cuban children arriving alone in the United States. The FSDPW then awarded subcontracts, effective March 1, to the Catholic Welfare Bureau, the Jewish Family and Children's Service (JFCS), and the (Protestant) Children's Service Bureau (CSB) in Miami.[39] Voluntary agencies received reimbursement for direct care costs and administrative expenses at a rate of $6.50 per day for each unaccompanied Cuban child placed in group care and $5.50 per day for each child in foster homes. Federal funds also covered transportation for children placed outside Miami and special services including medical treatment and psychiatric care.[40]

Part and parcel of Kennedy's overall response to the Cuban refugee crisis, the expansion of the Cuban Children's Program explicitly signaled for the first time the federal government's recognition of a responsibility to care for unaccompanied refugee minors. Financing the program through a one-time allocation from discretionary mutual security funds suggests that the president, confident in the quick demise of Castro's government, envisioned neither a permanent refugee minor assistance program nor long-term care for Cuban boys and girls. Together with the State Department's decision to prioritize visa waivers for unaccompanied children, this new opportunity for children without U.S. resident relatives or family friends who could afford to take them in converged with worsening conditions in Cuba to produce an unparalleled exodus from the island. The news that children were now eligible for federally funded *becas*, the catchall term by which Cubans unfamiliar with the public foster care described the "scholarships" for young people in the United States, spread like wildfire.[41]

Following Kennedy's announcement, the Children's Bureau raced to put in place basic standards and guidelines for the Cuban Children's Program. To avert the problems that arose when placing Hungarian youth, the bureau mandated that Cuban children only be placed with agencies licensed or approved by state child welfare departments. The FSDPW was required to keep a centralized record of all placements and develop other oversight procedures.[42] Children's Bureau chief Katherine Oetinger nonetheless understood that the Cuban Children's Program reversed the traditional relationship between the government and voluntary agencies in caring for unaccompanied refugee minors. Although she saw this change as "sound, appropriate and long overdue," she also recognized that voluntary agencies "understandably [had] a strong vested interest" in maintaining control in this arena. In order to ensure "fullest cooperation," agencies should be allowed to maintain as much autonomy as possible.[43]

As the Children's Bureau scrambled to define the parameters of the new program, the FSDPW confronted the unenviable task of seizing the reigns of a child evacuation scheme already in motion. By February 1, 1961, the Ruston network had sent 174 children to the United States; 53 were dispatched to homes of relatives and friends, 119 were under CWB care along with the 15 children previously taken in by the agency. Two more were placed in foster homes by the Jewish Family and Children's Service.[44] With growing numbers of children arriving in Miami, the overwhelming majority Catholic, the CWB established ad hoc policies and procedures of its own. The Children's Bureau's late entry into the game set the stage for ongoing confusion and reactive policy making, as well as disagreements between federal and state officials and voluntary agencies over who was actually in charge of the rapidly evolving Cuban Children's Program.

This dynamic first emerged when FSDPW director of Child Welfare Frances Davis realized that children admitted to the United States on student visas were not legally eligible for public assistance. Davis suggested admitting the children as "parolees," but Father Walsh and Cuban Refugee Center officials argued this would be "upsetting to parents" and that it "could bring about possible reprisals" in Cuba. After deliberation, Davis decided that the FSDPW would avoid raising questions about how children had entered the country and would simply "provide foster care . . . without reference to their immigration status." Although it troubled her to give "preferential treatment" for welfare services to a group of non-resident children, Davis reluctantly concluded it was justified for unaccompanied Cuban minors, who were "a particular and special group."[45]

Early disagreements also emerged among voluntary agencies over the purpose and parameters of the child evacuation effort, most notably between the Catholic Welfare Bureau, the International Rescue Committee, and the leaders of the Ruston Academy network in Cuba. In early January, finding

An Exception within an Exception

suitable Catholic foster homes in short supply, Father Walsh moved 140 teen-age boys and girls into the Kendall Children's Home, formerly the Dade County facility for African American children, under the care of a group of Ursuline nuns and Marist Brothers. With plans in the works to establish two more group homes in Miami, he also reached out to Catholic Charities agencies across the country to request beds for children in local boarding schools and orphanages.[46]

These arrangements were not at all what the Ruston Network or their IRC partners had in mind. On April 3, Penny Powers wrote to former ambas-sador to Cuba Philip Bonsal and HEW commissioner of Social Security William L. Mitchell to express displeasure with Father Walsh's handling of the program. She claimed parents were horrified to learn their sons and daughters were placed in isolated orphanages or other "charity" institutions where the standard of living was "not comparable to what children were accustomed to" in Cuba. Powers warned these substandard living arrange-ments did nothing to "further future Cuban-American relationships" or "give children an idea of a democratic way of life." She also claimed that, despite the participation of other sectarian agencies, Cuban parents saw the program as "a Catholic enterprise." Protestant families were thus "very reluctant to participate." Powers insisted that HEW take direct control of the program and make immediate arrangements to place children in coeducational board-ing schools in Florida or adjoining states where they would receive English classes and intensive courses on "democratic procedure" and where it would be easier to organize their repatriation "when the time [came] for them to return to Cuba."[47]

Later that month Powers made an IRC-funded trip to the United States, where she restated these complaints at a meeting with Frances Davis and Father Walsh. The priest vehemently rejected her claim to speak on behalf of "all parents," most of whom he understood were well satisfied with their children's care. He also pointed out that only half of the more than 600 chil-dren under his care arrived through the Ruston network; the others arranged travel through church contacts. And if the program had become a Catholic enterprise, this was because Protestant and Jewish Cuban parents were slow to recognize the "necessity to get the children out." Walsh dismissed outright any notion that the program's goal was to ensure the democratic formation of Cuba's future leaders, insisting that its "only purpose" was to avoid "the tragedies of earlier refugee situations" by providing "the best care possible" to unaccompanied children.[48] Following a flurry of letters between Ambassador Bonsal, HEW, and FSDPW officials, HEW and the FSDPW rallied to the priest's defense, turning down an offer from Powers' IRC colleagues to take a greater role in the program.

Powers wasn't the only one concerned about the dramatic evolution of the Cuban Children's Program. By early March, as the number of children entering the country surged to over one hundred per week, the INS field office in Miami informed Father Walsh that no more unaccompanied minors could be admitted until they received authorization from the State Department. By then the FSDPW was funding care for 348 children; 177 more were with U.S. relatives not receiving financial aid. If, as Walsh had hoped, visa waivers were granted for 500 additional children, the Florida State's budget would need to be quickly increased to cover program expenses until June 1961.

Davis conferred with her supervisor, FSDPW director Frank Craft, who agreed continuing the program was "essential." He also felt it necessary to clarify the program's scope and purpose and address its precarious financial situation before moving forward. Stressing these points in a letter to Mildred Arnold at HEW's Division of Social Services, he wrote, "the fundamental question is whether or not this country as a matter of policy wishes to guarantee care and protection to any Cuban child who is unaccompanied. This policy needs to be clearly determined at a Cabinet level with complete understanding between the Department of State and the Department of Health, Education, and Welfare. If it is our policy, then there should be a commitment of funds so as to carry it out without having to worry about how many children we take into care per week." Craft's letter essentially challenged the federal government to put its money where its mouth was. However, since he still saw the program as a limited, short-term initiative, Craft concluded that he found it "hard to believe" there would be "a mass exodus of unaccompanied children" from Cuba, "in such numbers that this country [could not] support them."[49] HEW's leaders, who similarly expected the program's caseload to soon stabilize at a maximum of 600 to 700 children, concurred. On April 14, they endorsed Walsh's request for 500 more visa waivers. The State Department approved his request the next day.[50]

The events of the next month shattered expectations that the children would be returning to Cuba in a matter of months. On April 20, the C.I.A.-sponsored Bay of Pigs Invasion was repelled by Castro's army and militias, and most of the 1,200 surviving members of the Cuban-exile invasion force, Brigade 2506, were taken prisoner. Rather than bringing about the collapse of the Castro regime, as counterrevolutionaries and their supporters had hoped, the attack dramatically increased the leader's popularity and provided the pretext for promulgating a new constitution prohibiting elections and proclaiming the revolution socialist.[51] This announcement, which coincided with the early closure of the island's schools and the beginnings of a nationwide literacy campaign, provoked an explosion in demand for visa waivers from parents beyond the Ruston network who now also wished to send their children away.[52]

In the United States the failed invasion set off a storm of criticism from congressional republicans, who lambasted Kennedy for not sending military aircraft and troops to support the exiles.[53] Humiliated but determined to avoid outright war against Cuba, Kennedy shifted to a policy mixing covert attacks against Castro with diplomatic efforts to isolate his regime, while promoting democracy and economic development in Latin America through a new Alliance for Progress.[54] To avoid being seen as weak on communism, Kennedy doubled down on his policy of welcoming Cuban refugees. Following the president's instructions, the State Department and Department of Justice further relaxed visa and eligibility requirements: Cubans no longer needed to present a valid passport when they arrived at a U.S. port of entry and adult access to visa waivers was expanded and made available to anyone eighteen and under. The State Department would also subsidize flights to the United States for refugees.[55]

Confronted with more and more children arriving alone, voluntary agencies found it increasingly difficult to secure placements in the Miami area. The overtaxed Jewish Family and Children's Service found itself compelled to rely on the HIAS's nationwide network of child welfare agencies to find foster homes further afield for the small number of Jewish children fleeing the island. The small Protestant Children's Service Bureau's caseload by October 1962 was only 267 but, without access to a national network of coreligionist child welfare agencies, they struggled to locate and conduct home studies on foster homes outside Dade County. The process was further complicated by Cuban parents and children that demanded placements with families sharing their same denomination.[56]

The persistent scarcity of Catholic foster homes meant Father Walsh bore the weight of improvising living arrangements for the majority of children. In July the priest opened a new facility at Camp Matecumbe, a rustic Catholic summer camp in south Miami. There were 350 boys ages twelve to fifteen that lived and studied at the camp. In October Walsh opened an even larger shelter at Florida City, where 700 boys under age twelve and girls of all ages lived together in a cluster of apartment buildings, under the care of lay parents and Cuban nuns from the Order of Saint Philip Neri from Cuba. Like Matecumbe, Florida City had its own makeshift school, but only for elementary students; older girls attended the local public high school.[57]

Meanwhile, private arrangements began breaking down as the financial and emotional burden of caring for children longer than anticipated weighed on relatives and family friends. After extended discussion, the FSDPW and HEW determined that boys and girls, if they were registered at the Cuban Refugee Center upon entering the United States, could subsequently be taken into federal care. Throughout the summer of 1961, expanding caseloads and resentment over government oversight led the CWB and its partner agencies across the country to sometimes relax placement standards and skimp on home studies. As a result, the quality of care received by unaccompanied children would vary dramatically from state to state, agency to agency, and individual placement to placement.[58]

Despite the White House's confidence in the impending collapse of the Castro regime, after the Bay of Pigs, it became clear unaccompanied children would be in federal care for longer than expected. The question of continued funding for the Cuban Children's Program—its budget now decidedly in the red—grew increasingly urgent. On May 17, Secretary Ribicoff wrote to Bureau of the Budget director David E. Bell telling him it was "necessary to continue this program in fiscal year 1962." Since Bell objected to additional support from the president's contingency funds, HEW was "glad to assist in any way" with developing the necessary legislation and appropriations requests. Failure to secure congressional authorization and funding for the program, Ribicoff warned, would have "extremely serious consequences from both a domestic standpoint and an international one."[59]

In July Commissioner William L. Mitchell and Father Walsh testified before the Senate Subcommittee to Investigate Problems Connected with Refugees and Escapees about the geopolitical importance of the Cuban Children's Program—behind closed doors, since Walsh continued to warn that publicity might cause Castro to clamp down on exit permits or endanger children's families on the island.[60] Ribicoff pressed the point at congressional hearings in August for H.R. 8291, the Migration and Refugee Assistance Act, to appropriate $26 million for the Cuban Refugee Program in 1962. Because of Cuban refugees' significance to the nation's foreign policy, the secretary argued, their resettlement "should not be dealt with through temporary expedients/half measures." Although many accepted this rationale, Ribicoff encountered early opposition from a powerful group of congressmen led by Francis Walter, whose anti-communism was exceeded only by his commitment to immigration restriction. Characterizing the legislation as "broad as a barn door," Walter speculated that some Cuban families were "using this situation" as a pretext for economic migration, and he warned of "over-Americanizing" unaccompanied children who then wouldn't want to return home. Otto Passman (D-La.), the isolationist chair of the House Appropriations Committee on Foreign Aid, also criticized the "excessive" daily per diem rate for the care of Cuban minors—which was, in fact, higher than the rate for U.S. foster children.[61]

Countering these objections, Ribicoff insisted that children had to leave Cuba because "their lives were in jeopardy." Revealing a pro-elite bias shared by many of the program's proponents, he emphasized the difference between Cubans and their poor, racialized Latin American immigrant cousins, stressing that most of the Cuban youth came from middle and "upper class" families that were better off than their American foster families. When pressed, the secretary conceded that HEW's vision of a limited short-term program changed after the Bay of Pigs; all involved were now preparing for the "contingency" that the children might be in the United States "for a period of time." But it remained the president's desire that children continue to be welcomed so Americans could "show the rest of the world . . . how we treat people who flee tyranny and communism."[62]

Unmoved by these arguments, Congress adjourned on September 27 without passing legislation authorizing the Cuban Refugee Program. Two days later, an alarmed Abraham Ribicoff wrote to Secretary of State Dean Rusk, urgently requesting $21.3 million from the mutual security fund to keep the federal refugee response going through June 1962.[63] On October 6, Kennedy authorized only an additional $8.9 million to support the program to the end of 1961. The number of children needing care had risen much more rapidly than HEW's capacity to finance them. In order to stay on budget, Commissioner Mitchell advised the Children's Bureau to develop "equitable and socially sound" guidelines for determining who qualified—and who didn't—for federal support.[64] He also directed the bureau to prepare a justification of the program's per diem rates, examine the CWB policy of retaining fifty cents per day per child to cover operational costs, and require the Catholic agency to reform haphazard accounting procedures which made it "impossible for the agency to report in detail on administrative procedures."[65]

At a second round of Senate Judiciary Subcommittee hearings in December, Senator Philip Hart (D-Mich.) reminded his peers of the foreign policy consequences if Congress failed to enact legislation authorizing the Cuban Refugee Program.[66] But not everyone was on the same page. While exile community leaders praised Kennedy's program as "eloquent and unforgettable proof" of U.S. generosity, senators raised questions about possible communist sympathies among Cubans coming to the United States. South Florida leaders decried the economic and social disruption caused by the ongoing influx, warning of a possible increase in juvenile delinquency among displaced youth.[67] As the year drew to a close, still lacking statutory authorization and running out of money, the future of the Cuban Children's Program remained uncertain. Secretary Ribicoff again requested contingency funding, noting that a transfer needed to be made by December 20 in order for the FSDPW to meet the next month's expenses.[68]

When Kennedy approved another last-minute appropriation at the end of 1961 to allow the program to continue for another six months, more than $2 million already had been spent on children's care, and the number of unaccompanied minors in federally funded homes surpassed 2,300.[69] But the number of children arriving alone in Miami continued to grow. With Cuban public schools set to reopen in January 1962, the government's announcement that high school students would be sent to new boarding schools in the countryside, where they would alternate classroom instruction with ideological education and agricultural labor, further accelerated the exodus of unaccompanied minors from the island.[70] As the Castro regime cracked down further on emigration, more parents made clear to children they were going to the United States to initiate the family's emigration; accordingly, as soon as they arrived the majority of children applied for visa waivers for parents.[71] Many also took part-time jobs to save for their parents' travel. These children were joined by a growing number of youth from lower socioeconomic backgrounds who asked to be sent to the United States to advance educational or career goals; many of them, like fifteen-year-old José Luís Hernández, the son of an impoverished single mother, wrote letters to the president and Mrs. Kennedy begging for *becas* outside Miami, where they hoped attending school would help them learn English and achieve the dream of attending a U.S. college.[72]

More children initially sent to live with relatives or friends were now also entering federal care, as host families' changing circumstances made them unwilling or unable to continue supporting them. Such was the case of a newly widowed elderly Cuban American man from the Bronx, who wrote to President Kennedy requesting a *beca* for his "obedient and well mannered" eleven-year-old grandson, whom he feared leaving unsupervised while at work.[73] A couple in Covington, Kentucky, similarly wrote to commissioner of Social Security Robert M. Ball asking how to apply for federal aid for a

Cuban friend's teenage son who'd been staying with them for more than six months; they were fond of the boy, but the expense of his Catholic school fees and medical care meant they could no longer afford their own children's college tuition.[74] Growing numbers of Cuban children "turning up across the country" and living "in very bad situations," helped Children's Bureau's leader convince Secretary Ribicoff to further relax program requirements to allow some children who had not been initially registered at the Cuban Refugee Center to apply for retroactive reclassification as "refugees," making them eligible for foster care.[75]

By spring 1962 the Cuban Children's Program primarily served as the first step in a process of family migration for Cubans who could no longer imagine a future on the island. This was implicitly recognized by leaders in HEW and the FSDPW, who no longer expected children's return to Cuba. Instead, they directed voluntary agencies to focus on expediting the reunion of children with parents, some of whom were now in Miami but delayed resuming custody because of inadequate living arrangements or uncertain employment prospects.[76]

Voluntary agency staff also observed demographic changes in the youth exodus. Despite class-conscious program proponents' continued insistence that Cubans were different from the "deprived children" in American foster care, greater numbers of working-class and rural children, including a small number of teenaged "boat boys" who left the island of their own volition in fisherman's boats, were arriving in the United States.[77] More than 50 percent of boys entering federal care during these months had left school after the fifth or sixth grade.[78] A growing number of "emotionally disturbed" youth and some with physical or mental disabilities also arrived, as did a few "negro" and Chinese Cuban children and others of "mixed racial background." Although in Cuba many of these children had been seen as white, U.S. child welfare workers did not consider them suitable for placement in "all-white" homes or communities; they couldn't be placed with African American families, either, since agency staff felt this would be "frightening" to them. The difficulty of placing minors who confounded Americans' binary notions of race was even more pronounced when searching for placements for siblings from families that included "many different shades of children."[79] A small number of stateless children—sons and daughters of European Jews who sought asylum in Cuba during and after World War II—only added to the confusion, requiring additional policy improvisation by the FSDPW's Frances Davis. Following several months of discussion, HEW eventually ruled that any Jewish refugee minor who resided in Cuba for five years and entered the United States after

January 1, 1959, was eligible for placement by the HIAS in federally funded foster homes.[80]

HEW Commissioner Mitchell attempted to put a positive spin on the challenges of caring for the ever-increasing and increasingly diverse unaccompanied minors arriving in the country, declaring that providing for Cuban refugees of all ages offered an "opportunity to demonstrate this country's humane dynamics, competence and capacity for constructive social action." But by then many local welfare agencies were reluctant to assume responsibility for the complex needs of a rapidly expanding group of foreign children whose lower socioeconomic status and ambiguous racial identities invited association with the stigmatized poor and minority youth already in U.S. foster care.[81] In April 1962, HEW Secretary Ribicoff privately acknowledged how changes over the past few months had complicated an already difficult placement process, noting the need for homes, especially for adolescent boys, was now "acute."[82]

On February 22, a reporter at the *Cleveland Plain Dealer* defied Father Walsh's entreaties to maintain silence and broke the story of the youthful Cuban exodus, setting off a wave of national coverage about "children saved from Castro's brainwashing" over the next several months.[83] Hoping to take advantage of the breach and new widespread public interest in the media-christened "Operation Pedro Pan," Ribicoff appealed for Americans to open their homes to Cuban youth. A week later he released another statement, urging patriotic citizens to join forces with their government to "frustrate the evil of Castro's Cuba" and protect the nation's "reputation in the eyes of the free world" by taking in refugees of all ages.[84] Motivated by both anti-communism and humanitarianism, several hundred families responded to Ribicoff's call, as did some who hoped to supplement their household income by becoming foster parents. Offers also came from married women, some childless or grieving the loss of a son or daughter, who hoped a Cuban child might be a source of companionship and comfort. But most offers, as in the past, were only for children under six and specified a desired gender or other personal characteristics.[85] Or, like Mrs. Edward Bates of Brookfield, Connecticut, they stressed they were only interested in taking in "small babies," and "with the financial help."[86] Many of these offers came from Protestant families; even if they were willing to care for Catholic boys and girls, Father Walsh, for whom the preservation of children's religious identity was the central purpose of the program, vigorously resisted interfaith placements.[87]

The lack of available home placements meant that almost 80 percent of Cuban unaccompanied minors remained in Catholic institutions, makeshift group homes, or severely overcrowded camps. The failure of Ribicoff's appeals to inspire a significant surge in home offers was due in part to Americans' general reluctance to take teenage boys into their homes as foster children.[88] This aversion was likely exacerbated by American insistence on associating even fair-skinned Cuban adolescent boys with supposedly "delinquent" Puerto Rican and Black youth, an assumption heightened by the recent success of moral panic–inducing movies like *Blackboard Jungle* (1955) and *West Side Story* (1961).[89] It was also consistent with Americans' response to Cuban refugees of all ages, which the IRC characterized as "apathetic" from the beginning. At best lukewarm before the Bay of Pigs, public support for anti-communist refugees cooled off rapidly when most Americans realized that Cubans would not in fact be temporary guests.[90]

This new antagonism toward refugees of all ages spilled out in heated school board debates about the expense of educating "nonresident" students as well as in letters by private citizens who wrote to HEW, congressional representatives, and the president to complain the federal government was doing more for Cuban youth than needy American children.[91] It was also reflected in growing suspicion about the refugees and the reluctance of some state and local welfare agencies to dedicate already scarce resources to the Cuban Children's Program. The Montana Board of Public Welfare flatly stated it did not have money for staff to provide services to unaccompanied Cuban minors—nor, in any case, did it want "Communistically oriented" youth placed in their state.[92]

Mounting anti-Cuban sentiment also took on explicitly religious overtones after April 23, 1962, when Boston's archbishop Cardinal Richard Cushing announced at a Knights of Columbus breakfast that one hundred children were being brought to Massachusetts to be "adopted" by the Marist Missionary Sisters. Newspapers nationwide picked up Cushing's statement, reinforcing Americans' persistent confusion about the difference between fostering and adoption and generating a storm of protest.[93] Letters flooded into HEW, the Children's Bureau, and to congressional representatives, objecting to federal funds being dedicated to an expensive and "unconstitutional" program that lacked congressional approval and had no clear end date. In a letter to Senator Thomas Kuchel (R-Calif.), an irate Herbert Goldsworthy of Santa Monica, California, asked "what is the matter that the church cannot take care of these refugees themselves?"[94] B. F. Fisk, a self-identified Pentecostal from Sanger, California, sent an equally angry letter to President Kennedy, asking the nation's first Catholic president if the Cuban Children's Program was "an example of the campaign promises we have heard so much about?

What about separation of Church and state?"[95] A furious Conrad V. Henshaw of Tyler, Texas, wrote to Representative Lindley Beckworth about the program's high per diem rate, accusing the Catholic church of seeking "to make a profit on human misery."[96]

By August so many complaints had been referred to HEW that it became impossible for Children's Bureau staff to respond individually. In a form letter prepared to assist congressmen responding to objections from constituents, the bureau noted that media coverage of Cardinal Cushing's announcement had been "misleading;" "at no time" were any of the Cuban children available for adoption, by Catholic nuns or anyone else. And while foster care per diem rates were high, this was because "an emergency program is always more expensive than an established program." Crucially, the letter stressed that at no time did the church receive money from the federal government to provide for children; children's care was handled by four "licensed and approved child placing agencies" whose collaboration they described as "a commendable example of cooperation in [sic] behalf of frightened and confused children in a strange land." Taking a page from USCOM's 1940 playbook, the Children's Bureau attempted to deflect religiously motivated criticism by emphasizing the nonsectarian character of what was in fact primarily a one-faith program—a reality confirmed by the dramatic expansion of the Catholic Welfare Bureau, which by March 1962 boasted a staff of more than 300, most of them involved in the care of the thousands of Cuban Catholic unaccompanied minors on the agency's caseload.

Strain from mounting program demands took a toll on state-level overseers. The Florida State Department of Public Welfare staff who had worked intensely on the federal Cuban Children's Program since its founding began to lose patience with voluntary agencies' lax application of Children's Bureau standards. Mildred Arnold of HEW's Division of Social Services shared these frustrations. Responding to a letter of complaint from the FSDPW's Frances Davis, she noted "we all agree that the public welfare agencies must be more involved in the planning for the unaccompanied Cuban children," before encouraging Davis to continue to "stimulate a feeling of greater responsibility for determining that the placement agency is licensed or approved."[97] But the FSDPW fought a losing battle, as voluntary agencies under intense pressure to find homes for children continued to loosely interpret placement standards. Efforts at maintaining a centralized record of the whereabouts of all unaccompanied Cuban children were also compromised by other agencies, including the National Catholic Welfare Conference, Church World Service, and the International Rescue Committee, who sometimes resettled

An Exception within an Exception

minors on their own rather than referring them to one of the four agencies contracted by the Cuban Children's Program.[98]

Frances Davis and her colleagues had also begun to openly express discomfort with the inequities between funding provided for the care of unaccompanied Cuban minors and for U.S. children. In August Mildred Arnold noted that FSDPW leaders and staff wished "agencies throughout the country could do as much for our teen-age dependent American boys as they are doing for the Cubans."[99] In the coming months, Davis would become more forceful in articulating her displeasure with the inconsistent quality of care provided to unaccompanied children, which she felt resulted from the "mass purchase of care with a minimum of accountability."[100] She was especially frustrated that the Catholic Welfare Bureau had yet to establish "satisfactory accounting procedures" that would allow HEW to reach a final determination on the appropriateness of the program's controversial per diem rates, nor provided a detailed justification for withholding a percentage of federal care stipends to cover the agency's operational expenses.[101] These frustrations were compounded by state officials' resentment of the media's exclusive focus on voluntary agencies' role in the Cuban Children's Program, which, as Mildred Arnold recognized in a letter to FSDPW director Frank Craft, totally disregarded the "greater responsibility . . . carried by your child welfare staff under the most effective leadership of Frances Davis."[102]

Tensions were also on the rise between HEW and Congress. In April 1962, the House Appropriations Committee released a report calling the program's per diem rates paid to voluntary agencies for children's care "excessive." HEW still believed the cost actually exceeded the daily per diem allotted but since the voluntary "institutions and agencies involved [did] not keep adequate records," they were unable to prove this.[103] The Migration and Refugee Assistance Act passed on June 28, finally providing legislative authorization and funding for federal refugee assistance. Budget negotiations continued until October 23, when Congress approved $70 million for the Cuban Refugee Program for fiscal year 1963. The unaccompanied children's program received $13.8 million, more than double the previous annual budget but representing a drastic per-capita funding reduction as the number of children in federal care had soared in 1962 from 650 to 4,000.[104] Congress further stipulated the funding had to be reauthorized annually.[105]

The FSDPW's new contract with voluntary agencies also reflected intensifying congressional concerns and opposition. The revised agreement established stricter eligibility guidelines and mandated children's care be cut off at nineteen rather than twenty-one, as in several previous programs for unaccompanied refugee minors.[106] HEW also directed the FSDPW to crack down on parents who delayed resuming custody after arriving in Miami, suggesting that agencies adopt a policy of returning children to their families within two to three weeks. Frances Davis pushed back on this—as did Walsh, recently named monsignor by Pope John XXIII in honor of his child-saving efforts, arguing reunification decisions should be made on an individual basis taking into consideration the newly arrived parents' housing and employment as well as their physical and mental health. Disagreement also arose between federal and state officials and the CWB over whether parents should be required to relocate to wherever children had resettled, a practice which Monsignor Walsh resisted.

Pressure from HEW to impose top-down policy directives put into stark relief the gap between the geopolitics of compassion driving the Cuban Children's Program and what voluntary agencies considered the children's best interest, further straining the relationship between the FSDPW and those charged with minors' day-to-day care.[107] In the absence of major policy changes, the program continued to grow. By fall 1962, 4,100 children were in federal care.[108] Something had to give—and it did—creating new pressures on everyone involved in the children's program.

On October 14, American U-2 reconnaissance flights documented Soviet ballistic missile silos at several sites in Cuba. A week later President Kennedy ordered an immediate naval blockade of the island, and the threat of a nuclear showdown between the superpowers sent shock waves across the world. After thirteen terrifying days the USSR agreed to withdraw its missiles. In return the United States promised it would not invade the island, effectively guaranteeing the survival of Castro's government. Exiles still angry about the failed Bay of Pigs Invasion understood the Kennedy-Khrushchev pact as proof that the White House had abandoned their cause.[109] But adult exiles weren't the only ones who felt betrayed.

The outcome of the Missile Crisis was devastating to Cuban minors who had clung to hopes of reunion with their families through years of loneliness and culture shock. Commercial flights between Cuba and the United States ended, meaning parents would have to travel to Mexico or Spain to apply for a U.S. visa, an expensive trip requiring U.S. dollars from relatives or friends outside Cuba. The State Department ruled that Cubans in Spain counted against that country's quota, making the wait for a visa a year or longer. Some desperate Cuban parents would choose instead to travel overland to the U.S.-Mexico border at Brownsville, Texas, where sympathetic INS officers paroled them into the country; a few more left the island without exit permits to make the dangerous sea crossing to Florida on small boats.[110]

For most Cuban children in federal care, separation from their parents was now indefinite. This harsh realization caused many to plunge into deep depression. Other youth, conscious of their role as the advance guard of their family's migration plan, dutifully followed instructions cabled from Cuba to "claim" their parents through the Red Cross, in the mistaken belief this would prioritize their evacuation.[111] Others launched letter writing campaigns begging the U.S. government to reinstate commercial travel, but the State Department held firm; isolating the Castro regime superseded pleas for family reunification.[112]

The Cuban Children's Program now entered a demanding two-year transition period, in which all involved struggled to meet minors' changing needs while grappling with how to bring the program to a responsible end. Frances Davis directed agencies to focus energies toward reducing persistent inconsistencies in the quality of care.[113] She also worked to expand diagnostic and treatment options for children with physical or mental special needs and to address the need for additional casework to handle issues stemming from minors' maturation.

Both the FSDPW and the CWB were particularly concerned about older working-class and rural teens living in camps. Because many were several years behind in school and aging out of care before graduation, Davis and Monsignor Walsh worried about delinquency, a fear reinforced by a rising number of juvenile court cases involving Cuban youth in late 1962. Walsh was also troubled by adolescents' burgeoning sexuality, especially a group of "overt homosexual" boys in the Opa-locka Camp, whom he felt should be broken up and sent for psychiatric treatment. Walsh and Davis also worried about heterosexual teens, fearing that unsupervised Cuban girls might fall into prostitution while boys' adventures produced a surge in American girls giving birth to "babies of dark color."[114] The CWB grappled as well with more serious behavioral issues among a small number of mentally ill children, including a "paranoid schizophrenic" eighteen-year-old girl at the Florida City group home who tried to smother her two younger roommates.[115]

After 1962 program leaders began to grasp the extent of children's challenges in foster care. Although many established caring relationships with host families, some struggled to communicate and adapt to unfamiliar household routines and expectations. For their part, American host parents who praised the "high class" origins that distinguished many Cuban minors also could perceive them as overly gregarious, picky about food, and reluctant to help with household chores.[116] While younger children usually adapted quickly to new living arrangements, they also tended to suffer more intense feelings of anxiety and abandonment. Prolonged foster care also contributed to diminished Spanish fluency, loss of cultural identity, and weakened familial bonds among smaller children.[117] Older teens struggled to balance the demands of homework in a second language, after-school jobs, and repeated trips to consuls and public welfare offices, while also being called upon to serve as their community's "best ambassadors" at an endless series of community events, parades, and Rotary Club meetings.[118] For their part, working-class male youth who were seen as young adults on the island often resented household rules that restricted their independence or challenged Cuban gender roles that excused men from housework. Teens of both genders reported to agency staff more serious placement problems, including cases of physical and sexual abuse.[119] When agencies failed to adequately resolve complaints, some youth abandoned bad *becas* and moved in with relatives, friends, or sympathetic community members without informing agency staff. The FSDPW lost track of an undetermined number of such unaccompanied minors.[120]

By fall 1963 Cuban youth started turning nineteen in greater numbers. Scrambling to provide vocational guidance, training, and college opportunities, agencies also had to reach out to the FSDPW to clarify selective service requirements; after extensive discussion with HEW, those boys who entered the country as parolees (after June 1962) were considered eligible for the draft, whereas those who arrived earlier as "students" were not.[121] Improvisation was also needed for youth who entered the United States as "students," because their immigration status prohibited full-time employment; after another round of consultation with HEW and the INS, the FSDPW informed agencies that children could travel to Canada and reenter as parolees.

But program directors and agency personnel continued to face opposition from Congress. In response to ongoing criticism from Representative Passman, on November 26, 1962, the Government Accounting Office (GAO) launched an audit of the Cuban Children's Program.[122] The Senate Judiciary Subcommittee scheduled additional hearings the following month, at which commissioner of Social Security Robert M. Ball attempted to convince legislators to maintain current levels of federal refugee assistance.[123] But by then the public had grown weary of the exile cause. More and more Americans wrote to congressmen complaining about the continuation of "unfair" welfare payments to resettled Cubans, which in many cases were higher than the unemployment benefits received by U.S. citizens.[124] As of March 1963, anti-Cuban feeling in Miami reached the point that Cuban Refugee Center director John F. Thomas warned "a certain segment of the population would protest violently against flight renewals."[125] Before the end of the year, even the *Miami Herald* advocated "a gradual termination of the federal dole" for Cuban exiles.[126] Sympathy was running short for unaccompanied minors as well, evidenced by letters of complaint to congressmen from foster parents wondering why children were still in their care when some had relatives in the United States—even parents—to claim them.[127]

The backlash deepened that summer, when the American and Cuban governments agreed to include the parents of 348 unaccompanied children on Red Cross ships bringing Bay of Pigs prisoners to the United States in exchange for food and medical supplies.[128] But media attention to the Red Cross ships' arrival further fueled congressional opposition. At another round of Senate Judiciary Subcommittee and House Appropriations Committee hearings in May, legislators expressed anger at not being consulted about the decision to provide visa waivers and parole status to new Cuban arrivals. Representative Passman and his allies took the opportunity to renew their criticisms of the Cuban Children's Program's generous eligibility policies and high per diem rates, claiming there were "too many asking for help" and that voluntary agencies were "trying to make a profit" from the care of unaccompanied minors.[129] After the hearings the Departments of State and Justice conducted a contentious internal review of the visa waiver program. Over the objections of some who maintained that a flexible immigration policy was crucial to demonstrating the United States' commitment to anti-communist Cubans, on August 19, the Interdepartmental Coordinating Committee on Cuban Affairs recommended cancelling the visa waiver program.[130]

By October 1963, the Cuban Children's Program was in limbo: intake was almost at zero, necessitating significant staff reductions at the CWB. Parents weren't arriving either, and the fate of the 2,950 children still in federal care was uncertain. Frustrated leaders at both the Protestant CSB and the Catholic Welfare Bureau made their resentment clear over "directives" from the FSDPW on how to do their job.[131] At the same time, HIAS representatives made their displeasure known to the Children's Bureau over how media attention to Monsignor Walsh's efforts overshadowed their own successful placement record.[132] Even the Catholic Welfare Bureau, which was finalizing plans to close five of its Miami shelters in the next year and find foster families for children under twelve, was eager to end their involvement "as quickly as possible."[133]

The FSDPW also wanted out. At a confidential meeting on October 17 in Washington, D.C., Director Frank Craft stressed the need to clarify the intent of the program—which, he noted, had initially been established to "demonstrate democracy to the future leaders of the new Cuba"—and asked HEW to take over its administration by February 1964.[134] Florida, he argued, had devoted too much time to Cuban refugees to the detriment of its own citizens. Moreover, it was "unsound" for a state welfare office to oversee a program involving other states, an anomaly that created a bewilderingly complex organizational structure and "crazy" lines of reporting and communications. In his opinion, the federal government needed to take responsibility for establishing and directing a permanent refugee program. Mildred Arnold flatly rejected this possibility, insisting that direct operation of the Cuban refugee response by the federal government would "seriously upset precedents." The FSDPW had no choice but to see the program through to its conclusion.[135]

By summer 1965, recognizing the unlikely prospect of significant future emigration from the island, the Bureau of the Budget mandated an additional $2.3 million cut to the Cuban Refugee Program.[136] Many unaccompanied minors feared they would never see their families again. But once again, history took an unexpected turn. On September 28, 1965, Fidel Castro announced that he would open the port at Camarioca so Cubans in the United States could pick up any relatives who wished to leave. A few days later, at the October 3 signing of a long-awaited immigration reform bill abolishing the internationally maligned racial and national origins quota system, President Lyndon B. Johnson reinforced the United States' commitment to anti-Castro refugees and stated that "those who seek refuge here in America will find it."[137] However, although the 1965 Hart-Celler Immigration Act established for the first time a permanent refugee category—limited mostly to those fleeing persecution or fear of persecution in communist-dominated countries—admission under this designation was restricted to Eastern Hemisphere applicants.[138] To get around this, Johnson disregarded the act's recommendation that future use of the parole authority be limited to "emergent, individual and isolated" situations, declaring he would continue to parole into the United States as many Cubans as wished to come.[139]

In response more than a thousand ships sailed for Cuba, bringing 5,083 Cubans to the United States in a matter of weeks.[140] Alarmed by the ensuing chaos and with weather conditions in the Straits of Florida raising the risks of an already dangerous crossing, the U.S. government negotiated frantically to bring the boatlift to an end. On November 6, in exchange for a U.S. promise to provide two flights a day to safely evacuate exiles' relatives from the island,

CHURCH GROUP HELPS REUNITE FAMILY -- Calm joy of being together again is registered by the Cuban family, shown here in an Indianapolis bus station. Over two years ago Dr. William Gonzalez and his wife, Celia, bade good-by to daughter, Celia, then 11, in Havana. They planned to join her soon in the U.S. But events delayed their plans. Only recently they reached this country via Spain. Looking on happily at the reunion scene was Albert Diaz, a Cuban refugee whose days are dedicated to helping unaccompanied Cuban children, as a worker of the Catholic Charities Bureau, Indianapolis. Celia, on the honor roll of St. Agnes Academy, is one of some 100 children in which Diaz and his associates have helpful interest, regarding homes, schooling, general welfare -- and reunions like that of Celia and her parents. (Photo Courtesy TIMES, Indianapolis.)

After the Freedom Flights were launched, newspapers across the United States celebrated the reunion of unaccompanied Cuban children like Celia González with parents whose migration they helped facilitate. *Image from the Cuban Refugee Centers Records, courtesy of the Cuban Heritage Collection, University of Miami Libraries, Coral Gables, Florida.*

Castro agreed to close the port at Camarioca. Beginning on December 1, 1965, the "Freedom Flights" would bring another 273,000 Cubans to the United States before concluding in 1973.[141]

The flights were a godsend for unaccompanied minors and those charged with their care; by prioritizing the parents of children alone in the United States, they finally ended a prolonged separation most had expected to last for only a few months.[142] As another wave of Cubans entered the United States, local newspapers across the United States featured heart-warming stories of local Pedro Pan children reunited with their families.

But reunification proved trickier than anticipated; anxious and remorseful parents and their Americanized sons and daughters often required family counseling, psychotherapy, and long-term casework to help them learn to live together again.[143] In some cases, youth who resented parents they felt had abandoned them or were unhappy about being returned to Miami's "Cuban ghetto" asked to go back to their foster homes.[144] Through voluntary agencies' determined efforts, by April 30, 1967, the number of children in federal care had been reduced to 375.[145]

By 1967 the Florida State Department of Public Welfare and its four voluntary agency partners, in collaboration with 137 child welfare agencies across the country, had placed 8,331 children in 40 states as well as Washington, D.C., and Puerto Rico.[146] The majority of those children had been returned to their parents, but several hundred remained in federal care; most would never be reunited with their families. In some cases, parents were unwilling or unable to leave Cuba; in other cases, mothers and fathers already in the United States were unable to overcome their own financial or emotional difficulties and would never be able to provide care for their children. A small number of youth with severe psychological, mental, or physical disabilities would require life-long institutionalization. These unforeseen eventualities demanded one final round of policy improvisation from leaders at the FSDPW and HEW, a sobering reminder that a program set up to meet an emergency could not hope to offer "ideal solutions" for the long-term needs of dependent Cuban children.[147]

When the Cuban Children's Program finally began to wind down in 1966, it had evolved into something none of its early proponents ever envisioned. Originally a temporary, limited, and elite child evacuation scheme that sought to demonstrate support for Cuban parents in the anti-Castro underground and to safeguard the ideological and spiritual purity of the island's future leaders, it quickly ballooned into a comprehensive child welfare program with a legislative mandate to provide indefinite care to thousands of unaccompanied Cuban minors—most of them sent to the United States to begin a process of chain migration for their families. Part of a broader geopolitically motivated federal effort to resettle hundreds of thousands of Cuban refugees, the "exception within an exception" provided to the so-called Pedro Pan children also reflected the U.S. government's growing recognition of the importance of children to its Cold War foreign policy goals. It also represented the beginning of a new public-private partnership in the care of unaccompanied refugee minors.

But official reports lauding the program's success hid the fact that the road traveled had, in truth, been a rocky one for all involved.[148] Tasked with seizing the reins of an ill-defined and hastily conceived child-evacuation scheme already in motion, leaders at HEW and the FSDPW quickly found themselves trapped in an endless cycle of policy improvisation as they worked feverishly to respond to the changing needs of the ever-increasing and increasingly diverse children in federal care. They struggled to balance the program's competing goals and interests with persistent congressional opposition and anti-Cuban public sentiment; they sought in vain to coordinate multiple participating federal, state, and local agencies and actors and enforce Children's Bureau placement standards; and hold voluntary agencies accountable for establishing adequate record-keeping and accounting procedures. Overworked voluntary staff who struggled to maintain their morale in the face of public apathy, congressional opposition, and constant budget uncertainty increasingly resented government officials' attempts to curtail their traditional autonomy—while privately acknowledging their failure to care for unaccompanied minors "as well and as completely" as they would have liked.[149]

By 1963 some of those involved in the Cuban Children's Program, including the thousands of rapidly maturing youth whose chances of family reunification seemed impossibly slim, wondered if bringing them to the United States had really been in their best interests.

Although Monsignor Walsh publicly insisted until his death in 2001 that the Cuban Children's Program was part of a "life and death struggle" for the souls of the island's children, other voluntary agency staff and government officials recognized that reports of Cuban boys and girls being forcibly removed from their homes or shipped off to Russia were only panicked rumors. The early reservations of their Jewish colleagues took on a disturbing new weight.[150]

In an official retrospective of the program, Children's Bureau director Katherine Oetinger blithely maintained that most youth had taken their new lives "in their stride." But many bureau personnel quietly asked the "recurring question" of whether children should have been separated from their parents in the first place. An HEW-sponsored history of the program ultimately disavowed any U.S. responsibility for incentivizing the exodus, concluding the government had "no choice" but to get involved; by fall 1960, Cuban parents of their own volition had begun sending unaccompanied minors to Miami. If harm befell them in the United States, the federal government would have been morally responsible. And it would also have caused irreparable damage to the nation's international reputation.[151] The narrative made no mention of the role of age-based immigration accommodations and the provision of federally funded *becas* in creating the new group of unaccompanied child migrants served by the program.

Oetinger sought to dispel any lingering doubts about the program's outcomes. She wrote in the *Social Service Review* that its positive impacts would be felt "long after its termination;" it had helped forge new "links of understanding" which would "mean much to relations between Latin America and the United States in the future." In the long run, she concluded, the "peace of the world and the preservation of free societies" depended on the development of the individual capacities of children. The Cuban Children's Program was thus "a long-term investment on this side of the ledger."[152] Despite continued claims to the contrary by hard-line exile organizations and the mainstream media, Oetinger's starkly geopolitical logic makes clear that not even those professional social workers who might be expected to prioritize children's well-being imagined the program primarily in humanitarian terms.[153]

Moreover, this concern never applied equally to all children fleeing communist states, as evidenced by official U.S. indifference to the thousands of unaccompanied minors among the 1 million refugees who fled to Hong Kong in the decade after the 1949 Chinese Revolution. Despite Kennedy's 1962 executive action admitting 500 babies and toddlers to the United States on nonquota visas, as was the case for Korean "war orphans," they were to be admitted as adoptees, rather than as refugees in their own right. Neither the U.S. Children's Bureau nor any other public or private American organization ever proposed extending federally funded foster care to Chinese unaccompanied minors.

Oetinger's comments in the *Social Service Review* vividly illustrate how the diverse public and private efforts converging over time into what became known as Operation Pedro Pan or the Cuban Children's Program were brought together primarily by a set of overlapping geopolitical, ideological, and spiritual—not humanitarian—concerns. However, this doesn't mean that the program should be understood as the product of a coherent policy-making process, through which a monolithic U.S. government sought to exploit refugee minors as pawns in its battle against global communism.[154] Instead, like previous child-saving schemes and those that would soon follow, the Cuban Children's Program was ultimately the product of a multivalent and improvisational process, shaped by the nation's evolving geopolitics of compassion as well as the competing interests of all who participated in it. It would nonetheless set the precedent for the federal government's progressive assumption of responsibility for the care and protection of unaccompanied refugee minors, further testing the racial limits of American sympathy for the youngest victims of communism when the Cold War reached into Southeast Asia.

6

The Most Difficult
Type of Refugee

Southeast Asian Unaccompanied Minors and the
Reinvention of U.S. Refugee Policy, 1975–1989

The end of the Vietnam War in April 1975 touched off an exodus from South-east Asia that brought more than 1 million refugees to the United States—including approximately 25,000 unaccompanied minors.[1] This prolonged refugee crisis would serve as a catalyst for the passage of the 1980 Refugee Act, encompassing both the United States' first permanent and comprehensive refugee law and guaranteed federal funding for refugee resettlement. This historic legislation also created a permanent federal foster care system for unaccompanied refugee minors of all nationalities. Representing the culmination of a process that began in 1934 with private Jewish American child-saving efforts, the creation of the new Office of Refugee Resettlement's (ORR) URM program reflected a by-then widely accepted belief that unaccompanied refugee minors had a unique age-based claim on priority admissions as well as a right to special forms of state-sponsored care and protection. Opening the doors to a massive influx of Southeast Asian children fleeing their homelands alone, the new URM program would also spur on a dramatic professionalization of minors' care in the United States by the end of the 1980s.

This was by no means a straightforward process. Between 1975 and the end of the 1980s, a changing foreign policy and domestic political context, exacerbated by a resurgence of anti-Asian and anti-immigrant sentiment, fueled disagreements over the extent of the United States' obligation to those displaced by the Vietnam War. These factors also drove the constantly shifting policy toward unaccompanied children fleeing the region. Inadvertently admitted as part of the massive and poorly coordinated exodus from Vietnam in April 1975, the first unaccompanied minors presented an unwelcome surprise to federal officials coordinating the evacuation of Saigon. In the absence of federal direction and additional funding for the children's resettlement, overwhelmed voluntary agencies that had long advocated for unaccompanied minors hesitated to assume long-term responsibility for those they considered the "most difficult type of refugee." For their part, immigration officials suspicious that Vietnamese youth were sent abroad to facilitate their families' later migration proved similarly reluctant to admit unaccompanied minors—a policy supported by a restrictionist Congress and Department of Justice (DOJ), but one that put them at odds with a State Department determined to continue using refugee policy against the spread of communism in Southeast Asia.

The Refugee Act granted unaccompanied refugee minors a new preferential admission status as well as guaranteed access to federally funded foster care; but, in its immediate aftermath, the Haitian and Mariel refugee crises sparked new fears that the nation had lost control of its borders as well as a growing backlash against Vietnamese refugees. With restrictionist sentiment on the rise, unaccompanied Southeast Asian children remained vulnerable to the vicissitudes of changing foreign policy and domestic political interests that led to declining refugee admissions after 1981. In the years to come, even as efforts to improve the quality of care provided by the federal URM program began to bear fruit, the widespread perception of unaccompanied Vietnamese youth as "anchors" lead the United States to join the Association of Southeast Asian Nations (ASEAN) and the UN High Commissioner for Refugees (UNHCR) in implementing policies that reimagined children as a tool for deterring the ongoing exodus from the region. Echoing FDR-era discourses that framed endangered European Jewish children as an "entering wedge" to force open the nation's gates for their adult coreligionists, proponents of this new policy approach sought to deny a new generation of unaccompanied refugee minors the right to be evaluated for admission on the basis of their actual individual circumstances rather than their potential impact on subsequent immigration from their homelands.

By the spring of 1975, American military intervention in Southeast Asia had entered its last days. South Vietnam's collapse was imminent after the

U.S.-backed regime in Cambodia fell to the Khmer Rouge.[2] In April, fearing that orphans already approved for adoption in the United States might not escape the country before the fall of Saigon, several private agencies joined forces with U.S. ambassador Graham Martin to petition the South Vietnamese and U.S. governments for permission to airlift 1,400 children to the United States.[3] Minister for Social Welfare Dr. Phan Quang Đán swiftly gave approval, in the desperate hope media attention might inspire the United States to provide last-minute support to his embattled nation. U.S. president Gerald Ford similarly hoped a highly publicized orphans airlift might motivate a Democratic-majority Congress to approve his request for last-minute military aid, thereby stabilizing the regime just long enough to allow the United States to negotiate a dignified end to the war.[4] Authorizing the U.S. Agency for International Development (USAID) to oversee the airlift, Ford appropriated $2.6 million for children's transportation on military aircraft and instructed the attorney general to parole them into the country.[5] Departing on April 4, the first official Operation Babylift flight crashed shortly after takeoff, killing seventy-eight minors and several of their adult escorts. The airlift continued without even a day's operational pause, bringing 2,547 Vietnamese and Cambodian children to the United States by the end of the month.[6]

As hoped, the operation sparked a deluge of positive media coverage; heartwarming stories about the arrival of orphans at U.S. military bases, featuring an iconic photograph of President Ford cradling a Vietnamese baby girl in his arms, ran on the front page of newspapers across the nation.[7] Celebratory coverage of Operation Babylift worked to reinforce the cherished notions of American paternal benevolence and military virtue that had been shattered by revelations of U.S. wartime atrocities against women, children, and the elderly.[8] But news stories also obscured the U.S. role in the violence that created orphans and displaced children in the first place. Media coverage covered up another inconvenient truth: while adoption workers and the media used the terms "orphan" and "refugee" interchangeably to refer to the Operation Babylift children, they were not actually refugees; they were children destined for adoptive homes.[9]

Journalists may have unintentionally failed to make this distinction; however, intercountry adoption advocates since the late 1940s sought to blur the conceptual boundaries between unaccompanied refugee minors and adoptable overseas children, exploiting public confusion about the differences to generate political support for their efforts and gild the private desires of prospective adoptive parents with a humanitarian veneer. They took this approach again during the final days of the Vietnam War, asserting children left behind in Vietnamese orphanages (and especially the Amerasian children fathered by U.S. service members) needed to be "rescued" before they fell victim to northern communist army atrocities—despite an utter lack of evidence to corroborate their claims.[10] By conflating the categories of orphan and unaccompanied refugee minor, adoption proponents privileged the desires of prospective U.S. citizen parents who since the 1950s had come to see war-stricken and impoverished Asian nations as a source of "children on demand" over endangered minor's need for protection. Additionally, adoption workers and journalists' descriptions of squalid orphanage conditions and children's poor health evoked long-standing racist and classist assumptions, justifying removal of children from their home communities by arguing middle-class white U.S. families could provide better lives for impoverished nonwhite children than their mothers or extended families ever could.[11]

In the past similar discursive strategies encouraged Americans to not look too closely at the details of "rescue" missions that placed "endangered" overseas children in adoptive homes. But this time, not everyone was convinced. A significant number of Americans dismissed Operation Babylift as a cynical ploy to generate last-minute sympathy for the collapsing U.S.-backed South Vietnamese government.[12] Others denounced claims that the children were endangered if they remained in Vietnam as rhetorical window dressing intended to cover up a massive baby-kidnapping campaign they likened to a "taking of war souvenirs."[13] At an April 8, 1975, Senate hearing, Senator Edward Kennedy (D-Mass.) lambasted the airlift, arguing the highly publicized evacuation served mostly to "assuage the American conscience" while disregarding the needs of "millions of people" displaced by war in Indochina. Professional aid workers representing the American Friends Service Committee (AFSC), the Lutheran Immigration and Refugee Service (LIRS), and Church World Service similarly testified that the mission distracted from the broader scope of humanitarian need in the combat zone.[14] These critiques were borne out in the coming weeks, after revelations that not all the children brought to the United States were in fact orphans, nor had all parents consented to evacuation.[15]

The controversy provoked by Operation Babylift revealed how much American assumptions about the ethics and efficacy of cross-border child evacuation had evolved since the early 1960s, when a perceived communist threat to youth led an overwhelming majority of government officials, voluntary agency personnel, and private citizens to embrace asylum for Cuban children. The belief that resettlement in the United States was always in endangered foreign children's best interest was no longer, it seemed, an absolute. But mounting public antipathy to the continued influx of Cubans motivated by the desire for family reunification and economic opportunity rather than fear of persecution had also diminished the ideological value of anti-communist refugees of all ages. Moreover, by the midseventies the crisis of national confidence provoked by the Vietnam debacle and the Watergate scandal, a prolonged economic recession, and the emergence of a new détente between the United States and the USSR, weakened the Cold War consensus that bolstered Americans' always-tentative support for refugee admissions.[16]

In April 1975 the Republic of Vietnam teetered on the verge of collapse, threatening to touch off a massive refugee crisis in the region.[17] Congressional leaders agreed the United States must take action: conservatives because they shared President Ford's conviction the United States must demonstrate its unwavering commitment to its anti-communist allies and anti-war liberals out of a desire to atone for some of the harm caused by the nation's intervention in Southeast Asia.[18] However, in light of public sentiment, the president and Congress also felt that an overly generous admissions policy would be politically risky. After weeks of internal debate, they finally agreed on a rescue mission of limited scope and duration, strictly focused on evacuating U.S. citizens and their Vietnamese relatives as well as people affiliated with the U.S. military or government.[19]

Ford appeared on television on April 17 to announce he was authorizing the parole of 150,000 Vietnamese into the country. In this and subsequent public statements, the president sought to generate public support by representing the evacuation in language that transcended ideological divides and appealed broadly to Americans' sense of themselves and their nation as virtuous and benevolent world leaders.[20] Echoing Truman, Eisenhower, and Johnson before him, Ford repeatedly reminded Americans of their nation's tradition of welcoming those fleeing oppression, stressing the United States' humanitarian duty to provide asylum to victims of communism.[21] Practically speaking, the president's understanding of that duty was more limited. Like many in Congress, Ford felt that the Kennedy-era Cuban Refugee Program, which continued to provide long-term welfare benefits to Cubans in the United States, cost too much and lasted too long.[22] Secretary of State Henry Kissinger held up the Eisenhower-era President's Committee for Hungarian Refugee Relief (PCHRR) as "an effective organization" that "did the job and then went out of business" and advised the staunchly Republican president that a similar committee should coordinate private efforts by the

American people to resettle refugees "in the quickest possible time frame."[23] Disregarding infrastructure and expertise developed by HEW while over-seeing Cuban resettlement efforts, Ford opted to create a new Interagency Task Force (IATF) for Indochina, bringing together representatives from a dozen federal agencies to oversee privately managed resettlement of South-east Asian refugees.

Following the Eisenhower program's model, President Ford tasked the military with evacuating and providing reception care to Vietnamese parol-ees at U.S. bases. Nine voluntary agencies, including the U.S. Catholic Con-ference (USCC), the Lutheran Immigration and Refugee Service, Church World Service, HIAS and the International Rescue Committee, would han-dle matching refugees to individual or community sponsors.[24] In return, they would receive $500 per refugee to cover administrative and relocation costs.[25] However, the IATF deliberately did not account for follow-up services to Vietnamese refugees. Referring to the President's Committee for Hungarian Refugee Relief in their own briefing materials, the task force reiterated its mandate to follow the PCHRR's model of "maximum reliance" on private voluntary agencies, during what the president expected to be a quick and stripped-down resettlement process.[26]

Several leading agencies agreed to accept IATF contracts—but their lack of enthusiasm revealed the corrosive impact of the Vietnam War on the tra-ditional public-private relationship for refugee resettlement. Deeply opposed to the nation's conduct during the war, many humanitarian organizations had concluded by the early 1970s that their reasons for aiding refugees were differ-ent than the state's. Moreover, the high caseloads, bureaucratic inefficiencies, and congressional opposition that plagued the Cuban Refugee Program left many agency personnel fatigued, frustrated, and disillusioned. Even some of the most staunchly anti-communist Catholic agencies had come to see cooperation with the government as a necessary evil to be approached with caution.[27] They nonetheless began gearing up for another wave of refugees.

And just in time: on April 21, the U.S. military began a ten-day evacua-tion to carry approximately 65,000 Vietnamese, many of whom were U.S.-affiliated elites or former government officials, out of Saigon.[28] After receiving emergency medical care and initial screening at military bases in the Philip-pines or Guam, evacuees were paroled into the United States.[29] They were then sent to makeshift reception centers at Camp Pendleton in Southern California; Fort Indiantown Gap, Pennsylvania; Fort Chaffee, Arkansas; and Eglin Air Force Base in Florida.[30] Another 65,000 Southern Vietnamese made their own panicked arrangements, fleeing aboard rented or stolen planes or boats, or overland into Thailand. On April 30, North Vietnamese tanks rolled into Saigon; the following day, American rescue operations terminated, leaving hundreds of thousands of U.S. supporters at their mercy.[31]

The American public initially reacted positively to the arriving refugees, suggesting the evacuation might, in fact, touch off the process of national reconciliation President Ford was hoping for. Government officials, high school bands, and sympathetic townspeople gathered at reception centers to welcome displaced Vietnamese to "the land of immigrants."[32] Building on early public sympathy, media coverage of Operations "New Life" and "New Arrivals"—terms associating refugees with notions of birth, childhood, and the Operation Babylift evacuation—sought to generate further support by focusing attention on Vietnamese children. As during Operation Babylift, photos of First Lady Betty Ford visiting refugee boys and girls and of kindly U.S. Marines taking a break to play games with delighted toddlers appeared in newspapers across the country. These child-centric discourses and images reinforced paternalistic notions of refugees of all ages as passive, dependent, and in need of rescue by the U.S. military, while emphasizing the difference between supposedly evil North Vietnamese Communists and their innocent South Vietnamese victims.[33] Representations of innocent and childlike refugees also worked to assuage Americans' racialized suspicions of Asians by framing them as apolitical and malleable, and therefore capable of assimilating. Together, they played an important role in inspiring ordinary Americans to welcome the Vietnamese—and to see their gestures of support toward them as evidence of national benevolence and virtue. The public responded in kind: during the first weeks of May 1975, more than 20,000 Americans offered to sponsor Vietnamese refugees.[34]

Behind the scenes, though, resettlement was off to a rocky start. Voluntary agencies, under pressure from the IATF to move refugees into U.S. communities as quickly as possible, scrambled as they had after the 1956 Hungarian Uprising to establish procedures for matching new arrivals with sponsors. Few of the regional agency directors or staff assigned to the camps had experience working with refugees.[35] Even fewer spoke Vietnamese. The IATF's determination to follow the PCHRR model only added to the chaos. Frustrated representatives of the Department of Health, Education, and Welfare faulted the "amateur" resettlement efforts, criticizing that the per-diem payment scheme adopted from the "crash" Hungarian program incentivized the hasty placements; voluntary agencies received a "bounty" of $500 per person, whether successfully relocated or not.[36] Local welfare agencies, community organizations, and religious congregations also soon

The Most Difficult Type of Refugee

found themselves overwhelmed by the demands of rapidly resettling such a large number of refugees.

Voluntary personnel were frustrated with the Interagency Task Force's ineffective leadership as well as the $500 stipend, which they claimed wasn't enough to cover even basic relocation costs. Of more grave concern, a month after the evacuation began, agencies were still operating without a formal contractual agreement with the federal government. In a May 1975 meeting with White House special advisor Theodore Marrs, agency representatives outlined their preexisting obligations to other needy communities and expressed doubts about their capacity to "deal effectively with the large number of refugees requiring service" without "clarification of the government's policy for utilization of recent appropriations." When Marrs suggested that private donors make up for some of the shortfalls, agency representatives curtly responded that "no special fundraising appeal would be made . . . for [the] Vietnamese refugee effort."[37]

Voluntary agencies' refusal to seek private donations, as they had in the past, reflected a pragmatic awareness that an increasingly anti-refugee public (who donated significantly less for the resettlement of racially ambiguous Cubans than for white European Hungarians) were unlikely to assume the burden of resettling the Vietnamese—especially during a prolonged economic recession.[38] Agency intransigence on this point helped propel the passage of the Indochina Migration and Refugee Assistance Act on May 23, providing $405 million of resettlement funding for an Indochinese Refugee Assistance Program (IRAP). Like the Cuban Refugee Program, the IRAP provided 100 percent reimbursement to states for all resettlement-related services, including health care, income maintenance, and other needed social services. However, unlike its open-ended predecessor, the Indochinese program was set to expire in 1977.[39]

President Ford and refugee advocates in the State Department and Congress publicly called for America to fulfill its moral obligations to Vietnamese refugees. Privately though, U.S. leaders continued to demand quick and limited resettlement; under no circumstances should they "develop into a permanent federal undertaking similar to the present Cuban Program."[40] Concerned that a prolonged refugee influx would hurt him politically, Ford directed the IATF to step up pressure on voluntary agencies to move Vietnamese out of the reception centers and into communities as swiftly as possible.[41] By June public support for resettlement was rapidly fading; 54 percent of Americans opposed the admission of Vietnamese refugees, and offers of sponsorship in communities near the reception centers had slowed to a trickle.[42] With less than half of refugees relocated and early plans for a government-sponsored public relations campaign, like those that inspired Americans to welcome Hungarians and Cubans, fallen victim to bureaucratic infighting, voluntary agencies were compelled to search far and wide for sympathetic sponsors, sending those remaining in camps to communities thousands of miles from other Southeast Asian families.[43]

At precisely this inopportune moment, voluntary agencies personnel made an unwelcome discovery: there were unaccompanied minors in the camps. On July 6 the *Los Angeles Times* reported 106 unattached children between the ages of two and seventeen, approximately two-thirds in the care of unrelated adults or distant relatives, living at Camp Pendleton.[44] By late July authorities at Camp Pendleton "discovered" a total of 250 minors living with people other than their parents.[45] Another seventy-nine unaccompanied children were found at Fort Indiantown Gap, thirty-eight more at Fort Chaffee, and eighteen at Eglin Air Force Base. Another twenty-eight were identified on Guam.[46] In some cases, the children were separated from parents during their escape; in others, children were sent with relatives or family friends when parents were unwilling or unable to flee. The final count determined that approximately 800 unaccompanied minors were paroled into the county as part of the Saigon evacuation.[47]

As startling as this oversight might seem, it was actually unsurprising that these unaccompanied minors went unnoticed so long. From the beginning, the State Department–sponsored IATF was far more focused on the geopolitics and logistics of evacuation than on refugees' welfare. They were even less concerned with children's well-being. As during Eisenhower's "crash" program, unaccompanied minors were admitted inadvertently, as part of a massive and poorly coordinated influx of refugees of all ages. Age had played no role in their admission, nor was it seen as significant during initial processing, except inasmuch as widespread assumptions about children's innocence and political inactivity exempted those under seventeen from security screenings designed to root out suspected criminals and Communists. Nor had INS officials in Guam and the Philippines gathered any but the most cursory demographic data before sending displaced Vietnamese on to the United States. As a result, although almost 50 percent of these first-wave refugees were children or teens, no information was gathered to determine if they were accompanied by relatives. Despite their highly publicized presence in previous refugee influxes, nothing in the IATF's initial plans suggested they had contemplated the likelihood of unaccompanied minors among the Vietnamese arriving in the United States.[48]

The Most Difficult Type of Refugee

Camp personnel similarly failed to plan in advance for meeting the needs of those especially traumatized and disoriented children arriving without their families. At Pendleton, after hasty consultation with the Red Cross and local church groups, voluntary agency staff decided to allow minors in the care of distant relatives or family friends to remain together in general housing; thirty-three children without appropriate adult guardians were moved to a closed barracks under military guard and the supervision of an on-call Red Cross nurse. A group of volunteers from the local Church of Latter-day Saints—a newcomer to national refugee resettlement efforts—quickly organized educational and recreational programs and took around-the-clock shifts caring for the children. At the other camps, bilingual refugees assisted with unaccompanied minors.[49] With these makeshift services in place, a spokesperson at Pendleton told the *Los Angeles Times* that the emotional state of the lonely and frightened children was "improving." Fifteen-year-old Phan Xuan Hoang, whose Army of the Republic of Vietnam (ARVN) colonel father had sent alone to the United States, disagreed. "We miss our parents," he told the *Times* reporter. "Especially after it gets dark. There are many boys and girls crying every night."[50]

Voluntary agencies next turned to the federal government for direction. However, the IATF was at a loss on how to proceed. On July 28—more than six weeks after unaccompanied minors were first identified at the reception centers—spokesperson Elinor Green told the *New York Times* that the Vietnamese children presented "a problem that has never been faced before that I know of." She further admitted their resettlement posed "serious legal and moral problems" that the IATF had yet to resolve. Green's statements betrayed a complete ignorance of previous public-private programs to care for unaccompanied minors. Coming from a blithely uninformed spokesperson, and in the context of mounting hostility toward Southeast Asian refugees, her remarks are emblematic of IATF incompetence and indifference to the minors' well-being. They may also suggest a racialized understanding of Vietnamese refugee children—like Jewish boys and girls forty years before them—as a "problem."[51] Neither boded well for the future of the children stranded alone in the camps.

After two months of consultations and the IATF's transfer to the Department of Health, Education, and Welfare, HEW issued an Action Transmittal (AT) clarifying procedures for resettling unaccompanied Southeast Asian minors. Whenever feasible, the children were to remain with adult refugees to whom they had become attached; otherwise, they were to be placed with foster families. Because most were assumed to have living parents in

Vietnam, the children were considered ineligible for adoption, and efforts would be made to reunite them with their families, should they be located in the United States. The AT further specified that 100 percent of the cost of placement and child welfare services would be reimbursed by the federal government. Foster care for Southeast Asian unaccompanied children would be regulated according to state-level welfare standards. HEW also requested states' assistance in finding foster homes, conducting home studies, and arranging for transference of custody, as well as providing follow up services.[52] Bypassing Children's Bureau oversight, these measures reduced federal costs at the expense of the children's well-being, since they did not guarantee any consistent minimum standard of care or even establish a centralized registry of placements. Moreover, continuity of care for the children remained an open question since the AT's legislative authority only lasted for two years.

The Action Transmittal set in motion yet another ad hoc program to resettle unaccompanied minors inadvertently admitted to the United States.[53] The children's resettlement proceeded more slowly than during the Hungarian and Cuban programs. In many cases voluntary agency efforts to resettle unaccompanied children with their surrogate refugee families were met with resistance since, in most states, refugees could not be approved as foster parents and, therefore, not receive financial support for the child.[54] Custody issues sidestepped in the past presented a new obstacle after the Immigration and Naturalization Service (INS) ruled it would not release Vietnamese minors for resettlement until an approved foster parent or voluntary agency assumed legal responsibility for them. Agencies were reluctant to do so since federal funding for care was only guaranteed until September 30, 1977. Even when an agency or foster family wished to take on guardianship, problems arose if they were located far from reception centers since local family courts could not easily make custody rulings when children were outside their geographic jurisdiction. In addition, legal mechanisms for establishing custody varied from state to state, further complicating the placement process. Confusion over custody issues remained unresolved for several years.[55]

Lack of guaranteed long-term funding for the program also made many sympathetic Americans reluctant to open their homes to Vietnamese refugee minors. Many of those who were willing preferred, as in the past, to foster small and hopefully adoptable children. Americans' historic reticence to take in older youth, exacerbated in this case by perceptions of Vietnamese racial, cultural, and religious difference, meant voluntary agency staff confronted more pronounced difficulties than previous resettlement workers finding homes for adolescent boys, who again made up the majority of the youth needing placements.

As refugee families continued to be relocated across the country, many unaccompanied minors remained in limbo—provoking some Americans who visited the camps and established connections with specific children to publicly condemn bureaucratic delays to their placement and demand the right to foster or adopt them.[56] Frustrated at being left behind, children also increasingly demanded the right to be resettled as quickly as possible. Phan Xuan Hoang, after six weeks at Camp Pendleton, was eager to leave the Marine Corps base as soon as he could; he told the *Los Angeles Times* he wanted to be placed with the Smith family in Thousand Oaks, California. Mr. and Mrs. Leonard Smith were equally impatient to bring Phan home so he could begin learning English before the school year began in September.[57]

By December 1975, although most of the evacuees had been relocated, 183 unattached children remained in Fort Chaffee. Only after a special appeal for help was issued and agencies with long experience placing unaccompanied minors, including the Lutheran Immigration and Refugee Service, stepped in to offer last-minute assistance, were foster homes finally secured for the last of the unaccompanied minors.[58] Having overcome this final hurdle, resettlement workers breathed a sigh of relief—assuming, like most Americans, that the refugee crisis had ended and the nation's duty to the Vietnamese had been fulfilled.[59] Disbanding the Interagency Task Force, President Ford shifted responsibility for overseeing follow-up refugee services to a new Indochina Refugee Task Force within HEW.[60] The message from Washington was clear: it was time to forget the war and move forward.

With the nation still deeply mired in economic and political malaise, Jimmy Carter's 1977 inauguration and his promise of a new human-rights inspired foreign policy offered a desperately needed sense of purpose and direction.[61] But Carter's humanitarian commitments were quickly tested by the growing numbers of "boat people" building up in camps in Hong Kong and across Southeast Asia. Polls showed as few as a third of Americans approved of admitting more Vietnamese to the United States. With Congress determined to prevent more refugee admissions, Carter recognized his ability to continue paroling Southeast Asians into the country was limited.[62] At the same time international and domestic pressures to admit more refugees were mounting. By autumn 1977, the growing exodus of boat people stirred up a backlash across Southeast Asia, and a number of ASEAN members adopted hard-line refugee policies, forcing ships back to sea and calling on the United States to take Vietnamese escapees off their hands.[63] Back in the

United States, Vietnamese exiles, voluntary agency directors, civic and business leaders, and refugee advocates within the State Department also mobilized. Led by chairman of the International Rescue Committee Leo Cherne, the new Citizens' Commission on Indochinese Refugees began lobbying for an expanded Indochinese resettlement program.

In response Carter paroled 7,000 more refugees into the country in December. In March 1978, following the nationalization of the Vietnamese economy and expulsion of the nation's remaining ethnic Chinese, boat departures surged again leading the president to announce parole for an additional 25,000.[64] In November of the same year, under attack from the *Wall Street Journal* and the *New York Times* for not doing enough and barraged by complaints from ASEAN nations accusing the United States of saddling them with a crisis, President Carter announced the United States would admit 21,000 more refugees—including 7,000 Cambodians fleeing the brutal Pol Pot regime—in the next six months.[65]

Privately, however, a besieged Carter was fed up with using the parole system to facilitate an open-ended Southeast Asian resettlement effort along the lines of the Cuban Refugee Program. And he wasn't willing to continue setting the nation's refugee quotas by executive order. He directed the State Department to work with key lawmakers to develop permanent policy in the form of legislation for a comprehensive and uniform approach to refugee admissions. He similarly urged that resettlement services and funding support to voluntary agencies and states be provided "on a uniform basis for all refugees."[66] In light of persistent anti-Vietnamese public sentiment, the president hoped legislation encompassing refugees from all nations—including the Soviet Jews and anti-communist dissenters of pressing concern to many Republican congressmen—would facilitate its passage.

Carter also hoped the new law might address inequities between the levels of assistance provided to different groups of refugees. This would help placate increasingly restive voluntary agencies who continued to complain about the lack of federal direction and support, especially after the stipend for resettling Southeast Asians was cut from $500 to $350 in March 1978—much less than for Cuban and Eastern European refugees, and which Secretary of State Cyrus Vance privately admitted was "seriously inadequate."[67] To make things worse delays extending the Indochina Migration and Refugee Act funding forced private agencies and state welfare offices to operate in debt to meet commitments to refugees already on their caseloads, heightening frustrations over the insufficient federal commitment to resettlement efforts.

The Most Difficult Type of Refugee

Tepid federal support for Southeast Asian refugee resettlement in general continued to impact unaccompanied minors. By mid-1978 voluntary agencies were struggling to meet the increasingly complex needs of the growing numbers of elderly and severely ill refugees, as well as illiterate laborers and peasants from isolated mountain communities, and were more and more reluctant to assume long-term responsibility for unaccompanied children's care.[68] At the same time, ongoing confusion over procedures for establishing custody and financial responsibility for children only intensified agency directors' resentment of HEW's attempt to "saddle them with permanent legal responsibility for minors." Tensions finally came to a breaking point in the summer of 1978, when agencies refused to bring any more unaccompanied children to the United States until these issues were resolved.[69]

The need for greater federal leadership increased that fall with a sudden uptick in boat departures from Vietnam, including a growing number of unaccompanied minors. Many of the "boat people" in this third wave of Southeast Asian migration were fleeing political persecution and ethnically based discrimination against Vietnam's Chinese minority.[70] But many escapees also cited economic hardship or the hope of a better life as a key reason for emigrating.[71] This intertwining of political and economic motives drove the increase in unaccompanied child migration, most of whom continued to be adolescent boys. However, unlike previous unaccompanied minors inadvertently separated from parents during flight, most children who fled after 1976 left of their own volition and with parental support. Some parents sent their children away fearing they would be blocked from attending university or punished for their family ties to the former Republic of Vietnam or the United States. In other cases, they hoped to prevent boys' conscription into the military. Families who couldn't afford smugglers' fees of up to $1,500 U.S. per person chose to send only the eldest son or other favored child overseas—in most cases, smugglers charged half price for children.

Despite the increase in unaccompanied minors among boat people, only forty-six were admitted to the United States in 1978.[72] Few voluntary agencies working in Southeast Asian camps provided specific services for refugee minors, making their selection for resettlement ad hoc and infrequent. Even still, as early as 1976, U.S. immigration officials had been reluctant to take in unaccompanied Vietnamese children, seeing them as "anchors" sent to facilitate family migration. These suspicions were not entirely unwarranted; whether minors' departure was politically or economically motivated—or a product of both—parents' expectation often *was* that minors would forge a path to the United States for the family.[73] But fears of Vietnamese children serving as an "entering wedge" emerged after only a few hundred unaccompanied minors were admitted. This is striking when contrasted with the INS's utter lack of concern with the similarly mixed motives of Cuban parents who sent children alone to the United States the previous decade. Persistent anti-Asian sentiment (which, like prewar anti-Semitism, included racialized assumptions of inscrutability and duplicity) likely helped fuel this early discourse about Vietnamese unaccompanied minors as "anchors," working against their admission the same way it had worked against Jewish children fleeing Nazism in the 1930s.[74]

But domestic demands for limited refugee admissions soon gave way to pressures emerging from geopolitical developments in Southeast Asia. The region's refugee crisis expanded dramatically in December 1978, when Vietnam invaded neighboring Cambodia; within weeks, Pol Pot's dictatorship fell and the Vietnam-aligned Heng Samrin regime was established. With the Cambodia-Thai border opened for the first time since 1975, tens of thousands of refugees streamed into Thailand. Among them were an undetermined number of unaccompanied minors. Some were orphans, others were adolescents taken from their families to perform slave labor in Khmer Rouge mobile work brigades, and still others were forced conscripts into Pol Pot's army.[75] As the U.S. nightly news filled with images of starving Cambodian women and children, U.S. churches and voluntary organizations mobilized to raise millions of dollars to send food and medicine to the Thai camps and lobbied Congress to increase the admission of Cambodian refugees.[76]

In February 1979, with conditions in Southeast Asia deteriorating further, Senator Edward Kennedy, Representative Peter Rodino Jr. (D-N.J.), and Representative Elizabeth Holtzman (D-N.Y.) introduced legislation in Congress for a comprehensive framework for refugee admissions and resettlement.[77] At Refugee Act hearings lasting into 1980, church leaders, child welfare professionals, and voluntary agency representatives argued unaccompanied refugee minors should no longer be treated as an afterthought or exception, but instead permanently incorporated within the new law. They also called for improvements to the frequency and quality of communication between the Departments of State and Justice, HEW, and the states, as well as the development of state-level policies and procedures for integrating unaccompanied refugee minors into local foster care systems.[78]

A changing foreign policy climate worked in favor of these demands. By 1978, multiple agencies within the executive branch had openly embraced a geopolitics of compassion, arguing publicly that the United States should do more to relieve pressure on Southeast Asian nations of first asylum as well as

The Most Difficult Type of Refugee

to alleviate the dangers and hardships faced by children in refugee camps.[79] As a first step, in December of that year, the State Department, INS, and HEW adopted a joint policy granting priority to unaccompanied children within existing refugee quotas and confirmed their eligibility for federally funded foster care. HEW was once again vested with authority for coordinating the activities of the multiple public and private agencies involved in resettling children. However, responsibility for Southeast Asian children remained with the Indochina Refugee Task Force, once again bypassing the Children's Bureau. It's unclear why this was done. While it's possible the bureau's experience with the Cuban Children's Program left it reluctant to assume leadership of what could become an equally intensive, contentious, and precariously funded program, its exclusion was nonetheless striking.[80]

On February 6, 1979, a newly proactive HEW issued an Action Transmittal to voluntary agencies and state social services administrators declaring that all children under the age of eighteen from Vietnam, Laos, and Cambodia, lawfully admitted as parolees, and without immediate adult relatives in the United States would henceforth be eligible for the same welfare benefits as U.S. citizen children in foster care.[81] The AT also clarified procedures for establishing legal custody of unaccompanied refugee minors and handling their movement across state lines, specifying HEW would from now on partner exclusively with the U.S. Catholic Conference and the Lutheran Immigration and Refugee Service, the only two of ten currently active resettlement agencies with their own national child welfare service networks, in placing children.[82]

The February 6 AT marked the official end of the grassroots and decentralized approach to resettling unaccompanied refugee minors, even as it institutionalized a central role for faith-based organizations in providing federally funded care to unaccompanied children. Together with State Department guidelines granting Southeast Asian refugee minors priority admission status, the decision to quietly reassume federal financial responsibility for their care at this time, something done only once before under the Cuban Children's Program, recognized for the first time a unique age-based claim on admission and protection for children from the region. These policy changes and the dramatic expansion of the refugee exodus caused unaccompanied minors' resettlement to skyrocket. Whereas only 48 had been granted visas in 1978, in 1979, 1,983 children were admitted to the United States.[83]

However, the incipient program to provide care for unaccompanied children had temporary legal authority and limited funding; HEW's authority to reimburse voluntary agencies and states for expenditures on children's behalf expired on September 30, 1979.[84] The program hit an additional road-block after President Carter announced a new parole to admit an additional 7,000 refugees per month in April.[85] Objecting to the ongoing executive abuse of the parole authority and the ballooning cost of resettlement, already exceeding $1 billion, Congress balked at approving an additional supplemental budget request.[86] The State Department was forced to borrow from its own emergency fund and deferred contributions to UNHCR refugee relief efforts. They also asked voluntary agencies to temporarily forgo resettlement grants, forcing many heavily into debt.[87]

As Refugee Act hearings continued in the spring and summer of 1979, the number of refugees fleeing Vietnam and Cambodia continued to rise. Unable to keep apace, the United States stepped up calls for assistance from the United Nations, ASEAN nations, and Western allies. They faced resistance from the UNHCR, which feared the United States' relatively generous admission policies to date had served as a magnet to encourage Vietnamese to take to the seas, and also from Southeast Asian nations who maintained they would only provide asylum to refugees if the United States guaranteed resettlement in a third country.[88] With Congress divided and the international community at odds over how to manage the crisis, the situation grew more dire by the day. By June more than 330,000 refugees crowded into camps around the region, and Indonesia and Malaysia announced they would turn new boat arrivals back to sea. Thailand similarly began to forcibly repatriate Cambodian refugees and refused to accept any arriving by boat. Hong Kong continued to accept refugees but by the summer of 1979, with tens of thousands of Vietnamese squeezed into horrifically crowded camps, the small urban enclave was reaching a breaking point.[89]

Public awareness was also on the rise, nurtured by extensive coverage of the crisis in the *New York Times* and other major news outlets, culminating with the CBS's explosive documentary *Vietnamese Boat People: The Price of Freedom*, in June 1979. By midsummer media attention turned American sympathies back toward the refugees.[90] Vietnamese exile groups, religious leaders, and a growing bipartisan coalition of refugee advocates renewed their demands for increased monthly admissions.[91] Faced by mounting political pressures at home, legislators backed down and approved supplemental funding to process refugees approved under the April quota. In July they also supported the president's decision to double the monthly quota to 14,000.[92]

Formerly reticent Western nations, including Canada, Australia, France, and Germany, subsequently pledged to admit tens of thousands more Southeast Asian refugees, including small numbers of unaccompanied minors.[93] At the same time, after prolonged negotiation, Vietnam agreed to crack down on the nation's extensive refugee smuggling network and collaborate with the UNHCR in implementing a legal "orderly departure" emigration program. As a result of these breakthroughs, the number of boat departures abruptly decreased. Still, by fall 1978 more than 347,000 refugees remained waiting resettlement.[94]

Among these were between 4,000 and 5,000 unaccompanied children: approximately 2,500 in camps in Malaysia, with smaller numbers in other ASEAN nations including Thailand, Indonesia, and the Philippines. Even though they qualified for priority admission, U.S. voluntary agencies remained hesitant to sponsor the children. This reluctance was largely pragmatic, a by-product of the ever-increasing challenges of running a prolonged and under-resourced resettlement effort. Exhausted voluntary personnel that already resettled more than 200,000 Southeast Asian refugees were working around the clock to deal with the recent increase in arrivals.[95] And the capacity of local congregations and community agencies to meet the needs of refugees of all ages, especially recent Laotian and Cambodian arrivals who required additional services and support, was rapidly being depleted.[96]

These challenges were especially pronounced for the U.S. Catholic Conference and Lutheran Immigration and Refugee Service, who had led resettlement efforts since 1975 and now carried sole responsibility for unaccompanied children. Strain on the USCC's local resources came also from the steep decline in religious vocations since the mid-1960s which left them struggling to replace religious sisters who traditionally performed much of the church's social welfare work.[97] States were also not willing to commit additional resources; recalling Congress' inconsistent support for the Cuban Children's Program, they voiced concerns they would be "stuck holding the bill" for unaccompanied minors' long-term support. By the summer of 1979, only nine states had agreed to participate.[98]

Despite voluntary agencies' reservations, the federal government remained committed to the priority admission of unaccompanied Southeast Asian children. Local voluntary agencies, preparing for the inevitable, stepped up efforts to find homes for the influx of minors expected to begin arriving that fall. But placements continued to be in short supply. Some families, motivated by religious principles or moved by television documentaries about the suffering of boat people, did offer to foster unaccompanied children.[99] However, as a frustrated spokesperson for Philadelphia's Lutheran Children and Family Service noted in May 1979, hopeful inquiries about "any Vietnamese babies to adopt" were more frequent than offers to take in the mostly adolescent boys in need of resettlement.[100] Agencies found themselves relaxing eligibility requirements and turning to the media for assistance recruiting families. On July 17, the *Minneapolis Tribune* reported forty "boat children" were coming to the Twin Cities in August or September, noting that the local Catholic Charities and Lutheran Social Service were seeking foster families "without regard to religious affiliation." While these agencies preferred placing the children with Southeast Asian families, the article stressed applications from prospective host families of all backgrounds would be considered.[101]

But not all children were prioritized for resettlement in the United States. As late as August 1979, overseas relief workers complained that only Vietnamese "boat cases" were being expedited for admission; although media coverage had sparked greater sympathy for the plight of "orphans" in the land camps, little had been done to process the thousands of unaccompanied Cambodian and Laotian minors in Thailand.[102] This was partly due to opposition from local caregivers advocating to keep the children—few of whom were actually orphans—in the camps, where relatives might turn up to claim them. But a coalition of U.S. religious and political leaders, including First Lady Rosalynn Carter, lobbied the U.S. government and UNHCR to expedite their resettlement, arguing that the overflowing camps, which lacked food and medicine, represented an imminent threat to children's well-being. They called especially for the swift resettlement of adolescents who had already lost crucial formative years of education or vocational training and were at risk of "aging out" of priority admission and foster care.[103] Hopeful parents, driven by altruism and self-interest, also began to visit the camps in search of adoptable Cambodian children. Following a storm of protest by local child welfare workers, on December 5, 1979, the UNHCR placed a temporary moratorium on evacuations until all Cambodian minors had been thoroughly documented and efforts to trace their parents had been exhausted.[104] Vietnamese refugees would nonetheless continue flowing into the United States: more than 165,000, including 4,077 unaccompanied minors, in 1980 alone.[105] But the temporary upsurge in sympathy for the boat people was fast declining. Distracted by a series of new international crises, including the Soviet invasion of Afghanistan, leftist revolutions in Central America, and a prolonged hostage crisis in Iran, public approval for Carter's human-rights focused foreign policy plummeted. At the same time, persistent economic malaise fueled concerns about the expansion of unauthorized immigration during the previous decade.[106] Differences between conservatives and progressives over how to address these new challenges deepened the polarization of American society created by the Vietnam War, feeding ongoing disagreements over the nation's refugee policy. A small but influential bipartisan congressional coalition, supported by Southeast Asian exile groups and civic, religious, and humanitarian leaders, worked to maintain support for high admission rates, while those opposed to ongoing paroles began to openly voice suspicions that many refugees were actually economic migrants. Majority-white communities in Southern California and elsewhere also began to voice their opposition to Vietnamese resettlement in their neighborhoods.[107]

Growing polarization over the admission of refugees provided the background for the March 2 passage of the 1980 Refugee Act. The culmination of more than a year of congressional hearings, the act finally adopted an internationally accepted definition of refugees and established for the first time a clear distinction in U.S. law between immigrants and refugees. It also set an annual quota of 50,000, almost tripling the 17,400 yearly refugees eligible under the 1965 Hart-Celler Immigration Act, and established procedures for granting asylum to those already in the country. Putting an end to the legal limbo endured by previous generations of parolees, the act stipulated future refugees be admitted as conditional residents and upgraded to permanent residency one year later following a successful INS interview. In addition, it created permanent mechanisms for funding resettlement services, placing them under the authority of a federal Office of Refugee Resettlement within the new Department of Health and Human Services (HHS), which replaced HEW in late 1979.[108] In response to congressional insistence that all refugees be resettled via a single program and have access to the same resources, the act stipulated the stand-alone Cuban Refugee Program be wrapped up by 1983.[109]

Passed with little opposition despite flagging support for Southeast Asian admissions, the Refugee Act marked a major paradigm shift for U.S. lawmakers and the public alike, signaling a majority of Americans had finally accepted the need for a comprehensive refugee policy and endorsed the principle of federal responsibility to provide for the basic needs of refugees once in the country.[110] Equally important, by expanding resettlement services currently offered only to Southeast Asian children to encompass unaccompanied minors of all nationalities, the legislation conferred an unprecedented acknowledgement of the unique needs and rights of unaccompanied refugee minors. The culmination of a process beginning in 1934 with private Jewish American child-saving efforts, the establishment of a permanent and comprehensive federal URM program under the 1980 Refugee Act, which authorized the Office of Refugee Resettlement to sign long-standing contracts with the USCC and LIRS to provide foster homes to refugee children arriving alone, both reflected and reinforced the belief that unaccompanied refugee minors were entitled to priority admissions as well as special forms of care and protection.

Important gaps remained in the Refugee Act's provisions for unaccompanied minors. The legislation failed to articulate age-appropriate guidelines for determining whether children qualified for refugee status, requiring instead the same screenings as adults.[111] It also limited eligibility for the URM program to those classified as "unaccompanied" by the ORR upon admission, defining this term narrowly to mean only those children who did not arrive as part of a family unit containing an adult relative of any degree or those who were not destined to the home of an adult relative. It thus left many precariously accompanied minors without access to child welfare services if living arrangements broke down—an easily foreseeable eventuality given the frequency of failed relative placements in previous programs.[112] The Refugee Act also failed to establish procedures for dealing with unaccompanied minors who arrived as part of a major refugee influx entering the country without pre-authorization.[113] This oversight likely stemmed from legislators' assumption that future refugees would continue to be selected for admission through an orderly overseas process. Congress's failure to address the possibility that the United States might again become a nation of first asylum, as after the Cuban Revolution, became glaringly apparent only two months after the law's passage.

Between May and October of 1980, more than 130,000 Cubans and Haitians (including small numbers of unaccompanied minors) took to the Caribbean on unseaworthy vessels, seeking freedom and security in the United States. However, where previous generations of anti-Castro Cubans were welcomed with mostly open arms, 57 percent of Americans now opposed the admission of the less educated, darker-skinned "Marielitos." Public opposition to the Black and desperately impoverished Haitians was even higher.[114] An increasingly powerful exile political lobby demanded Cubans continue being admitted without restrictions, while outraged allies of the Haitian boat people condemned opposition as racially motivated and argued the migrants were fleeing political repression far worse than anything experienced by the Mariel Cubans. President Carter ordered both groups detained in camps in South Florida and across the country, including Ford Indiantown Gap, Pennsylvania, and Fort Chafee, Arkansas, bases which had recently housed Vietnamese refugees. At the end of June, he directed the INS to create a new immigration status, "Cuban/Haitian Entrant (Status Pending)," to parole

The Most Difficult Type of Refugee

both groups into the country for two years while individual status determinations were conducted.[115]

The massive influx of Caribbean boat people in the spring and summer of 1981 crushed hopes that the United States had finally established an effective refugee policy, pushed public sentiment back toward restrictionism, and exacerbated mounting concerns about unauthorized immigration. It also fueled backlash against Southeast Asian refugees, who continued to be admitted at a rate of 14,000 per month. The passage of the Refugee Act thus represented the culmination and also the end point for Americans' flirtation during the 1970s with a human-rights inspired foreign policy. A burgeoning neoconservative movement seized the moment, calling for the nation to stop atoning for imagined sins, reassert its power in the international arena, and protect its borders at home. Americans' hunger to feel strong and proud again contributed to Jimmy Carter's decisive electoral defeat later that year and propelled Ronald Reagan into the White House.[116] Impatient with the moral complexities of détente and determined to reassert a strong Cold War agenda, during his first year in office the new Republican president continued admitting high numbers of Southeast Asian refugees—but where Carter's refugee policy sought to balance a complex mix of foreign policy interests, humanitarian ideals, and the demands of competing domestic lobbies, Reagan returned to previous administrations' policy of admitting anti-communist escapees to draw attention to the evils of communism. At the same time, he directed the INS to crack down on irregular entrants from Latin America and the Caribbean, many of whom were fleeing persecution under U.S.-aligned right-wing leaders.[117]

Under Reagan's orders more than 100,000 Vietnamese and almost 30,000 Cambodians were admitted to the United States in 1981.[118] Among these were 5,964 unaccompanied minors—including a small number of the 840 Cambodian children remaining in Thai camps whose parents could not be traced.[119] Reagan's tougher overall stance on immigration opened up new fissures between the Departments of State and Justice over whether those fleeing Southeast Asia should still be considered refugees. Leaders within the State Department recognized that "some might term such refugees economic," yet maintained they were still "victims" of the political policies of the communist Vietnamese government.[120] On the other hand, DOJ leaders argued the Indochinese refugee program had developed into a preferential migration program for those seeking economic opportunity and demanded all Southeast Asian escapees undergo individual screening as required by the 1980 Refugee Act.[121]

In early 1981 INS officials overseas began rejecting high numbers of Southeast Asians they claimed didn't meet the new act's individual definition of "refugee."[122] A number of unaccompanied minors were rejected because they could not articulate their motives in "adult" terms. This directly contravened UNHCR guidance on age-specific approaches to determining minors' refugee status, which stated if parents wished "their child to be outside the country of origin on grounds of well-founded fear of persecution, the child himself may be presumed to have such fear."[123] An outraged Secretary of State Alexander Haig immediately directed the attorney general to determine whether there were in fact categories of persons who shared "common characteristics that identif[ied] them as targets of persecution in a particular country."[124] Although the attorney general declined to offer a definitive ruling, the two executive branch offices reached their own agreement in the spring of 1981. INS officers were to subject adult refugees to rigorous individual screening; unaccompanied Southeast Asians would be informally recognized as possessing a special claim on refugee status and once again expedited for resettlement.

As a result of these age-based exceptions, although overall Vietnamese admissions were reduced to approximately 50,000 per year between 1982 and 1985, unaccompanied minors continued to enter the United States in high numbers: 4,041 in 1982, another 3,425 in 1983, and 2,695 in 1984.[125] This included a small but steadily growing number of Cambodian minors, totaling 897 in these three years.[126] After 1982, following more than a decade of advocacy by religious and humanitarian organizations, the Amerasian Immigration Act also allowed children of American fathers and Southeast Asian mothers to immigrate to the United States. However, the act callously excluded their mothers as the postwar Displaced Persons Act of 1948 had excluded the surviving parents of European "half orphans"—presumably to prevent Amerasian minors from initiating a process of chain migration for opportunistic relatives seeking to follow in their footsteps. Those seeking to claim their narrowly defined right to U.S. residence were thus forced to migrate alone, effectively being converted by U.S. law into unaccompanied minors.[127]

Children's continued preferential admission remained a source of tension between the State Department and INS officials in the camps, some of whom continued to violate DOJ guidance that unaccompanied minors be given the benefit of the doubt during the refugee screening process.[128] In January 1984, the Immigration and Naturalization Service in Thailand rejected two unaccompanied Cambodian minors who had served as Khmer Rouge army messengers when they were eleven and twelve years old, citing State Department guidelines barring members of the Pol Pot regime and military forces from entering the United States. International and U.S. children's advocates protested that admission criteria that failed to distinguish between adults and young children forced into military service would jeopardize the resettlement of hundreds of endangered Cambodian minors.[129] With national media coverage threatening to fuel further controversy, the DOJ quickly conceded, ruling that conscripted minors' age and individual circumstances would henceforth be taken into consideration. However, these age-based accommodations would remain informal and inconsistently applied.

Over time, however, this vague commitment increasingly flew in the face of hardening international and domestic public sentiment. As early as 1981, other resettlement nations, including France, Canada, Germany, and Australia, began shutting down programs for youth they increasingly viewed as "anchors."[130] In 1983 Australian welfare officials recommended the UNHCR actively work to disincentivize underage migration by minimizing media attention and deliberately slowing resettlement procedures. U.S. and international voluntary agency personnel quickly objected, arguing that whether or not unaccompanied minors were technically refugees, prolonging their stay in camps was neither ethically justifiable nor an effective deterrent to youth migration.[131] In the United States, perceptions of unaccompanied Vietnamese children as migrants of opportunity were so pervasive that a State Department spokesman told the *New York Times* in 1984 that INS officers needed to be "on the watch for minors who misrepresented themselves as being separated" in order to "become 'anchors' in another country."[132]

Notions of Southeast Asian minors as "anchors" both emerged from and further fueled the broader anti-immigrant backlash in the United States and other wealthy nations during the 1980s. They also echoed the anti-Semitic logic of the 1930s used to justify exclusion of Jewish children by framing them as an "entering wedge" through which adult Jews might flood the United States. In each instance, these discourses implicitly denied unaccompanied minors' right to be considered for asylum based on their own individual circumstances. The consequences for children were very real: even as the numbers of unaccompanied Southeast Asian children remaining in the camps declined—to 2,800 by July of 1984 and to 1,300 by March 1985—their claims on refugee status became increasingly adjudicated in light of their relationship to their (nonwhite) families and communities of origin. As a result, the United States and other resettlement nations grew increasingly reluctant to admit them.[133]

In 1982, as the admission of Southeast Asian URMs began to slow, the Office of Refugee Resettlement, the USCC and LIRS would begin to refine their initial "crash" model of operations, undertaking comprehensive efforts to ensure resettled minors received adequate and consistent care. An urgent first step for the ORR was creating standardized forms for collecting data on children served by the program. They also reached an agreement with the State Department on new procedures for monitoring the growing number of minors placed with relatives or refugee families to whom they had become informally attached after leaving home. When in May 1983 HHS lifted the prohibition on unaccompanied refugee minors' adoption, agencies also developed processes for reclassifying children as adoptable after parents or close relatives had not been located within two years. However, gaps in the provision of care remained, especially at the state level where procedures for placing and monitoring children varied significantly and were inconsistently implemented.[134]

The USCC and LIRS also recognized the need to ease the acculturation process for resettled youth. Beginning in 1982 both agencies made greater efforts to place children with families of similar cultural backgrounds, especially in the case of Cambodian minors who, because of their mostly impoverished rural origins and extreme experiences of trauma and deprivation, were seen as requiring additional support to adapt to U.S. life.[135] Persistent shortages of culturally similar foster families meant this was often impossible. Agencies experimented with ways of addressing cultural needs, including providing initial stays with co-ethnic reception foster families, placing children in homes where a successfully integrated refugee minor was already living, or "clustering" groups of children in the same geographic areas.[136]

Local agencies also developed new programs designed to preserve minor's ethnic identities and foster ties to the local refugee community. One exceptional program in New Hampshire, supported by Congregationalist minister Peter Pond, worked with local high schools to organize intensive Cambodian studies courses for Cambodian refugee minors; visits from Khmer refugee musicians, artists, and political leaders; and regular sessions with a Cambodian Buddhist monk who provided counseling and spiritual guidance.[137] More characteristic were efforts by the Catholic Charities Bi-County Center of Suffolk County in New York State, which organized a 1982 Christmas party for Southeast Asian children and their foster families, inaugurating a series of social events to give refugee minors an opportunity to interact with peers who shared their migration and resettlement experiences, home languages, and cultures.[138] A departure from decades of "Americanization" efforts, these strategies reflected the growing influence of new notions of multiculturalism within the social work profession in the post–civil rights era.[139]

Voluntary agency and child welfare workers also began to proactively address the psychological needs of unaccompanied Southeast Asian minors living with foster families. Traumatized by flight and unfamiliar with the idea of government-funded foster care, many children were suspicious of host parents they viewed as being "hired" to take care of them.[140] Others grappling with extreme survivor's guilt and fears for family members still trapped in Vietnam or Cambodia or in refugee camps, felt guilty about forming emotional ties with host parents and feared their biological parents would see this as disloyalty.[141] These complex psychosocial challenges were often compounded by minors' limited English language skills, as well as Euro-American foster parents and caseworkers' lack of familiarity with culturally specific ways of expressing distress. As a result, even when caregivers were well intended, many children with depression, anxiety, and PTSD did not receive appropriate mental health care.[142]

Even the most resilient and well-adjusted refugee minors struggled to adapt to an unfamiliar familial context. Despite forming affectionate relationships with their host families, they often remained confused by American family dynamics, including children's lack of deference toward their parents and older siblings as well as the expectation that both boys and girls perform household chores.[143] Older boys, including the not-insignificant numbers who claimed to be younger to expedite resettlement, faced gender-based difficulties integrating with their foster families. Accustomed to living on their own in the camps, many insisted on maintaining their emotional distance and demanded a level of independence unacceptable to their foster parents.[144] Conflicts of this kind became a common cause of placement breakdowns, leaving social workers scrambling to make alternative arrangements.[145] In a few cases, older minors unhappy in their placements made their own plans to move in with relatives or friends. Unlike previous programs, youth often did better living with relatives, although breakdowns still occurred when family members' changing circumstances made them unable or unwilling to assume or continue care. In a few cases, relatives abandoned youth after deciding to move to another state or "returned" them to voluntary agencies complaining of bad behavior.[146]

Whether placed in foster homes or with relatives, unaccompanied Southeast Asian minors faced formidable challenges adjusting to their new educational and social contexts. Most experienced significant disruptions to their education; one 1985 study found that only three in ten completed more than an elementary school education, and one quarter had less than five years of school.[147] The already-difficult return to the classroom was exacerbated by linguistic and cultural differences, as well as by racial discrimination. Like Cuban youth before them, Southeast Asian minors struggled to accept their new identities in America as members of a racialized minority, while negotiating expectations that they perform the role of "the good refugee" by demonstrating gratitude to the United States for taking them in. These pressures made it virtually impossible for young people to speak freely about their experiences of U.S. racism or publicly express grief and longing for their homeland, the loss of cherished cultural traditions, religious practices, and ways of life.[148] They made it difficult for youth to make American friends. At the same time many Vietnamese youth reported being bullied by Asian American classmates and Cambodian youth by their Vietnamese peers. By the mid-1980 academic failure and social isolation led to rising substance abuse and school dropout rates among teenage URMs. When combined with limited job prospects and pressures to make money to support families back home, these factors drove some youth into gangs and criminal activity, including selling marijuana, theft, and extortion, especially in the San Francisco Bay area.[149]

With time many unaccompanied minors successfully adjusted to their new lives in the United States. One study found that of the 1,896 Southeast Asian children resettled in New York State between 1979 and the mid-1990s, approximately 50 percent completed or were enrolled in a university undergraduate program—numbers well above the average for white U.S. citizen youth.[150] In 1984, the *Christian Science Monitor* reported on similar successes among the Cambodian minors resettled in New Hampshire after August 1980. Soneat Hong, Arn Chorn, and Lekhana Seri, three boys who were fostered and then adopted by Reverend Peter Pond and his wife Shirley, arrived in the United States with less than three years of formal schooling and speaking only a few words of English learned in the Thai refugee camps. Four years later, they had been promoted to ninth grade and were exceeding their American peers in math and French classes.[151]

The boys' accomplishments speak to the determination of many youth who struggled to fulfill expectations that they pursue higher education and achieve the financial independence necessary to bring their families to the United States. But they were not representative of most unaccompanied children's experiences. Despite media coverage that vacillated between praising Southeast Asian refugee students' "legendary" academic achievements and condemning them as violent juvenile delinquents, the reality was in fact more complex.[152] As a staff member at the San Francisco Chinatown Youth Center succinctly noted, most Vietnamese and Cambodian URMs were neither "Straight A students nor . . . gang members."[153]

By the mid-1980s efforts to provide more targeted support to resettled Southeast Asian children were bearing fruit. In November 1984, the USCC and LIRS held a joint conference bringing together more than 300 persons involved in the care of unaccompanied minors nationwide; armed with findings from multiple studies of program outcomes, they discussed strategies for how to best meet children's multiple needs.[154] In February 1985 the Office of Refugee Resettlement convened a national Unaccompanied Minors Workgroup, which included representatives of the U.S. Catholic Conference, Lutheran Immigration and Refugee Service, Church World Service, the American Branch of the International Social Service (ISS), and the Pearl S. Buck Foundation, as well as representatives from the UNHCR, the Children's Bureau, the INS, and members of the House Judiciary Committee and Senate Subcommittee on Immigration and Refugee Policies.[155] In March 1987 a new National Association for Vietnamese American Education convened a conference to discuss the adjustment challenges of refugee children, unaccompanied minors, and Amerasian youth.[156] These efforts were representative of a process of dramatic professionalization in the care of unaccompanied refugee children in the United States after the middle of the decade, one that both reflected and reinforced a growing recognition among humanitarian and child welfare workers of the specific age-based needs and rights of underage solo migrants.

However, these advancements coincided with a significant contraction in URM admissions. In 1986, only 1,657 unaccompanied minors were admitted to the United States, leaving an estimated 1,400 children alone in camps throughout Southeast Asia.[157] Despite another uptick in boat departures from Vietnam late that year, including at least 800 additional unaccompanied minors, overall U.S. admission of refugees of all ages continued to decline— to 40,000 in 1986, 35,000 in 1987, and further in subsequent years.[158] URM admissions also fell to 1,338 in 1987.[159]

Returning to a more stringent interpretation of which youth met the 1980 act's definition of refugee, INS officers began to reject a growing number of unaccompanied minors with relatives in the United States. This included some especially bewildering cases in which Vietnamese children with previously resettled siblings were denied admission.[160] Pressed by voluntary agencies, leaders at the State Department's Bureau of Refugee Programs once again reminded the INS that current policy called for leniency toward minors.[161] But support for the admission of even the youngest refugees was waning fast. Within the State Department, a growing number of officials appeared to support frontline INS officials' understanding of Southeast Asian youth as migrants of opportunity. Taking this harder line, an embassy official in Bangkok argued that local INS officers should only admit minors without relatives still in Vietnam, in order to prevent families from "throwing out an anchor" by sending a child overseas alone.[162]

Between 1988 and 1992, along with another surge of departures from Vietnam, international sympathy for Southeast Asian refugees continued to decline.[163] So too would the geopolitical importance of Vietnam to U.S. foreign policy. In January 1989 George H. W. Bush took over as president of a nation whose priorities had changed dramatically since Reagan's inauguration. With the USSR's withdrawal from Afghanistan and the Soviet Union on the verge of collapse, Bush's geopolitical concerns pivoted toward the middle east. As a result, Southeast Asian refugee admissions would drop even further.[164] Frustrated by the slowing pace of resettlement, Thailand and Indonesia reverted in 1988 to pushing Vietnamese refugee boats back to sea. Malaysia threatened to do so as well. This latest backlash against boat people came to a head in the spring of 1989, when the ASEAN states successfully pressured the UNHCR and the United States to accept a new Comprehensive Plan of Action (CPA) designed to deter further departures from Vietnam. After March of that year, the CPA designated all Southeast Asian asylum seekers as economic migrants until proven otherwise and relocated all who were not classified as "genuine" refugees to prison-like "closed" camps until they could be repatriated.[165]

The CPA also stipulated that all unaccompanied minors remaining in the camps would be individually assessed by a panel of UNHCR representatives and international child welfare professionals to determine "the best durable solution" for their case.[166] Although the best interests of children, including their own expressed wishes, were granted primary importance, UNHCR guidelines made clear that voluntary repatriation should be encouraged whenever possible.[167] This new position reflected the UNHCR's growing conviction that the ongoing resettlement of Southeast Asian youth was diverting resources from the rising problem of unaccompanied refugee minors in other regions of the world—particularly in Africa, where new efforts to document unaccompanied children and provide them with appropriate services were underway.[168] It also reflected many frontline UN workers' belief that children living in difficult and dangerous conditions in the camps would be better off in Vietnam.[169] But the CPA's explicit concern with deterring further youth migration also rested upon the racialized assumption that the majority of the minors in camps were there because they'd been sent out as anchors. Reflecting this understanding of Vietnamese parents as concerned only with their own desire to emigrate, senior United Nations officer Christine Mougne wrote in an editorial in the UNHCR magazine *Refugees* that "the horrific realities of loss of life at sea" had "no apparent impact on the numbers of unaccompanied minors being put on boats by their parents." According to Mougne, the exodus of unaccompanied minors would only end "when parents in Viet Nam finally realize that sending their children out alone will no longer lead to their own resettlement."[170]

The U.S. government's acceptance of the CPA provoked outrage among refugee and child welfare advocates and inspired a burst of grassroots advocacy by Vietnamese American exiles. They were led by Nguyen D. Huu, a former South Vietnamese army officer turned social worker and the founder of the San Jose–based Aid to Refugee Children Without Parents, Inc. (ARCWP), who beginning in 1989 ceaselessly lobbied the U.S. State Department to admit more Southeast Asian unaccompanied minors.[171] Huu also wrote directly to Christine Mougne to challenge her public characterization of Vietnamese parents as indifferent to the dangers faced by children sent out alone as "anchors." Instead, he insisted the decision "to risk the lives of their children by arranging for their flight from Vietnam" was an act of love. "Those who have not lived under the conditions of present-day Vietnam cannot realize how desperate parents must be to send their children out of the country on a perilous escape," he wrote. "These children mean more to these parents than anything else in the world."[172]

Huu's advocacy appeared to have paid off when, on May 1, 1990, INS commissioner Gene McNary issued a press release announcing that an additional 700 unaccompanied Vietnamese youth would be admitted to the United States.[173] However, this was the final large-scale accommodation made on behalf of Southeast Asian children. Henceforth the U.S. State Department and Department of Justice held firm to the policy of accepting all children with U.S. links and 50 percent of those without, maintaining that the UNHCR needed to work with the international community to find homes for the "small number of unaccompanied minors that the United States [did] not resettle."[174] When those homes failed to materialize, the UNHCR announced in August 1992 that it would begin implementing the Comprehensive Plan of

Action's provisions for returning unaccompanied minors in Southeast Asian camps to Vietnam.

Between 1975 and 1992, more than 25,000 unaccompanied Southeast Asian children were admitted to the United States. The challenges confronted by voluntary agencies caring for this "most difficult type of refugee" served as the catalyst for the United States' first permanent program to provide federally funded foster care to unaccompanied refugee minors of all nationalities. The culmination of a process that began in 1934 with private Jewish American child-saving efforts, the establishment of the new federal URM program codified for the first time an understanding of unaccompanied refugee minors as possessing a unique age-based claim on priority admission as well as the right to special forms of state-sponsored, developmentally appropriate, and culturally sensitive care. But decisions about the admission or exclusion of unaccompanied children from Southeast Asia remained in the hands of political leaders driven more by foreign policy and domestic political considerations than by humanitarian concern for the children's well-being.

As early as 1976 INS officers tried to limit admission to the United States of unaccompanied Southeast Asian refugee minors who they saw as "anchors." Acting at first in defiance of State Department guidance, these rogue INS officials were at the forefront of a growing anti-refugee coalition in the federal government after 1981. By the end of the decade, they joined with allies in ASEAN nations and the UNHCR to implement new policies that reimagined children as a tool for deterring the ongoing exodus from the region. At the heart of these policies were discourses that framed Vietnamese unaccompanied children—as they had Jewish children during the FDR era—as an "entering wedge" through which their adult relatives might flood the nation. In both the 1930s and 1980s, these discourses implicitly sought to deny racially undesirable unaccompanied minors the right to be considered for admission to the United States based on their individual circumstances. They also provided justification for policies that adjudicated nonwhite children's asylum claims in light of their relationship to their stigmatized families and communities, rather than on the basis of the children's best interests. The reemergence of this racialized logic of deterrence immediately following the passage of the 1980 Refugee Act revealed the limits of Americans' newly legislated humanitarian commitment to unaccompanied refugee minors as it foreshadowed the federal government's increasingly punitive approach to children migrating alone after the 1980s.

7

The Origins of a Crisis

Unaccompanied Refugee Minors and Unaccompanied Alien Children, 1980–2018

Although the 1980 Refugee Act institutionalized federal responsibility toward unaccompanied refugee minors (URMs), the geopolitics of compassion have continued to shape decisions about which children are deemed worthy of admission and protection in the United States. Since the 1990s, admitted URM children have become increasingly diverse as their numbers were severely curtailed, revealing the declining political utility of unaccompanied minors in the post–Cold War era. However, despite direct linkages between U.S. Cold War interventions in Latin America and the Caribbean and ongoing political and economic instability in the region, few among the growing numbers of underage migrants flowing north from the Americas (excluding Cuba) have been deemed eligible for the URM program. Instead, most of the carefully curated population of unaccompanied minors in federal care continue to be refugees designated by the UN High Commissioner for Refugees (UNHCR) and preselected overseas.

Far from accidental, recent URM resettlement patterns are a direct result of the Refugee Act's failure to account for the possibility of a significant flow of unregulated refugee seekers from south of the U.S. border. This glaring omission in the otherwise paradigm-shifting legislation appeared within weeks of its passage, when new waves of anti-Castro Cubans and Haitians fleeing the U.S.-aligned Duvalier dictatorship sought asylum in the United States. Among them were hundreds of a new kind of child migrant—unaccompanied alien children (UACs)—for whom the new act had also failed to account. Notwithstanding the Refugee Act's universal framing, the ambivalence about UACs' legal rights, together with ideologically and racially charged perceptions of Cubans as legitimate political refugees and Haitians as opportunistic economic migrants meant this first wave of unauthorized child migrants often received inadequate and inconsistent treatment from Immigration and Naturalization Service (INS) officers whose pro-deterrence biases shaped their responses to children of different races and national origins.

Between 1980 and 2018, the differential treatment accorded to the United States' small URM population and successive waves of Haitian, Central American, and Mexican UACs has become ever more apparent. Despite sustained legal advocacy seeking to bring the United States into conformity with international law detailing the rights of all unaccompanied migrant children, underage unauthorized border crossers continue to confront an enforcement regime that treats them first as "illegal" immigrants and only secondarily as children, and this is not accidental. Instead, the emergence of a vastly inequitable two-tier system for processing unaccompanied child migrants is the inevitable result of the U.S. government's disavowal of its own role in creating massive and ongoing displacement in the Americas and of the decision to prioritize public demands to secure the southern border over the protection needs of Western Hemisphere asylum seekers. This latest variant of a geopolitics of compassion that reaches far back into the twentieth century continues to fuel the ongoing legal violence against Mexican and Central American child migrants today.

Promulgated after two years of intense debate, the passage of the 1980 Refugee Act did not end Americans' disagreements about which refugees—regardless of age—should be admitted to the United States.[1] Instead these debates reached a new intensity when, only a week after the act was signed, anti-Castro exiles launched an emergency boatlift of disaffected Cubans from the port of Mariel. Between April and October, 120,000 more Cubans arrived in Florida, including over 2,000 unaccompanied minors.[2] At the same time approximately 20,000 Haitians followed on the heels of countrymen and women who since the early 1970s sought asylum in the United States from political repression at the hands of the U.S.-allied anti-communist Duvalier regime.

President Carter, confronted by intense public opposition to poor and darker-skinned "Marielitos" stigmatized by the unsympathetic media as deviants and criminals, broke with a Cold War geopolitical precedent dating back to Eisenhower and refused to extend *prima facie* refugee status to this latest wave of anti-Castro exiles.[3] Instead he mandated detention in closed camps until a decision could be made about their status. In the face of intense pressure from Florida's politically powerful exile community and under assault by voluntary agencies, religious and civil rights groups, and the Congressional Black Caucus, all of whom accused the immigration service of racial discrimination against the Black Haitian asylum seekers, Carter quickly gave in. In June 1980, he instructed the INS to temporarily admit all Cubans who had entered between April and June of 1980, as well as Haitians who had entered before June 19, under a new classification: "Cuban/Haitian Entrant (Status Pending)."[4]

Temporary authorization to remain in the country was just a first step. Voluntary agencies struggled to place the stigmatized Mariel Cubans in American communities.[5] Figuring out what to do with the children proved even more difficult. During the first month of the influx, INS officials who were ill qualified to identify unaccompanied minors or make arrangements for their care simply released them to unverified individual sponsors, without conducting advance screenings or arranging for follow-up supervision. After Miami's Community Relations Service complained of multiple cases of abuse, minors whose placements had failed were sent to the Krome North Detention Center where they were detained alongside children unclaimed by relatives or sponsors. On May 23, 1980, however, Florida's government—which had to date received no federal funds for the children's care—declared it would no longer accept this responsibility. Placed under the jurisdiction of the Federal Emergency Management Agency (FEMA), the children were relocated to camps on the same military bases that had housed Vietnamese refugees five years earlier and released into the general population alongside adult Marielitos. Although the Department of Health and Human Services (HHS) tasked the Office of Refugee Resettlement (ORR) with providing additional services to the children, in the absence of age-appropriate supervision and protection, they became victims of violence, abuse, and harassment by INS officers, military police, and fellow exiles.[6]

Despite the dire conditions of minors in the camps, voluntary agencies resisted adding unaccompanied Marielitos to their caseloads until the federal government issued clear directions on how their resettlement was to proceed—and how it was to be funded. Following several months of negotiations between voluntary agencies and the Departments of State, Justice, and HHS, the INS reluctantly agreed in July to retain legal custody of Cuban

URMs until they were placed; however, ongoing confusion and conflict over who held long-term financial responsibility for the children drove voluntary agencies to declare a temporary moratorium on children's resettlement later that month. This latest stalemate between the government and resettlement agencies delayed the placement of underage Marielitos, including several hundred who had relatives eager to take them in. It wasn't until August 18, after HHS tasked the Office of Refugee Resettlement with oversight of the children's care and authorized ORR to reimburse states for 75 percent of the related expenses up to a maximum of $20 million, that agencies began placing this new wave of Cuban children with foster families. Homes remained in short supply until after October 1980, when the passage of the hotly contested Refugee Education Assistance Act made Cuban and Haitian entrants eligible for the full range of Refugee Act benefits and services and required the federal government to reimburse state and local governments for 100 percent of the cost of caring for children admitted under this provisional status.[7]

While federal, state, and local governments clashed with voluntary agencies over how to handle unaccompanied Cuban entrant minors, neither the INS nor ORR recognized the need for a similar program for Haitian minors. Haitian children were mostly detained in the general population until the INS could place them in the community, releasing them to any adult who claimed to be a relative or offered to be a sponsor. By October, having identified at least 340 unaccompanied Haitian children, they established a separate facility at Krome South Detention Center. However, although they'd abandoned this practice with underage Marielitos, the INS continued to release unaccompanied Haitian minors to unscreened adults, without creating a procedure for conducting follow-up welfare checks. Only after the State of Florida raised concerns that unaccompanied Haitian children were being placed in homes where they were exploited or abused and that some children had been abandoned after their placements failed, was their care placed under ORR jurisdiction in December.

In an effort to facilitate family reunifications and secure appropriate foster homes for Haitian children without relatives in the United States, the ORR contracted the Miami Association of Black Social Workers to initiate a tracing program and establish state-approved procedures for home studies. Placements continued to proceed slowly; U.S. relatives could only be located for 116 children, and state and local governments remained reluctant to accept responsibility for the rest of the unaccompanied Haitian entrant minors. The majority were transported in 1981 to an institution in New York State, where most remained for an average of seven months before placements could be found for them in New York City's Haitian community.[8]

The trajectories of unaccompanied Cuban and Haitian entrant minors diverged even further in 1984, when an amendment to the 1966 Cuban Adjustment Act made Cuban entrants eligible for permanent residency, providing unaccompanied Marielitos with the legal status and security to facilitate their integration into U.S. society. In contrast, having determined that Haitian entrants were strictly "economic" migrants with no claim on asylum, the INS summarily revoked their provisional status. An undetermined number of unaccompanied minors who had been cared for by the ORR were subsequently placed in deportation proceedings until the 1986 Immigration Reform and Control Act (IRCA) granted amnesty to Haitian entrants arbitrarily rendered "illegal" two years earlier.[9]

After Mariel, the geopolitics of compassion continued to produce disparities in the reception of different groups of endangered children. During the rest of the 1980s the exploding global refugee population became increasingly diverse, including new displaced populations from the Horn of Africa, Afghanistan, and Central America. President Reagan deferred to restrictionist sentiment by steadily reducing overall refugee admissions while allocating the overwhelming number of visas to anti-communist refugees from Southeast Asia and Eastern Europe.[10] Throughout the decade over 95 percent of children admitted to the URM program continued to come from Vietnam, Cambodia, and Laos.[11] This pattern began to change by the midnineties when, although overall URM admissions were severely curtailed, hundreds more unaccompanied children from Cuba and Haiti were admitted. As a result, by 1995, 1,123 Haitian URMs lived in federally funded homes in New York State.[12]

Public debate over the nation's humanitarian obligations to endangered overseas children also resurfaced in the nineties, especially after more than 32,000 Cuban *balseros* (rafters) of all ages took to the seas in the summer of 1994, becoming the catalyst for the Clinton administration's new hardline policy toward those fleeing the island.[13] Interdicted at sea, rafters were transported to tent cities aboard U.S. naval facilities at Guantanamo and in Panama; approximately 500 "humanitarian" cases, including the elderly, severely ill, and unaccompanied minors, were quickly granted parole, but the rest were detained pending individual asylum screenings. By the end of the year, however, Clinton yielded to pressure from the Cuban American community and its conservative allies, instructing Attorney General Janet

Reno to authorize the parole of up to 3,000 children and their immediate relatives—a total between 8,000 and 10,000 people—provided they secured full financial sponsorship in the United States.[14] Despite these newly rigid policies, exceptions continued to be made for Cubans of all ages, approximately 300,000 of whom were granted asylum in the United States between the 1980s and 1990s.[15]

Neither the Clinton nor Bush administrations took meaningful efforts to resettle refugees from Central America and Africa in the United States, despite growing displacement crises in the regions. Responding to continued foreign policy priorities, which included concern for European stability in the aftermath of the USSR's dissolution and the desire to help former victims of Soviet regimes, as well as strong lobbying by ethnic organizations in the United States, both presidents reserved most of the more than 1 million refugee visas allocated between 1990 and 2000 for asylum seekers from the former Soviet Union, East Asia, and Eastern Europe. At the same time, public anger at the perceived "loss of control" at the southern border and racialized fears about the cultural and economic implications of an influx of poor nonwhite people on U.S. society worked against the admission of more than a few thousand refugees per year from Latin America, Africa, and the Middle East.[16] This started to shift mid-decade, as new foreign policy concerns with Africa emerged, leading to the admission of small but steadily increasing numbers of refugees from the continent's sub-Saharan nations. At the same time, small numbers of unaccompanied minors from China, Afghanistan, and Honduras were admitted, further diversifying the URM population except with respect to gender—adolescent males continued to make up the great majority.[17]

Between 1999 and 2005, although only 782 new URMs were admitted, changing geopolitics and domestic political conditions continued to broaden the URM program's demographics.[18] In particular, a convergence between new U.S. military interventions in Africa and transnational activism on behalf of the continent's estimated 120,000 child soldiers, culminating with the presentation of the 1996 Machel report to the UN General Assembly, led to a significant increase in the admission of unaccompanied African refugee minors. During this period sixty-three unaccompanied refugee minors from Liberia, twenty-seven from Somalia, fourteen from Sierra Leone, and another thirty-five from Ethiopia, Congo, Burundi, and Yemen, many of whom had participated in armed conflicts, were admitted.[19] After 9/11, when refugee admissions were temporarily suspended, growing U.S. foreign policy concerns in Africa and increased lobbying by NGOs, celebrity activists concerned with the Darfur crisis, and conservative evangelicals who pushed for the admission of persecuted Sudanese Christians spurred modestly increased refugee admissions from Somalia, Liberia, and Sudan.[20]

Small numbers of Liberian unaccompanied minors were admitted to the United States in the early 2000s as part of this new emphasis on African refugees.[21] This small population paled, however, in comparison to the 407 Sudanese "Lost Boys" selected for the URM program from among the roughly 10,000 male youth who fled a fractious civil war in their homeland for asylum in Kenya in 1992. Benefiting from sustained advocacy, sympathetic media coverage, and public awareness sparked by the publication of memoirs documenting their experiences, these highly visible Sudanese unaccompanied minors made up 52 percent of the URMs admitted to the United States between 1999 and 2005.[22] During this period, the ORR also resettled an additional 3,100 Lost Boys who had reached the age of majority.[23]

Despite overwhelmingly positive U.S. media coverage, not everyone supported the Lost Boys' resettlement in the United States—including Sudanese political and community leaders who suggested that the State Department's money would be better spent discouraging further displacement by encouraging peace in Sudan.[24] Activists and scholars pointed out the regional, gendered, and age-based disparities reflected by new international campaigns on behalf of child soldiers, criticizing media misrepresentations of youth combatants as preteen African boys, despite the fact that children had long participated in armed conflict around the world, most were adolescents, and up to 40 percent were girls. Others challenged humanitarians' reliance on a "transnational politics of age" that represents all child soldiers as helpless (and therefore blameless) victims, uncritically reifying Western notions of childhood as time of innocence and dependence as well as understandings of endangered overseas children as in need of the protection of benevolent white nations. Still others sought in vain to draw attention to the equally urgent protection needs of underaged conscripts (male and female) in Central and South America.[25]

New laws and policies after the mid-1990s further diversified the nation's URM population. In 2000, the Trafficking Victims Protection Act (TVPA) made trafficked unaccompanied children eligible for T visas and granted them access to federal benefits and services on the same basis as refugees. However, very few children—only thirty-two, mostly Mexican and Central American adolescents, between 2001 and 2004—were subsequently made eligible for the URM program.[26] The TVPA also guaranteed unaccompanied minors apprehended after entering the country without authorization the right to apply for asylum via an affirmative (non-adversarial) process, while other unauthorized border crossers were compelled to undergo defensive (adversarial) asylum hearings in immigration court. Children whose asylum applications were approved then became eligible for placement as URMs.[27]

Together with the nation's changing foreign policy and domestic political contexts, legal and administrative changes broadened the scope of the URM program in the new millennium. Although total numbers remained circumscribed, by 2012 the program was serving children from almost fifty nations.[28] Still almost 90 percent of unaccompanied minors in ORR care continued to be UNHCR-designated refugees selected from overseas. Only 2.2 percent of children in the program were trafficking victims. Asylum seekers represented a similarly scant 2.3 percent of the program's beneficiaries.[29] And despite decades of violence and political and economic instability in Latin America, between 1999 and 2005 only sixty-eight children from all of Latin America (excluding Cuba) were admitted to the program. Thirty-nine were from Honduras, eleven from Guatemala, ten from Mexico, and six from Nicaragua. Only two were from war-devastated El Salvador.[30]

After 1979, a socialist revolution in Nicaragua and the beginnings of prolonged warfare in El Salvador intensified the regional displacement set in motion in the sixties by the Guatemalan Civil War. During the 1980s, hundreds of thousands of Nicaraguans and Guatemalans, as well as more than 500,000 Salvadorans, fled state-sponsored violence, terror, and extreme poverty—all inextricably linked to more than a century of U.S. intervention in the region—for the United States.[31] But following on the heels of more than a decade of Southeast Asian resettlement and then the Mariel crisis, this wave of unauthorized asylum seekers were met with alarm and hostility. For many Americans, as well as restrictionist legislators like Representative Romano Mazzoli (D-Ky.) and Senator Alan Simpson (R-Wyo.), Central Americans were not legitimate refugees but rather self-interested economic migrants seeking to take advantage of the country's overly generous refugee laws.[32] The fact that the refugees were poor, nonwhite, and fleeing right-wing U.S.-aligned regimes only increased conservative skepticism about the validity of their asylum claims. By 1981, Reagan's determination to limit refuge primarily to anti-communist escapees who served the nation's reinvigorated Cold War foreign policy led him to order the mandatory detention of all Haitian asylum seekers, the interdiction of their boats at sea, and their forcible return to Haiti.[33]

Consistent with this new hard-line approach, throughout the 1980s the Reagan administration systematically denied asylum to Salvadorans and Guatemalans fleeing repressive military governments.[34] The estimated 70,000 Nicaraguans who claimed persecution by the socialist Sandinista regime fared somewhat better; still, less than 10 percent of their asylum petitions were successful.[35] During the remainder of the decade, despite sustained protest by U.S.-resident Central Americans and their allies in the religiously motivated Sanctuary movement, hundreds who fled the region were deported to their homelands where they faced imprisonment, torture, and execution—even as the INS continued to approve at much higher rates the asylum petitions of Iranians, Eastern Europeans, and Ethiopians.[36] Those who evaded removal were forced into the shadows, where they struggled to survive as low-wage workers and lived in constant fear of deportation. This politicized and racially discriminatory asylum process laid the groundwork for enduring structures of legal violence against U.S. residents from Latin American and Caribbean communities, especially those of Central American origin. Together with the exclusion of most from the 1986 Immigration Reform and Control Act, which provided amnesty to approximately 3 million undocumented immigrants, the asylum process compounded the trauma of war survivors and ensured they would pass along the consequences of their "illegality" to their U.S. born children.[37]

An asylum system designed for adults presented even more obstacles for unaccompanied alien children.[38] The first to suffer the disparate effects of this system, Haitian youth who arrived after the June 1980 cutoff for admission as "entrants," were transported to Miami's Krome detention facilities. There they were stripped, showered, and forced to dress in orange prison jumpsuits before being released into the general population until they could be placed into the care of relatives or sponsors. They then waited long months for the adjudication of their asylum petitions, the overwhelming majority of which were denied. Although IRCA provided a path to legalization for some Haitian minors who arrived before January 1, 1982, those that came after remained subject to removal. Beginning in 1987, as many of the youth were nearing high school graduation or had entered college, the INS began to deport them back to Haiti.[39]

Hard-line policies were also callously implemented against a growing number of Central American minors making the long and dangerous overland journey to *el norte* alone during the 1980s.[40] Arriving exhausted, malnourished, and traumatized, but determined to find security and opportunity or to reunite with family in the United States, these children instead met formidable obstacles to their admission. Whether apprehended by the U.S. Border Patrol or taken into custody after presenting themselves at a checkpoint, most were placed in removal proceedings and transported to area detention facilities to wait—from a few days to several months—for their day in an Executive Office for Immigration Review (EOIR) immigration court.

INS policy during the 1980s allowed those minors over fifteen to remain in detention among the general population. Younger children were sent to INS-contracted facilities, not always licensed by states, that varied dramatically in the quality of care offered. Some more adequate homes were run by churches or other humanitarian organizations, while others were run by for-profit institutions that made little provision for children's comfort, recreation, or education. Younger children could be bonded out to relatives or community sponsors; however, many remained in detention because U.S. resident parents without papers feared to come forward because doing so meant they could themselves be apprehended and deported.[41] And in any case, being released was not necessarily preferable; unaccompanied alien children who were bonded out to inadequately screened community members were sometimes pressed into forced labor or physically or sexually abused.[42]

Asylum proceedings also failed to take into account minors' age-specific vulnerabilities. Since the Refugee Act lacked statutory provisions for adjudicating the asylum claims of unaccompanied minors, their processing was left in the hands of frontline INS officers untrained on how to make age determinations and assess children's protection needs.[43] Institutional barriers to asylum were further exacerbated by frontline agents' occupational culture, which prioritized immigration enforcement and deterrence over humanitarian considerations. In the absence of clear procedural guidelines or oversight, many INS agents knowingly or unknowingly ignored federal guidance to treat children with sensitivity, adopting instead the adversarial approach they used when dealing with unauthorized adult border crossers. This included failing to inform some children of their right to request asylum or coercing them into accepting voluntary departure despite their experiences or well-founded fears of persecution.[44]

In 1984 repeated complaints of INS mistreatment led legal advocates to file a class action suit on behalf of Salvadoran minors in a Los Angeles district court. In *Perez-Funez v. District Director*, the plaintiffs conclusively demonstrated an INS pattern of actively working to deny unaccompanied Central American children access to asylum or other forms of deportation relief.[45] As a result of the case, the INS was ordered to make UACs aware of their right to an asylum hearing and access to legal counsel.[46] These new guidelines were nonetheless routinely disregarded. In a tragic repetition of another historical pattern, the deliberate denial of refuge to Central American children fleeing

The Origins of a Crisis

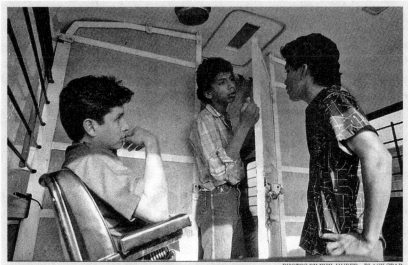

Exiles from war and poverty: *Brothers on a bus in Texas with Border Patrol agent (left)*

Like most unaccompanied minors who have come to the United
States since the 1930s, the overwhelming majority of Central
American UACs apprehended in 1989 were adolescent males.
Image by Phil Huber for Newsweek; *provided courtesy of the University
of Minnesota Immigration History Archives, Minneapolis.*

war and human rights violations coincided with a dramatic uptick in intercountry adoptions, many of them ethically dubious or outright illegal, from
Guatemala and El Salvador.[47]

The United States' hard-line approach continued after spring 1988 when
a sudden upsurge of unaccompanied Central American minors attempted
to cross the border. By July 1989, the Rio Grande Valley district INS office
alone had detained 1,333 minors; during the same period, 30 UACs were
apprehended daily in California. INS estimates further suggested that for
each apprehension, two more minors entered the country without getting
caught.[48] As in previous waves, the majority were teenage boys, approximately 75 percent of whom had U.S. relatives; still, girls and small children
as young as three years old, many of whom had been beaten or raped before
being abandoned by smugglers at the border, were among those detained.
Although some of the children cited economic opportunity and family reunification as their motives, immigration officials believed that the upsurge was
due in large part to the growing prevalence of forced conscription of boys as
young as twelve by both government and opposition forces in Guatemala,
El Salvador, Nicaragua, and Honduras.[49]

Central American advocacy groups, including Los Angeles's Central American Resource Center (CARECEN) and the South Texas Proyecto Libertad, as well as national humanitarian organizations like the U.S. Catholic Conference and Lutheran Immigration and Refugee Service, the ISS-American Branch, the U.S. Committee for Refugees and Immigrants, and the National Center for Immigrants' Rights, quickly organized on behalf of this latest wave of children. Demanding improved facilities and care for those in detention, they also called for congressional hearings to guarantee the rights of UACs in INS custody. Advocates also mobilized to provide minors with free legal representation and to locate sponsor families for those without U.S. relatives.[50]

Their efforts produced a few hard-won victories, including a November 1988 affirmative asylum decision for Proyecto Libertad client José Galindo, an adolescent Salvadoran boy who had been forcibly recruited into the army at the age of thirteen. Citing political and religious objections to military mistreatment of civilians, he deserted two years later and fled to the United States. But since U.S. immigration law did not consider draft refusal or desertion—even in the case of a forcibly conscripted minor—as grounds for asylum, most cases like Galindo's were denied.[51] Revealing of the continued geopolitics of compassion that underlay asylum adjudications, minors fleeing induction into socialist Nicaragua's Sandinista Patriotic Military Service (two-years' service was obligatory for males over age fourteen) had a much better chance. In 1988 approximately 50 percent of Nicaraguan UAC's petitions, as opposed to only 26 percent of adults from the same nation, were granted; in contrast, the INS denied asylum to 94 percent of Salvadorans, regardless of age.[52]

After the region's wars came to an end in the mid-1990s, much of Central America was left in political and economic ruin. Extreme poverty and rampant familial breakdown in an only partially demilitarized region created ideal conditions for expanded criminal gang and drug trafficking activity—trends also fueled by the Clinton administration's new policy of deporting U.S.-resident gang members back to the region.[53] However, with the Cold War officially over, U.S. foreign policy priorities shifted elsewhere; the little remaining official interest in the region would be channeled toward promoting neoliberal economic reforms that benefitted the United States at the expense of increasing local poverty and inequality, furthering conditions for social violence.[54] Together these factors escalated the migratory flow northward. Central Americans seeking security and opportunity in the United States were joined by a growing number of unauthorized Mexican immigrants fleeing economic dislocation produced by the 1992 North American

Free Trade Agreement (NAFTA), as well as violence linked to the expanded drug trade and warfare between rival cartels.[55] Among both of these populations were a growing number of unaccompanied minors.

But an evolving geopolitics of compassion, increasingly sensitive to public demands to "regain control of the border," meant that growing migration from south of the border was met by an ever-more punitive response. Beginning in 1993, President Bill Clinton directed the INS to deploy thousands more agents to the southwest, ordered the construction of border fences and the installation of military surveillance technologies in heavy-crossing areas. Over the next six years, the INS budget grew from $1.5 to $4.2 billion, while provisions of the 1996 Illegal Immigration Reform and Immigrant Responsibility Act further criminalized unauthorized entry and broadened the conditions under which deportations could take place.[56] At the same time, an explosion of new asylum applications—during most of the 1990s, the United States received more than 100,000 petitions per year—abetted perceptions that many unauthorized immigrants were abusing the asylum provision as a "back door" through which to unfairly gain admission to the United States.[57]

During the nineties as the geopolitics of compassion became increasingly circumscribed by anti-immigrant and anti-Latinx public sentiment, a growing number of politicians rode the nativist wave into state and federal office, decrying unauthorized immigrants as criminals and freeloaders seeking to take advantage of the nation's public education and welfare benefits.[58] Some specifically targeted Mexican and Central American children, framing them as runaways, juvenile delinquents and gang members, as well as through narratives that accused undocumented Latina mothers of deliberately giving birth to "anchor babies" through which they would supposedly gain access to permanent residence.[59] These claims couldn't be further from the truth; to date, U.S. immigration law denies minors the right to petition for the admission of their foreign-born parents.[60] Indeed, since 1980 the Board of Immigration Appeals reasserted on multiple occasions that having a U.S.-born child did not entitle an alien to "*any* favored status in seeking discretionary relief." The corresponding increase in deportations after 1996 has forced many parents under deportation orders to choose between taking children with them—thereby depriving them of the benefits of their U.S. citizenship—or of surrendering them to relatives or foster families. This willful disregard for the rights of U.S. citizen children, enshrined in U.S. law, has actually served to create an untold number of unaccompanied and separated children.[61]

New representations of Latinx children as a threat in their own right fueled the ongoing mistreatment of unaccompanied alien children during the nineties, prompting repeated class action lawsuits against the INS. However, even after the landmark 1996 Flores Settlement Agreement, which required the INS to establish clear guidelines and procedures for the detainment, release, and repatriation of unaccompanied alien children, frontline agents continued to prioritize enforcement over minors' welfare.[62] Investigations by legal advocates and federal agencies uncovered hundreds of cases of children deprived of information about their right to an asylum hearing or access to legal representation and of minors detained within adult population in facilities in California, New York, and Texas, as well as other serious deficiencies in their care.[63] In the aftermath of 9/11, rhetoric framing unauthorized immigrants of all ages as criminals, gang members, and potential terrorists further intensified, reinforcing public perceptions of the U.S.-Mexico border as a space of violence, lawlessness, and danger. Reinforcing the growing understanding of immigration as a national security issue, border enforcement was moved to the newly formed U.S. Customs and Border Protection (CBP) agency of the Department of Homeland Security (DHS).[64] This bureaucratic reorganization of the nation's immigration, refugee, and naturalization services under the jurisdiction of separate agencies after 2002 meant that the CBP and Border Patrol officers who were the official point of contact for most underage border crossers represented an organization whose mission was exclusively enforcement-based.[65] Despite the Flores Settlement Agreement guidelines for the humane treatment of UACs, in practice, the CBP and Border Patrol maintained the pattern of mistreatment initiated by their INS predecessors, keeping children in their own mixed-use detention facilities for weeks or months before transferring them to the Office of Refugee Resettlement, as required by the 2002 Homeland Security Act.[66] Even then, despite the act's provisions for an Alien Minors Shelter Care program designed to mirror the URM program, the legislation's lack of oversight and enforcement mechanisms meant that UACs continued to receive variable care even in ORR custody.[67]

As the flow of UACs crept steadily upward in the 2000s, the CBP's determination to subsume children's statutory rights within their enforcement priorities quickly led to tensions between the new agency and the child-welfare oriented ORR, stimulating intra–executive branch conflicts over the handling of UACs in subsequent years.[68] At the same time similar disagreements spurred repeated congressional hearings as well as public debate over the government's obligation to endangered foreign-born children. Advocates' arguments that all unaccompanied alien children had experienced extreme forms of poverty and abuse that made them deserving of refugee status were drowned out by restrictionists who sought in increasingly explicit ways to frame children who migrated alone as a deviant and dangerous subgroup of the nation's already-criminalized undocumented community.[69] As the decade progressed, the lack of enforceable laws clearly delineating UACs' rights, together with persistent racialized ambivalence about unaccompanied minors of Latin American origin—like Southeast Asian and European Jewish children before them—laid the groundwork for further expansion of legal violence against Mexican and Central American children in the new millennium.[70]

Between 2004 and 2011, the CBP apprehended an average of 6,800 unaccompanied minors from Central America's Northern Triangle—30 percent from Honduras, 26 percent from El Salvador, and 20 percent from Guatemala—as well as 13,000 to 15,000 Mexican UACs per year. Of these, 74 percent were males and 80 percent were fifteen to eighteen years old.[71] Following a fact-finding mission to the region, a U.S. Conference of Catholic Bishops report attributed the continued youthful exodus from the region to a "perfect storm" of poverty and "generalized violence at the state and local levels," as well as a "corresponding breakdown of the rule of law [that] threatened citizen security and created a culture of fear and hopelessness." The report also noted the growing prevalence of forms of violence and coercion directed specifically at children, including forced recruitment into criminal gangs.[72] While many were fleeing danger, the majority of children also sought reunification with undocumented parents from whom they had been separated for years. Older boys also migrated north as part of a family survival strategy in which relatives saved money to pay for the trip to the United States, hoping the youth could secure employment and begin sending money home as quickly as possible.[73] During this period, in order to circumvent an increasingly militarized border-enforcement regime, more UACs were transported north by smugglers, some linked to transnational gangs; by 2006, *coyotes* charged as much as $6,000 per child.[74]

Although most of the youth arriving alone during this period articulated mixed motives for migrating, advocates widely agreed that many possessed legitimate claims on asylum. UNHCR interviews with more than 400 Mexican and Central American minors in ORR custody determined that approximately 58 percent had been forcibly displaced due to a threat of harm and 48 percent were at risk of violence from organized and armed criminal actors, including cartels and gangs. That number rose to 72 percent for children from El Salvador, where local UNHCR observers had reported widespread extralegal killing and human rights abuses, not only by transnational gangs like the MS-13 but also by the police, military, and other government agents. Thirty-eight percent of Mexican children had been recruited, often forcibly, to serve as couriers and guides to human smugglers, for forced labor or to participate in criminal activity. Of all the children, 20 percent had been exposed to violence or abuse in their home.[75] Mexican and Central American children also often experienced abuse during the dangerous journey northward, during which they risked being robbed, assaulted, or sexually violated by *coyotes*, gang members, and even Mexican law enforcement officers.[76] These findings concurred with those of other major advocacy organizations, including the U.S. Conference of Catholic Bishops.[77]

Despite the acute protection needs of many of the children arriving alone at the southern border, George W. Bush's administration cracked down further on UAC asylum seekers. Between 1999 and 2003 approval rates for affirmative cases dropped from 63 percent to 31 percent. How many more Central American minors were deported after unsuccessful defensive (adversarial) asylum hearings during the 2000s—even after the reauthorized TVPA made minors from noncontiguous countries exempt from immediate credible threat screenings—is unknown.[78] And even though the 2008 version of the act mandated that CBP officers interview all Mexican unaccompanied children to determine whether they were victims of trafficking or wished to file an asylum claim, the majority continued to be "voluntarily returned" to Mexico by frontline agents who prioritized enforcement over children's welfare needs.[79]

By 2007 UACs' low asylum approval rates had contributed to the dramatic expansion of a for-profit immigration detention system that held children in forty-two ORR "shelters" across the country—most of them strategically located in Arizona, California, and Texas.[80] At the same time, rising alarm over minors' prolonged detention in frequently inadequate facilities brought together a new coalition of children's advocates that founded national organizations to provide pro bono legal service to unaccompanied migrant children. The first of these, the National Center for Refugee and Immigrant Children, was established with a generous grant from actor and UNHCR goodwill ambassador Angelina Jolie. Beginning in 2005 the NCRIC advocated for children's rights in courtrooms across the country, as well as provided legal training for attorneys representing UACs in immigration cases.[81] Pressing for the implementation of UAC provisions in the reauthorized TVPA and other recent legislation, legal advocates by 2008 achieved a small increase in asylum petition success rates and in the number of Mexican and Central American children subsequently enrolled in the URM program.[82] But these modest gains were soon overshadowed by a dramatic acceleration of youthful migration from south of the border.

In 2012, 10,443 Central American and 15,709 Mexican unaccompanied children were apprehended at the border. In 2013 this sharp upward trend continued, when the apprehension of Central American minors (21,537) outnumbered their Mexican peers (18,754) for the first time.[83] Then, during 2014, 51,705 unaccompanied Central American minors arrived at the southern border.[84] As in the past, most of this latest wave of Mexican UACs were promptly returned after a day or two in CBP custody. But tens of thousands of Honduran, Salvadoran, and Guatemalan children were placed in detention to await asylum hearings.

This unprecedented surge in unaccompanied child migration put a severe strain on the nation's immigration enforcement bureaucracy as well as on ORR officers tasked with providing interim care. In Arizona and Texas warehouses and storage facilities were hastily converted into detention facilities; photographs of young children sleeping on concrete floors under Mylar blankets in chain-link fenced enclosures filled newspapers and magazines across the nation. Scholars and journalists published exposés and op-eds arguing that the children were fleeing violence and poverty that U.S. interventions in Central America had helped to create.[85] The surge also sparked protests from anti-immigrant public figures and organizations, who framed the crisis as an invasion of deviant and criminal youth encouraged to come to the United States by an overly generous asylum policy and President Obama's 2012 Deferred Action for Childhood Arrivals (DACA) executive order granting temporary deportation relief to undocumented youth. Stoking public fears about a supposedly out-of-control border (in fact, it was more secure than at any time in U.S. history), conservative politicians demanded DACA be suspended and draconian new immigration enforcement mechanisms be immediately put into place.[86]

Struggling to reconcile an increasingly fraught geopolitics of compassion with his own personal sympathy for migrant youth, President Obama sought to craft a policy response that incorporated elements of both deterrence and protection. He ordered immigrant courts to expedite removal hearings for unaccompanied minors and undocumented family units already in the United States, authorized raids to enforce deportation orders against unsuccessful asylum applicants, and funded three new for-profit detention facilities for women and children in Texas and New Mexico. He also pressured the Mexican and Guatemalan governments to aggressively apprehend and deport unaccompanied children in transit to the United States. However, the Obama administration also stressed that existing UAC legal protections should be upheld and provided federal funding for minors' legal representation. The president also established an in-country processing program to allow a small number of Central American children to apply for asylum from their home nations. Unaccompanied alien children who reached the United States between 2014 and 2016 thus stood a greater chance of being granted asylum than those who arrived before the surge.[87] In accordance with the Flores Settlement Agreement guidelines, approximately 90 percent of these UACs were released into the care of U.S.-resident parents or relatives while their claims on asylum, T visas, or Special Immigrant Juvenile Status (SIJS) were adjudicated.[88]

Importantly, in 2016 Obama also launched a new multiagency Strategy for Engagement in Central America, providing $2.1 billion in aid to promote democratization, institution building, and economic development in the region.[89] This new program represented a tacit recognition that Central American unaccompanied child migration was inextricably tied to widespread political, social, and economic deprivations in the region—although it stopped short of recognizing the United States' historic role in creating those conditions. Despite the president's concessions to those demanding a policy of deterrence, restrictionists lambasted his "soft" approach to the UAC crisis.[90] Although unauthorized crossings were estimated to be at their lowest rate since the early seventies, a growing anti-immigrant backlash fueled by discourses framing unaccompanied alien children as a national security threat helped propel former reality star and political provocateur Donald J. Trump into the White House.[91]

The new president immediately sought to fulfill campaign promises to dramatically reduce immigrant and refugee admissions, ban Muslims from entering the country, and build a Mexico-funded wall to seal off the entire southern border.[92] After only days in office, Trump issued an executive order calling on DHS to refer all unauthorized border crossers to the Department of Justice (DOJ) for criminal charges rather than processing them through the civil immigration enforcement system as was standard practice before 2017.[93] In 2018 he lowered the annual refugee admissions quota to 45,000, the lowest since the Refugee Act's passage in 1980.[94] He also revoked the Temporary Protective Status (TPS) that had allowed some Hondurans and Salvadorans to legally reside in the United States since the late 1980s and demanded further reductions in already-low asylum approval rates.[95]

Trump also specifically targeted unaccompanied minors. After shutting down the Obama-era Central American Minors Refugee and Parole Program, he issued a series of executive orders that systematically undercut UACs' existing legal protections by eliminating requirements that immigration judges consider children's developmental capacities when assessing their testimony in court and allowing them to challenge minors' designation as UACs after their cases were underway.[96] The Trump White House also instructed judges to exclude domestic violence and gang persecution as grounds for asylum and to give precedence to immigration regulations over the best interest of the child in all adjudications.[97] At the same time, Trump's supporters within and outside the government further undercut Central American children's claims on protection by repeatedly characterizing them—in the words of former attorney general Jeff Sessions—as "gang members . . . in sheep's clothing."[98]

In April 2017 the Trump administration took its anti-immigrant campaign to new heights. Sessions announced a new "zero tolerance" policy instructing border agents and prosecutors to criminally process all unauthorized border crossers, including asylum seekers and families with small children. Since U.S. law allowed UACs to be detained separately from criminal alien relatives or guardians, charging all adult unauthorized migrants with a criminal violation provided legal justification for the attorney general to order CBP agents to separate migrant children from their parents.[99] Within weeks as many as 3,000 children, most under the age of ten, were taken away from their mothers and fathers, often through deception or force.[100] Lest anyone be confused about the racialized logic of deterrence that inspired the zero-tolerance policy, DHS secretary John Kelly made clear that it was intended to discourage Central American adults from seeking asylum in the United States.[101]

On June 20, 2017, after horrifying media images of crying toddlers snatched from their mothers' arms produced a massive outcry, President Trump signed an executive order purporting to end family separation.[102] But an incalculable level of damage had already been done to thousands of migrant children and families. Despite the efforts of a nationwide coalition of advocates, including multiple grassroots and community organizations as well as the National Immigration Law Center, the American Civil Liberties Union (ACLU), and the Center for Human Rights and Constitutional Law, by the end of 2020, more than 500 children remained lost in the United States' vast immigration enforcement machinery.[103]

A steady chorus of journalists and public figures have condemned the separation of border-crossing children from their parents as a "new low" that violates the United States' historic tradition of opening its arms to the poor and oppressed.[104] Their outrage is legitimate. However, such protests obscure the harsh reality that Trump's zero-tolerance policy was in fact the logical, if grotesque, culmination of a geopolitics of compassion that has always elevated notions of the national interest above the welfare of both refugees and unaccompanied migrant children.

Between 1934 and 1980, the U.S. response to unaccompanied refugee minors evolved from a series of ad hoc, limited, specifically focused privately initiated and directed efforts into a more broadly conceived and institutionalized set of federal laws, policies, and programs. This complex and multivalent process was closely linked both to the growth of the federal government and to the emergence of an international consensus about the unique rights of both refugees and children during the 1970s and 80s. However, despite the prominent role of humanitarian organizations in establishing individual programs for unaccompanied refugee children, decisions about which boys and girls to admit and protect were consistently driven by a geopolitics of compassion that imagined these children as a tool of statecraft, whose admission to the United States advanced a range of foreign and domestic political objectives.

Beginning in 1934 when the small German Jewish Children's Aid (GJCA) society wrenched the first policy accommodations for unaccompanied refugee minors from a reluctant U.S. government, successive generations of child advocates, voluntary agency staff, and child welfare professionals argued that unaccompanied child refugees had a unique age-based claim on asylum as well as community (and later government) resources for their care. Impeded by America's racially restrictive immigration laws and pervasive anti-Semitism, the GJCA ultimately provided homes for a few hundred children fleeing Nazi terror. However, its well thought out operational model and the principles on which it rested would provide the foundation upon which subsequent wartime and postwar children's evacuation schemes spearheaded by the U.S. Committee for the Care of European Children (USCOM), the International Social Service, and other sectarian agencies would be built, while also raising for the first time the possibility of U.S. government involvement in facilitating the creation of programs to offer shelter to children at risk overseas.

During the World War II era, voluntary agencies driven by humanitarian aims as well as more pragmatic concerns collaborated and competed to bring Jewish, British, and other war-afflicted European children to the United States. Seeking to harmonize their ideals and interests with the nation's

The Origins of a Crisis

geopolitical and domestic political objectives, agencies walked a fine line in advocating for the admission of war-afflicted European children, regardless of their background, while avoiding openly criticizing the ethno-racial and religious boundaries of American humanitarian sentiment, the racialized logic of U.S. immigration law, and the assumption that refugee admissions should continue to be extremely limited. This led to practices of "collateral humanitarianism" through which voluntary-led programs succeeded in resettling a small but increasingly diverse group of endangered European children while simultaneously rendering themselves complicit with laws and policies that worked to actively exclude most other endangered children (and their parents) from the United States.

Voluntary initiatives were facilitated by successive administrations that understood the resettlement of small numbers of carefully selected endangered overseas children as a low-cost but high-impact means of placating powerful domestic lobbies and demonstrating political and moral solidarity with besieged allies. In the immediate postwar period, as the Cold War began to coalesce, the inclusion of "war orphans" in the 1948 Displaced Persons Act gave official form for the first time to an incipient notion of a state responsibility toward unaccompanied refugee minors, while creating new opportunities for the placement of a broader range of foreign-born children in American homes. These postwar efforts were supported by administrations that saw resettlement of unaccompanied children variously as a means of demonstrating the United States' humanitarian credentials and asserting the nation's political, economic, and moral superiority, as well as, in more practical terms, of providing material assistance to overburdened nations of first asylum in order to prevent economic and political instability that could open the door to Soviet influence or intervention. Official sanction for these voluntary resettlement efforts helped establish a new precedent within U.S. immigration policy for the provision of special treatment to unaccompanied refugee minors, regardless—at least in theory—of their racial, ethnic, or religious background.

At the same time, as early as 1950, these developments inspired a backlash as congressional defenders of the nation's prewar immigration laws worked to counter attempts by USCOM and its allies to define refugees and children's rights more broadly—in part by promoting intercountry adoptions from Europe and Asia as a way for Americans to "rescue" needy foreign boys and girls while growing their own families, at the same time as they imposed new restrictions on the admission of unaccompanied refugee minors. The growing popularity of intercountry adoption would encourage Americans to think of crisis-stricken developing nations as a source of "children on demand" while distracting them from more critical debates about their nation's obligation toward refugees of all ages.

By the midfifties, established voluntary agencies that harbored reservations about intercountry adoption were grappling with the sometimes-ambivalent outcome of their efforts, especially when this included separating children from living parents or relatives, and an awareness of the psychological and cultural impact of separation from home and homeland. Staff began to express quiet doubts about the efficacy and ethics of resettling endangered overseas children in the United States—and whether bringing them had really been in their best interests. They nonetheless remained convinced that resettlement in the United States remained a legitimate humanitarian strategy for responding to the needs of some endangered children. Voluntary agencies' continued belief in the legitimacy of resettlement and their continued willingness to work within the system would lay the groundwork for new Cold War–era collaborations between the federal government and voluntary agencies to facilitate the admission and care of displaced and endangered children to the United States. Beginning with Eisenhower's "crash" resettlement of anti-communist Hungarian escapees, the federal government played an increasingly proactive role initiating and, for the first time, funding the resettlement of Hungarian, Cuban, and later Southeast Asian children to the United States.

This new public-private model response to unaccompanied refugee minors emerged within the context of broader resettlement efforts seeking to repair credibility and secure goodwill for the United States following failed interventions (or the failure to effectively intervene) in local anti-communist uprisings in Hungary, Cuba, and Vietnam. The model also reflected new notions of children as the building blocks of democratic societies who needed to be protected from the ideological and spiritual threat of communism, as well as responded to pressure from powerful domestic lobbies that demanded the United States alleviate the suffering of groups of children who, by nature of their origins in Cold War battleground states, they had identified as uniquely deserving of American protection. These programs continued to provide, as in the World War II era, a source of particularly evocative public relations material; exploiting the propaganda value of images of suffering children redeemed by American benevolence, they worked to discredit the Soviet Union and confirm the moral superiority of American democratic capitalism.

As this public-private dynamic evolved, a growing number of federal officials and children's advocates began to question the efficacy of a refugee policy that effectively transferred the burden of implementing the nation's foreign policy onto the shoulders of private organizations and individuals. These debates reflected and reinforced a growing belief, first articulated by wartime child-saving activists, that the state's responsibility to displaced persons did not end with their admission to the United States. Together with the U.S. government's growing recognition of the importance of refugees to the nation's Cold War foreign policy goals, changing understandings of both refugees and children and their relationship to the state laid the groundwork, beginning in 1960, for the first-ever U.S. government–funded program for unaccompanied refugee minors.

The unprecedented and largely improvisational Cuban Children's Program marked a new stage in the deepening collaboration between governmental and nongovernmental actors in caring for unaccompanied refugee minors, accelerating the parallel expansion of federal funding and regulation of the nation's domestic child welfare system, and the institutionalization of programs for the care of unaccompanied refugee minors. Despite efforts by Republican president Gerald Ford to "walk back" the state's recently expanded commitment to refugee resettlement under the Cuban Refugee Program, a newly adversarial community of voluntary agency leaders and advocates maintained the federal government must provide similarly comprehensive benefits for the next generation of unaccompanied children as they had for Cuban children, leading to the establishment in 1979 of a similar program to provide federally funded foster care to unaccompanied Southeast Asian refugee minors—and then the following year, to the passage of a Refugee Act creating a permanent program to provide priority admission and federally funded foster care to unaccompanied refugee minors of all nationalities.

The culmination of a process that began in 1934 with private Jewish American child-saving efforts, the establishment of the new federal URM program codified for the first time an understanding of unaccompanied refugee minors as possessing a unique age-based claim on priority admission as well as the right to special forms of state-sponsored care and protection. But despite the 1980 Refugee Act's humanitarian aspirations, the geopolitics of compassion has continued to shape which children are seen as worthy of admission and protection in the United States. In fact, the differential treatment accorded to distinct groups of unaccompanied minors hardened in the eighties, as growing numbers of Mexican and Central American children began to seek security and opportunity in the United States. Since then, despite sustained legal advocacy seeking to bring the United States' treatment of unaccompanied minors into conformity with international law, the overwhelming majority of child migrants designated as "unaccompanied alien children" has continued to be confronted to an immigration enforcement regime that treats them first as illegal immigrants, and only secondarily as children.

Today's child migration crisis can be traced directly to the Refugee Act's failure to account for the possibility of a significant and unregulated flow of refugee seekers from south of the border—as well as to its failure to anticipate the presence of solo children among those fleeing north. However, the differential treatment of URM and UAC children that fueled the horrific expansion of a for-profit child detention industry in the United States is equally a product of Americans' deeply racialized ambivalence about unaccompanied child migrants. Whether demonized as juvenile delinquents, gang bangers, or "anchors," migrant youth from Latin American and the Caribbean, like European Jewish and Southeast Asian children before them, continue to be framed as a threat to the nation's political, economic, and cultural integrity by those who oppose their admission. This racial logic of deterrence once barred the nation's door to hundreds of thousands of children who later perished in the Holocaust. It is at the heart of the legal violence perpetuated today against tens of thousands of Central American and Mexican minors seeking asylum in the U.S. It is fundamental to a geopolitics of compassion that continues to value foreign policy and domestic political objectives above the welfare of endangered foreign-born children.

Epilogue

The Right to Have Rights? Migrant Children and the Geopolitics of Compassion in the Twenty-First Century

Since the 1930s, decisions about which unaccompanied minors are deemed worthy of admission to the United States have consistently prioritized the national interest over migrant children's welfare. This is the central argument I sought to make in this book. But there are a number of other trends in the history of unaccompanied child migration to the United States that merit a few final words of reflection.

First among these is the gap between the United States' self-ascribed identity as a supporter of human rights and its historic reluctance to embrace those ideals in practice. Since 1980, new laws have begun to articulate internationally accepted norms of refugees and children's rights. The United States nonetheless remains the only UN member nation to never ratify the 1989 Convention on the Rights of the Child. The corresponding unwillingness to codify a commitment to the best interests of children in immigration law is one of the reasons that the United States has lagged behind European nations in guaranteeing adequate protections to unaccompanied refugee minors and alien children.[1]

At the same time, the story of unaccompanied child migration told in this book also speaks to the limits of the law as the sole guarantor of rights. Since at least the 1930s, Americans' feelings of sympathy and obligation toward both refugees and endangered children have been at odds with their fears of foreign-born people's "otherness" and their purported negative political, economic, and cultural impact on U.S. society. Though infrequently acknowledged (especially by more progressive Americans), this persistent and racialized ambivalence has shaped the way laws and policies have been written and implemented. In a country with an immigration system as fragmented and decentralized as the United States, this has allowed individual government officials to exercise an extraordinary level of discretionary power over the fate of unaccompanied refugee minors and alien children. In the past, the most dramatic examples of this were a string of successive presidents who between 1960 and 1980 bypassed Congress to parole millions of anti-communist escapees into the country. In the present, an equally life-and-death power resides in the hands of frontline Custom and Border Protection (CBP) and Border Patrol officers who frequently choose to defy federal law and policies that guarantee unaccompanied alien children (UACs) access to a fair and age-appropriate asylum adjudication process.

Equally deserving of reflection is the extent to which intersecting notions of race, class, national origin, religion, gender, and age have influenced public opinion as well as the way that decision makers understood the foreign policy and domestic political stakes involved in admitting or excluding particular groups of children to the United States. Time and time again, children's racial, religious, and national identities have worked together to draw lines between those who were admitted for resettlement as refugees, those who were adopted, and those who were excluded. Even after the 1980 Refugee Act ostensibly extended the right to protection from persecution regardless of origins, notions of race in particular would continue to limit Americans' sense of obligation to children migrating alone from poor, nonwhite nations. In the decades to come, an equally racialized logic of deterrence motivated a growing number of immigration officials to seek out administrative methods of preventing the admission of unaccompanied Vietnamese, Haitian, Central American, and Mexican minors who they saw—as their restrictionist colleagues in the 1930s had seen Jewish children—as "anchors" and a threat to the nation's economy and social fabric. And even when geopolitical or domestic political interests trumped these biases to allow for the admission of "less desirable" children, finding homes for the nonwhite and non-Christian minors, and especially those who were also adolescent boys, has remained difficult. At the same time, decisions made by voluntary agency personnel about children's best interests—including whether to place them in homes that would facilitate their swift "Americanization" or provide living arrangements that preserved children's cultural and linguistic heritage—were also influenced by the diverse meanings that voluntary agency personnel ascribed to children's race, national origin, and religion.

On an even more fundamental level, the story of the unaccompanied refugee minors and alien children admitted to the United States compels us to think more deeply about who and what we imagine children to be. For many, the symbolic figure of the child carries deep emotional and moral resonance. But the seemingly universal notions of children (and refugees) as innocent, passive, and dependent that continue to inform much legal and humanitarian advocacy today fail to account for the experiences of most displaced young people, who before their displacement often played an active role in the political, economic, and social lives of their families and communities. These middle-class and western-centric constructions of childhood also fail to recognize the developmental differences and distinct welfare needs of younger and older children who, though still vulnerable to exploitation and abuse by adults, also exercise a much greater degree of agency.[2]

The tendency to imagine all children as a single undifferentiated group helps explain why successive generations of mostly teenaged Jewish, Hungarian, Cuban, and Southeast Asian URMs repeatedly confounded American expectations that they (like refugees of all ages) would be passive and grateful beneficiaries of American benevolence. The majority-adolescent UACs who have arrived in ever-greater numbers since 1980 departed even further from those expectations, simultaneously challenging the belief that children should wait patiently to be rescued by adults and refugees should languish in overseas camps until selected for admission. In the eyes of far too many people, Mexican and Central American minors' desperate attempts to save their own lives—evidence of the grave protection deficits that force many UACs to flee their home countries—render them ineligible for the sympathy reserved for "innocent victims," transforming them instead into deviants and criminals.

Children's advocates since the 1930s have nonetheless consistently made use of stories and images of victimized tender-age children in order to counter anti-immigrant and refugee sentiment and advance all minors' claims on admission and protection. The short-term value of this strategy is obvious: however, the sensationalist representations of displaced and suffering babies and toddlers favored by humanitarian organizations and progressives actually serve to undermine children's right to international protection in the long run. By reinforcing normative assumptions of childhood as a time of innocence and dependence, the representations further obscure and even pathologize the more complex identities, experiences, and vulnerabilities of the older children who make up the majority of the URM and UAC populations. They also provide ongoing justification for restrictionist efforts to limit minors' access to asylum, which continues to be framed in adult-centric terms. Those who insist on viewing all children as innocent victims are less likely to imagine that older youth might be persecuted for their political activities or targeted for specific rights violations—whether forced labor, sexual exploitation, or conscription into the military or criminal gangs—precisely because of their membership in a particular (age-based) social group. According to this logic, the abuse or exploitation of children, regardless of context, remains a national child welfare problem rather than an international protection issue.[3]

Perhaps most fundamentally, the story of unaccompanied child migration to the United States since the 1930s compels Americans to confront our ongoing failure to treat unaccompanied migrant children as individual rights-bearing subjects. From the FDR era to the present day—even after the explicit codification of children's individual human rights in international law in the 1980s—decision-making about unaccompanied minors has been driven by an understanding of children as an extension of their parents and communities. This has sometimes served to privilege the admission of certain groups of children when Americans wished to demonstrate solidarity or provide material aid to their parents or nations of origin. But in many other cases, it has worked to the detriment of children from poor and nonwhite nations, whose asylum claims were adjudicated not in terms of their individual circumstances or needs but rather in light of broader implications for refugee and immigrant flows from their homelands. This implicit denial of children's individual existence was at the heart of the racialized logic of deterrence that justified the decision to bar most endangered Jewish children from the prewar United States. It was also reflected in provisions of the 1948 Displaced Persons and 1982 Amerasian Immigration Acts that forced European "half-orphans" and the children of American GIs and Southeast Asian mothers to choose between lives of deprivation in their homelands or migrating to the United States alone. In more recent years, the persistent denial of children's individual rights has inspired a growing number of immigration officials to work to undercut unaccompanied Southeast Asian, Haitian, Central American, and Mexican minors' access to asylum, despite indisputable evidence of their acute need for protection.

It is clear that the United States needs to adopt a more consistent, more nuanced, and more rights-based approach to the growing phenomenon of unaccompanied child migration. As a nation, we need to craft a response that accounts for the nation's geopolitical and domestic political interests but balances them more compassionately with the best interests of children. But how?

Of course, we could begin by faithfully implementing the laws and policies already on the books. But that won't be enough. Broader reform will also be necessary, beginning with legislation to address two pressing deficiencies in current immigration law. First, despite the chaos surrounding the Mariel boatlift and the prolonged influx of Central American asylum seekers—both of which date back more than forty years—the United States still lacks an effective legal and logistical infrastructure for serving as a nation of mass first asylum. Second, we have yet to explicitly codify the internationally accepted principle of children's best interests in U.S. immigration law.[4] Because children who cross borders alone are in fact both individuals *and* members of communities, both of these omissions must be addressed.

We could begin to remedy the first by reserving a significant proportion of annual refugee allotments to those fleeing contiguous and nearby Latin American and Caribbean nations, as well as refugees from countries where U.S. intervention played a role in creating human rights violations and displacement. We also need to update the way we understand who has a valid claim on international protection. Whether applied to children or adults, our current statutory definition of refugees fails to take into consideration the multiple and intertwined political, economic, social, and environmental factors that cause people to cross borders in fear for their lives. A refugee policy for our new millennium should move beyond its Cold War preoccupation with political persecution to recognize the broader range of basic human rights deprivations that threaten human survival.[5]

There is both an ethical imperative and a pragmatic argument to be made for these actions. Since so much migration to the United States has been produced or exacerbated by our proximity to (and asymmetrical relations with) developing nations—particularly south of our border—it stands to reason that many of these migrants could be more efficiently and humanely processed through an expanded refugee resettlement program than through our expensive, inhumane, and ineffective immigration enforcement regime. After all, as recent history has made clear, refusing to acknowledge persistent political, economic, and social crises in our own hemisphere will not stop Latin American and Caribbean people of all ages from seeking asylum in the United States. As long as we continue to deny the existence of significant numbers of refugees among those labelled as "illegal" economic migrants, attempts to address the structural problem of unauthorized immigration will continue to fail—as will our overburdened asylum process. The result will be additional human suffering, billions more taxpayer dollars wasted on fruitless efforts to "secure the border," and further damage to our democratic and humanitarian ideals.

We also need to update our laws to bring treatment of unaccompanied migrant children more closely in line with international norms. Procedures that protect the human rights of unaccompanied minors can no longer be left to the discretion of individual immigration officers or judges; they need to be explicitly codified. As part of these reforms, just as U.S. law usually permits adult refugees and asylees to bring their spouses and dependent children with them, the parents, customary caretakers, and immediate family members of unaccompanied refugee minors and UACs who are granted asylum should also be admitted to the United States.

But just writing these provisions into law isn't enough. In order to ensure that new legal protections are rigorously enforced, we will need to mandate and fund an independent oversight agency that closely monitors detained children in federal custody. Consequences for failures to comply with standards and procedures encoded in the law should also be clearly articulated. At the same time, federal funding and other forms of support should be provided to promote the efforts of legal advocates and grassroots activists who play a significant role identifying violations of unaccompanied migrant children's rights and addressing them through the courts. Scholars, journalists, and other community leaders also have an important role to play. We need to address public misperceptions about unaccompanied migrant children and combat misinformation about their criminality and role as "anchors." It falls on us to lead our fellow citizens in critically reassessing our mythological belief in the United States as a historic haven for the oppressed. We need to confront the truth that to the extent that our country has established a humanitarian tradition of welcoming those forced to flee, it has been largely—in the words of Congresswoman Elizabeth Holtzman—"in spite of, not because of our laws relating to refugees."[6] We need to confront head-on our historical opposition to the admission of refugees and immigrants of all ages and commit to overcoming the racial, ethnic, and religious biases that have undergirded that opposition.[7]

Crafting a humane and effective response to the issue of unaccompanied child migration will require a sustained process of political and legal advocacy and grassroots social activism. Like all struggles to advance human rights, it promises to be a long and arduous one. However, those who wish to participate can find inspiration in the example of the diverse coalition of undocumented youth and their allies who since the late 1990s have drawn upon their multiple intersectional identities to build new alliances with other marginalized U.S. communities in combating legal violence against immigrants, people of color, and the LGBTQ community.[8] Following their lead, we can work together to promote the best interests of unaccompanied migrant children and demand they no longer be subsumed to our nation's geopolitical and domestic political interests. We can aspire to a future in which our national response to refugees and unaccompanied migrant children alike will be informed not by our selective and ephemeral sympathies, but by a shared commitment to justice.

NOTES

INTRODUCTION

1. Historians have no way of estimating how many thousands of unaccompanied children have migrated to the United States throughout the nation's history. Their numbers are unknown for many reasons: because of the paucity of immigration record keeping before the twentieth century, because many entered without official inspection, and because of shifting definitions of who has counted as a "child" at different moments in time. Kidnapped African children, legally classified as imported property rather than as immigrants, represent this most vivid example of the erasure of unaccompanied child migration from U.S. history; traces of their existence nonetheless appear in scholarly literature. See Paula S. Fass, "Children in Global Migrations," *Journal of Social History* 38, no. 4 (Summer 2005): 937–53; Gwyn Campbell, Suzanne Miers, and Joseph Calder Miller, eds., *Children in Slavery Through the Ages* (Athens: Ohio University Press, 2009); Farley Grubb, "Babes in Bondage? Debt Shifting by German Immigrants in Early America," *Journal of Interdisciplinary History* 37, no. 1 (Summer 2006): 1–34; Madeline Hsu, "Gold Mountain Dreams and Paper Son Schemes: Chinese Immigration Under Exclusion," *Chinese America: History and Perspectives* 11 (1997): 46–60; Barry Moreno, *Children of Ellis Island* (Charleston, S.C.: Arcadia Publishing, 2005); and Yolanda Chávez Leyva, "'¿Qué Son Los Niños?': Mexican Children along the U.S.-Mexico Border, 1880–1930," (PhD. diss., University of Arizona, 1999).

2. Legal scholars and social scientists have been at the forefront of analyzing the phenomenon of unaccompanied child migration to the United States; leading examples include Jacqueline Bhabha, *Child Migration and Human Rights in a Global Age* (Princeton, N.J.: Princeton University Press, 2014); Susan J. Terrio, *Whose Child Am I? Unaccompanied, Undocumented Children in U.S. Immigration Custody* (Berkeley: University of California Press, 2015). However, this work is overwhelmingly focused on the contemporary period. The few dedicated historical studies of unaccompanied child migration to the United States include Judith Tydor Baumel, *Unfulfilled Promise: Rescue and Resettlement of Jewish Refugee Children in the United States, 1934–1945* (Juneau, Alaska: Denali Press, 1990); Lynne Taylor, *In the Children's Best Interests: Unaccompanied Children in American-Occupied Germany, 1945–1952* (Toronto, Ont.: University of Toronto Press, 2017); María de los Angeles Torres, *The Lost Apple: Operation Pedro Pan, Cuban Children in the U.S., and the Promise of a Better Future* (Boston: Beacon Press, 2004); as well as Sabrina Thomas, *The Scars of War: The Politics of Paternity and National Responsibility for the Amerasians of Vietnam* (Lincoln: University of

Nebraska Press, 2020). But these books all focus on one specific historical moment or group of unaccompanied children.

3. Although they don't address unaccompanied child migration, historians widely recognize that foreign policy and domestic political objectives have shaped U.S. refugee policy more than humanitarian considerations. See Gil Loescher and John A. Scanlan, *Calculated Kindness: Refugees and America's Half-Open Door, 1945 to the Present* (New York: Free Press, 1986); Carl J. Bon Tempo, *Americans at the Gate: The United States and Refugees during the Cold War* (Princeton, N.J.: Princeton University Press, 2008); and Stephen R. Porter, *Benevolent Empire: U.S. Power, Humanitarianism, and the World's Dispossessed* (Philadelphia: University of Pennsylvania Press, 2017). "New" diplomatic histories that have explored the dynamic relationships between foreign policy objectives and the reception of immigrants in U.S. history, as well as the role of "everyday citizens," including women, children, and people of color in international relations, include Matthew Frye Jacobson, *Barbarian Virtues: The United States Encounters Foreign Peoples at Home and Abroad, 1876–1917* (New York: Hill and Wang, 2000); Amy Kaplan, *The Anarchy of Empire and the Making of U.S. Culture* (Cambridge, Mass.: Harvard University Press, 2002); and Emily S. Rosenberg and Shanon Fitzpatrick, eds., *Body and Nation: The Global Realm of U.S. Body Politics in the Twentieth Century* (Durham, N.C.: Duke University Press, 2014). Scholars that have advanced our understanding of young people's centrality to national life and of the evolving relationship between the American state and children include Paula S. Fass, *Children of a New World: Society, Culture, and Globalization* (New York: New York University Press, 2007); Helen Brocklehurst, *Who's Afraid of Children? Children, Conflict and International Relations* (New York: Routledge, 2006); Catherine E. Rymph, *Raising Government Children: A History of Foster Care and the American Welfare State* (Chapel Hill: University of North Carolina Press, 2017); Alice Boardman Smuts, *Science in the Service of Children, 1893–1935* (New Haven, Conn.: Yale University Press, 2006); and Geoff K. Ward, *The Black Child-Savers: Racial Democracy and Juvenile Justice* (Chicago: University of Chicago Press, 2012). But none have explicitly addressed how unaccompanied migrant children fit into these historical processes.

4. Jacqueline Bhabha and Susan Schmidt, "Seeking Asylum Alone: Unaccompanied and Separated Children and Refugee Protection in the U.S.," *Journal of the History of Childhood and Youth* 1, no. 1 (Winter 2008): 126–38. Most of the available archival records deal with "refugee" children brought to the United States through earlier privately led programs. There is very little data available on unaccompanied minor asylum seekers before 2001, when the UNHCR began collecting annual statistics on these children in developed countries. But because of U.S. reticence to share what little information is gathered here, the UN does not collect data on underage asylum seekers arriving at U.S. borders.

5. See Theda Skocpol, *Social Policy in the United States: Future Possibilities in Historical Perspective* (Princeton, N.J.: Princeton University Press, 1995), 167–68; Phil Orchard, *The Right to Flee: Refugees, States, and the Construction of International Cooperation* (Cambridge: Cambridge University Press, 2014), 201–2.

6. Loescher and Scanlan, *Calculated Kindness*; Bon Tempo, *Americans at the Gate*.

7. David Scott FitzGerald, *Refuge Beyond Reach: How Rich Democracies Repel Asylum Seekers* (New York: Oxford University Press, 2019), 1.

8. Justin Hart, *Empire of Ideas: The Origins of Public Diplomacy and the Transformation of U.S. Foreign Policy* (New York: Oxford University Press, 2013), 14.

9. See Brian Balogh, *The Associational State: American Governance in the Twentieth Century* (Philadelphia: University of Pennsylvania Press, 2015); Paul Pierson, *Politics in Time: History,*

Institutions, and Social Analysis (Princeton, N.J.: Princeton University Press, 2004); William J. Novak, *The People's Welfare: Law and Regulation in Nineteenth-Century America* (Chapel Hill: University of North Carolina Press, 1996); Margot Canaday, *The Straight State: Sexuality and Citizenship in Twentieth-Century America* (Princeton, N.J.: Princeton University Press, 2009); and Laura Nader, "Up the Anthropologist: Perspectives Gained from Studying Up," in *Reinventing Anthropology*, ed. Dell Hymes (New York: Pantheon Books, 1972), 284–311.

10. Wendy Brown, *States of Injury: Power and Freedom in Late Modernity* (Princeton, N.J.: Princeton University Press, 1995), 174–75.

11. Adam B. Cox and Cristina M. Rodríguez, *The President and Immigration Law* (New York: Oxford University Press, 2020), 44–46; Phil Orchard and Jamie Gillies, "Atypical Leadership: The Role of the Presidency and Refugee Protection, 1932–1952," *Presidential Studies Quarterly* 45, no. 3 (September 2015): 491.

12. Balogh, *The Associational State*, 8–11.

13. Porter, *Benevolent Empire*, 3.

14. David Kennedy, *The Dark Sides of Virtue: Reassessing International Humanitarianism* (Princeton, N.J.: Princeton University Press, 2005), xviii.

15. Joshua W. Busby, *Moral Movements and Foreign Policy* (Cambridge: Cambridge University Press, 2010), 1–16.

16. Michael Barnett, *Empire of Humanity: A History of Humanitarianism* (Ithaca, N.Y.: Cornell University Press, 2011), 132.

17. Rachel M. McCleary, *Global Compassion: Private Voluntary Organizations and U.S. Foreign Policy Since 1939* (New York: Oxford University Press, 2009), 80.

18. Paul Ginsborg, *Family Politics: Domestic Life, Devastation and Survival, 1900–1950* (New Haven, Conn.: Yale University Press, 2014), xiii; see also Elaine Tyler May, *Homeward Bound: American Families in the Cold War Era*, rev. ed. (New York: Basic Books, 2008).

19. "What is a Refugee?," UNHCR, accessed January 20, 2021, https://www.unhcr.org/what-is-a-refugee.html; see also David Scott FitzGerald and Rawan Arar, "The Sociology of Refugee Migration," *Annual Review of Sociology* 44 (2018): 389.

20. Phuong Tran Nguyen, *Becoming Refugee American: The Politics of Rescue in Little Saigon* (Urbana: University of Illinois Press, 2017), 5.

21. Yến Lê Espiritu, *Body Counts: The Vietnam War and Militarized Refuge(es)* (Berkeley: University of California Press, 2014), 3–7.

22. Tara Zahra, *The Lost Children: Reconstructing Europe's Families After World War II* (Cambridge, Mass.: Harvard University Press, 2011); Bruno Cabanes, *The Great War and the Origins of Humanitarianism, 1918–1924* (Cambridge: Cambridge University Press, 2014); Barbara Beatty and Julia Grant, "Entering into the Fray: Historians of Childhood and Public Policy," *Journal of the History of Childhood and Youth* 3, no. 1 (Winter 2010): 107–26; and Viviana A. Zelizer, *Pricing the Priceless Child: The Changing Social Value of Children* (Princeton, N.J.: Princeton University Press, 1994).

23. Laura Briggs, *Somebody's Children: The Politics of Transracial and Transnational Adoption* (Durham, N.C.: Duke University Press, 2012), 132–33.

24. Briggs, *Somebody's Children*, 132–35; Heather Marie Stur, *Beyond Combat: Women and Gender in the Vietnam War* (New York: Cambridge University Press, 2011), 142–82; Jana K. Lipman, "A Refugee Camp in America: Fort Chaffee and Vietnamese and Cuban Refugees, 1975–1982," *Journal of American Ethnic History* 33, no. 2 (Winter 2014): 63; see also Louis A. Pérez Jr., *Cuba in the American Imagination: Metaphor and the Imperial Ethos* (Chapel Hill: University of North Carolina Press, 2008).

25. Bhabha, *Child Migration and Human Rights*, 3.

26. Paula S. Fass, ed., *The Routledge History of Childhood in the Western World* (Oxford, U.K.: Routledge, 2013), 8; Elliot West and Paula Petrik, eds., *Small Worlds: Children and Adolescents in America, 1850–1950* (Lawrence: University of Kansas Press, 1992); Barrie Thorne, "Re-Visioning Women and Social Change: Where Are the Children?" *Gender and Society* 1, no. 1 (March 1987): 85–109. See also Peter N. Stearns, *Childhood in World History*, 3rd ed. (New York: Routledge, 2016) and Bianca Premo, "How Latin America's History of Childhood Came of Age," *Journal of the History of Childhood and Youth* 1, no. 1 (Winter 2008): 63–76.

CHAPTER 1

1. Richard Breitman and Alan M. Kraut, *American Refugee Policy and European Jewry, 1933–1945* (Bloomington: Indiana University Press, 1987), 12–13.

2. Phil Orchard and Jamie Gillies, "Atypical Leadership: The Role of the Presidency and Refugee Protection, 1932–1952," *Presidential Studies Quarterly* 45, no. 3 (September 2015): 498.

3. Bat-Ami Zucker, *In Search of Refuge: Jews and US Consuls in Nazi Germany, 1933–1941* (London: Vallentine Mitchell, 2001), 50.

4. Breitman and Kraut, *American Refugee Policy*, 11–12.

5. Breitman and Kraut, *American Refugee Policy*, 12.

6. Breitman and Kraut, *American Refugee Policy*, 12–18; Zucker, *In Search of Refuge*, 51–52. This reluctance to intervene in German affairs was echoed by the governments of Britain, France, and other League of Nations members, who similarly declined to take action in support of German refugees for fear of antagonizing the Nazi government. See Claudena M. Skran, *Refugees in Inter-War Europe: The Emergence of a Regime* (Oxford, U.K.: Clarendon Press, 1995); and Ari J. Sherman, *Island Refuge: Britain and Refugees from the Third Reich, 1933–1939* (Berkeley: University of California Press, 1973).

7. Ruth Ellen Wasem, "Immigration Governance for the Twenty-First Century," *Journal on Migration and Human Security* 6, no. 1 (2018): 101; Bat-Ami Zucker, "Frances Perkins and the German-Jewish Refugees, 1933–1940," *American Jewish History* 89, no. 1 (March 2001): 35–59; Breitman and Kraut, *American Refugee Policy*.

8. Richard Breitman and Allan J. Lichtman, *FDR and the Jews* (Cambridge, Mass.: Harvard University Press, 2013), 68–69.

9. Judith Tydor Baumel-Schwartz, "Jewish Refugee Children in the USA (1934–45): Flight, Resettlement, Absorption," in *The Young Victims of the Nazi Regime: Migration, the Holocaust and Postwar Displacement*, eds. Simone Gigliotti and Monica Tempian (London: Bloomsbury Publishing, 2016), 16.

10. Judith Tydor Baumel, *Unfulfilled Promise: Rescue and Resettlement of Jewish Refugee Children in the United States, 1934–1945* (Juneau, Alaska: Denali Press, 1990), 16.

11. Laura Briggs, *Somebody's Children: The Politics of Transracial and Transnational Adoption* (Durham, N.C.: Duke University Press, 2012), 133.

12. Michal Ostrovsky, "'Children Knocking at our Gates': The Activities of the German Jewish Children's Aid, 1933–39," *Journal of Jewish Studies* 66, no. 2 (2015): 387–411; and Baumel, *Unfulfilled Promise*, 13–14.

13. Elizabeth J. Clapp, *Mothers of All Children: Women Reformers and the Rise of Juvenile Courts in Progressive Era America* (University Park, Pa.: Penn State University Press, 1998); Anthony M. Platt, *The Child Savers: The Invention of Delinquency*, exp. 40th ann. ed. (New

Brunswick, N.J.: Rutgers University Press, 2009); and Geoff K. Ward, *The Black Child-Savers: Racial Democracy and Juvenile Justice* (Chicago: University of Chicago Press, 2012).

14. U.S. Congress, "An Act to Regulate the Immigration of Aliens To, And the Residence of Aliens In, The United States," *U.S. Statutes at Large, Volume 39 (1915–1916), 64th Congress.* H.R. 10384, no. 301, at 876 (February 5, 1917) https://www.loc.gov/item/llsl-v39; Max J. Kohler, *Immigration and Aliens in the United States: Studies of American Immigration Laws and the Legal Status of Aliens in the United States* (New York: Bloch Publishing Company, 1936), 57–58; Barry Moreno, *Children of Ellis Island* (Charleston, S.C.: Arcadia Publishing, 2005), 25–27; Baumel, *Unfulfilled Promise*, 11.

15. Breitman and Kraut, *American Refugee Policy*, 18–19, 23.

16. Biographical Note, *Papers of Cecilia Razovsky (1886–1968)*, undated, 1913–1971, P-290, American Jewish Historical Society, http://digifindingaids.cjh.org/?pID=109184.

17. Baumel-Schwartz, "Jewish Refugee Children," 22; and Baumel, *Unfulfilled Promise*, 17–18.

18. Baumel, *Unfulfilled Promise*, 17–18.

19. Baumel-Schwartz, "Jewish Refugee Children," 13, 20.

20. Breitman and Kraut, *American Refugee Policy*, 25; Baumel, *Unfulfilled Promise*, 19.

21. Andrea Hammel, "The Kinder's Children: Second Generation and the Kindertransport," in *The Young Victims of the Nazi Regime: Migration, the Holocaust and Postwar Displacement*, eds. Simone Gigliotti and Monica Tempian (London: Bloomsbury Publishing, 2016), 240–41.

22. Baumel-Schwartz, "Jewish Refugee Children," 13–14, 24; Baumel, *Unfulfilled Promise*, 19.

23. Breitman and Kraut, *American Refugee Policy*, 18–19, 25; Baumel, *Unfulfilled Promise*, 19.

24. Saul Friedländer, *Nazi Germany and the Jews, 1933–1945* (New York: Harper Collins, 2009), 50.

25. Breitman and Kraut, *American Refugee Policy*, 26–27.

26. Tara Zahra, *The Lost Children: Reconstructing Europe's Families After World War Two* (Cambridge, Mass.: Harvard University Press, 2011), 71, 73.

27. Zahra, *The Lost Children*, 62, 84.

28. Zahra, *The Lost Children*, 68.

29. Baumel-Schwartz, "Jewish Refugee Children," 14, 18; Breitman and Lichtman, *FDR and the Jews*, 147.

30. Frank Caestecker and Bob Moore, *Refugees from Nazi Germany and the Liberal European States* (New York: Berghahn Books, 2010), 245.

31. Timothy Snyder, *Black Earth: The Holocaust as History and Warning* (New York: Crown Publishing Group, 2015), 77–81; Martin Gilbert, *Kristallnacht: Prelude to Destruction* (London: HarperCollins, 2006), 13–14, 30–33.

32. Alan E. Steinweis, "The Trials of Herschel Grynszpan: Anti-Jewish Policy and German Propaganda, 1938–1942," *German Studies Review* 31, no. 3 (October 2008): 471–88; Gerald Schwab, *The Day the Holocaust Began: The Odyssey of Herschel Grynszpan* (New York: Praeger, 1990).

33. David S. Wyman, *Paper Walls: America and the Refugee Crisis, 1938–1941* (Amherst: University of Massachusetts Press, 1968), 74, 80.

34. Breitman and Lichtman, *FDR and the Jews*, 114.

35. Breitman and Kraut, *American Refugee Policy*, 62.

36. Breitman and Lichtman, *FDR and the Jews*, 114.

37. Breitman and Kraut, *American Refugee Policy*, 63–66.

38. Hammel, "The Kinder's Children," 240–41.

39. Baumel, *Unfulfilled Promise*, 20.

40. Breitman and Lichtman, *FDR and the Jews*, 147; Baumel, *Unfulfilled Promise*, 23.

41. Breitman and Kraut, *American Refugee Policy*, 62.

42. Briggs, *Somebody's Children*, 142–43.

43. Susan S. Forbes and Patricia Weiss Fagen, "Unaccompanied Refugee Children: The Evolution of U.S. Policies—1939 to 1984," (Washington, D.C.: Refugee Policy Group, August 1984), 3.

44. Breitman and Lichtman, *FDR and the Jews*, 147.

45. Breitman and Lichtman, *FDR and the Jews*, 147–48.

46. Daniel J. Steinbock, "The Admission of Unaccompanied Children into the United States," *Yale Law and Policy Review* 7, no. 1 (1989): 146.

47. Wyman, *Paper Walls*, 75.

48. Breitman and Kraut, *American Refugee Policy*, 73.

49. Breitman and Lichtman, *FDR and the Jews*, 149.

50. Breitman and Lichtman, *FDR and the Jews*, 149.

51. "Wagner-Rogers Bill," Holocaust Encyclopedia, United States Holocaust Museum, accessed February 8, 2018, https://encyclopedia.ushmm.org/content/en/article/wagner-rogers-bill.

52. "Hoover Backs Bill to Waive Quota Act for Reich Children," *New York Times*, April 23, 1939; quoted in Briggs, *Somebody's Children*, 6.

53. Breitman and Kraut, *American Refugee Policy*, 73.

54. Steinbock, "The Admission of Unaccompanied Children," 147.

55. Breitman and Kraut, *American Refugee Policy*, 74.

56. Briggs, *Somebody's Children*, 149.

57. Forbes and Fagen, "Unaccompanied Refugee Children," 6.

58. Zahra, *The Lost Children*, 70.

59. Breitman and Kraut, *American Refugee Policy*, 73.

60. Briggs, *Somebody's Children*, 147.

61. Gilbert Kraus to George Messerschmidt, assistant secretary of state, February 3, 1939, Decimal File 150.6265/610, RG-59, General Records of the Department of State, National Archives and Records Administration.

62. Philip K. Jason and Iris Posner, eds., *Don't Wave Goodbye: The Children's Flight from Nazi Persecution to American Freedom* (Westport, Conn.: Praeger, 2004), 17–18.

63. Patricia Heberer, ed., *Children During the Holocaust (Documenting Life and Destruction: Holocaust Sources in Context)* (Lanham, Md.: AltaMira Press in association with the United States Holocaust Memorial Museum, 2011), 364–65.

64. "Fifty German-Jewish Refugee Children," *Jewish Exponent*, June 9, 1939; Breitman and Kraut, *American Refugee Policy*, 107.

65. Michael H. Hunt, *The American Ascendancy: How the United States Gained and Wielded Global Dominance* (Chapel Hill: University of North Carolina Press, 2007), 120.

66. Breitman and Kraut, *American Refugee Policy*, 73.

67. "300 Cross Battle Zone: Spanish Rebels Said to Have Sent Refugees Into 'No Man's Land,'" *New York Times*, February 14, 1937, 34; and "Basques Halt Foe in Attack on Eibar," *New York Times*, April 18, 1937, 1.

68. Susanna Sabín Fernández, *The Niños Vascos of 1937 (UK)* (Bilbao, Sp.: Central de Publicaciones Euskal Herria, 2011), 65; see also "Dorothy Thompson," *Encyclopædia Britannica*, last modified July 5, 2021, https://www.britannica.com/biography/Dorothy-Thompson.

69. Eric R. Smith, *American Relief Aid and the Spanish Civil War* (Columbia: University of Missouri Press, 2013), 2–3, 126.

70. Donald F. Crosby, "Boston's Catholics and the Spanish Civil War: 1936–1939," *New England Quarterly* 44, no. 1 (March 1971): 83, 85–86; Smith, *American Relief Aid*, 79–80, 83–84.

71. Hunt, *The American Ascendancy*, 100–101; Smith, *American Relief Aid*, 80–89, 109–11, 126.

72. Martin Blinkhorn, *Democracy and Civil War in Spain 1931–1939* (London: Routledge, 1992), 48; George A. Finch, "The United States and the Spanish Civil War," *American Journal of International Law*, 31 no. 1 (January 1937): 74–75, 77–78; see also Hugh Thomas, *The Spanish Civil War*, rev. ed. (New York: Modern Library, 2001); Helen Graham, *The Spanish Republic at War, 1936–1939* (Cambridge: Cambridge University Press, 2003); Sabín Fernández, *The Niños Vascos*, 58.

73. Sabín Fernández, *The Niños Vascos*, 67; see also Marie José Devillard, Álvaro Pazos, Susana Castillo, and Nuria Medina, *Los Niños Españoles en la URSS (1937–1997): Narración y Memoria* (Barcelona: Editorial Ariel, 2001).

74. Graham, *The Spanish Republic at War*, 253; see also Gregorio Arrien, *La Generación del exilio: Genesis de las Escuelas Vascas y las Colonias Escolares 1932–1940* (Bilbao, Sp.: Colectivo Pedagógico Oruna, 1983).

75. "Washington May Admit 500 Basque Children on Visitors' Visas Granting Six-Month Stays," *New York Times*, May 22, 1937, 3; and "U.S. Visas Asked for 500 Refugee Children," *Washington Post*, May 22, 1937, 1.

76. "Washington May Admit 500 Basque Children," 3.

77. "U.S. Visas," 1.

78. Sabín Fernández, *The Niños Vascos*, 3; "U.S. Visas," 1.

79. "The Exile of the Children," *New York Times*, May 26, 1937, 24.

80. Crosby, "Boston's Catholics," 97; William V. Nessly, "Catholic Leaders in Massachusetts Protest Refuge Plan," *Washington Post*, May 26, 1937, 1.

81. Nessly, "Catholic Leaders in Massachusetts," 1.

82. Crosby, "Boston's Catholics," 97.

83. See Richard M. Linkh, *American Catholicism and European Immigrants, 1900–1924* (New York: Center for Migration Studies, 1974); James T. Fisher, *Communion of Immigrants: A History of Catholics in America* (New York: Oxford University Press, 2000); and John T. McGreevy, *Parish Boundaries: The Catholic Encounter with Race in the Twentieth Century Urban North* (Chicago: University of Chicago Press, 1996).

84. See David R. Roediger, *Working Toward Whiteness: How America's Immigrants Became White; The Strange Journey from Ellis Island to the Suburbs* (New York: Basic Books, 2005); and Matthew Frye Jacobson, *Whiteness of a Different Color: European Immigrants and the Alchemy of Race* (Cambridge, Mass.: Harvard University Press, 1999).

85. See Noel Ignatiev, *How the Irish Became White* (New York: Routledge Classics, 2009); see also Roberto R. Treviño, *The Church in the Barrio: Mexican American Ethno-Catholicism in Houston* (Chapel Hill: University of North Carolina Press, 2006); Jay P. Dolan and Gilberto Hinojosa, eds., *Mexican Americans and the Catholic Church, 1900–1965*, vol. 1 and Jay P. Dolan and Allan Figueroa Deck, eds., *Hispanic Catholic Culture in the U.S.: Issues and Concerns*, vol. 3 of *The Notre Dame History of Hispanic Catholics in the U.S.* (Notre Dame, Ind.: University of Notre Dame Press, 1994).

86. Fernando Molina, "Lies of our Fathers: Memory and Politics in the Basque Country Under the Franco Dictatorship, 1936–68," *Journal of Contemporary History* 49, no. 2 (April 2014): 297.

87. Gloria Totoricagüena, "Historical Aspects to Political Identity in the New York Basque Community," Euskonews & Media, December 12–19, 2003, http://www.euskonews .eus/0234zbk/kosmo23402.html.

88. "Fund for Basques Sought: $500,000 to Be Sought Here to Aid Child Refugees," *New York Times*, June 26, 1937, 6.

89. Dorothy Legaretta, *The Guernica Generation: Basque Refugee Children of the Spanish Civil War* (Reno: University of Nevada Press, 1985).

90. Jennie N. Haxton, "What is Being Done for Refugee Children?" *Childhood Education* 17, no. 3 (1940): 132.

CHAPTER 2

1. Ruth Inglis, *The Children's War: Evacuation 1939–1945* (London: William Collins Sons & Co. Ltd., 1989), 106.

2. Carlton Jackson, *Who Will Take Our Children?* (London: Methuen London Ltd., 1985), xiv.

3. Martin Parsons and Penny Starns, *The Evacuation: The True Story* (London: BBC/ DSM, 1999), 50.

4. Parsons and Starns, *The Evacuation*, 76.

5. Keith Parker, "British Evacuees in America During World War II," *Journal of American Culture* 17, no. 4 (December 1994): 34.

6. Parker, "British Evacuees," 34; Jackson, *Who Will Take Our Children?*, 76.

7. Bess Goodykoontz, "Our Guest Children from Europe," *The Education Digest* 6, no. 3 (November 1940): 20–21.

8. "The Immigration of Refugee Children to the United States," Holocaust Encyclopedia, United States Holocaust Memorial Museum, accessed September 18, 2019, https://encyclopedia .ushmm.org/content/en/article/the-immigration-of-refugee-children-to-the-united-states.

9. "The Immigration of Refugee Children."

10. Daniel J. Steinbock, "The Admission of Unaccompanied Children into the United States," *Yale Law and Policy Review* 7, no. 1 (1989): 147.

11. Jennie N. Haxton, "What is Being Done for Refugee Children?," *Childhood Education* 17, no. 3 (1940): 133.

12. Jackson, *Who Will Take Our Children?*, 65–73.

13. Jackson, *Who Will Take Our Children?*, 65–73.

14. Travis L. Crosby, *The Impact of Civilian Evacuation in the Second World War* (London: Croom Helm Ltd., 1986), 115.

15. Judith Tylor Baumel-Schwartz, "Jewish Refugee Children in the USA (1934–45): Flight, Resettlement, Absorption," in *The Young Victims of the Nazi Regime: Migration, the Holocaust and Postwar Displacement*, eds. Simone Gigliotti and Monica Tempian (London: Bloomsbury Publishing, 2016), 19; Patricia Heberer, ed., *Children During the Holocaust (Documenting Life and Destruction: Holocaust Sources in Context)* (Lanham, Md.: AltaMira Press in Association with the United States Holocaust Memorial Museum, 2011), 324, 347, 358; Mordecai Paldiel, "Fear and Comfort: The Plight of Hidden Children in Wartime Poland," *Holocaust and Genocide Studies* 6, no. 4 (1992): 397–413; Howard Greenfeld, *The Hidden Children* (New York: Ticknor & Fields, 1993); Ewa Kurek, *Your Life is Worth Mine: How Polish Nuns Saved Hundreds of Jewish Children in German Occupied Poland, 1939–1945* (New York: Hippocrene Books, 1997).

16. Catherine E. Rymph, *Raising Government Children: A History of Foster Care and the American Welfare State* (Chapel Hill: University of North Carolina Press, 2017), 3.

17. "Memorandum Concerning the Official Basis of the Program of the United States Committee for the Care of European Children, Inc.," n.d., box 23, folder 27, International Social Service United States of America Branch Records, Social Welfare History Archives, University of Minnesota, Minneapolis, 2–3.

18. "We Are Standing By: A Report of the United States Committees' Program Accomplishments and Present Status," (New York: U.S. Committee for the Care of European Children, Inc., May 1941), 26–27.

19. "We Are Standing By: A Report," May 1941.

20. "We Are Standing By: A Report," May 1941.

21. Excerpt from *Child Welfare League of American Bulletin*, June 1940, box 177, folder 5, United Way of Minneapolis Collection, Social Welfare History Archives, University of Minnesota, Minneapolis.

22. Excerpt from *Child Welfare League*, June 1940.

23. Excerpt from *Child Welfare League*, June 1940.

24. Excerpt from *Child Welfare League*, June 1940.

25. "We Are Standing By: A Report," May 1941, 4, 26–27.

26. "Admission of Refugee Children to the United States," July 7, 1945, box 23, folder 27, International Social Service United States of America Branch Records, Social Welfare History Archives, University of Minnesota, Minneapolis, 1; see also USCOM to the attorney general of the United States, July 25, 1944, U.S. Committee for the Care of European Children Papers, Folder 15, Franklin D. Roosevelt Presidential Library, www.fdrlibrary.marist .edu/_resources/images/wrb/wrb0941.pdf.

27. From the *New York Times*, quoted in excerpt from *Child Welfare League*, June 1940.

28. Joint press release, Department of Justice and Department of State, July 13, 1940, box 177, folder 5, United Way of Minneapolis Collection, Social Welfare History Archives, University of Minnesota, Minneapolis.

29. Joint press release, Department of Justice and Department of State, July 13, 1940.

30. Joint press release, Department of Justice and Department of State, July 13, 1940.

31. Michael H. Hunt, *The American Ascendancy: How the United States Gained and Wielded Global Dominance* (Chapel Hill: University of North Carolina Press 2007), 120–21.

32. Parker, "British Evacuees," 34; see also Michal Ostrovsky, "'We are Standing By': Rescue Operations of the United States Committee for the Care of European Children," *Holocaust and Genocide Studies* 29, no. 2 (Fall 2015): 230.

33. "We Are Standing By: A Report," May 1941, 12–13; "Memorandum Concerning the Care of European Children," n.d., 4.

34. Rymph, *Raising Government Children*, 67.

35. Rymph, *Raising Government Children*, 11, 32.

36. Rymph, *Raising Government Children*, 69; Susan S. Forbes and Patricia Weiss Fagen, "Unaccompanied Refugee Children: The Evolution of U.S. Policies—1939 to 1984," (Washington, D.C.: Refugee Policy Group, August 1984), 12.

37. Rymph, *Raising Government Children*, 80–82.

38. "We Are Standing By: A Report," 6; Robert Lang on behalf of the U.S. Committee for the Care of Unaccompanied Children to designated agencies, March 19, 1943, box 177, folder 6, United Way of Minneapolis Collection, Social Welfare History Archives, University of Minnesota, Minneapolis; see also Crosby, *The Impact of Civilian Evacuation*, 112.

39. Telegram from Eric H. Biddle to David C. Liggett, July 5, 1940, box 177, folder 4, United Way of Minneapolis Collection, Social Welfare History Archives, University of Minnesota, Minneapolis.

40. "United States Committee for the Care of European Children, General Memorandum No. 4," 8–9, n.d., box 177, folder 4, United Way of Minneapolis Collection, Social Welfare History Archives, University of Minnesota, Minneapolis.

41. Memorandum from David Liggett to Dr. S. Marx White, July 8, 1940, box 177, folder 4, United Way of Minneapolis Collection, Social Welfare History Archives, University of Minnesota, Minneapolis.

42. Mrs. John S. Dalrymple, chairman, and Charles E. Dow, secretary, to the members of the Minneapolis Local Information Committee of the U.S. Committee for the Care of European Children, August 8, 1940, box 177, folder 4, United Way of Minneapolis Collection, Social Welfare History Archives, University of Minnesota, Minneapolis.

43. Parsons and Starns, *The Evacuation*, 138; Jackson, *Who Will Take Our Children?*, 100.

44. Tara Zahra, *The Lost Children: Reconstructing Europe's Families After World War Two* (Cambridge, Mass.: Harvard University Press, 2011), 65.

45. Parsons and Starns, *The Evacuation*, 127–28.

46. Parsons and Starns, *The Evacuation*, 132.

47. Press release from United States Committee for the Care of European Children, July 16, 1940, box 177, folder 5, United Way of Minneapolis Collection, Social Welfare History Archives, University of Minnesota, Minneapolis.

48. Press release from USCOM, July 17, 1940, box 177, folder 5, United Way of Minneapolis Collection, Social Welfare History Archives, University of Minnesota, Minneapolis.

49. "Halt British Tot 'Shipping': Government Unable to Provide Ships," *Minneapolis Star-Journal*, July 10, 1940, 8, box 177, folder 5, United Way of Minneapolis Collection, Social Welfare History Archives, University of Minnesota, Minneapolis.

50. Jackson, *Who Will Take Our Children?*, 78–79.

51. "Why not Try to Save English Children?" *Minneapolis Star-Journal*, July 24, 1940, box 177, folder 5, United Way of Minneapolis Collection, Social Welfare History Archives, University of Minnesota, Minneapolis.

52. Congressional Record, vol. 86, part 9, July 25, 1940, 9627–9631, https://www.govinfo.gov/app/collection/crecb.

53. Congressional Record, July 25, 1940, 9629–9630.

54. Crosby, *The Impact of Civilian Evacuation*, 115–16.

55. "200,000 Children Seek Haven; Drive Here Asks Funds for Them," *New York Times*, August 2, 1940, 1.

56. Crosby, *The Impact of Civilian Evacuation*, 120.

57. Parsons and Starns, *The Evacuation*, 132.

58. Crosby, *The Impact of Civilian Evacuation*, 114; Jackson, *Who Will Take Our Children?*, 85.

59. Parker, "British Evacuees," 35.

60. "We Are Standing By: A Report," May 1941, 18–19.

61. Bulletin No. 1, Minneapolis Local Information Committee of the U.S. Committee for the Care of European Children, July 29, 1940, box 177, folder 4, United Way of Minneapolis Collection, Social Welfare History Archives, University of Minnesota, Minneapolis.

62. "We Are Standing By: A Report," May 1941, 14.

63. Parker, "British Evacuees," 35.

64. "Agenda for Placement Committee Meeting," Minneapolis Local Information Committee of the U.S. Committee for the Care of European Children, August 8, 1940, box 177, folder 4, United Way of Minneapolis Collection, Social Welfare History Archives, University of Minnesota, Minneapolis.

65. "Agenda for Placement Committee Meeting," August 8, 1940.

66. Zahra, *The Lost Children*, 62.

67. "Agenda for Placement Committee Meeting," August 8, 1940.

68. "We Are Standing By: A Report," May 1941, 19.

69. "We Are Standing By: A Report," May 1941, 19.

70. Goodykoontz, "Our Guest Children from Europe," 20–21.

71. Parker, "British Evacuees," 36.

72. Haxton, "What is Being Done for Refugee Children?," 133–34.

73. "United States Committee for the Care of European Children, General Memorandum No. 4," n.d., 6.

74. Bulletin No. 1, July 29, 1940, 2; Parker, "British Evacuees," 37.

75. Steinbock, "The Admission of Unaccompanied Children," 157; see also Bulletin No. 1, July 29, 1940, 2; "Memorandum Concerning the Care of European Children," n.d., 20–21.

76. Robert Rosen, *Saving the Jews: Franklin D. Roosevelt and the Holocaust* (New York: Basic Books, 2007), 196–97; Henry L. Feingold, *Bearing Witness: How America and Its Jews Responded to the Holocaust* (Syracuse, N.Y.: Syracuse University Press, 1995), 78–79; "The Immigration of Refugee Children"; "We Are Standing By: A Report," May 1941, 17.

77. Jackson, *Who Will Take Our Children?* 101–3.

78. Jackson, *Who Will Take Our Children?* 108.

79. Jackson, *Who Will Take Our Children?* 108.

80. Jackson, *Who Will Take Our Children?* 113.

81. Inglis, *The Children's War*, 124.

82. "Latest Information Re: the U.S. Committee for the Care of European Children," memorandum from National Office of Community Chests and Councils, Inc. to local Chests and Councils, October 8, 1940; Press release from USCOM, October 9, 1940, box 177, folder 5, United Way of Minneapolis Collection, Social Welfare History Archives, University of Minnesota, Minneapolis.

83. Press release from USCOM, October 9, 1940.

84. "Latest Information," October 8, 1940; Bernice B. Dalrymple to Mr. David Liggett, Council of Social Agencies, October 18, 1940, box 177, folder 5, United Way of Minneapolis Collection, Social Welfare History Archives, University of Minnesota, Minneapolis.

85. Zahra, *The Lost Children*, 57.

86. For more on the AFSC's mixed feelings about child evacuation, see Clarence Pickett, *For More Than Bread: An Autobiographical Account of Twenty-Two Years' Work with the American Friends Service Committee* (Boston: Little, Brown and Company, 1953).

87. Ostrovsky, "We are Standing By," 239.

88. Bat-Ami Zucker, *In Search of Refuge: Jews and US Consuls in Nazi Germany, 1933–1941* (London: Vallentine Mitchell, 2001), 54–55.

89. Franklin Delano Roosevelt Administration, "Statement on Political Refugees," October 17, 1939, https://www.jewishvirtuallibrary.org/roosevelt-statement-on-political-refugees.

90. Richard Breitman and Allan J. Lichtman, *FDR and the Jews* (Cambridge, Mass.: Harvard University Press, 2013), 177.

91. "We Are Standing By: A Report," May 1941, 2, 25.

92. "We Are Standing By: A Report," May 1941, 32.

93. "The Immigration of Refugee Children."

94. Robert Lang to designated agencies, March 19, 1943.

95. Steinbock, "The Admission of Unaccompanied Children," 141.

96. "Safe!" U.S. Committee for the Care of European Children, Inc., Member Agency of the National War Fund, Inc., University of Minnesota Libraries Manuscript Division, Minneapolis, http://special.lib.umn.edu/manuscripts.

97. Robert Lang to designated agencies, March 19, 1943, 4–5.

98. "The Vélodrome d'Hiver (Vél d'Hiv) Roundup," Holocaust Encyclopedia, United States Holocaust Memorial Museum, accessed October 31, 2019, https://encyclopedia.ushmm.org/content/en/article/the-velodrome-dhiver-vel-dhiv-roundup.

99. Heberer, *Children During the Holocaust*, 96; Robert Lang to designated agencies, March 19, 1943.

100. Telegram from Adolf Freudenberg to USCOM, September 7, 1942, box 23, folder 27, International Social Service United States of America Branch Records, Social Welfare History Archives, University of Minnesota, Minneapolis.

101. Breitman and Lichtman, *FDR and the Jews*, 202–3.

102. USCOM Memorandum, n.a., n.d., box 23, folder 27, International Social Service United States of America Branch Records, Social Welfare History Archives, University of Minnesota, Minneapolis.

103. Memorandum on telephone conversation with Dr. Schwartz on September 22, 1942, regarding emigration of children from unoccupied France, September 22, 1942; and Cable from Joseph Schwartz to Mr. Leavitt, September 26, 1942, box 23, folder 27, International Social Service United States of America Branch Records, Social Welfare History Archives, University of Minnesota, Minneapolis.

104. Samuel McCrea Cavert, "Memorandum on Refugee Children Project," November 4, 1942, box 23, folder 27, International Social Service United States of America Branch Records, Social Welfare History Archives, University of Minnesota, Minneapolis.

105. Telephone conversation with Dr. Schwartz, September 22, 1942.

106. Ruth Larned to Robert Lang, October 30, 1942, box 23, folder 27, International Social Service United States of America Branch Records, Social Welfare History Archives, University of Minnesota, Minneapolis; Robert Lang to designated agencies, March 19, 1943.

107. Telephone conversation with Dr. Schwartz, September 22, 1942.

108. Telephone conversation with Dr. Schwartz, September 22, 1942.

109. Breitman and Lichtman, *FDR and the Jews*, 202–3.

110. Cavert, "Memorandum on Refugee Children," November 4, 1942.

111. Cavert, "Memorandum on Refugee Children," November 4, 1942.

112. USCOM to the attorney general, July 25, 1944.

113. Breitman and Lichtman, *FDR and the Jews*, 202–3; see also Christopher R. Browning, *The Origins of the Final Solution: The Evolution of Nazi Jewish Policy, September 1939-March 1942* (Lincoln: University of Nebraska Press, 2007).

114. Robert Lang to designated agencies, March 19, 1943, 2.

115. Breitman and Lichtman, *FDR and the Jews*, 203.

116. Robert Lang to designated agencies, March 19, 1943, 2.

117. Gunnar M. Berg, "Finding Aid to the German-Jewish Children's Aid," archival collection, Center for Jewish History, April 2000, http://findingaids.cjh.org/?pID=109118; Baumel-Schwartz, "Jewish Refugee Children," 21.

118. Robert Lang to designated agencies, March 19, 1943.

119. Robert Lang to designated agencies, March 19, 1943.

120. Richard Breitman and Alan M. Kraut, *American Refugee Policy and European Jewry, 1933–1945* (Bloomington: Indiana University Press, 1987), 245–47; see also Rebecca Erbelding, *Rescue Board: The Untold Story of America's Efforts to Save the Jews of Europe* (New York: Doubleday, 2018).

121. USCOM to the attorney general, July 25, 1944; USCOM to Mr. Howard K. Travers, July 26, 1944; and USCOM to Mr. John W. Pehle, July 28, 1944, U.S. Committee for the Care of European Children Papers, Folder 15, Franklin D. Roosevelt Presidential Library, www.fdrlibrary.marist.edu/_resources/images/wrb/wrb0941.pdf.

122. Robert Lang to designated agencies, March 19, 1943, 14.

123. Crosby, *The Impact of Civilian Evacuation*, 119.

124. Parker, "British Evacuees," 36–38.

125. Inglis, *The Children's War*, 109; Parker, "British Evacuees," 36.

126. Robert Lang to designated agencies, March 19, 1943, 4–5.

127. Jackson, *Who Will Take Our Children?*, 90, 139, 153.

128. Judith Tydor Baumel, *Unfulfilled Promise: Rescue and Resettlement of Jewish Refugee Children in the United States, 1934–1945* (Juneau, Alaska: Denali Press, 1990), 5.

129. Zahra, *The Lost Children*, 76.

130. Baumel-Schwartz, "Jewish Refugee Children," 21–22.

131. Mary Fraser Kirsh, "Remembering the 'Pain of Belonging': Jewish Children Hidden as Catholics in Second World War France," in *The Young Victims of the Nazi Regime: Migration, the Holocaust and Postwar Displacement*, eds. Simone Gigliotti and Monica Tempian (London: Bloomsbury Publishing, 2016), 258.

132. Zahra, *The Lost Children*, 69.

133. Robert Lang to designated agencies, March 19, 1943.

134. Zahra, *The Lost Children*, 74–76; Baumel-Schwartz, "Jewish Refugee Children," 22, 24.

CHAPTER 3

1. Judith Hemmendinger and Robert Krell, *The Children of Buchenwald: Child Survivors of the Holocaust and Their Post-War Lives* (Jerusalem: Gefen Press, 2000), 21, 27–31, 180.

2. Everett M. Ressler, Neil Boothby, and Daniel J. Steinbock, *Unaccompanied Children: Care and Protection in Wars, Natural Disasters, and Refugee Movements*, (1988; repr., Oxford, U.K.: Oxford University Press, 2018), 23–28; Tara Zahra, *The Lost Children: Reconstructing Europe's Families After World War Two* (Cambridge, Mass.: Harvard University Press, 2011), 6; Kathryn Close, *Transplanted Children: A History* (New York: U.S. Committee for the Care of European Children, 1953), 37; "Official Basis of the Program of the United States Committee," report prepared for USCOM, April 1953, box 23, folder 27, International Social Service United States of America Branch Records, Social Welfare History Archives, University of Minnesota, Minneapolis, 11.

3. "Official Basis," April 1953, 11; Ressler, Boothby, and Steinbock, *Unaccompanied Children*, 29.

4. Very Reverend Monsignor Aloysius J. Wycislo, "The Refugee and United States Legislation," *Catholic Lawyer* 2, no. 4 (Spring 1958): 135.

5. Zahra, *The Lost Children*, 8; Lynne Taylor, *In the Children's Best Interests: Unaccompanied Children in American-Occupied Germany, 1945–1952* (Toronto, Ont.: University of Toronto Press, 2017), 5.

6. Ressler, Boothby, and Steinbock, *Unaccompanied Children*, 31; "Official Basis," April 1953, 14.

7. "International Placement of Children," *Social Service Review* 22, no. 4 (December 1948): 508.

8. Angelika Sauer, "Children Who Are Not Children: Finding a Place for the Displaced Children of Europe, 1945–1948," Chapter 2 of *Suffer the Little Children: American Lutherans and the Border-Crossing Child, 1939–1987* (unpublished manuscript, cited with permission of the author), 9; see also Close, *Transplanted Children*, 41.

9. Sauer, "Children Who are Not Children," 15–17; Susan T. Pettiss and Lynne Taylor, *After the Shooting Stopped: The Story of an UNRRA Welfare Worker in Germany 1945–1947* (Victoria, B.C.: Trafford, 2004), 119; Close, *Transplanted Children*, 37; Frances Bagley, "Rebuilding Life for Homeless Children," *The Child* 11, no. 1 (July 1946), 20; Taylor, *In the Children's Best Interests*, 88.

10. Taylor, *In the Children's Best Interests*, 52, 57; Ressler, Boothby, and Steinbock, *Unaccompanied Children*, 30.

11. Ressler, Boothby, and Steinbock, *Unaccompanied Children*, 33.

12. Sauer, "Children Who are Not Children," 19; Richard Solberg, *Open Doors: The Story of Lutherans Resettling Refugees* (St. Louis, Mo.: Concordia Publishing House, 1992), 26–27; Mark Wyman, *DPs: Europe's Displaced Persons, 1945–51* (Ithaca, N.Y.: Cornell University Press, 1998), 48–50.

13. Memorandum from Miss Castendyck to Miss Lenroot, "Admission of Refugee Children to the United States," July 7, 1945, box 23, folder 27, International Social Service United States of America Branch Records, Social Welfare History Archives, University of Minnesota, Minneapolis, 3.

14. Memorandum from Miss Castendyck to Miss Lenroot, "Admission of Refugee Children," July 7, 1945, 3.

15. Memorandum from Miss Castendyck to Miss Lenroot "Admission of Refugee Children," July 7, 1945, 3.

16. Memorandum from Miss Castendyck to Miss Lenroot, "Outline of Minimum Social Data Needed by Child Welfare Agencies in Planning for and in Placement of Children Referred for Resettlement," July 7, 1945, box 23, folder 27, International Social Service United States of America Branch Records, Social Welfare History Archives, University of Minnesota, Minneapolis, 1–2.

17. Memorandum from Miss Castendyck to Miss Lenroot, "Admission of Refugee Children," July 7, 1945, 2–3.

18. Memorandum from Miss Castendyck to Miss Lenroot, "Admission of Refugee Children," July 7, 1945, 3.

19. Taylor, *In the Children's Best Interests*, 104.

20. Catherine E. Rymph, *Raising Government Children: A History of Foster Care and the American Welfare State* (Chapel Hill: University of North Carolina Press, 2017), 7.

21. Rymph, *Raising Government Children*, 79; Aristide R. Zolberg, *A Nation by Design: Immigration Policy in the Fashioning of America* (Cambridge, Mass.: Harvard University Press, 2008), 305.

22. Zolberg, *A Nation by Design*, 305.

23. Zolberg, *A Nation by Design*, 304–6.

24. Phil Orchard and Jamie Gillies, "Atypical Leadership: The Role of the Presidency and Refugee Protection, 1932–1952," *Presidential Studies Quarterly* 45, no. 3 (September 2015): 502–4.

25. Carl J. Bon Tempo, *Americans at the Gate: The United States and Refugees during the Cold War* (Princeton, N.J.: Princeton University Press, 2008), 23.

26. Zolberg, *A Nation by Design*, 293, 298–302.

27. Zolberg, *A Nation by Design*, 294.

28. "Official Basis," April 1953, 6.

29. "Official Basis," April 1953, 6; Wycislo, "The Refugee," 134.

30. Gil Loescher and John A. Scanlan, *Calculated Kindness: Refugees and America's Half-Open Door, 1945 to the Present* (New York: Free Press, 1986), 5–6.

31. "Official Basis," April 1953, 7; Susan S. Forbes and Patricia Weiss Fagen, "Unaccompanied Refugee Children: The Evolution of U.S. Policies—1939 to 1984," (Washington, D.C., Refugee Policy Group, August 1984), ii; "International Placement of Children," 508.

32. "Official Basis," April 1953, 7.

33. "Official Basis," April 1953, 7.

34. "Official Basis," April 1953, 7.

35. Close, *Transplanted Children*, 39; Forbes and Fagen, "Unaccompanied Refugee Children," 14.

36. "Official Basis," April 1953, 15, 33.

37. "Official Basis," April 1953, 11.

38. Zahra, *The Lost Children*, 43–45.

39. Todd Scribner, "'Pilgrims of the Night': The American Catholic Church Responds to the Post-World War II Displaced Persons Crisis," *American Catholic Studies* 124, no. 3 (2013): 4, 9. Despite U.S. Catholics' late entry into the field of refugee relief work—a significant departure for a church whose lack of institutional capacity, concerns for the economic well-being of Depression-era Catholic families, anti-Semitism, and anti-communism had underlaid its resistance to resettlement during the 1930s—the organization that became known as the Catholic Relief Services (CRS) in 1955 quickly became one of the United States' most important refugee resettlement organizations.

40. "International Placement of Children," 511; "European Children Brought to America," *Social Service Review* 21, no. 2 (June 1947): 240.

41. Daniel J. Steinbock, "The Admission of Unaccompanied Children," *Yale Law and Policy Review* 7, no. 1 (1989): 141.

42. "Official Basis," April 1953, 11.

43. Close, *Transplanted Children*, 51.

44. Cornelia Goodhue, "We Gain New Candidates for Citizenship," *The Child* 11, no. 1 (July 1946): 2–7.

45. Close, *Transplanted Children*, 41, 51.

46. "European Children Brought to America," 239.

47. Goodhue, "We Gain New Candidates," 2–7; Close, *Transplanted Children*, 49.

48. Steinbock, "The Admission of Unaccompanied Children," 153; for more on mid century intercountry adoption see Rachel Winslow, *The Best Possible Immigrants: International Adoption and the American Family* (Philadelphia: University of Pennsylvania Press, 2017).

49. Angelika Sauer, "Our Direct Responsibility: American Lutherans and Europe's Displaced Children, 1945–1951," Chapter 3 of *Suffer the Little Children: American Lutherans and the Border-Crossing Child, 1939–1987* (unpublished manuscript, cited with permission of the author), 3; Forbes and Fagen, "Unaccompanied Refugee Children," 15.

50. "European Children Brought to America," 239.

51. Steinbock, "The Admission of Unaccompanied Children," 151; Louise Wilhelmine Holborn, *The International Refugee Organization: A Specialized Agency of the United Nations, Its History and Work, 1946–1952* (Oxford, U.K.: Oxford United Press, 1956), 505–7.

52. "Official Basis," April 1953, 16–18; Close, *Transplanted Children*, 40.

53. "International Placement of Children."

54. "Many DP Children in Germany Are Too Old to Qualify for Immigration to the United States," *New York Times*, August 16, 1948.

55. Close, *Transplanted Children*, 40–41.

56. Close, *Transplanted Children*, 39–40.

57. "Official Basis," April 1953, 8.

58. Close, *Transplanted Children*, 41; Sauer, "Children Who are Not Children," 9; Wyman, *DPs*, 99; Zahra, *The Lost Children*, 47.

59. Close, *Transplanted Children*, 45.

60. Taylor, *In the Children's Best Interests*, 93.

61. "International Placement of Children," 508.

62. "Hopes to Adopt 3 Abroad," *New York Times*, May 3, 1947.

63. Taylor, *In the Children's Best Interests*, 103.

64. Heide Fehrenbach, *Race After Hitler: Black Occupation Children in Postwar Germany and America* (Princeton, N.J.: Princeton University Press, 2005), 133, 140.

65. Bon Tempo, *Americans at the Gate*, 22.

66. Bon Tempo, *Americans at the Gate*, 23.

67. Harry S. Truman, "Annual Message to the Congress on the State of the Union," January 6, 1947, https://www.infoplease.com/primary-sources/government/presidential-speeches/state-union-address-harry-s-truman-january-6-1947.

68. Michael H. Hunt, *The American Ascendancy: How the United States Gained and Wielded Global Dominance* (Chapel Hill: University of North Carolina Press, 2007), 123, 167; Zolberg, *A Nation by Design*, 307; Bon Tempo, *Americans at the Gate*, 23.

69. Scribner, "'Pilgrims of the Night,'" 10.

70. Forbes and Fagen, "Unaccompanied Refugee Children," 15.

71. Scribner, "'Pilgrims of the Night,'" 11–13.

72. André Gerolymatos, *An International Civil War: Greece, 1943–1949* (New Haven, Conn.: Yale University Press, 2016), 258, 303.

73. Bon Tempo, *Americans at the Gate*, 21–26.

74. Scribner, "'Pilgrims of the Night,'" 11–13.

75. Wycislo, "The Refugee," 138; Kathryn Hulme, *The Wild Place* (New York: Little, Brown and Company, 1953), 227; Pettiss and Taylor, *After the Shooting Stopped*, 223; Loescher and Scanlan, *Calculated Kindness*, 9–10.

76. Scribner, "'Pilgrims of the Night,'" 16.

77. Sauer, "Children Who are Not Children," 21; Gertrude Samuels, "Children Who Have Known No Childhood," *New York Times*, March 9, 1947.

78. Laura Briggs, *Somebody's Children: The Politics of Transracial and Transnational Adoption* (Durham, N.C.: Duke University Press, 2012), 138–40, 143–44, 152.

79. "International Placement of Children," 508.

80. Rachel Winslow, "Immigration Law and Improvised Policy in the Making of International Adoption, 1948–1961," *Journal of Policy History* 24, no. 2 (2012): 323.

81. "Would Let Orphans Enter for Adoption," *New York Times*, March 11, 1947, 1.

82. Winslow, "Immigration Law," 323; "War Orphans," *New York Times*, March 21, 1947, 20.

83. Winslow, "Immigration Law," 323.

84. Emily A. Benfer, "In the Best Interest of the Child? An International Human Rights Analysis of the Treatment of Unaccompanied Minors in Australia and the United States," *Indiana International & Comparative Law Review* 14, no. 3 (2004): 732–34; see also Office of the United Nations High Commissioner for Human Rights, "Universal Declaration of Human Rights (1948)," https://www.un.org/ruleoflaw/files/ABCannexesen.pdf.

85. Orchard and Gillies, *Atypical Leadership*, 505.

86. Bon Tempo, *Americans at the Gate*, 24, 26.

87. Forbes and Fagen, "Unaccompanied Refugee Children," 15.

88. Loescher and Scanlan, *Calculated Kindness*, 19; Roger Daniels, *Guarding the Golden Door: American Immigration Policy and Immigrants Since 1882* (New York: Hill and Wang, 2004), 109.

89. Loescher and Scanlan, *Calculated Kindness*, 21; Harry S. Truman, "Statement by the President Upon Signing the Displaced Persons Act," June 25, 1948, https://www.trumanlibrary.gov/library/public-papers/142/statement-president-upon-signing-displaced-persons-act.

90. "International Placement of Children," 509–11; Forbes and Fagen, "Unaccompanied Refugee Children," ii; Steinbock, "The Admission of Unaccompanied Children," 151; "Official Basis," April 1953, 8.

91. Close, *Transplanted Children*, 44.

92. Fehrenbach, *Race After Hitler*, 141.

93. "Official Basis," April 1953, 9–10; Close, *Transplanted Children*, 44.

94. "Many DP Children."

95. Close, *Transplanted Children*, 45.

96. "Official Basis," April 1953, 20.

97. Close, *Transplanted Children*, 51.

98. Steinbock, "The Admission of Unaccompanied Children," 151.

99. Zahra, *The Lost Children*, 48–57; Steinbock, "The Admission of Unaccompanied Children," 150–51.

100. Pettiss and Taylor, *After the Shooting Stopped*, 187–93.

101. Taylor, *In the Children's Best Interests*, 290–91.

102. Zahra, *The Lost Children*, 36; "Official Basis," April 1953, 18.

103. Steinbock, "The Admission of Unaccompanied Children," 151.

104. "DP Children Dazzled but Happy," *New York Times*, March 17, 1949, 1.

105. "International Placement of Children," 510.

106. Sauer, "Our Direct Responsibility," 15.

107. "International Placement of Children."

108. Close, *Transplanted Children*, 53, 63.

109. Close, *Transplanted Children*, 53.

110. Close, *Transplanted Children*, 53–63; Lucy Hansson and Arnold Layslo, "The Distribution and Adjustment of 150 Unaccompanied Refugee Children Brought to the United States Under the Joint Auspices of U.S. Committee for the Care of European Children, Inc., and

the National Lutheran Council" (unpublished master's thesis, Columbia School of Social Work, 1952), 39–40, quoted in Sauer, "Our Direct Responsibility," 17.

111. Ressler, Boothby, and Steinbock, *Unaccompanied Children*, 34.

112. Taylor, *In the Children's Best Interests*, 244, 250.

113. Hunt, *The American Ascendancy*, 127.

114. Wycislo, "The Refugee," 144.

115. Wycislo, "The Refugee," 143; Bon Tempo, *Americans at the Gate*, 25; Loescher and Scanlan, *Calculated Kindness*, 22.

116. Bon Tempo, *Americans at the Gate*, 25; Loescher and Scanlan, *Calculated Kindness*, 22.

117. "Official Basis," April 1953, 21, 33.

118. "Official Basis," April 1953, 9.

119. Close, *Transplanted Children*, 68.

120. Taylor, *In the Children's Best Interests*, 253; Close, *Transplanted Children*, 68.

121. "Official Basis," April 1953, 30; Gerolymatos, *An International Civil War*, 198–99, 217, 221; Ressler, Boothby, and Steinbock, *Unaccompanied Children*, 41.

122. Ressler, Boothby and Steinbock, *Unaccompanied Children*, 43; Joy Damousi, "Building 'Healthy Happy Family Units': Aileen Fitzpatrick and Reuniting Children Separated by the Greek Civil War with Their Families in Australia, 1949–1954," *The History of the Family* 22, no. 4 (2017): 473.

123. "Official Basis," April 1953, 31.

124. "Official Basis," April 1953, 31.

125. "Washington Conference Clarifies D.P. Problems," *The AHEPAN* (April-May-June 1951), 8, 11.

126. Close, *Transplanted Children*, 47; United States Committee for the Care of European Children, "Greek Children Who Arrived on U.S. Committee Assurances," August 28, 1952; Margaret A. Valk, "U.S. Committee for the Care of European Children—Joint Program with Hellenic Education Progressive Association (HEPA), Re: [MINOR CHILD'S NAME OMITTED]," November 6, 1952, box 23, folder 27, International Social Service United States of America Branch Records, Social Welfare History Archives, University of Minnesota, Minneapolis.

127. Gonda Van Steen, *Adoption, Memory, and Cold War Greece: Kid Pro Quo?* (Ann Arbor: University of Michigan Press, 2019), 96.

128. Taylor, *In the Children's Best Interests*, 245; Close, *Transplanted Children*, 46, 47.

129. Valk, "Joint Program with HEPA," November 6, 1952.

130. Van Steen, *Kid Pro Quo?*, 77.

131. Close, *Transplanted Children*, 46; Damousi, "Healthy Happy Family Units," 467.

132. "Official Basis," April 1953, 33.

133. Statement by Ingeborg Olsen, executive director, ISS, to Ruth H. Carter, notary public, State of New York, June 29, 1953, box 23, folder 27, International Social Service United States of America Branch Records, Social Welfare History Archives, University of Minnesota, Minneapolis.

134. Fehrenbach, *Race After Hitler*, 140–43.

135. Fehrenbach, *Race After Hitler*, 144–45.

136. Rymph, *Raising Government Children*, 10.

137. Cybelle Fox, *Three Worlds of Relief: Race, Immigration, and the American Welfare State, from the Progressive Era to the New Deal* (Princeton, N.J.: Princeton University Press, 2012), 3; Rymph, *Raising Government Children*, 124–25.

138. Fehrenbach, *Race After Hitler*, 148.

139. Idean Salehyan, "Safe Haven: International Norms, Strategic Interests, and U.S. Refugee Policy," Working Paper 40 (Center for Comparative Immigration Studies, University of California, San Diego, June 2001), 16.

140. Orchard and Gillies, *Atypical Leadership*, 505.

141. Wycislo, "The Refugee," 144; Bon Tempo, *Americans at the Gate*, 29, 32; Loescher and Scanlan, *Calculated Kindness*, 40.

142. Sauer, "Our Direct Responsibility," 20.

143. "Official Basis," April 1953, 9.

144. Dicy Dodds to Jeanne Douine, Ella Laursen, Joy Rutherford, and Frances Windsor, April 7, 1952, box 23, folder 27, International Social Service United States of America Branch Records, Social Welfare History Archives, University of Minnesota, Minneapolis.

145. Dicy Dodds to Dr. Kitz, February 26, 1952; M. S. to Mr. Kirk, February 8, 1952; and Memorandum of telephone call, Mr. Malin to Mr. Kirk, January 30, 1952, box 23, folder 27, International Social Service United States of America Branch Records, Social Welfare History Archives, University of Minnesota, Minneapolis.

146. Ingeborg Olsen to Miss Ruth Larned, April 2, 1953, box 23, folder 27, International Social Service United States of America Branch Records, Social Welfare History Archives, University of Minnesota, Minneapolis.

147. "Official Basis," April 1953, 35; "Report of the Executive Director to the Board of Directors," U.S. Committee for the Care of European Children, Inc., Annual Meeting of the Board of Directors, May 14, 1952, box 3, folder 23, Marion E. Kenworthy Papers (P-511), American Jewish Historical Society Archives, New York.

148. Loescher and Scanlan, *Calculated Kindness*, 45.

149. Bon Tempo, *Americans at the Gate*, 31–32, 36; Loescher and Scanlan, *Calculated Kindness*, 27, 38–39.

150. Forbes and Fagen, "Unaccompanied Refugee Children," 15; Bon Tempo, *Americans at the Gate*, 38.

151. Forbes and Fagen, "Unaccompanied Refugee Children," 15; Bon Tempo, *Americans at the Gate*, 38.

152. Forbes and Fagen, "Unaccompanied Refugee Children," 15; Bon Tempo, *Americans at the Gate*, 45, 48; Stephen R. Porter, *Benevolent Empire: U.S. Power, Humanitarianism, and the Displaced* (Philadelphia: University of Pennsylvania Press, 2017), 128.

153. Bon Tempo, *Americans at the Gate*, 46–47.

154. Steinbock, "The Admission of Unaccompanied Children," 144.

155. Chad C. Haddal, *Unaccompanied Refugee Minors. CRS Report for Congress* (Washington, D.C.: Congressional Research Service, March 14, 2008), 2; Steinbock, "The Admission of Unaccompanied Children," 143–44; Loescher and Scanlan, *Calculated Kindness*, 46.

156. Winslow, "Immigration Law," 325. For more on the complex relationship between public and private interests in shaping the evolution of intercountry adoption, see Winslow, *The Best Possible Immigrants*.

157. Forbes and Fagen, "Unaccompanied Refugee Children," 19–20; Fehrenbach, *Race After Hitler*, 162; Winslow, "Immigration Law," 334.

158. Zahra, *The Lost Children*, 58.

159. Close, *Transplanted Children*, 66.

160. Steinbock, "The Admission of Unaccompanied Children," 141, 144.

161. Howard Altstein and Rita J. Simon, eds., *Intercountry Adoption: A Multinational Perspective* (New York: Praeger, 1991), 3; Ressler, Boothby, and Steinbock, *Unaccompanied Children*, 57.

162. Eleana Kim, *Adopted Territory: Transnational Korean Adoptees and the Politics of Belonging* (Durham, N.C.: Duke University Press, 2010), 64; Kim Park Nelson, *Invisible Asians: Korean American Adoptees, Asian American Experiences, and Racial Exceptionalism* (New Brunswick, N.J.: Rutgers University Press, 2016), 43–44; Arissa Oh, "From War Waif to Ideal Immigrant: The Cold War Transformation of the Korean Orphan," *Journal of American Ethnic History* 31, no. 4 (2012): 34–55.

163. Briggs, *Somebody's Children*, 153; Park Nelson, *Invisible Asians*, 59.

164. Ressler, Boothby, and Steinbock, *Unaccompanied Children*, 57.

165. Park Nelson, *Invisible Asians*, 57; for more on these critiques, see Jodi Kim, *Ends of Empire: Asian American Critique and the Cold War* (Minneapolis: University of Minnesota Press, 2010).

166. Bon Tempo, *Americans at the Gate*, 25; Porter, *Benevolent Empire*, 128; "Official Basis," April 1953, 10; Steinbock, "The Admission of Unaccompanied Children," 141.

167. Orchard and Gillies, *Atypical Leadership*, 491.

168. Louis A. Pérez Jr., *Cuba in the American Imagination: Metaphor and the Imperial Ethos* (Chapel Hill: University of North Carolina Press, 2008); Matthew Frye Jacobson, *Barbarian Virtues: The United States Encounters Foreign Peoples at Home and Abroad, 1876–1917* (New York: Hill and Wang, 2001); Park Nelson, *Invisible Asians*, 3–6; Corrine Chaponnière, "A Question of Interests: Intercountry Adoption," *International Children's Rights Monitor* 1, no. 1 (1983): 3.

CHAPTER 4

1. Dwight D. Eisenhower, staff memorandum, December 1956 Diary, box 19, Papers as President of the United States, 1953–1961 (Ann Whitman File) DDE Diary Series, Dwight D. Eisenhower Presidential Library and Archives.

2. Johanna C. Granville, *The First Domino: International Decision Making during the Hungarian Crisis of 1956* (College Station: Texas A&M University Press, 2004), 196.

3. "Notes by Mr. Ugo Carusi on Possible Closing of Kilmer," March 25, 1957, box 7, President's Committee for Hungarian Refugee Relief, Dwight D. Eisenhower Presidential Library.

4. Granville, *The First Domino*; "'Caught With Jam on Our Fingers': Radio Free Europe and the Hungarian Revolution of 1956," *Diplomatic History* 29, no. 5 (2005): 811–39; Paul Lendvai, *One Day That Shook the Communist World: The 1956 Hungarian Uprising and its Legacy* (Princeton, N.J.: Princeton University Press, 2008); Marjoleine Zieck, "The 1956 Hungarian Refugee Emergency, an Early and Instructive Case of Resettlement," *Amsterdam Law Forum* 5, no. 2 (2013): 45–63; Gil Loescher and John A. Scanlan, *Calculated Kindness: Refugees and America's Half-Open Door, 1945 to the Present* (New York: Free Press, 1986), 27, 50–56; Carl J. Bon Tempo, *Americans at the Gate: The United States and Refugees during the Cold War* (Princeton, N.J.: Princeton University Press, 2008), 71–74, 105–12; Stephen R. Porter, *Benevolent Empire: U.S. Power, Humanitarianism, and the Displaced* (Philadelphia: University of Pennsylvania Press, 2017), 143–45; see also Arthur A. Markowitz, "Humanitarianism versus Restrictionism: The United States and the Hungarian Refugees," *International Migration Review* 7, no. 1 (1973): 46–59; Peter Pastor, "The American Reception and Settlement of Hungarian Refugees in 1956–1957," *Hungarian Cultural Studies* 9 (2016): 197–205;

Vera Sheridan, "Support and Surveillance: 1956 Hungarian Refugee Students in Transit to the Joyce Kilmer Reception Center and to Higher Education Scholarships in the USA," *History of Education* 45, no. 6 (2016): 775–93.

5. "Notes by Mr. Ugo Carusi," March 25, 1957.

6. Maxwell Rabb, "Proposal to Accept Up to 5,000 Hungarian Refugees Under Terms of the Refugee Relief Act," memorandum to Governor Adams, November 8, 1956, box 678, White House Confidential File-Official-1953–1961, Hungarian Refugee Relief 1, Dwight D. Eisenhower Presidential Library, 2; John B. Hollister to Tracy S. Voorhees, February 5, 1957, box 678, White House Confidential File-Official-1953–1961, Hungarian Refugee Relief 3, Dwight D. Eisenhower Presidential Library.

7. Murrey Marder, "Voorhees to Direct Refugee Aid, Ike Asks Support for Red Cross," *Washington Post*, November 30, 1956, 1; "Now Let's Go," *New York World-Telegram and Sun*, November 30, 1956.

8. Press release, December 1, 1956, box 678, White House Confidential File-Official-1953–1961, Hungarian Refugee Relief 1, Dwight D. Eisenhower Presidential Library.

9. Anita Casavantes Bradford, "'With the Utmost Practical Speed': Eisenhower, Hungarian Parolees, and the 'Hidden Hand' Behind U.S. Immigration and Refugee Policy, 1956–1957," *Journal of American Ethnic History* 39, no. 2 (Winter 2020): 15.

10. Memorandum from Harry B. Lyford to James Hagerty, "First Arrivals of Hungarian Escapees," November 19, 1956, box 678, White House Confidential File-Official-1953–1961, Hungarian Refugee Relief 1, Dwight D. Eisenhower Presidential Library, 2.

11. Bon Tempo, *Americans at the Gate*, 73.

12. McCann Worldgroup, "Truth Well Told," accessed January 19, 2017, https://www.mccannworldgroup.de/en; Tracy S. Voorhees, "The Freedom Fighters: Hungarian Refugee Relief, 1956–1957," essay prepared 1961, revised 1968 and 1971, 6, Tracy Voorhees Papers, Rutgers University, https://doi.org/doi:10.7282/T3930SNZ.

13. Voorhees, "The Freedom Fighters," 11, 26.

14. "What About the Others?," *New York Times*, December 21, 1956, 22C.

15. In late December the parole selection process would be adjusted: Catholic agencies were granted the right to sponsor 62 percent of the applicants, Protestant agencies 22 percent, Jewish agencies 10 percent, and "specialized agencies" the remaining 6 percent. In January a system of priorities was established to admit first those who were of "special interest" to congressmen or other "influential persons;" refugees with close U.S. relatives; and those with special skills. Resettlement Department of the International Rescue Committee, *Resettling Hungarian Refugees: A Report on the Resettlement Activities of the International Rescue Committee, Inc. in the United States, 1957–1959*, (New York: International Rescue Department, May 1960), 10, http://www.refugees1956.org/2016/12/06/resettlement-of-hungarian-refugees-1957-1959; "Observations on Agency Experiences at Camp Kilmer, submitted by Fact Finding Committee of the Committee on Migration and Refugee Problems, American Council of Voluntary Agencies for Foreign Service, Inc.," January 14, 1958, box 24, Folder 2A-Hungary, U.S. Committee for Refugees and Immigrants Papers, Social Welfare History Archives, University of Minnesota, Minneapolis, 2; "Report of Fact Finding Committee of the Committee on Migration and Refugee Problems on Hungarian Youth," American Council of Voluntary Agencies for Foreign Service, Inc., February 14, 1958, box 4-Hungarians, American Immigration and Citizenship Conference Records, Social Welfare History Archives, University of Minnesota, Minneapolis, 2.

16. "Observations on Agency Experiences," January 14, 1958, 2.

17. "'Mercy' Plan for Refugees Reported Approved," *Washington Post and Times-Herald*, December 5, 1956, A11.

18. American Branch-Mrs. Pettiss to HG Geneva-Miss Dodds, Re: Hungarian Refugee Situation, November 19, 1956; and William T. Kirk to Pierce J. Gerety, November 15, 1956, box 15, folder 21, International Social Service United States of America Branch Records, Social Welfare History Archives, University of Minnesota, Minneapolis.

19. William T. Kirk to Pierce J. Gerety, November 15, 1956.

20. Lawrence A. Dawson to William T. Kirk, November 23, 1956, box 15, folder 21, International Social Service United States of America Branch Records, Social Welfare History Archives, University of Minnesota, Minneapolis.

21. This photo and caption appeared, for example, in the *Kansas City Star*, on December 3. See Mrs. William Guthrie to Tracy Voorhees, Kansas City, Mo., December 6, 1956, box 3, folder-Adoption, President's Committee for Hungarian Refugee Relief, Dwight D. Eisenhower Presidential Library.

22. "'Mercy' Plan for Refugees."

23. "Air Force Brings 199 Exiles to U.S.," *New York Times*, December 13, 1956.

24. "Hungarian Refugees: Arrivals Mostly Young Men," *Washington Post and Times-Herald*, December 12, 1956, D1.

25. "First of 9,500 From Munich: 199 Hungarian Refugees Fly In," *New York Herald Tribune*, December 13, 1956, 1.

26. See, for example, "President Lifts Refugee Ceiling on 'Parole' Basis," *Washington Evening Star*, January 2, 1957, 1; "Transport Lands 1,716 Hungarians," *New York Times*, January 8, 1957, 1.

27. Anita Casavantes Bradford, *The Revolution is for the Children: The Politics of Childhood in Havana and Miami, 1959–1962* (Chapel Hill: University of North Carolina Press, 2014); Laura Briggs, *Somebody's Children: The Politics of Transracial and Transnational Adoption* (Durham, N.C.: Duke University Press, 2012), 132–35; "Mother, Child, Race, Nation: The Visual Iconography of Rescue and the Politics of Transnational and Transracial Adoption," *Gender and History* 15, no. 2 (August 2003): 179–200.

28. Karen Dubinsky, *Babies without Borders: Adoption and Migration across the Americas* (Toronto, Ont.: University of Toronto Press, 2010), 12; "Children, Ideology and Iconography: How Babies Rule the World," *Journal of the History of Childhood and Youth* 5, no. 1 (Winter 2012): 5–13.

29. Mrs. Pettiss to Miss Dodds, November 19, 1956.

30. President Richard P. Saunders on behalf of Save the Children Federation, December 10, 1956, box 15, folder 21, International Social Service United States of America Branch Records, Social Welfare History Archives, University of Minnesota, Minneapolis.

31. ISS-American Branch Report, "Information for Individuals Asking about Hungarians: Hungarian Unaccompanied Children or Orphans," November 26, 1956, box 15, folder 21, International Social Service United States of America Branch Records, Social Welfare History Archives, University of Minnesota, Minneapolis.

32. See, for example, Mrs. William Guthrie to Tracy Voorhees, December 6, 1956.

33. Mrs. Lillian M. Mazzetta to President Eisenhower, February 12, 1957, box 3, folder-Adoption, President's Committee for Hungarian Refugee Relief, Dwight D. Eisenhower Presidential Library; Mr. and Mrs. David L. Hallstrom to President Eisenhower, December 12, 1956, box 3, folder-Adoption, President's Committee for Hungarian Refugee Relief, Dwight D. Eisenhower Presidential Library.

34. C. E. Olds to Tracy Voorhees, January 3, 1957, box 3, folder-Adoption, President's Committee for Hungarian Refugee Relief, Dwight D. Eisenhower Presidential Library.

35. Mr. and Mrs. William Dominish to President Eisenhower, January 28, 1957, box 3, folder-Adoption, President's Committee for Hungarian Refugee Relief, Dwight D. Eisenhower Presidential Library.

36. Mrs. John Wilson to President Eisenhower, December 27, 1956, box 3, folder-Adoption, President's Committee for Hungarian Refugee Relief, Dwight D. Eisenhower Presidential Library.

37. Mrs. W. Jack Hunsucker to President Eisenhower, December 9, 1956, box 3, folder-Adoption, President's Committee for Hungarian Refugee Relief, Dwight D. Eisenhower Presidential Library; Mrs. Albert Hester to President Eisenhower, December 14, 1956, box 3, folder-Adoption, President's Committee for Hungarian Refugee Relief, Dwight D. Eisenhower Presidential Library.

38. See, for example, W. H. Hieterich to Tracy S. Voorhees, March 8, 1957, box 12, folder-Adoption B, President's Committee for Hungarian Refugee Relief, Dwight D. Eisenhower Presidential Library.

39. W. H. Hieterich to Tracy S. Voorhees, March 8, 1957.

40. Mrs. William Mains to Tracy Voorhees, March 8, 1957, box 12, folder-Adoption B, President's Committee for Hungarian Refugee Relief, Dwight D. Eisenhower Presidential Library; Mr. and Mrs. James W. Thompson to Tracy Voorhees, January 9, 1957, box 12, folder-Adoption B, President's Committee for Hungarian Refugee Relief, Dwight D. Eisenhower Presidential Library.

41. Faye Blumberg to Leo Beebe, January 31, 1957, box 3, folder-Adoption, President's Committee for Hungarian Refugee Relief, Dwight D. Eisenhower Presidential Library.

42. Mrs. Lillian M. Mazzetta to President Eisenhower, February 12, 1957; Mr. and Mrs. Allen Norris to President Eisenhower, December 30, 1956, box 3, folder-Adoption, President's Committee for Hungarian Refugee Relief, Dwight D. Eisenhower Presidential Library; Mr. and Mrs. Robert Schuerger to President Eisenhower, February 14, 1957, box 3, folder-Adoption, President's Committee for Hungarian Refugee Relief, Dwight D. Eisenhower Presidential Library.

43. Memorandum from D. Dodds to Mr. Warren A. Pinegar, Subject: ISS Service to Unaccompanied Hungarian Refugee Youths, March 7, 1957, box 15, folder 21, International Social Service United States of America Branch Records, Social Welfare History Archives, University of Minnesota, Minneapolis, 7.

44. Susan Pettiss to Miss Luft, December 14, 1956, box 15, folder 21, International Social Service United States of America Branch Records, Social Welfare History Archives, University of Minnesota, Minneapolis.

45. "Refugee Airlift Sets U.S. Record," *New York Times*, December 15, 1956, 1; "3000 Offer to Aid Fleeing Children," *New York Times*, December 16, 1956, 1.

46. J. Lawton Collins to Mrs. E. A. Peacock, January 15, 1957, box 3, folder-Adoption, President's Committee for Hungarian Refugee Relief, Dwight D. Eisenhower Presidential Library; J. Lawton Collins to Mrs. Albert Hester, January 28, 1957, box 3, folder-Adoption, President's Committee for Hungarian Refugee Relief, Dwight D. Eisenhower Presidential Library.

47. International Rescue Committee, *Resettling Hungarian Refugees*, 5.

48. Jonathan P. Herzog, *The Spiritual-Industrial Complex: America's Religious Battle Against Communism in the Early Cold War* (New York: Oxford University Press, 2011), 54–64, 85;

Patrick McNamara, *A Catholic Cold War: Edmund A. Walsh, S.J., and the Politics of American Anti-Communism* (New York: Fordham University Press, 2005).

49. Miss H. M. Luft to Mrs. S. Pettiss, December 7, 1956, box 15, folder 21, International Social Service United States of America Branch Records, Social Welfare History Archives, University of Minnesota, Minneapolis.

50. ISS-Austria Branch, "Unattached Hungarian Youth in Austria and Survey of Their Situation in Spring 1958: Report to the United Nations High Commissioner for Refugees," September 1958, box 15, folder 22, International Social Service United States of America Branch Records, Social Welfare History Archives, University of Minnesota, Minneapolis, 2, 5, 27; "Observations on Agency Experiences," January 14, 1958, 7.

51. Memorandum from Etta Deutsch to members of the Fact Finding Committee, American Council of Voluntary Agencies for Foreign Service, Inc., Subject: "Summary of Notes of Meeting of Subcommittee of Fact Finding Committee Dealing with Youth and Teen-Age Problems; and Full committee on General Problems," May 21, 1957, box 24, folder 1A--Hungary, U.S. Committee for Refugees and Immigrants Papers, Social Welfare History Archives, University of Minnesota, Minneapolis, 2.

52. Memorandum from D. Dodds to Mr. Warren A. Pinegar, Subject: ISS Service to Unaccompanied Hungarian Refugee Youths, January 9, 1957, box 15, folder 21, International Social Service United States of America Branch Records, Social Welfare History Archives, University of Minnesota, Minneapolis, 1–2.

53. Memorandum from D. Dodds to Mr. Warren A. Pinegar, January 9, 1957, 6–7; Memorandum from D. Dodds to European Branches, Subject: "Question of Special ISS Service in relation to unaccompanied children and youths among the Hungarian refugees," December 7, 1956, box 15, folder 21, International Social Service United States of America Branch Records, Social Welfare History Archives, University of Minnesota, Minneapolis; ISS-Austria Branch, September 1958.

54. Hildegard M. Luft to the Honorable Llewellyn E. Thompson, December 24, 1956, box 15, folder 21, International Social Service United States of America Branch Records, Social Welfare History Archives, University of Minnesota, Minneapolis.

55. Memorandum from American Branch-Susan Pettiss to ISS Headquarters-Miss Dicy Dodds, Subject: "American Branch Service in Regard to Hungarian Refugees," February 26, 1957, box 15, folder 21, International Social Service United States of America Branch Records, Social Welfare History Archives, University of Minnesota, Minneapolis.

56. Tracy S. Voorhees, *Joyce Kilmer Reception Center: Manual of Policies and Procedures, 1957*, 176, Tracy Voorhees Papers, 1956–1957, Hungarian Refugee Relief Files, Rutgers University Community Repository, https://rucore.libraries.rutgers.edu/partnerportal/search/results.php?q1=joyce%20kilmer%20reception%20center&q1field=mods:titleInfo&q1bool=AND&q2=1956&q2field=mods:dateCreated&orderby=title&numresults=25&key=6Lu-6Ia3By.

57. "Observations on Agency Experiences," January 14, 1958, 7.

58. *Joyce Kilmer Reception Center*, 152; "Observations on Agency Experiences," January 14, 1958, 6.

59. *Joyce Kilmer Reception Center*, 154.

60. Kathryn Close, "Speed in Resettlement: How Has it Worked?" *Children* 4, no. 4 (July/August 1957): 124; "Observations on Agency Experiences," January 14, 1958, 3.

61. "Report of the Fact Finding Committee of the Committee on Migration and Refugee Problems on Hungarian Youth and Teenage Problems," American Council of Voluntary

Agencies for Foreign Service, Inc., January 14, 1958, box 24, folder 2A-Hungary, U.S. Committee for Refugees and Immigrants Papers, Social Welfare History Archives, University of Minnesota, Minneapolis.

62. Memorandum from Etta Deutsch to members of the Fact Finding Committee, May 21, 1957, 6; "Observations on Agency Experiences," January 14, 1958, 2; "Report of the Fact Finding Committee," January 14, 1958, 2.

63. "Observations on Agency Experiences," January 14, 1958, 7.

64. Voorhees, "The Freedom Fighters," 26; Close, "Speed in Resettlement," 127.

65. Willis D. Gradison Jr. to General J. Lawton Collins (Ret.), February 27, 1957, box 1, President's Committee for Hungarian Refugee Relief, Dwight D. Eisenhower Presidential Library.

66. Close, "Speed in Resettlement," 126, 130; "Report of the Fact Finding Committee," January 14, 1958, 5–6.

67. "Report of the Fact Finding Committee," January 14, 1958, 2.

68. International Refugee Committee, "To Keep Open a Unique Home for Refugee Children: The Unfinished Story of the IRC Children's Home at Hainbach, Austria," n.d.; accessed June 18, 2020, www.refugees1956.org/2016/12/06/program-for-minor-refugees/, 1; "Report Prepared by the Joint Committee on Integration of the American Immigration Conference and the National Council on Naturalization and Citizenship," n.d., box 4, folder-Hungarians, American Immigration and Citizenship Conference Collection, Social Welfare History Archives, University of Minnesota, Minneapolis, 14.

69. "Report Prepared by the Joint Committee," n.d.

70. "Report Prepared by the Joint Committee," n.d., 1, 7.

71. Close, "Speed in Resettlement," 127; Memorandum from Etta Deutsch to members of the Fact Finding Committee, May 21, 1957, 5.

72. "Report of the Fact Finding Committee," January 14, 1958, 5.

73. "He's Still Stranger Among His Friends," *Miami Herald*, January 3, 1957, box 15, folder 21, International Social Service United States of America Branch Records, Social Welfare History Archives, University of Minnesota, Minneapolis.

74. Memorandum from Etta Deutsch to members of the Fact Finding Committee, May 21, 1957, 6.

75. Memorandum from Etta Deutsch to members of the Fact Finding Committee, May 21, 1957, 3–4.

76. Summary of minutes of the Meeting on Youth (special committee of the Fact Finding Committee), American Council of Voluntary Agencies for Foreign Service, Inc., May 8, 1957, box 24, folder 1A-Hungary, U.S. Committee for Refugees and Immigrants Papers, Social Welfare History Archives, University of Minnesota, Minneapolis, 2.

77. Memorandum from Etta Deutsch to members of the Fact Finding Committee, May 21, 1957, 6.

78. Memorandum from Etta Deutsch to members of the Fact Finding Committee, May 21, 1957, 5.

79. Attorney general to Congressman Francis E. Walter, February 27, 1957, Rogers box 16—January 57–February 57, Dwight D. Eisenhower Presidential Library.

80. Statement from the White House to the Congress of the United States, January 31, 1957, box 9, folder-Press Releases: White House, President's Committee for Hungarian Refugee Relief, Dwight D. Eisenhower Presidential Library.

81. Attorney general to Congressman Francis E. Walter, February 27, 1957.

82. Memorandum from M. Pages, director of UNREF, to all UNHCR branch offices, subject: "Unattached Children and Adolescents among Hungarian Refugees," February 1957, box 24, folder 1B-Hungary, U.S. Committee for Refugees and Immigrants Papers, Social Welfare History Archives, University of Minnesota, Minneapolis, 3.

83. Memorandum from M. Pages to all UNHCR branch offices, February 1957, 1.

84. Memorandum from M. Pages to all UNHCR branch offices, February 1957, 2.

85. ISS-Austria Branch, September 1958, 9–10.

86. "Refugee Centers Scored by Priest," *New York Times*, February 20, 1957.

87. Memorandum from Harold H. Healy Jr. to Brigadier General A. J. Goodpaster, staff secretary, the White House, April 5, 1957, Rogers box 16—January 57–February 57, Dwight D. Eisenhower Presidential Library.

88. Meeting on Youth, May 8, 1957.

89. Robert N. Sturdevant, "Refugees in Austria Decreasing: Hungarians Go to Other Nations," *New York Herald-Tribune*, May 8, 1957.

90. The Department of State, Office of Refugee and Migration Affairs, "Confidential: Admission of Hungarian Escapees into the United States, After April 1957 (Appendix: Paraphrase of Cable from the United States Embassy, Vienna)," box 32, older-HC 5, White House Circular Files—Confidential—1953–61, Dwight D. Eisenhower Presidential Library.

91. "Hungarian Fast in Exile Pressed," *New York Times*, May 10, 1957, 1.

92. "Camp for Refugees is Closed at Kilmer" and "44 Children Repatriated," *New York Times*, May 10, 1957.

93. ISS-Austria Branch, September 1958, 53.

94. Minutes of meeting of June 20, 1957 of the American Council of Voluntary Agencies with Mr. Robert McCollum of the State Department, box 24, folder 1C-Hungary, U.S. Committee for Refugees and Immigrants Papers, Social Welfare History Archives, University of Minnesota, Minneapolis, 1.

95. ISS Case Notes 57–944/DA, June 26, 1957; ISS Case Notes 57–963/DA, June 26, 1957; and ISS Case Notes 57–936, June 27, 1957, box 15, folder 22, International Social Service United States of America Branch Records, Social Welfare History Archives, University of Minnesota, Minneapolis.

96. "To Aid Hungarian Children: Admission to this Country of Those in Austria is Advocated," *New York Times*, August 6, 1957, box 24, folder 1D-Hungary, U.S. Committee for Refugees and Immigrants Papers, Social Welfare History Archives, University of Minnesota, Minneapolis.

97. "Conscience on Hungary," *New York Times*, June 26, 1957, box 24, folder 1D-Hungary, U.S. Committee for Refugees and Immigrants Papers, Social Welfare History Archives, University of Minnesota, Minneapolis.

98. "To Aid Hungarian Children," August 6, 1957.

99. "Migrants and Refugees-Hungarian Unaccompanied Minors Coming to Relatives in the U.S. 1957," June 27, 1957, box 15, folder 18, International Social Service United States of America Branch Records, Social Welfare History Archives, University of Minnesota, Minneapolis.

100. Joshua Mather, "Champions of Compassion: The American Council of Voluntary Agencies for Foreign Service and Cold War-Era U.S. Foreign Policy," April 25, 2016, http://www.baas.ac.uk/usso/champions-of-compassion-the-american-council-of-voluntary-agencies-for-foreign-service-and-cold-war-era-u-s-foreign-policy; Minutes, June 20, 1957, 1.

101. Minutes, June 20, 1957, 2.

102. Minutes, June 20, 1957.

103. "Migrants and Refugees," June 27, 1957.

104. Memorandum from Etta Deutsch to members of the Fact Finding Committee, May 21, 1957, 3, 7.

105. "Statement of Fact Finding Committee for Review by Members of the Committee in Advance of June 10 Meeting with DHEW: Youth and Teen-Ager Problems," June 4, 1957, box 24, folder 1B-Hungary, U.S. Committee for Refugees and Immigrants Papers, Social Welfare History Archives, University of Minnesota, Minneapolis, 1–2.

106. "Migrants and Refugees," June 27, 1957; Minutes, June 20, 1957, 2.

107. "Ad Hoc Committee on Children: Program for Unaccompanied Hungarian Minors," n.d., 2, Collection 024–2, Center for Migration Studies Archives, New York City.

108. "Minutes of Meeting Held at State Department Tuesday, July 9, 1957, at 11:00 a.m.," American Council of Voluntary Agencies for Foreign Service, Inc., n.d., box 24, folder 1A-Hungary, U.S. Committee for Refugees and Immigrants Papers, Social Welfare History Archives, University of Minnesota, Minneapolis.

109. "Minutes," July 9, 1957.

110. "Report of Fact Finding Committee," February 14, 1958, 8.

111. "Ad Hoc Committee on Children," n.d., 2.

112. "Ad Hoc Committee on Children," n.d., 4.

113. "Ad Hoc Committee on Children," n.d., Appendix II, 1.

114. "Ad Hoc Committee on Children," n.d., 7–10.

115. "Draft Recommendations for Final Report on Unaccompanied Hungarian Minor Children Program," American Council of Voluntary Agencies for Foreign Service, Inc., n.d, 1–2, Collection 024–2, Center for Migration Studies Archives, New York City.

116. ISS-Austria Branch, September 1958, 22.

117. "Draft Recommendations," n.d., 1–2.

118. "Observations on Agency Experiences," January 14, 1958, 7.

119. "Minutes of Meeting on Hungarian Unaccompanied Minors Coming to Relatives in the United States," October 2, 1957, box 15, folder 18, International Social Service United States of America Branch Records, Social Welfare History Archives, University of Minnesota, Minneapolis.

120. Memorandum from Margaret S. Little to Ad Hoc Committee on Children, n.d.; and "Letter of October 15th from L. W. Williams . . . ," October 10, 1957, box 15, folder 18, International Social Service United States of America Branch Records, Social Welfare History Archives, University of Minnesota, Minneapolis.

121. Memorandum from Etta Deutsch to the ACVAFS ad hoc Committee on Children, "Tentatively Arranged Discussion with INS Re: Movement of Unaccompanied Youth to Join U.S. Relatives," September 3, 1957, box 15, folder 18, International Social Service United States of America Branch Records, Social Welfare History Archives, University of Minnesota, Minneapolis.

122. "Ad Hoc Committee on Children," n.d., Appendix III.

123. "Ad Hoc Committee on Children," n.d., Appendix IV.

124. Bette R. Sprung to Mrs. Susan T. Pettiss, February 19, 1958, box 15, folder 22, International Social Service United States of America Branch Records, Social Welfare History Archives, University of Minnesota, Minneapolis.

125. "Ad Hoc Committee on Children," n.d., 5; ISS-Austria Branch, September 1958, 25.

126. "Report of Fact Finding Committee," February 14, 1958, 3.

127. "Observations on Agency Experiences," January 14, 1958, 3–4.

128. "Report of Fact Finding Committee," February 14, 1958, 1–3.

129. "Report of Fact Finding Committee," February 14, 1958, 4.

130. "Report of Fact Finding Committee," February 14, 1958, 4.

131. "Report of Fact Finding Committee," February 14, 1958, 4.

132. "Report of Fact Finding Committee," February 14, 1958, 1.

133. "Report of Fact Finding Committee," February 14, 1958, 4.

134. "Report of Fact Finding Committee," February 14, 1958, 3.

135. Tracy S. Voorhees, "Notes on Present Hungarian Refugee Relief Problem," July 19, 1958, Correspondence 1958 (Situation of Hungarian Refugees), 1958–1959, Tracy Voorhees Papers, Rutgers University Library, https://rucore.libraries.rutgers.edu/rutgers-lib/33444/PDF/1/play.

136. Tracy S. Voorhees, "Memorandum for Lewis M. Hoskins," June 17, 1958, Correspondence 1958 (Situation of Hungarian Refugees), 1958–1959, Tracy Voorhees Papers, Rutgers University Library, https://rucore.libraries.rutgers.edu/rutgers-lib/33444/PDF/1/play.

137. "The Role of the Department of Health, Education, and Welfare in Connection with Refugees and Immigrants," report of Task Force on Health, Education, and Welfare of Refugees and Immigrants, U.S. Department of Health, Education, and Welfare, Office of the Secretary, Office of Program of Analysis, June 1958, box 761, folder 1, National Archives, 102, Children's Bureau, ii, 2–4.

138. "Department of Health, Education, and Welfare," June 1958, ii, 2–4.

139. "Department of Health, Education, and Welfare," June 1958, 20.

140. "Department of Health, Education, and Welfare," June 1958, 29–30.

141. "Public Law 85–559: An Act to Authorize the Creation of a Record of Admission for Permanent Residence in the Case of Certain Hungarian Refugees," July 25, 1958, https://www.govinfo.gov/content/pkg/STATUTE-72/pdf/STATUTE-72-Pg419.pdf#page=1.

CHAPTER 5

1. Karen Dubinsky, *Babies without Borders: Adoption and Migration across the Americas* (Toronto, Ont.: University of Toronto Press, 2010), 22.

2. Ramón Torreira Crespo and José Buajasán Marrawi, *Operación Peter Pan: Un Caso de Guerra Psicológica contra Cuba* (Havana: Editora Política, 2000), 26, 91–92, 94; Lillian Guerra, *Visions of Power in Cuba: Revolution, Redemption, and Resistance, 1959–1971* (Chapel Hill: University of North Carolina Press, 2012), 212–13; Leslie Dewart, *Cuba, Church and Crisis: Christianity and Politics in the Cuban Revolution* (London: Sheed and Ward, 1964), 160.

3. Anita Casavantes Bradford, *The Revolution is for the Children: The Politics of Childhood in Havana and Miami, 1959–1962* (Chapel Hill: University of North Carolina Press, 2014).

4. U.S. Department of Health, Education, and Welfare, "Cuban Refugee Program," fact sheet, Social and Rehabilitation Service, Miami, Fla., December 1, 1969, box 1, Data on Unaccompanied Refugee Children, Records of the Social and Rehabilitation Services, RG 363, National Archives at College Park, Md.

5. Memorandum from Katherine D. Goodwin, director, Bureau of Public Assistance, "Cuban Refugees," to Jarold A. Kieffer, assistant to the secretary, through the commissioner of Social Security, November 9, 1960, box 167, folder 2, Records of the Department of Health, Education, and Welfare, RG 235, National Archives at College Park, Md.

6. Thomas D. Boswell and James R. Curtis. *The Cuban-American Experience: Culture, Images, and Perspectives* (Totowa, N.J.: Rowman & Allanheld, 1984), 45–47, 71–78; María Cristina García, *Havana USA: Cuban Exiles and Cuban Americans in South Florida, 1959–1994* (Berkeley: University of California Press, 1996), 15.

7. Robert Ingalls, *Urban Vigilantes in the New South: Tampa, 1882–1936* (Knoxville: University of Tennessee Press, 1988); Gene Burnett, "Death and Terror Scar Tampa's Past," *Florida Trend* 18 (1975): 76–80; James S. Olson and Judith E. Olson, *Cuban Americans: From Trauma to Triumph* (New York: Twayne Publishers, 1995).

8. "Cuban Refugees in Florida," n.a., November 8, 1960, box 38, folder 71, Records of the Cuban Refugee Center, 0218, Series 4, Cuban Heritage Collection, University of Miami Otto G. Richter Library.

9. María de los Angeles Torres, *The Lost Apple: Operation Pedro Pan, Cuban Children in the U.S., and the Promise of a Better Future* (Boston: Beacon Press, 2004), 60.

10. Memorandum from Katherine D. Goodwin to Jarold A. Kieffer, November 9, 1960.

11. James Hennessy, Al McDermitt, and John Hurley, "Cuban Refugee Situation in Dade County," November 8, 1960, box 42, Confidential Files, Subject Series, Mutual Security Assistance, 1960–1963, Dwight D. Eisenhower Presidential Library.

12. Katherine Oetinger, "Cuba's Children in Exile: The Story of the Unaccompanied Cuban Refugee Children's Program," Department of Health, Education, and Welfare, 1967, box 35, folder 8, Records of the Cuban Refugee Center, CHC0218, Cuban Heritage Collection, University of Miami Otto G. Richter Library, 1; Memorandum from T. E. Winterstee to Tracy Voorhees, "Report of the Welfare Planning Council," November 22, 1960, box 42, Confidential Files, Cuba, National Security, 1960–1963, Dwight D. Eisenhower Presidential Library.

13. Oetinger, "Cuba's Children in Exile," 2.

14. Oetinger, "Cuba's Children in Exile," 1; Memorandum from T. E. Winterstee to Tracy Voorhees, November 22, 1960.

15. Torres, *The Lost Apple*, 67.

16. Memorandum from Monsignor Bryan O. Walsh to Father Dominick Adessa, "Dissertation, Chapter IV, P.31," April 22, 1964, box 3, folder 1, Records of the Cuban Refugee Center, RG 353, National Archives at College Park, Md.

17. Deborah Schnookal, *Operation Pedro Pan and the Exodus of Cuba's Children* (Gainesville: University of Florida Press, 2020), 137–38; Torres, *The Lost Apple*, 49–55.

18. Schnookal, *Operation Pedro Pan*, 134; Torres, *The Lost Apple*, 65–66.

19. Eric Thomas Chester, *Covert Network: Progressives, the International Rescue Committee, and the CIA* (Armonk, N.Y.: M.E. Sharpe, 1995), 185–87; Robert Scheer, "Leo Cherne, Our Man with the CIA: The Ruling Class," *New York Times*, April 30, 1976, 16.

20. Torres, *The Lost Apple*, 64.

21. Jonathan P. Herzog, *The Spiritual-Industrial Complex: America's Religious Battle Against Communism in the Early Cold War* (New York: Oxford University Press, 2011), 54–64, 85; Patrick McNamara, *A Catholic Cold War: Edmund A. Walsh, S.J., and the Politics of American Anti-Communism* (New York: Fordham University Press, 2005).

22. Anita Casavantes Bradford, "'Let the Cuban Community Aid their Haitian Brothers': Monsignor Bryan Walsh, Miami's Immigrant Church, and the Making of a Multiethnic City, 1960–2000," *U.S. Catholic Historian* 34, no. 3 (Summer 2016): 49–76; David A. Badillo, "Catholicism and the Search for Nationhood in Miami's Cuban Community," *U.S. Catholic Historian* 20, no. 4 (Fall 2002): 79; Monsignor Bryan O. Walsh to Francisco J. Carreras, June

4, 1979, box 1, folder 6, Monsignor Bryan O. Walsh Collection, Barry University Archives, Miami Shores, Fla.

23. Susan S. Forbes and Patricia Weiss Fagen, "Unaccompanied Refugee Children: The Evolution of U.S. Policies—1939 to 1984," (Washington, D.C.: Refugee Policy Group, August 1984), 27.

24. Torres, *The Lost Apple*, 67–68.

25. Louis A. Pérez Jr., *On Becoming Cuban: Identity, Nationality, and Culture* (Chapel Hill: University of North Carolina Press, 1999), 160–61.

26. Pérez, *On Becoming Cuban*, 404.

27. Tracy S. Voorhees, *Report to the President of the United States on the Cuban Refugee Problem* (Washington, D.C.: U.S. Government Printing Office, January 18, 1961), 5–6.

28. Torres, *The Lost Apple*, 68.

29. Casavantes Bradford, "'Let the Cuban Community,'" 58.

30. Torres, *The Lost Apple*, 69.

31. "En Manos de los Profesores, Como en las Manos del Pueblo, Está el Porvenir de la Revolución," *Revolución*, February 6, 1961, 6.

32. Oetinger, "Cuba's Children in Exile," 1.

33. Torres, *The Lost Apple*, 55–57, 75–78.

34. Oetinger, "Cuba's Children in Exile," 2.

35. Torres, *The Lost Apple*, 76, 85.

36. William L. Mitchell, "The Cuban Refugee Program," *Social Security Bulletin*, March 1962, 4, box 4, folder "Miscellaneous-2," Records of the Cuban Refugee Center, RG 353, National Archives at College Park, Md.

37. Memorandum from Abraham Ribicoff to the president, "Determination Under Section 451 (a) of the Mutual Security Act of 1954, Permitting Additional Assistance to Cuban Refugees," February 15, 1961, box 167, folder 2, Records of the Department of Health, Education, and Welfare, RG 235, National Archives at College Park, Md.

38. Torres, *The Lost Apple*, 78.

39. Department of Health, Education, and Welfare, Children's Bureau, "History of the Federal Unaccompanied Cuban Refugee Children's Program," n.a., n.d., box 1, Cuban Refugee Children's Files, 1961–67, Records of the Social and Rehabilitation Services, RG 363, National Archives at College Park, Md., 58.

40. Oetinger, "Cuba's Children in Exile," 2.

41. Kathryn Close, "Cuban Children Away from Home," *Children* 10, no. 1 (January/February 1963): 10; Torres, *The Lost Apple*, 81–83.

42. Forbes and Fagen, "Unaccompanied Refugee Children," 31.

43. Betty Barton to Mrs. Katherine B. Oetinger, January 31, 1961, box 761, folder 1, Records of the Children's Bureau, 1912–69, RG 102.2, National Archives at College Park, Md.

44. Dwight H. Ferguson to Mildred Arnold, February 28, 1961, box 2, folder 15, Records of the Cuban Refugee Center, RG 353, National Archives at College Park, Md.; Oetinger, "Cuba's Children in Exile," 2.

45. Frances Davis to Miss Mildred Arnold, April 17, 1961, box 760, folder 3, Records of the Children's Bureau, 1912–69, RG 102.2, National Archives at College Park, Md.

46. Torres, *The Lost Apple*, 68, 155; Oetinger, "Cuba's Children in Exile," 2.

47. P. H. Powers to Mr. Bonsal, April 3, 1961; and P. H. Powers to W. L. Mitchell, April 3, 1961, box 760, folder 2, Records of the Children's Bureau, 1912–69, RG 102.2, National Archives at College Park, Md.

48. Father Bryan O. Walsh, "Catholic Welfare Bureau, Inc., Program for Cuban Children," n.d., box 3, folder 4, Records of the Cuban Refugee Center, RG 353, National Archives at College Park, Md.

49. Frank M. Craft to Mildred Arnold, March 13, 1961, box 3, folder 4, Records of the Cuban Refugee Center, RG 353, National Archives at College Park, Md.

50. Robert F. Hale, director, Visa Office, to Katherine B. Oetinger, chief, Children's Bureau, March 27, 1961, box 760, folder 3, Records of the Children's Bureau, 1912–69, RG 102.2, National Archives at College Park, Md.

51. Tad Szulc, "Castro's Regime Moves to Solidify Links to Soviet" and "Castro Rules Out Elections in Cuba," *New York Times*, May 2, 1961.

52. Torres, *The Lost Apple*, 129; Ramón Grau Alsina and Valerie Ridderhof, *Mongo Grau: Cuba Desde 1930* (Madrid: Agualarga Editores, 1997), 137.

53. Walter Lippmann, "An Inquiry on Cuba Is Essential," *Los Angeles Times*, May 4, 1961; Drew Pearson, "How CIA Staged Cuban Fiasco," *Washington Post*, May 5, 1961.

54. Asa McKercher, "Steamed Up: Domestic Politics, Congress, and Cuba, 1959–1963," *Diplomatic History* 38, no. 3 (2014): 601, 603, 612.

55. Carl J. Bon Tempo, *Americans at the Gate: The United States and Refugees during the Cold War* (Princeton, N.J.: Princeton University Press, 2008), 114; Torres, *The Lost Apple*, 126–27, 133.

56. Close, "Cuban Children Away from Home," 5.

57. Torres, *The Lost Apple*, 156.

58. "Minutes of Meeting for Consideration of Problems Arising in Program for Unaccompanied Cuban Refugee Children," September 26, 1962, box 5, folder 1, Records of the Cuban Refugee Center, RG 353, National Archives at College Park, Md.

59. Abraham Ribicoff to David E. Bell, May 17, 1961, n.a., n.d., box 167, folder 3, Records of the Department of Health, Education, and Welfare, RG 235, National Archives at College Park, Md.; "Estimate: Unaccompanied Children," n.a., n.d., box 167, folder 3, Records of the Department of Health, Education, and Welfare, RG 235, National Archives at College Park, Md.

60. Testimony of William Mitchell to U.S. Congress, Senate Subcommittee to Investigate Problems Connected with Refugees and Escapees, Committee on the Judiciary, World Refugee Problems, 87th Cong., 1st sess., 1961, 53; and Testimony of Bryan O. Walsh, U.S. Congress, Senate Subcommittee to Investigate Problems Connected with Refugees and Escapees, Committee on the Judiciary, Cuban Refugee Problems, 87th Cong., 1–2nd sess., 1961–1962, 229.

61. Memorandum from Mildred Arnold to W. L. Mitchell, "Rates for Payment for Foster Care of Unaccompanied Cuban Children," November 17, 1961, box 760, folder 3, Records of the Children's Bureau, 1912–69, RG 102.2, National Archives at College Park, Md.

62. Statement of Hon. Abraham Ribicoff, secretary of Health, Education, and Welfare, hearing before subcommittee no. 1 of the Committee of the Judiciary, House of Representatives, 87th Cong., 1st Sess. on H.R. 8291, August 3, 1961, box 5, folder 5, Records of the Cuban Refugee Center, RG 353, National Archives at College Park, Md., 7–15.

63. Abraham Ribicoff to Dean Rusk, September 29, 1961, box 167, folder 3, Records of the Department of Health, Education, and Welfare, RG 235, National Archives at College Park, Md.

64. Memorandum from W. L. Mitchell to Mildred Arnold, October 31, 1961, box 3, folder 7, Records of the Cuban Refugee Center, RG 353, National Archives at College Park, Md.

65. Memorandum from Mildred Arnold to W. L. Mitchell, November 17, 1961.

66. "Cuban Refugee Problems: Hearings before the Subcommittee to Investigate Problems Connected with Refugees and Escapees of the Committee of the Judiciary United States Senate, 87th Cong., First Sess.," Washington, D.C., U.S. Government Printing Office, December 6–7, 13, 1961, 12, https://catalog.hathitrust.org/Record/100679664.

67. "Cuban Refugee Problems," 4–6; Martha H. Hynning to Miss Arnold and Mr. Green, December 27, 1961, box 760, folder 2, Records of the Children's Bureau, 1912–69, RG 102.2, National Archives at College Park, Md.; Zaid Jilani, "Cruz's Smearing of Syrian Refugees Echoes Attacks on Cuban Refugees during His Father's Era," *The Intercept*, December 24, 2015, https://theintercept.com/2015/12/24/cruzs-smearing-of-syrian-refugees-echoes-his-fathers-attacks-on-cuban-refugees.

68. Abraham Ribicoff to Mr. Hamilton, December 11, 1961, box 167, folder 3, Records of the Department of Health, Education, and Welfare, RG 235, National Archives at College Park, Md.

69. Mitchell, "The Cuban Refugee Program," 7; Close, "Cuban Children Away from Home," 4.

70. Schnookal, *Operation Pedro Pan*, 59, 113, 125, 177.

71. Close, "Cuban Children Away from Home," 6.

72. José L. Hernández to Mrs. Jacqueline Kennedy, August 24, 1962, box 2, folder 17, Records of the Cuban Refugee Center, RG 353; and Lyle Birks, "Cuban Refugee Boy Now Living with Berriers Near Eldora," *Marshalltown Times-Republican*, July 5, 1963, box 5, folder 4, Records of the Cuban Refugee Center, RG 353, National Archives at College Park, Md.

73. Daniel Carrillo to the U.S. Department of State, July 10, 1962; and Mildred Arnold to Alfred H. Schultz, August 27, 1962, box 760, folder 2, Records of the Children's Bureau, 1912–69, RG 102.2, National Archives at College Park, Md.

74. Mrs. Catherine A. Bahr to Mr. Robert M. Ball, September 12, 1962, box 2, folder 12, Records of the Cuban Refugee Center, RG 353, National Archives at College Park, Md.

75. Memorandum to Joseph H. Meyers and Mildred Arnold, "Unaccompanied Cuban Refugee Children: Need for Conference," October 11, 1962, box 760, folder 3, Records of the Children's Bureau, 1912–69, RG 102.2, National Archives at College Park, Md.

76. Memorandum from Mildred Arnold to State Public Welfare administrators and Child Welfare directors, May 24, 1962, box 1, folder 6, Records of the Cuban Refugee Center, RG 353, National Archives at College Park, Md.; Mitchell, "The Cuban Refugee Program," 7; Close, "Cuban Children Away from Home," 6.

77. Close, "Cuban Children Away from Home," 6–7.

78. Mildred Arnold to Alfred H. Schultz, August 27, 1962.

79. Child Welfare League of America, "Notes on Meeting Regarding Placement of Cuban Children," May 28, 1962, box 2, folder 21, Records of the Cuban Refugee Center, RG 353; Arthur J. Lesser, M.D., "Report of Conference on Cuban Refugee Children," May 6, 1962, box 1, folder 8, Records of the Cuban Refugee Center, RG 353; and Mildred Arnold to Betty Eldridge, June 25, 1962, box 760, folder 3, Records of the Children's Bureau, 1912–69, RG 102.2, National Archives at College Park, Md.

80. Mildred Arnold to Frances Davis, October 11, 1962, box 760, folder 3, Records of the Children's Bureau, 1912–69, RG 102.2, National Archives at College Park, Md.

81. Mitchell, "The Cuban Refugee Program," 8; Thomas J. B. Waxter to Mildred Arnold, June 1, 1962, box 2, folder 13, Records of the Cuban Refugee Center, RG 353, National Archives at College Park, Md.

82. Abraham Ribicoff to Reverend Charles I. Kretz Jr., April 13, 1962, box 2, folder 13, Records of the Cuban Refugee Center, RG 353, National Archives at College Park, Md.

83. Torres, *The Lost Apple*, 150.

84. "For Release in a.m. Papers," U.S. Department of Health, Education, and Welfare, March 8, 1962, box 3, folder 4, Records of the Cuban Refugee Center, RG 353; and Address by Abraham Ribicoff, May 15, 1962, box 5, folder 4, Records of the Cuban Refugee Center, RG 353, National Archives at College Park, Md.

85. Mrs. Nancy Massiette to Governor Ribicoff, n.d., box 760, folder 2, Records of the Children's Bureau, 1912–69, RG 102.2, National Archives at College Park, Md.

86. Mrs. Edward Bates, June 5, 1962, box 760, folder 1, Records of the Children's Bureau, 1912–69, RG 102.2, National Archives at College Park, Md.

87. Close, "Cuban Children Away from Home," 5.

88. Forbes and Fagen, "Unaccompanied Refugee Children," 31–32; Arnold to Schultz, August 27, 1962, box 760, folder 2, Records of the Children's Bureau, 1912–69, RG 102.2, National Archives at College Park, Md.

89. Carlos Eire, *Learning to Die in Miami: Confessions of a Refugee Boy* (New York: Free Press, 2010), 17, 99–100.

90. Memorandum from William J. Vanden Heuvel to Arthur M. Schlesinger Jr., April 17, 1962, box 167, folder 1, Records of the Department of Health, Education, and Welfare, RG 235, National Archives at College Park, Md.

91. Close, "Cuban Children Away from Home," 8–9.

92. Memorandum from Anna E. Sundwall to Mildred Arnold, "Subject: Montana— Cuban Refugee Program," July 3, 1962, box 760, folder 1, Records of the Children's Bureau, 1912–69, RG 102.2, National Archives at College Park, Md.

93. "Nuns Adopt Refugee Children," *Florida Times Union*, April 30, 1962, box 167, folder 1, Records of the Department of Health, Education, and Welfare, RG 235, National Archives at College Park, Md.

94. Herbert Goldsworthy to Senator Thomas Kuchel, April 30, 1962, box 760, folder 1, Records of the Children's Bureau, 1912–69, RG 102.2, National Archives at College Park, Md.

95. B. F. Fisk to John F. Kennedy, June 22, 1962, box 760, folder 1, Records of the Children's Bureau, 1912–69, RG 102.2, National Archives at College Park, Md.

96. Conrad V. Henshaw to Hon. Lindley Beckworth, June 29, 1962, box 760, folder 2, Records of the Children's Bureau, 1912–69, RG 102.2, National Archives at College Park, Md.

97. Mildred Arnold to Frances Davis, May 9, 1962, box 760, folder 3, Records of the Children's Bureau, 1912–69, RG 102.2, National Archives at College Park, Md.

98. Frances Davis to Mildred Arnold, March 13, 1962, box 3, folder 4, Records of the Cuban Refugee Center, RG 353, National Archives at College Park, Md.

99. Arnold to Schultz, August 27, 1962.

100. "Meeting for Consideration of Problems," September 26, 1962.

101. Mildred Arnold to Frances Davis, May 9, 1962.

102. Mildred Arnold to Frank M. Craft, December 19, 1962, box 760, folder 3, Records of the Children's Bureau, 1912–69, RG 102.2, National Archives at College Park, Md.

103. Memorandum from Robert M. Ball to the acting secretary, "Cuban Refugee Problem," July 26, 1962, box 167, folder 1, Records of the Department of Health, Education, and Welfare, RG 235, National Archives at College Park, Md.

104. Close, "Cuban Children Away from Home," 4; Department of Health, Education, and Welfare, Social Security Administration, "Assistance to Refugees in the United States:

Justification," n.d., box 167, folder 1, Records of the Department of Health, Education, and Welfare, RG 235, National Archives at College Park, Md.

105. "Meeting for Consideration of Problems," September 26, 1962.

106. Memorandum from Joseph Meyers to Mildred Arnold, April 16, 1962, box 3, folder 8, Records of the Cuban Refugee Center, RG 353, National Archives at College Park, Md.

107. Memorandum to Joseph H. Meyers and Martha N. Hynning, August 22, 1962, box 760, folder 3, Records of the Children's Bureau, 1912–69, RG 102.2, National Archives at College Park, Md.

108. Oetinger, "Cuba's Children in Exile," 4.

109. McKercher, "Steamed Up," 624.

110. "Minutes of the Conference on October 10, 1963 on Questions on the Unaccompanied Cuban Children's Program," October 14, 1963, box 3, folder 7, Records of the Cuban Refugee Center, RG 353, National Archives at College Park, Md.

111. Lucille Batson, "Report on Field Trip to Miami, Florida, November 13–20," November 27, 1962; and Batson, "Field Report: January 29–February 5, 1963," February 11, 1963, box 5, folder 3, Records of the Cuban Refugee Center, RG 353, National Archives at College Park, Md.

112. Torres, *The Lost Apple*, 186.

113. Batson, February 11, 1963.

114. Batson, November 27, 1962; Batson, "Field Report: May 27–31, 1963," June 7, 1963, box 5, folder 3, Records of the Cuban Refugee Center, RG 353; Frances Davis to Lucille Batson, December 14, 1964; and Lucille Batson to Miss Frances Davis, January 5, 1965, box 3, folder 2, Records of the Cuban Refugee Center, RG 353, National Archives at College Park, Md.

115. Batson, November 27, 1962.

116. U.S. Department of Health, Education, and Welfare, Welfare Administration, and Children's Bureau, "Annual Report of the Interdepartmental Committee of Children and Youth, July 1, 1963–June 30, 1964," 1964, 66, https://babel.hathitrust.org/cgi/pt?id=osu.324 35028869451&view=1up&seq=3; Oetinger, "Cuba's Children in Exile," 8.

117. Oetinger, "Cuba's Children in Exile," 8.

118. Orville Crays to Martha Hynning, August 9, 1962, box 2, folder 21, Records of the Cuban Refugee Center, RG 353, National Archives at College Park, Md.; Oetinger, "Cuba's Children in Exile," 8.

119. Yvonne M. Conde, *Operation Pedro Pan: The Untold Exodus of 14,048 Cuban Children* (New York: Routledge, 1999), 156–57.

120. Memorandum from Mildred Arnold to State Public Welfare administrators and Child Welfare directors, May 24, 1962.

121. Mildred Arnold to Mr. Frank M. Craft, May 28, 1965, box 3, folder 2, Records of the Cuban Refugee Center, RG 353, National Archives at College Park, Md.

122. Note from Lucille Batson to Mrs. Hynning, June 25, 1963, box 4, folder "Children's Bureau-History," Records of the Cuban Refugee Center, RG 353, National Archives at College Park, Md.

123. Statement of Robert M. Ball, commissioner of Social Security, before the Special Subcommittee on Refugees and Escapees of the Senate Judiciary Committee on the Cuban Refugee Program, December 3, 1962, box 167, folder 1, Records of the Department of Health, Education, and Welfare, RG 235, National Archives at College Park, Md.

124. Frank Thompson Jr. to Jim G. Akin, January 4, 1963, box 167, folder 1, Records of the Department of Health, Education, and Welfare, RG 235, National Archives at College Park, Md.

125. Memorandum from John F. Thomas to Dr. Ellen Winston, March 18, 1963, box 167, folder 1, Records of the Department of Health, Education, and Welfare, RG 235, National Archives at College Park, Md.

126. "Reason and the Refugees," *The Miami Herald*, December 14, 1963, 6A.

127. Jim G. Akin to Senator John G. Tower, May 16, 1963, box 167, folder 1, Records of the Department of Health, Education, and Welfare, RG 235, National Archives at College Park, Md.

128. Torres, *The Lost Apple*, 190–91.

129. "Questions on the Unaccompanied Cuban Children's Program," October 14, 1963.

130. Torres, *The Lost Apple*, 192–95.

131. Batson, June 7, 1963.

132. Batson, February 11, 1963.

133. Batson, "Field Report: October 16–18, 1963," October 21, 1963, box 3, folder 5, Records of the Cuban Refugee Center, RG 353; and "C-75D CWB 1964," box 1, folder 1, Records of the Cuban Refugee Center, RG 353, National Archives at College Park, Md.

134. Batson, October 21, 1963.

135. Dwight H. Ferguson, "Conference with Representatives from the Florida State Department of Public Welfare Regarding the Cuban Program," October 31, 1963, box 2, folder 15, Records of the Cuban Refugee Center, RG 353, National Archives at College Park, Md.

136. "U.S. Aims to End Exile Aid, Hopes Dade Can Carry Load," *The Miami Herald*, March 10, 1965, 1.

137. Oetinger, "Cuba's Children in Exile," 4.

138. U.S. Citizenship and Immigration Services, "1965: The 1965 Amendments to the Immigration and Nationality Act (INA)," https://www.uscis.gov/about-us/our-history /history-office-and-library/featured-stories-from-the-uscis-history-office-and-library /refugee-timeline.

139. Deborah E. Anker and Michael H. Posner, "The Forty Year Crisis: A Legislative History of the Refugee Act of 1980," *San Diego Law Review* 19, no. 1 (1981): 17–19.

140. Torres, *The Lost Apple*, 207.

141. Everett M. Ressler, Neil Boothby, and Daniel J. Steinbock, *Unaccompanied Children: Care and Protection in Wars, Natural Disasters, and Refugee Movements*, (1988; repr., Oxford, U.K.: Oxford University Press, 2018), 69; Bon Tempo, *Americans at the Gate*, 114, 128.

142. Ressler, Boothby, and Steinbock, *Unaccompanied Children*, 74.

143. "Conference of Representatives from CWB, CSB, FSDPW, and CB on Problems the Agencies are Having in Reuniting Children with Parents," February 17, 1966, box 3, folder 5, Records of the Cuban Refugee Center, RG 353, National Archives at College Park, Md.

144. Martha H. Hynning to Frances Davis, August 13, 1962, box 3, folder 5, Records of the Cuban Refugee Center, RG 353, National Archives at College Park, Md.; Arnold to Schultz, August 27, 1962; and "Reuniting Children with Parents," February 17, 1966.

145. Oetinger, "Cuba's Children in Exile," 5.

146. Oetinger, "Cuba's Children in Exile," 6.

147. "Reuniting Children with Parents," February 17, 1966; Howard Croom to Mildred Arnold, September 28, 1966, box 3, folder 1, Records of the Cuban Refugee Center, RG 353, National Archives at College Park, Md.

148. Children's Bureau, "Annual Report, July 1, 1963–June 30, 1964," 66.

149. Batson, June 7, 1963.

150. Monsignor Bryan O. Walsh, untitled paper, 1973, box 1, folder 6, Walsh Collection, Barry University Archives, Miami Shores, Fla.; Bryan O. Walsh, "Cuban Refugee Children,"

Journal of Inter-American Studies 13, nos. 3/4 (July/October 1971): 395; Oetinger, "Cuba's Children in Exile," 7; Orville Crays to Martha Hynning, August 9, 1962.

151. Children's Bureau, "Cuban Refugee Children's Program," n.d., 101.

152. Katherine Brownell Oetinger, "Services to Unaccompanied Cuban Refugee Children in the United States," *Social Service Review* 36, no. 4 (1962): 384, box, 4, folder "Miscellaneous-2," Records of the Cuban Refugee Center, RG 353, National Archives at College Park, Md.

153. For in-depth discussion of the competing narratives surrounding the children's exodus, see Anita Casavantes Bradford, "Remembering Pedro Pan: Childhood and Collective Memory Making in Havana and Miami, 1960–2000," *Cuban Studies* 11, no. 44 (2016): 283–308.

154. Torres, *The Lost Apple*, 66.

CHAPTER 6

1. Shivani Ekkanath, "8 Facts About the Vietnam War and Vietnamese Refugees," The Borgen Project, accessed December 22, 2020, https://borgenproject.org/vietnam-war-and-vietnamese-refugees; U.S. Department of State, Refugee Data Center, "East Asia/Admissions: Unaccompanied Minors: Numbers Entering U.S.," October 1987, box 46, folder 43, International Social Service United States of America Branch Records, Social Welfare History Archives, University of Minnesota, Minneapolis.

2. Gil Loescher and John A. Scanlan, *Calculated Kindness: Refugees and America's Half-Open Door, 1945 to the Present* (New York: Free Press, 1986), 104.

3. Susan S. Forbes and Patricia Weiss Fagen, "Unaccompanied Refugee Children: The Evolution of U.S. Policies—1939 to 1984," (Washington, D.C.: Refugee Policy Group, August 1984), 33–40.

4. Loescher and Scanlan, *Calculated Kindness*, 105–6.

5. Everett M. Ressler, Neil Boothby, and Daniel J. Steinbock, *Unaccompanied Children: Care and Protection in Wars, Natural Disasters, and Refugee Movements*, (1988; repr., Oxford, U.K.: Oxford University Press, 2018), 100; Forbes and Fagen, "Unaccompanied Refugee Children," 33–35.

6. Ressler, Boothby, and Steinbock, *Unaccompanied Children*, 101; Forbes and Fagen, "Unaccompanied Refugee Children," 35.

7. "Gerald Ford Presidential Library A3860–35A" image A3854-03A, April 5, 1975, Gerald R. Ford Presidential Library & Museum, National Archives, https://www.fordlibrarymuseum.gov/museum/exhibits/babylift/photography.

8. Alexandra Young, "Developments in Intercountry Adoption: From Humanitarian Aid to Market-Driven Policy and beyond," *Adoption & Fostering Quarterly Journal* 36, no. 2 (July 2012): 70; Barbara J. Keys, *Reclaiming American Virtue: The Human Rights Revolution of the 1970s* (Cambridge, Mass.: Harvard University Press, 2014), 48; Christian G. Appy, *American Reckoning: The Vietnam War and Our National Identity* (New York: Penguin Random House, 2015), 59, 144, 183–85, 204.

9. "Yes, There is Something You can Do for the Children of Vietnam," advertisement in the *New York Times*, April 7, 1975, The Adoption History Project, https://pages.uoregon.edu/adoption/archive/NYTOBad.htm; Harry Minetree, "Heroes of the Vietnam Orphan Lift," *People*, June 16, 1975; "Save the Children," *Hartford Times*, April 5, 1975; "A Cool and Wary Reception," *Time*, May 12, 1975, 30, 32.

10. Daniel J. Steinbock, "The Admission of Unaccompanied Children," *Yale Law and Policy Review* 7, no. 1 (1989): 149. For examples of alarmist media coverage, see Richard Steele,

"Orphans of the Storm," *Newsweek* 14, April 1975, 29–30; and Joyce Gemberlein, "Callers Swamp Adoption Agencies," *Pittsburgh Post-Gazette*, April 8, 1975, 1.

11. Yến Lê Espiritu, *Body Counts: The Vietnam War and Militarized Refuge(es)* (Berkeley: University of California Press, 2014), 42. For more on the history of white American women as "mothers" to children of color, including U.S. Indigenous people, see Margaret Jacobs' *White Mother to a Dark Race* (Lincoln: University of Nebraska Press, 2009).

12. Forbes and Fagen, "Unaccompanied Refugee Children," 39; Agency for International Development, "Operation Babylift Report (Emergency Movement of Vietnamese and Cambodian Orphans for Intercountry Adoption, April – June 1975)," Washington, D.C., 5–6, The Adoption History Project, https://pages.uoregon.edu/adoption/archive/AIDOBR.htm.

13. Ressler, Boothby, and Steinbock, *Unaccompanied Children*, 101.

14. U.S. Congress, Senate, Subcommittee to Investigate Problems Connected with Refugees and Escapees, Committee on the Judiciary, "Part I: Indochina Evacuation and Refugee Problems: Operation Babylift & Humanitarian Needs," 94th Cong., 1st sess., 1975, 11, 27–28, 51.

15. Ressler, Boothby, and Steinbock, *Unaccompanied Children*, 101, 103.

16. Peter H. Koehn, *Refugees from Revolution: U.S. Policy and Third World Migration* (Boulder, Colo.: Westview Press, 1991), 101; Loescher and Scanlan, *Calculated Kindness*, 74–78.

17. Michael H. Hunt, *The American Ascendancy: How the United States Gained and Wielded Global Dominance* (Chapel Hill: University of North Carolina Press, 2007), 244; Yanek Mieczkowski, *Gerald Ford and the Challenges of the 1970s* (Lexington: University Press of Kentucky, 2005), 293–94.

18. Carl J. Bon Tempo, *Americans at the Gate: The United States and Refugees during the Cold War* (Princeton, N.J.: Princeton University Press, 2008), 138.

19. Loescher and Scanlan, *Calculated Kindness*, 102.

20. Loescher and Scanlan, *Calculated Kindness*, 107, 108.

21. Heather Marie Stur, "'Hiding Behind the Humanitarian Label': Refugees, Repatriates, and the Rebuilding of America's Benevolent Image After the Vietnam War," *Diplomatic History* 39, no. 2 (April 2015): 223–44, 224; Yến Lê Espiritu, "Toward a Critical Refugee Study: The Vietnamese Refugee Subject in US Scholarship," *Journal of Vietnamese Studies* 1, nos. 1/2 (February/August 2006): 410–33; Loescher and Scanlan, *Calculated Kindness*, 110.

22. Norman L. Zucker, "Refugee Resettlement in the United States: Policy and Problems," *Annals of the American Academy of Political and Social Science* 467 (May 1983): 174.

23. "Memorandum for the President," from Secretary of State Henry A. Kissinger, subject "National Committee for Vietnamese and Cambodian Refugees," (May 1975), box 11, folder: Indochina Refugees-President's Advisory Committee: General (1), Theodore C. Marrs Files, Gerald R. Ford Presidential Library.

24. Edwin B. Silverman, "Indochina Legacy: The Refugee Act of 1980," *Publius* 10, no. 1 (Winter 1980): 27–41, 29; Bon Tempo, *Americans at the Gate*, 163.

25. Forbes and Fagen, "Unaccompanied Refugee Children," 41.

26. "Functions of the President's Committee for Hungarian Refugee Relief," addendum to "The President's Advisory Committee on Refugees: Background Papers," Interagency Task Force, May 19, 1975, box 11, folder: Indochina Refugees-President's Advisory Committee: Background Papers (1), Theodore C. Marrs Files, Gerald R. Ford Presidential Library.

27. Rachel M. McCleary, *Global Compassion: Private Voluntary Organizations and U.S. Foreign Policy Since 1939* (New York: Oxford University Press, 2009), 65, 76, 80, 92, 94; Keys, *Reclaiming American Virtue*, 171; J. Bruce Nichols, *The Uneasy Alliance: Religion, Refugee Work*

and U.S. Foreign Policy (New York: Oxford University Press, 1988), 104, 107, 115; Michael Barnett, *Empire of Humanity: A History of Humanitarianism* (Ithaca, N.Y.: Cornell University Press, 2011), 147–49.

28. Paul James Rutledge, *The Vietnamese Experience in America* (Bloomington: Indiana University Press, 1992), 4–5; Min Zhou and Carl L. Bankston III, *Straddling Two Social Worlds: The Experience of Vietnamese Refugee Children in the United States*. Urban Diversity Series, no. 111 (New York: ERIC Clearinghouse on Urban Education, 2000), 4.

29. Bon Tempo, *Americans at the Gate*, 158, 160.

30. Zhou and Bankston III, *Straddling Two Social Worlds*, 6; Phuong Tran Nguyen, *Becoming Refugee American: The Politics of Rescue in Little Saigon* (Urbana: University of Illinois Press, 2017), 38.

31. Loescher and Scanlan, *Calculated Kindness*, 112.

32. Nguyen, *Becoming Refugee American*, 39.

33. Jana K. Lipman, "A Refugee Camp in America: Fort Chafee and Vietnamese and Cuban Refugees, 1975–1982," *Journal of American Ethnic History* 33, no. 2 (Winter 2014): 62–63; Espiritu, *Body Counts*, 34; see also Mimi Thi Nguyen, *The Gift of Freedom: War, Debt, and Other Passages* (Durham, N.C.: Duke University Press, 2012).

34. Nguyen, *Becoming Refugee American*, 45.

35. Nguyen, *Becoming Refugee American*, 35.

36. John M. Campbell to Mr. Roger D. Semerad, executive director, President's Advisory Committee on Refugees, July 11, 1975, box 11, folder: Indochina Refugees-President's Advisory Committee: General (4), Theodore C. Marrs Files, Gerald R. Ford Presidential Library.

37. "May 22, 1975: Meeting with Voluntary Agencies, Roosevelt Room;" and "Memorandum for President's Advisory Committee on Refugees, Subject: Meeting with Voluntary Agencies, May 22, 1975," box 10, folder: Indochina Refugees-Meeting with Voluntary Agencies, 5/22/75, Theodore C. Marrs Files, Gerald R. Ford Presidential Library.

38. Bon Tempo, *Americans at the Gate*, 146.

39. "Ford Signs $405 Million Bill to Resettle Refugees," *Los Angeles Times*, May 25, 1975, 6; Zucker, "Refugee Resettlement," 175; Loescher and Scanlan, *Calculated Kindness*, 114; Silverman, "Indochina Legacy," 32.

40. Zucker, "Refugee Resettlement," 175.

41. Bon Tempo, *Americans at the Gate*, 164.

42. Bella Stumbo, "Idleness, Frustration in a Refugee Camp," *Los Angeles Times*, May 6, 1975, B3; Nguyen, *Becoming Refugee American*, 4, 38, 39.

43. Jack Walsh to John Eisenhower, June 23, 1975; and John S. D. Eisenhower to Mr. Jack Walsh, June 26, 1975, box 11, folder: Indochina Refugees-President's Advisory Committee: General (3), Theodore C. Marrs Files, Gerald R. Ford Presidential Library.

44. "'We Miss our Parents': Viet Children at Pendleton Sit and Wait," *Los Angeles Times*, July 6, 1975, B1.

45. "250 Refugee Children Found Without Parents," *San Diego Union*, July 31, 1975, 1.

46. Douglas E. Kneeland, "Unaccompanied Children Pose a Refugee Problem," *New York Times*, July 28, 1975, 1.

47. Forbes and Fagen, "Unaccompanied Refugee Children," 42; Steinbock, "The Admission of Unaccompanied Children," 141.

48. "The President's Advisory Committee on Refugees: Background Papers," Interagency Task Force, May 19, 1975, box 11, folder: Indochina Refugees-President's Advisory Committee: Background Papers (1), Theodore C. Marrs Files, Gerald R. Ford Presidential Library.

49. Kneeland, "Unaccompanied Children," 1.

50. "'We Miss our Parents.'"

51. Jonathan Freedman, "Transgressions of a Model Minority," *Shofar: An Interdisciplinary Journal of Jewish Studies* 23, no. 4 (2005): 83–84, 87, 91. A small number of scholars have begun to note the distinct but related processes of racialization which have defined the Jewish and Asian American communities. Imagined as intelligent and industrious even as they were stigmatized for their presumed avarice, scheming, and materialism, both were reimagined later as "model minorities" whose thrift, family cohesion, and educational achievement explained how they accessed an "American dream" ostensibly available to all minority groups—even though they have remained under suspicion as a lingering threat to the nation's political and cultural integrity.

52. Forbes and Fagen, "Unaccompanied Refugee Children," 44–45.

53. Chad C. Haddal, *Unaccompanied Refugee Minors. CRS Report for Congress* (Washington, D.C.: Congressional Research Service, March 14, 2008), 2.

54. Kneeland, "Unaccompanied Children," 1.

55. Forbes and Fagen, "Unaccompanied Refugee Children," 43.

56. Ressler, Boothby, and Steinbock, *Unaccompanied Children*, 106; Linda W. Gordon, "Asian Immigration since World War II," in *Immigration and U.S. Foreign Policy*, eds. Robert W. Tucker, Charles B. Keely, and Linda Wrigley (New York: Routledge, 2019), 183.

57. "'We Miss our Parents.'"

58. Forbes and Fagen, "Unaccompanied Refugee Children," 44–45.

59. Aristide R. Zolberg, *A Nation by Design: Immigration Policy in the Fashioning of America* (Cambridge, Mass.: Harvard University Press, 2008), 346.

60. Silverman, "Indochina Legacy," 32.

61. Hunt, *The American Ascendancy*, 245; Keys, *Reclaiming American Virtue*, 104, 110, 177.

62. Loescher and Scanlan, *Calculated Kindness*, 129; Rutledge, *The Vietnamese Experience*, 62.

63. "Intelligence Memorandum Prepared in the Central Intelligence Agency. Refugees and Human Rights: An Issue in US-ASEAN Relations," December 16, 1977, in *Southeast Asia and the Pacific*, eds., David P. Nickles and Melissa Jane Taylor, vol. 22 of Adam M. Howard, ed. *Foreign Relations of the United States 1977–1980* (Washington, D.C.: U.S. Government Publishing Office, 2017), (hereafter *FRUS 1977–1980*, vol. 22), 409–14.

64. Loescher and Scanlan, *Calculated Kindness*, 130–33, 136.

65. Bon Tempo, *Americans at the Gate*, 151; Loescher and Scanlan, *Calculated Kindness*, 137–38; "Letter from Secretary of State Vance to Representative Clement J. Zablocki," September 30, 1978, *FRUS 1977–1980*, vol. 22, 95.

66. "Memorandum from the President's Assistant for National Security Affairs (Brzezinski) to President Carter. Subject: Emergency Parole for Indochinese Refugees," December 19, 1977, *FRUS 1977–1980*, vol. 22, 414–15; and "Paper Prepared in the Department of State: The Status of National Policy on Indochinese Refugees," n.d., *FRUS 1977–1980*, vol. 22, 417–18; see also "President Agrees to Admit 7,000 Indochinese Refugees," *Washington Post*, December 23, 1977, A11.

67. "Memorandum from Secretary of State Vance to Vice President Mondale. Subject: Initiatives to Help in the Resettlement of Indochinese Refugees," n.d., *FRUS 1977–1980*, vol. 22, 450–52.

68. Frances Grandy, "A Refugee Now Helps Others Begin Anew," *New York Times*, October 14, 1979, CN2; Ressler, Boothby, and Steinbock, *Unaccompanied Children*, 113.

69. Haddal, *Unaccompanied Refugee Minors*, 3; Forbes and Fagen, "Unaccompanied Refugee Children," 47.

70. Aristide R. Zolberg, Astri Suhrke, and Segrio Aguayo, *Escape from Violence: Conflict and the Refugee Crisis in the Developing World* (New York: Oxford University Press, 1989), 164–65.

71. Koehn, *Refugees from Revolution*, 102.

72. U.S. Department of State, "East Asia/Admissions."

73. Rutledge, *The Vietnamese Experience*, 16–17; Ressler, Boothby, and Steinbock, *Unaccompanied Children*, 106–7; see also "Paper Prepared in the Department of State: The Status of National Policy on Indochinese Refugees," n.d., *FRUS 1977–1980*, vol. 22; and "Memorandum to the Files. Subject: Refugees," December 12, 1978, *FRUS 1977–1980*, vol. 22, 459.

74. Yuko Kawai, "Stereotyping Asian Americans: The Dialectic of the Model Minority and the Yellow Peril," *The Howard Journal of Communications* 16, no. 2 (2005): 112–13; see also Robert G. Lee, *Orientals: Asian Americans in Popular Culture* (Philadelphia, Pa.: Temple University Press, 1999), 2, 4, 8–11.

75. Ressler, Boothby, and Steinbock, *Unaccompanied Children*, 130.

76. Loescher and Scanlan, *Calculated Kindness*, 147, 152–53, 156–57.

77. Silverman, "Indochina Legacy," 34; Loescher and Scanlan, *Calculated Kindness*, 154.

78. Forbes and Fagen, "Unaccompanied Refugee Children," 53–55.

79. Steinbock, "The Admission of Unaccompanied Children," 152.

80. Forbes and Fagen, "Unaccompanied Refugee Children," 46–47, 52–53.

81. Angela Shen Ryan, "Lessons Learned from Programs for Unaccompanied Refugee Minors," *Journal of Multicultural Social Work* 5, nos. 3/4 (1997): 186.

82. Forbes and Fagen, "Unaccompanied Refugee Children," 46, 48; Rosalind Harris to Audrey Moser, November 7, 1979; and Rosalind Harris to Petrina Slaytor, June 18, 1979, box 16, folder 26, International Social Service United States of America Branch Records, Social Welfare History Archives, University of Minnesota, Minneapolis; Ryan, "Lessons Learned," 195–96.

83. U.S. Department of State, "East Asia/Admissions."

84. Forbes and Fagen, "Unaccompanied Refugee Children," 51–52.

85. Loescher and Scanlan, *Calculated Kindness*, 142; Nguyen, *Becoming Refugee American*, 72.

86. "At the End of the Rainbow—Holes in the Ceiling," *The Philadelphia Inquirer*, May 26, 1979, 4A.

87. Loescher and Scanlan, *Calculated Kindness*, 142.

88. Loescher and Scanlan, *Calculated Kindness*, 140; Zolberg, Suhrke, and Aguayo, *Escape from Violence*, 166.

89. "Memorandum from the U.S. Coordinator for Refugee Affairs (Clark) to Vice President Mondale. Subject: Indochina Refugees," June 18, 1979, *FRUS 1977–1980*, vol. 22, 469–74; Kwok B. Chan and David Loveridge, "Refugees 'In Transit': Vietnamese in a Refugee Camp in Hong Kong," *International Migration Review* 21, no. 3 (Autumn 1987): 749.

90. Silverman, "Indochina Legacy," 35; Sixty Minutes (CBS), "The Vietnamese Boat People: The Price of Freedom," June 24, 1979, https://www.youtube.com/watch?v=-TsZVgQf4Ss.

91. "Memorandum from the U.S. Coordinator for Refugee Affairs (Clark) to President Carter. Subject: Indochinese Refugees: Tokyo and Beyond," June 20, 1979; *FRUS 1977–1980*, vol. 22, 474–79.

92. Loescher and Scanlan, *Calculated Kindness*, 142, 144.

93. "Briefing Paper Prepared in the Department of State. UN Conference on Indochinese Refugees," July 25, 1979, *FRUS 1977–1980*, vol. 22, 479–82; Ressler, Boothby, and Steinbock, *Unaccompanied Children*, 113, 116.

94. "Intelligence Assessment Prepared in the Central Intelligence Agency. The Indochina Refugee Situation: An Update," November 1979, *FRUS 1977–1980*, vol. 22, 487–95.

95. "At the End of the Rainbow."

96. Nichols, *The Uneasy Alliance*, 112, 115.

97. Rodney Stark and Roger Finke, "Catholic Religious Vocations: Decline and Revival," *Review of Religious Research* 42, no. 2 (December 2000): 125.

98. Rosalind Harris to Audrey Moser, November 7, 1979.

99. "For a Boy All Alone, a Foster Family with Open Arms," *The Philadelphia Inquirer*, May 26, 1979, 4A.

100. "For a Boy All Alone."

101. Peter Blau, "40 'Boat Children' to Come to Twin Cities," *The Minneapolis Tribune*, July 17, 1979.

102. Ressler, Boothby, and Steinbock, *Unaccompanied Children*, 134.

103. Rosalind Harris to Audrey Moser, August 1, 1979, box 16, folder 26, International Social Service United States of America Branch Records, Social Welfare History Archives, University of Minnesota, Minneapolis; Ressler, Boothby, and Steinbock, *Unaccompanied Children*, 132–34; "Report Prepared in the Office of the First Lady. Report of Mrs. Rosalynn Carter on Cambodian Relief," November 8–10, 1979, *FRUS 1977–1980*, vol. 22, 248–52.

104. Ressler, Boothby, and Steinbock, *Unaccompanied Children*, 140.

105. Nguyen, *Becoming Refugee American*, 5; Gordon, "Asian Immigration since World War II," 177; United States Department of State, "East Asia/Admissions."

106. Zolberg, *A Nation by Design*, 339.

107. Nguyen, *Becoming Refugee American*, 101, 109.

108. Steinbock, "The Admission of Unaccompanied Children," 162–63; Bon Tempo, *Americans at the Gate*, 174, 178–79; Forbes and Fagen, "Unaccompanied Refugee Children," 53.

109. Zucker, "Refugee Resettlement," 174.

110. Silverman, "Indochina Legacy," 27.

111. Bon Tempo, *Americans at the Gate*, 192; Forbes and Fagen, "Unaccompanied Refugee Children," 58.

112. Steinbock, "The Admission of Unaccompanied Children," 156, 158.

113. Forbes and Fagen, "Unaccompanied Refugee Children," 60.

114. Bon Tempo, *Americans at the Gate*, 179–80.

115. Bon Tempo, *Americans at the Gate*, 114–15.

116. Keys, *Reclaiming American Virtue*, 243, 267; Hunt, *The American Ascendancy*, 249–50.

117. Russell H. Fifield, "The Reagan Administration and Southeast Asia," *Southeast Asian Affairs* (1983): 42, 43–46; Phil Orchard, *A Right to Flee: Refugees, States, and the Construction of International Cooperation* (Cambridge: Cambridge University Press, 2014), 212–13.

118. Rutledge, *The Vietnamese Experience*, 37; Loescher and Scanlan, *Calculated Kindness*, 104, 165.

119. U.S. Department of State, "East Asia/Admissions;" Ressler, Boothby, and Steinbock, *Unaccompanied Children*, 155–58; John Hail, "Kitty Dukakis Stirs Refugee Issue," *Boston Globe*, June 27, 1981, 5.

120. "Telegram from the Embassy in Thailand to the Department of State. Subject: Motivations of Vietnamese Boat Refugees," December 30, 1980, *FRUS 1977–1980*, vol. 22, 516–21.

121. Loescher and Scanlan, *Calculated Kindness*, 168; Steinbock, "The Admission of Unaccompanied Children," 163.

122. Bon Tempo, *Americans at the Gate*, 192.

123. Steinbock, "The Admission of Unaccompanied Children," 165.

124. Steinbock, "The Admission of Unaccompanied Children," 163.

125. Bon Tempo, *Americans at the Gate*, 187–88; Rutledge, *The Vietnamese Experience*, 37; U.S. Department of State, "East Asia/Admissions."

126. Ressler, Boothby, and Steinbock, *Unaccompanied Children*, 159.

127. Rutledge, *The Vietnamese Experience*, 134; Sabrina Thomas, *The Scars of War: The Politics of Paternity and National Responsibility for the Amerasians of Vietnam* (Lincoln: University of Nebraska Press, 2021), 168.

128. Forbes and Fagen, "Unaccompanied Refugee Children," 59.

129. "U.S. Entry for Pol Pot Youths Debated," *New York Times*, January 15, 1984, 3.

130. "ISS Unaccompanied Minors Committee: Notes of the Meeting," April 9, 1985, box 46, folder 42, International Social Service United States of America Branch Records, Social Welfare History Archives, University of Minnesota, Minneapolis.

131. Ressler, Boothby, and Steinbock, *Unaccompanied Children*, 124.

132. "U.S. Entry for Pol Pot Youths."

133. Ressler, Boothby, and Steinbock, *Unaccompanied Children*, 117.

134. Forbes and Fagen, "Unaccompanied Refugee Children," 56–58; Ryan, "Lessons Learned," 196.

135. Ryan, "Lessons Learned," 198.

136. Ressler, Boothby, and Steinbock, *Unaccompanied Children*, 112, 118, 120–21.

137. Connally C. Tolland, "From Cambodian Jungle to New Hampshire's Mountains," *Christian Science Monitor*, August 3, 1981, 16; Hilary DeVries, "New Lives," *Christian Science Monitor*, December 21, 1984, 16.

138. Scott Minerbrook, "Joyful Respite for Refugees," *Newsday*, December 17, 1982, 4.

139. Ressler, Boothby, and Steinbock, *Unaccompanied Children*, 120.

140. "For a Boy All Alone."

141. Ressler, Boothby, and Steinbock, *Unaccompanied Children*, 121; Earl E. Huyck and Rona Fields, "Impact of Resettlement on Refugee Children," *International Migration Review* 15, nos. 1/2 (Spring/Summer 1981): 249; Ryan, "Lessons Learned," 197–98, 201.

142. Ryan, "Lessons Learned," 197–98, 200; Ressler, Boothby, and Steinbock, *Unaccompanied Children*, 278.

143. Ryan, "Lessons Learned," 199, 201.

144. Ryan, "Lessons Learned," 199, 201.

145. Ressler, Boothby, and Steinbock, *Unaccompanied Children*, 123.

146. "Unaccompanied Refugee Minors in Family Reunification Cases: A 90-Day Follow-Up Study," Migration and Refugee Services, U.S. Catholic Conference, March 1985, box 46, folder 43, International Social Service United States of America Branch Records, Social Welfare History Archives, University of Minnesota, Minneapolis.

147. "Unaccompanied Refugee Minors."

148. Nguyen, *Becoming Refugee American*, 10, 30, 34.

149. Beverly Beyette, "Agency Softens Clash of Cultures: Asian-American Organization Fills a Social-Service Gap," *Los Angeles Times*, December 15, 1985, H12; "Replanting Uprooted Youth: Proceedings, National Conference on Refugee Youth," Lutheran Immigration and Refugee Service, December 4–6, 1988, Vertical File Collection, MS-SEA020, Southeast Asian Archive, UC Irvine Libraries, Irvine, Calif., 24–25.

150. Ryan, "Lessons Learned," 198.

151. Tolland, "From Cambodian Jungle;" DeVries, "New Lives," 16.

152. Espiritu, *Body Counts*, 6.

153. "Replanting Uprooted Youth," December 4–6, 1988, 24–25.

154. "Unaccompanied Minor Refugees: Nine Years of Achievement," Proceedings of the Unaccompanied Minor Refugee Conference, November 13–16, 1984, Chevy Chase, Md., Lutheran Immigration and Refugee Service, U.S. Catholic Conference and U.S. Office of Refugee Resettlement, box 46, folder 43, International Social Service United States of America Branch Records, Social Welfare History Archives, University of Minnesota, Minneapolis.

155. "Unaccompanied Minors Workgroup: Minutes of February 14–15 (1985) Meeting," box 46, folder 42, International Social Service United States of America Branch Records, Social Welfare History Archives, University of Minnesota, Minneapolis.

156. Evelyn Hsu, "'Americanization' Problems of Viet Youth to Be Explored," *Washington Post*, March 27, 1987, C2.

157. U.S. Department of State, "East Asia/Admissions;" Rutledge, *The Vietnamese Experience*, 37; Maira Farrow, "Orphans Trapped in Camps," *The Ottawa Citizen*, September 18, 1986, B7.

158. "Thailand Flooded With New Asian Refugees," *The Globe and Mail*, December 28, 1987, A12; Rutledge, *The Vietnamese Experience*, 37; Executive Committee of the High Commissioner's Programs, "Report on Refugee Children," 40th Session, July 21, 1989, 9, Series 1, folder: "Vietnamese American Organization - CA - San Jose - Aid to Refugee Children Without Parents Inc.—Ephemera," Vertical File Collection, MS-SEA020, Southeast Asian Archive, UC Irvine Libraries, Irvine, Calif.; Sara E. Davies, "Realistic Yet Humanitarian? The Comprehensive Plan of Action and Refugee Policy in Southeast Asia," *International Relations of the Asia-Pacific* 8, no. 2 (2008): 192.

159. Steinbock, "The Admission of Unaccompanied Children," 163; U.S. Department of State, "East Asia/Admissions."

160. William A. Garland, director of the Office of Asian Refugee Assistance, U.S. Department of State, to Mr. Huu Nguyen, n.d., Series 1, folder: "Vietnamese American Organization - CA - San Jose - Aid to Refugee Children Without Parents Inc.—Ephemera," Vertical File Collection, MS-SEA020, Southeast Asian Archive, UC Irvine Libraries, Irvine, Calif.

161. "Highlights of ISS Committee on Minors in Migration," February 3, 1987, box 46, folder 43, International Social Service United States of America Branch Records, Social Welfare History Archives, University of Minnesota, Minneapolis.

162. Joel Keehn, "Vietnam's Boat Refugees," *East/West News*, February 11, 1988, folder: "Refugees: Vietnamese-Clippings-1975–1988," Vertical File Collection, MS-SEA020, Southeast Asian Archive, UC Irvine Libraries, Irvine, Calif.

163. Zhou and Bankston III, *Straddling Two Social Worlds*, 5; Nguyen, *Becoming Refugee American*, 6.

164. Hunt, *The American Ascendancy*, 259–62, 271.

165. Davies, "Realistic Yet Humanitarian," 192, 194–98, 205, 209, 212.

166. Christine Mougne, "Difficult Decisions," *Refugees* (November 1989): 12–13, 13, Series 1, folder: "Vietnamese American Organization - CA - San Jose - Aid to Refugee Children Without Parents Inc.—Ephemera," Vertical File Collection, MS-SEA020, Southeast Asian Archive, UC Irvine Libraries, Irvine, Calif.

167. Steinbock, "The Admission of Unaccompanied Children," 164–65.

168. Executive Committee, "Report on Refugee Children," 9.

169. Executive Committee, "Report on Refugee Children."

170. Nguyen D. Huu to Mr. Thorvald Stoltenberg, March 5, 1990, Series 1, folder: "Vietnamese American Organization - CA - San Jose - Aid to Refugee Children Without Parents Inc.—Ephemera," Vertical File Collection, MS-SEA020, Southeast Asian Archive, UC Irvine Libraries, Irvine, Calif; Mougne, "Difficult Decisions," 13.

171. "Vietnamese Social Worker Dedicated to Helping Refugees," *AsianWeek* 11, no. 21 (January 5, 1990), 21; "James Montague Freeman," Emeritus and Retired Faculty Biographies, San José State University, accessed October 18, 2020, https://scholarworks.sjsu.edu /erfa_bios/299; Nguyen D. Huu to Mr. Thorvald Stoltenberg, March 5, 1990.

172. Nguyen D. Huu to Ms. Christine M. Mougne, May 15, 1990, Series 1, folder: "Vietnamese American Organization - CA - San Jose - Aid to Refugee Children Without Parents Inc.—Ephemera," Vertical File Collection, MS-SEA020, Southeast Asian Archive, UC Irvine Libraries, Irvine, Calif.

173. "INS to Grant Refugee Status for Vietnamese Unaccompanied Minors," U.S. Department of Justice, Immigration and Naturalization Service, Press Information Office, May 1, 1990, Vertical File Collection, MS-SEA020, Southeast Asian Archive, UC Irvine Libraries, Irvine, Calif.

174. William A. Garland to Mr. Huu Nguyen, n.d.

CHAPTER 7

1. Aristide R. Zolberg, *A Nation by Design: Immigration Policy in the Fashioning of America* (Cambridge, Mass.: Harvard University Press, 2008), 339.

2. Susan S. Forbes and Patricia Weiss Fagen, "Unaccompanied Refugee Children: The Evolution of U.S. Policies—1939 to 1984," (Washington, D.C.: Refugee Policy Group, August 1984), 64, 66.

3. Jana K. Lipman, "A Refugee Camp in America: Fort Chafee and Vietnamese and Cuban Refugees, 1975–1982," *Journal of American Ethnic History* 33, no. 2 (Winter 2014): 71–74; Robert Pear, "As Castro Zigged and Zagged on the Refugees, So Did Carter," *New York Times*, May 18, 1980, E4.

4. Deborah E. Anker and Michael H. Posner, "The Forty Year Crisis: A Legislative History of the Refugee Act of 1980," *San Diego Law Review* 19, no. 1 (1981): 64–65.

5. Norman L. Zucker, "Refugee Resettlement in the United States: Policy and Problems," *Annals of the American Academy of Political and Social Science* 467 (May 1983): 179.

6. Forbes and Fagen, "Unaccompanied Refugee Children," 64–65.

7. Zucker, "Refugee Resettlement," 180; Forbes and Fagen, "Unaccompanied Refugee Children," 62–63, 66–68.

8. Forbes and Fagen, "Unaccompanied Refugee Children," 71–73; Jonathan Mandell, "A Closing Door," *Newsday*, June 30, 1987, A4.

9. Anker and Posner, "The Forty Year Crisis," 64; Zucker, "Refugee Resettlement," 179; Mandell, "A Closing Door," A4.

10. Carl J. Bon Tempo, *Americans at the Gate: The United States and Refugees during the Cold War* (Princeton, N.J.: Princeton University Press, 2008), 185–86.

11. Daniel J. Steinbock, "The Admission of Unaccompanied Children into the United States," *Yale Law and Policy Review* 7, no. 1 (1989): 164.

12. Angela Shen Ryan, "Lessons Learned from Programs for Unaccompanied Refugee Minors," *Journal of Multicultural Social Work* 5, nos. 3/4 (1997): 197.

13. "10,000 Detained Cuba Rafters May Be Let into the US on Parole," *Philadelphia Inquirer*, December 3, 1994, A17.

14. "10,000 Detained Cuba Rafters."

15. Bon Tempo, *Americans at the Gate*, 199.

16. Anker and Posner, "The Forty Year Crisis," 70; Bon Tempo, *Americans at the Gate*, 198–99.

17. Chad C. Haddal, *Unaccompanied Refugee Minors*. *CRS Report for Congress* (Washington, D.C.: Congressional Research Service, March 14, 2008), i, 8, 12–13.

18. Haddal, *Unaccompanied Refugee Minors*, i, 10.

19. "Report on Impact of Armed Conflict on Children Exposes Moral Vacuum, Secretary-General's Expert Tells Third Committee" United Nations General Assembly Press Release, November 8, 1996, https://www.un.org/press/en/1996/19961108.gash3382.html; see also David M. Rosen, *Child Soldiers in the Western Imagination: From Patriots to Victims* (New Brunswick, N.J.: Rutgers University Press, 2015), 104–5, 182; and Haddal, *Unaccompanied Refugee Minors*, 12, 13.

20. Bon Tempo, *Americans at the Gate*, 204; see also Ted Dagne, *Sudan: The Crisis in Darfur and Status of the North-South Peace Agreement. CRS Report for Congress* (Washington, D.C.: Congressional Research Service, June 11, 2015).

21. Susan Schmidt, "Liberian Refugees: Cultural Considerations for Social Services Providers," Bridging Refugee Youth and Children's Services, June 2011, https://brycs.org/wp-content/uploads/2018/09/Liberian_Cultural_Considerations.pdf.

22. Laura Bates, Diane Baird, Deborah J. Johnson, Robert E. Lee, Tom Luster, and Christine Rehagen, "Sudanese Refugee Youth in Foster Care: The 'Lost Boys' in America," *Child Welfare* 84, no. 5 (September/October 2005): 631–48; United States Conference of Catholic Bishops (USCCB), "The United States Unaccompanied Refugee Minor Program: Guiding Principles and Promising Practices," 2013, https://www.usccb.org/about/children-and-migration/unaccompanied-refugee-minor-program/upload/united-states-unaccompanied-refugee-minor-program-guiding-principles-and-promising-practices.pdf, 6–7; Haddal, *Unaccompanied Refugee Minors*, i, 12, 13.

23. Sara Corbett, "The Lost Boys of Sudan; The Long, Long, Long Road to Fargo," *New York Times*, April 1, 2001, 48.

24. Corbett, "The Lost Boys of Sudan."

25. Stacey Hynd, "Trauma, Violence, and Memory in African Child Soldier Memoirs," *Culture, Medicine, and Psychiatry* 45, no. 1 (March 2020): 74–96; Rosen, *Child Soldiers*, 104–5, 182.

26. Olga Byrne, *Unaccompanied Children in the United States: A Literature Review* (New York: VERA Institute of Justice, 2008), 22; Jacqueline Bhabha and Susan Schmidt, "Seeking Asylum Alone: Unaccompanied and Separated Children and Refugee Protection in the U.S.," *Journal of the History of Childhood and Youth* 1, no. 1 (Winter 2008): 126–38.

27. Chiara Galli, "No Country for Immigrant Children: From Obama's 'Humanitarian Crisis' to Trump's Criminalization of Central American Unaccompanied Minors" (California Immigration Research Initiative Brief Series 6, University of California, Los Angeles, Spring 2018), 3; USCCB, "Unaccompanied Refugee Minor Program," 3–5.

28. USCCB, "Unaccompanied Refugee Minor Program," 6.

29. Haddal, *Unaccompanied Refugee Minors*, 11.

30. Haddal, *Unaccompanied Refugee Minors*, 12–13.

31. Walter LaFeber, *Inevitable Revolutions: The United States in Central America* (New York: W. W. Norton, 1984), 166–77; Felix Masud-Piloto, *From Welcomed Exiles to Illegal Immigrants:*

Cuban Migration to the U.S., 1959–1995 (Lanham, Md.: Rowman & Littlefield, 1996), 120; Philippe Fournier, "The Boomerang Effect in US-Northern Triangle Relations" (CÉRIUM Working Paper, no. 16, Center for International Studies, Université de Montréal, Montreal, Que., June 2019), 2–5.

32. Zucker, "Refugee Resettlement," 181.

33. Zucker, "Refugee Resettlement," 181.

34. Fournier, "The Boomerang Effect," 4–5.

35. *The Miami Herald*, September 15, 1984, 26a.

36. María Cristina García, *Seeking Refuge: Central American Migration to Mexico, the United States, and Canada* (Berkeley: University of California Press, 2006); see also Susan Bibler Coutin, *The Culture of Protest: Religious Activism and the U.S. Sanctuary Movement* (Boulder, Colo.: Westview Press, 1993); and "U.S. Churches Offer Sanctuary to Aliens Facing Deportation," *New York Times*, April 8, 1983, box 54, folder 19, Walsh Collection, Barry University Archives, Miami Shores, Fla.

37. Cecilia Menjívar and Leisy J. Abrego, "Legal Violence: Immigration Law and the Lives of Central American Immigrants," *American Journal of Sociology* 117, no. 5 (March 2012): 1381; Miranda Cady Hallett and Lynnette Arnold, "Compounding the Crisis: Understanding Legal Violence Against Central American Families," *NACLA*, July 24, 2018, https://nacla.org/news/2018/07/24/compounding-crisis; Zolberg, *A Nation by Design*, 371; see also Laura E. Enriquez, "Multigenerational Punishment: Shared Experiences of Undocumented Immigration Status within Mixed-Status Families," *Journal of Marriage and Family* 77, no. 4 (August 2015): 939–53.

38. Bhabha and Schmidt, "Seeking Asylum Alone," 14.

39. Mandell, "A Closing Door," A4.

40. Bhabha and Schmidt, "Seeking Asylum Alone," 22.

41. Forbes and Fagen, "Unaccompanied Refugee Children," 82.

42. Forbes and Fagen, "Unaccompanied Refugee Children," 76–77.

43. Bhabha and Schmidt, "Seeking Asylum Alone," 18.

44. Irene I. Vega, "Toward a Cultural Sociology of Immigration Control: A Call for Research," *American Behavioral Scientist* 63, no. 9 (2019): 1173–76; Jennifer Lee Koh, "Executive Defiance and the Deportation State," *Yale Law Journal* 130, no. 4 (February 2021): 778–1049.

45. Steinbock, "The Admission of Unaccompanied Children," 167.

46. Forbes and Fagen, "Unaccompanied Refugee Children," 77.

47. Alexandra Young, "Developments in Intercountry Adoption: From Humanitarian Aid to Market-Driven Policy and Beyond," *Adoption & Fostering Quarterly Journal* 36, no. 2 (July 2012): 71; Karen Dubinsky, *Babies without Borders: Adoption and Migration across the Americas* (Toronto, Ont.: University of Toronto Press, 2010), 104–8.

48. Ralph Winningham, "Illegal Alien Juveniles Hoping for Better Life in U.S.," *San Antonio Express-News*, June 6, 1989, 1.

49. Border Association for Refugees from Central America (BARCA) to supporters, Edinburgh, Tex., June 1989; and "Asylum Won for Minor," *Proyecto Libertad Newsletter* (May–June 1989), 2–3, box 24, folder 3, U.S. Committee for Refugees and Immigrants Papers, Social Welfare History Archives, University of Minnesota, Minneapolis; see also "Plight of the 'Border Orphans,'" *Newsweek*, July 24, 1989, 18; and "Illegal Alien Kids Flooding South Texas," *San Antonio Express-News*, June 25, 1989, 1.

50. CARES Newsletter, Diocese of Brownsville, May 1988; and "Children in Detention," n.a., n.d., box 24, folder 3, U.S. Committee for Refugees and Immigrants Papers, Social Welfare History Archives, University of Minnesota, Minneapolis.

51. "Plight of the 'Border Orphans,'" 18; "Asylum Won for Minor," 3.

52. Dianna Solis, "Memories of War in Central America Haunt Young Aliens," *Wall Street Journal*, August 4, 1989, A1, A8; Lisa Belkin, "U.S. Providing Shelters for Young Illegal Aliens," *New York Times*, May 25, 1989, A16.

53. Fournier, "The Boomerang Effect," 7, 12–13; Bhabha and Schmidt, "Seeking Asylum Alone," 19.

54. Fournier, "The Boomerang Effect," 4, 13.

55. Fournier, "The Boomerang Effect," 17.

56. José Palafox, "Introduction to 'Gatekeeper's State: Immigration and Boundary Policing in an Era of Globalization,'" *Social Justice* 28, no. 2 (84) (Summer 2001): 2; Ruth Ellen Wasem, "Immigration Governance for the Twenty-First Century," *Journal on Migration and Human Security* 6, no. 1 (2018): 104.

57. Bon Tempo, *Americans at the Gate*, 201.

58. Zolberg, *A Nation by Design*, 402–7.

59. Leo R. Chavez, *The Latino Threat: Constructing Immigrants, Citizens, and the Nation*, 2nd ed. (Stanford, Calif.: Stanford University Press, 2013), x, 4, 75, 181–84.

60. UNICEF, "Convention on the Rights of the Child," accessed January 14, 2021, https://www.unicef.org/child-rights-convention/convention-text.

61. Jacqueline Bhabha, *Child Migration and Human Rights in a Global Age* (Princeton, N.J.: Princeton University Press, 2014), 86–88, 116.

62. United States District Court for the Central District of California, Flores v. Reno: Stipulated Settlement Agreement, C.D. Cal. 85-4544 RJK (1997), https://cliniclegal.org/sites/default/files/attachments/flores_v._reno_settlement_agreement_1.pdf; Byrne, *Unaccompanied Children*, 22.

63. Chad C. Haddal, *Unaccompanied Alien Children: Policies and Issues. CRS Report for Congress* (Washington, D.C.: Congressional Research Service, 2007), 4.

64. Fournier, "The Boomerang Effect," 14; Zolberg, *A Nation by Design*, 387; Bon Tempo, *Americans at the Gate*, 203.

65. Wasem, "Immigration Governance," 106, 109.

66. Haddal, *Unaccompanied Refugee Minors*, 5; Miriam Jordan and Manny Fernandez, "Judge Rejects Long Detentions of Migrant Families, Dealing Trump Another Setback," *New York Times*, July 9, 2018.

67. Wasem, "Immigration Governance," 110; Haddal, *Unaccompanied Refugee Minors*, 7.

68. Haddal, *Unaccompanied Alien Children*, 14–15.

69. Bhabha and Schmidt, "Seeking Asylum Alone," 20.

70. For more on contemporary ambivalence toward unaccompanied migrant children, see Bhabha, *Child Migration*, 11–14.

71. Committee on Migration and USCCB, "Mission to Central America: The Flight of Unaccompanied Children to the United States," November 2013, 2, https://www.usccb.org/about/migration-policy/upload/Mission-To-Central-America-FINAL-2.pdf; Susan Schmidt and Aryah Somers, "Children on the Run: Unaccompanied Children Leaving Central America and Mexico and the Need for International Protection," (Washington, D.C.:UNHCR Regional Office for the United States and the Caribbean, 2014), 4–5, 7, 9, 11,

https://resourcecentre.savethechildren.net/node/8302/pdf/532180c24.pdf; Betsy Cavendish and Maru Cortazar, *Children at the Border: The Screening, Protection and Repatriation of Unaccompanied Mexican Minors*, (Washington, D.C.: Appleseed, 2011), 16; Tim Gaynor, "Mexican Minors Crossing Border at Risk: Study," *Reuters*, April 28, 2011; Haddal, *Unaccompanied Alien Children*, 23–24.

72. Committee on Migration and USCCB, "Mission to Central America," 2.

73. Sylvia Moreno, "A Set of Borders to Cross, For Children Seeking Immigrant Relatives in U.S., Journey is Twofold," *Washington Post*, October 23, 2006, A1.

74. Tim Gaynor, "Children Cross U.S. Border Solo as Security Rises," *Reuters*, December 4, 2006.

75. Schmidt and Somers, "Children on the Run," 4–5, 7, 9, 11; Agnes Callamard, "El Salvador End of Mission Statement," February 5, 2018, Office of the United Nations High Commissioner for Human Rights, https://www.ohchr.org/EN/NewsEvents/Pages/DisplayNews.aspx?NewsID=22634&LangID=E; Cavendish and Cortazar, *Children at the Border*, 16.

76. Cavendish and Cortazar, *Children at the Border*, 13.

77. Committee on Migration and USCCB, "Mission to Central America," 8.

78. Bhabha and Schmidt, "Seeking Asylum Alone," 188, 190.

79. Gaynor, "Mexican Minors Crossing Border;" Galli, "No Country for Immigrant Children," 2.

80. Haddal, *Unaccompanied Alien Children*, 10.

81. See National Center for Refugee and Immigrant Children, "Executive Summary," accessed December 10, 2020, https://sites.google.com/site/ncricmanagement/Home.

82. USCCB, "Unaccompanied Refugee Minor Program," 6.

83. Schmidt and Somers, "Children on the Run," 5–6; Cavendish and Cortazar, *Children at the Border*, 16.

84. Galli, "No Country for Immigrant Children," 3.

85. See, for example, Leisy Abrego, "Intervention and Displacement: How U.S. involvement in Central America Pushes Children and Families to Migrate," Moral-Imperialism, August 21, 2014, https://moralimperialism.wordpress.com/2014/08/21/intervention-and-displacement-how-u-s-involvement-in-central-america-pushes-children-and-families-to-migrate; Óscar Martínez, "Why the Children Fleeing Central America Will Not Stop Coming," *The Nation*, July 30, 2014, https://www.thenation.com/article/archive/why-children-fleeing-central-america-will-not-stop-coming; and Donald Kerwin, "Migrant Children, Uninvited Guests, and Welcoming the Stranger," HuffPost, October 13, 2014, https://www.huffpost.com/entry/migrant-children-uninvited-immigration_b_5673300.

86. Mark Binelli, "The GOP's Fake Border War. How the Far Right Has Used the Refugee Crisis—and Ignored Suffering Children—for Short-Term Political Gain," Rolling Stone, August 13, 2014, https://www.rollingstone.com/politics/politics-news/the-gops-fake-border-war-235887/#ixzz3AJATRobo.

87. Hallett and Arnold, "Compounding the Crisis"; Galli, "No Country for Immigrant Children," 1–4; see also Cecilia Menjívar and Krista M. Perreira, "Undocumented and Unaccompanied: Children of Migration in the European Union and the United States," *Journal of Ethnic and Migration Studies* 45, no. 2 (2019): 200.

88. Galli, "No Country for Immigrant Children," 2.

89. Fournier, "The Boomerang Effect," 20–21.

90. Galli, "No Country for Immigrant Children," 4.

91. Wasem, "Immigration Governance," 113.

92. Julia Preston, "Many What-Ifs in Donald Trump's Plan for Migrants," *New York Times,* June 18, 2016.

93. American Civil Liberties Union, "Fact Sheet: Criminal Prosecutions for Unauthorized Border Crossing," 1, accessed January 15, 2021, https://www.aclu.org/sites/default/files/field_document/15_12_14_aclu_1325_1326_recommendations_final2.pdf; Hallett and Arnold, "Compounding the Crisis."

94. Wasem, "Immigration Governance," 113.

95. Fournier, "The Boomerang Effect," 22; Cynthia S. Gorman, "Singled Out: Scaling Violence and Social Groups as Legal Borderwork in U.S. Asylum Law," *Geographical Review* 109, no. 4 (October 2019): 488–89.

96. Wasem, "Immigration Governance," 113; Galli, "No Country for Immigrant Children," 2.

97. Galli, "No Country for Immigrant Children," 7; Hallett and Arnold, "Compounding the Crisis."

98. Galli, "No Country for Immigrant Children," 4.

99. Haddal, *Unaccompanied Alien Children,* 30.

100. Hallett and Arnold, "Compounding the Crisis."

101. Daniella Diaz, "Kelly: DHS Is Considering Separating Undocumented Children from Their Parents at the Border," CNN, March 7, 2017, https://www.cnn.com/2017/03/06/politics/john-kelly-separating-children-from-parents-immigration-border/index.html.

102. Donald J. Trump, "Affording Congress an Opportunity to Address Family Separation," Executive Order 13841 dated June 20, 2018, https://www.federalregister.gov/documents/2018/06/25/2018-13696/affording-congress-an-opportunity-to-address-family-separation.

103. "Parents of 545 Children Separated at the Border Cannot Be Found," *New York Times,* October 21, 2020.

104. Michelle Chen, "Separating Children from Their Parents is a New Low for Our Immigration System," *The Nation,* June 8, 2018, https://www.thenation.com/article/archive/separating-children-parents-new-low-immigration-system.

EPILOGUE

1. Jacqueline Bhabha, *Child Migration and Human Rights in a Global Age* (Princeton, N.J.: Princeton University Press, 2014).

2. Heather Montgomery, *An Introduction to Childhood: Anthropological Perspectives on Children's Lives* (West Sussex, U.K.: Wiley-Blackwell, 2009), 14; David M. Rosen, *Child Soldiers in the Western Imagination: From Patriots to Victims* (New Brunswick, N.J.: Rutgers University Press, 2015), 157.

3. Bhabha, *Child Migration,* 210.

4. Olga Byrne, *Unaccompanied Children in the United States: A Literature Review* (New York: VERA Institute of Justice, 2008), 13.

5. Alexander Betts, *Survival Migration: Failed Governance and the Crisis of Displacement* (Ithaca, N.Y.: Cornell University Press, 2013), 4–5.

6. Statement of Congresswoman Elizabeth Holtzman, hearing on H.R. 2816 before the Subcommittee on Immigration, Refugees and the International Law of the House Comm. of the Judiciary, 96th Cong., 1st Sess., 1979, quoted in Deborah E. Aner and Michael H.

Posner, "The Forty Year Crisis: A Legislative History of the Refugee Act of 1980," *San Diego Law Review* 19, no. 1 (1981): 9.

7. María Cristina García, *The Refugee Challenge in Post-Cold War America* (New York: Oxford University Press, 2017), 203.

8. See Kevin Escudero, *Organizing while Undocumented: Immigrant Youth's Political Activism under the Law* (New York: New York University Press, 2020), 3.

INDEX

Action Transmittal (AT), 175–76, 181
ACVAFS (American Council of Voluntary Agencies for Foreign Service), 119, 123–29
Afro-European refugee children, 92–93; adoption by African American families of, 93
AFSC. *See* American Friends Service Committee
Aguirre, José, 33
AHEPA (American Hellenic Educational Progressive Association), 90–92
Aid to Refugee Children Without Parents, Inc., 195
Alien Minors Shelter Care program, 210
Allen, Theodora, 94
Alliance for Progress, 147
Amerasian refugee children, 169, 188, 193; Amerasian Immigration Act (1982) effects on, 188, 224
American Board of Guardians for Basque Refugee Children of New York, 34, 36, 38
American Chamber of Commerce, Havana, 138–39
American Coalition of Patriotic, Civic and Fraternal Societies, 22, 30
American Committee for the Evacuation of British Children, 41, 49–50, 52
American Council of Voluntary Agencies for Foreign Service, 119, 123–29

American Friends Service Committee, 27, 38, 43, 57–58, 61–64, 72, 80, 169
American Hellenic Educational Progressive Association (AHEPA), 90–92
Americanization, 54, 190, 222
American Jewish Joint Distribution Committee, 24, 60–62, 64, 72
American Legion, 30, 83
"anchors," 9, 15, 167, 179, 180, 189, 195–96, 209, 220, 222, 226. *See also* chain migration; "entering wedge"
anti-Semitism, 11, 21, 26, 37, 42, 44, 62, 76–77, 180, 189, 216, 243n39. *See also* Nazis; Zionism
Arnold, Mildred, 146, 154–55, 160
ASEAN (Association of Southeast Asian Nations), 15, 167, 177–78, 182–83, 194, 196
Auerbach, Frank, 140–41

Baker, James, 138–41. *See also* Walsh-Baker program
Ball, Robert M., 150, 158
Bay of Pigs, 146, 148–49, 153, 156, 159
becas, 143, 150, 158, 164
behavioral problems, of refugee children, 25, 88, 157
Beisser, Paul, 29
Bell, David E., 148
Berlin Children's Emigration Office, 22
Biden, Joseph R., Jr., 2

B'nai B'rith, 18, 20
"boat people," 177, 179, 182–84,
    186–87, 194
Bonsal, Philip, 145
B'rith Sholom, 31, 37
British Foreign Office, 41, 46
British Home Office, 51, 67
Brown, Wendy, 6
Bureau of the Budget, 148, 160
Bush, George H. W., 194, 202
Bush, George W., 212

Cambodia, 168, 180–82, 191, 201;
    Cambodians, 168, 180, 182–84, 187–90,
    192–93; Cambodia-Thai border, 180.
    See also Khmer Rouge
Camp Kilmer (Joyce Kilmer Reception
    Center), 3, 103, 105, 114–16, 121, 128
Camp Matecumbe, 147–48
Camp Pendleton, 171, 174–75, 177
Caribbean, 5, 8, 186–87, 197, 205,
    220, 225
Carr, Wilbur, 18
cartels, 209, 211
Carter, Jimmy, 177–78, 182, 186, 198–99
Carter, Rosalynn, 184
Castendyck, Elsa, 48, 74
Castro, Fidel, 14, 133–35, 138, 141,
    146–48, 150, 157, 160, 162; opposition to,
    14, 133, 135, 137–39, 141–42, 162–63, 186,
    197–99
Catholic agencies: Catholic Charities,
    87, 145, 184, 190; Catholic Committee
    for Refugees, 79, 90; Catholic Relief
    Service, 78, 121, 243n39; Catholic War
    Relief Services, 72, 78; Catholic Welfare
    Bureau, 136–37, 139, 143–44, 148–49,
    154–57, 159; Centro Hispano Católico,
    137, 139; League of Catholic Women, 35;
    National Catholic Welfare Conference,
    90, 113, 116, 121, 124, 126, 154; U.S. Catholic
    Conference, 171, 181, 183, 186, 190, 193, 208,
    211; U.S. Conference of Catholic Bishops,
    2, 211–12
Catholic Cuban children, 137–38, 152–54
Catholicism, hostility toward, 35, 36,
    134–35

Catholic leaders: opposition to child-saving
    efforts, 33, 34–36, 38, 94–95; support for
    child-saving efforts, 28–29, 136, 147
Catholic schools, 78, 113, 140, 151
Central America, 8, 184, 201–3, 208, 211,
    213–14; Central American Minors
    Refugee and Parole program, 215;
    Central American Resource Center, 208;
    Central Americans, 1–2, 5, 10, 15, 198,
    204–7, 211–15, 220, 222–25. See also Latin
    America
certificate of abandonment, 91–92
chain migration, 9, 142, 163, 188. See also
    "anchors;" "entering wedge"
children, adoptable, 29, 75, 79, 84, 88–89,
    97–98, 109, 112, 168, 176, 184, 190;
    children, unadoptable, 88
Children's Overseas Reception Board, 41,
    50, 52, 56
Children's Service Bureau (CSB),
    143, 159
child soldiers, 4, 15, 202–3. See also Lost
    Boys
Child Welfare Division, 72. See also UN
    Relief and Rehabilitation Administration
    (UNRRA)
Child Welfare League of America, 29, 37,
    45–46
Chinese Cuban children, 151
Chinese Revolution, 164
Christianity, 10, 83, 138; Anglo-Saxon
    Christians, 42, 54, 57, 60; British
    Christians, 41, 47–48; Christian
    Hungarians, 13, 101; evangelical
    Christians, 98; non-Aryan Christians, 63;
    non-Christian children, 10, 222; Sudanese
    Christians, 203; white Christians, 39. See
    also Protestantism
Churchill, Winston, 42, 50, 56
Church World Service, 72, 79, 112, 121, 124,
    154, 169, 171, 193
CIA, 102, 134, 138, 142, 146
Citizens' Commission on Indochinese
    Refugees, 178
Clapper, Raymond, 51
Clinton, Bill, 201–2, 208–9
Close, Kathryn, 97

Cold War foreign policy, 14, 70, 100, 107, 130, 133, 163, 204, 219

Collins, J. Lawton, 116

communism, 22, 70, 89, 107, 164, 169; anti-communism, 5, 33–34, 85, 88, 95, 98, 101–2, 122–23, 142, 218; anti-communist allies, 5; anti-communist Catholics, 34, 113, 171; anti-communist Cubans, 131, 139, 159; anti-communist dissenters, 178; anti-communist Duvalier regime, 198; anti-communist escapees, 104, 187, 204, 222; anti-communist foreign policy, 95; anti-communist Hungarians, 8, 112, 122, 218; anti-communist Irish American Catholics, 38; anti-communist refugees, 106, 115, 131, 153, 170, 201; communist brainwashing, 141; communist-controlled nations, 128, 160; Communist forces in China, 89; Communist guerrillas, 90; communist indoctrination, 134, 136, 138; communist North Korea, 98; communist refugees, 105–6, 115, 131, 153, 164, 170, 201; communist sympathies, 83, 150; communist Vietnam, 187; "fast-tracked" communist escapees, 105

Comprehensive Plan of Action (CPA), 194–95

CORB (Children's Overseas Reception Board), 41, 50, 52, 56

corporate affidavit, 27, 36–37, 39, 47, 64, 73–74, 76–77, 81, 91, 95

Craft, Frank, 146, 155, 160

crash resettlement program, 104–6, 115, 118–19, 121, 123, 126, 129, 174

Cuban Adjustment Act (1966), 201

"Cuban/Haitian Entrant (Status Pending)," 186, 199

Cuban Refugee Center, 136, 144, 148, 151, 159

Cuban Refugee Program, 148–49, 155, 160, 170–71, 173, 178, 185, 219

Cuban Revolutionary Council, 142

Cushing, Richard, 153–54

DACA (Deferred Action for Childhood Arrivals), 1, 213

Davis, Frances, 136–37, 139, 144–46, 151, 154–57

Deferred Action for Childhood Arrivals, 1, 213

Department of Health, Education, and Welfare, 2; and anti-Cuban public feeling, 154–56, 158, 160, 162–64; and Cuban refugees, resettlement of, 133, 135–37, 145–46, 148–49, 151–53; as Department of Health and Human Services, 185, 190, 199–200; and Southeast Asian refugees, 171–72, 175–77, 179–81, 185; and unaccompanied Hungarian minors, resettlement of, 114, 116, 124, 129–30

Department of Homeland Security, 3, 210, 214–15

Department of Justice, 2, 19, 21; and Cuban refugees, 141, 147, 159; and Eisenhower, 103–4, 123; and Hungarian refugees, 103–4, 129–30; and Southeast Asian refugees, 167, 180, 187–89, 195, 199; and Trump, 214–15; and U.S. Committee for the Care of European Children, 46–47, 64–65, 68

Department of Labor, 19, 21–22, 23, 27; Miami, 136

Department of State, 19; and Cuban children, 141, 146, 159; and Eisenhower, 103–4, 106, 123, 125; and Hungarian refugees, 129–30; and Southeast Asian refugees, 180, 187, 199; and U.S. Committee for the Care of European Children, 46–47, 61, 64–65, 68,

deportation, 25, 60–62, 112, 201, 205–6, 209, 213

DHS (Department of Homeland Security), 3, 210, 214–15

Dickstein, Samuel, 51–52

Dillon, Douglas, 135

disabilities, 25, 88, 151, 162

Displaced Persons (DP), 71, 75, 82–83, 85, 89, 105; Displaced Persons Act (1948), 8, 85–87, 88–92, 94–96, 99–100, 103, 188, 217, 224; displaced persons camps,

Displaced Persons (DP) (*continued*)
71–72, 76, 80–81, 84, 88; Displaced
Persons Commission, 78, 86, 92, 103
Dodds, Dicey, 113
DOJ. *See* Department of Justice

economic migration, 91, 149; economic
migrants, 8, 185, 194, 198, 201, 204, 225
education: in boarding schools, 115, 134,
137–39,141, 145, 150; Catholic faith and,
113; in high schools, 117, 137, 148, 150,
172, 190, 205; in public schools, 54, 134,
150; and Ruston Academy, 138, 140–42,
144–45, 147; in the United States, 54, 137
Eglin Air Force Base, 171, 174
Eisenhower, Dwight D., 95, 101–3, 109–111;
commitment to anti-Castro Cubans,
135–36, 140–42; commitment to anti-
communist Hungarians, 123, 131, 170–71;
and crash resettlement program, 104, 115,
119; and resettlement program, 13, 102,
112. *See also* crash resettlement program
EJCA (European Jewish Children's Aid),
11–12, 64, 70, 72–73, 79
El Salvador, 204, 207, 211; Salvadoran
children, 204, 206, 208, 213–14
"entering wedge," 10, 22, 167 180, 189, 196.
See also "anchors;" chain migration
European Jewish children, 12, 25, 31, 36,
39–40, 42–44, 47, 57–58, 64, 67–68, 151,
167, 211, 220
European Jewish Children's Aid, 11–12, 64,
70, 72–73, 79
Executive Office for Immigration Review
(EOIR), 206

Fabian, Béla, 122
fascism, 17, 38, 68. *See also* Nazis
federal care, 148, 150–51, 155–57, 159, 162–63,
197; federally funded foster care, 14, 152,
164, 167, 181, 191, 195–96, 219
FEMA (Federal Emergency Management
Agency), 199
Field, Marshall, 44–45, 50, 56
FitzGerald, David, 4
Florida City, 147–48, 157

Florida State Department of Public
Welfare, 133, 136–37, 143–46, 148, 150–51,
154–60, 162–63
Folsom, Marion B., 130
Ford, Betty, 172
Ford, Gerald R., 14, 168, 170–73, 177,
186, 219
Fort Chaffee, 171, 174, 177, 186
Fort Indiantown Gap, 171, 174, 186
foster parents, 7, 22, 42, 55, 66–67, 79, 81, 88,
92, 128, 152, 159, 176, 191
Foster Parents' Plan for Spanish Children,
38, 83
Freedom Flights, 162
Freud, Anna, 50
FSDPW (Florida State Department of
Public Welfare), 133, 136–37, 143–46, 148,
150–51, 154–60, 162–63

gang, 192, 211, 215, 220; criminal, 208,
224; members, 193, 209, 210, 212, 215;
MS-13, 212
Gerety, Pierce J., 106
German Jewish Children's Aid, 11–12,
20–27, 33–34, 37, 39, 48, 58, 62, 64, 68,
216; and British child-saving committees,
43, 46–47, 54–55; first model of a
comprehensive program of the, 36–37;
opposition to the B'rith Sholom child
evacuation scheme, 31. *See also* European
Jewish Children's Aid
German League of Jewish Women, 23
GJCA. *See* German Jewish Children's Aid
Gradison, Willis D., Jr., 116
Grammer, Mabel, 93
Great Depression, 23, 35
group homes, 25, 38, 67, 115, 137, 145, 153, 157
Guam, 171, 174
Guatemala, 204, 207, 211; Guatemalan
children, 213; Guatemalan Civil War, 204

Haiti, 201, 204–5; Haitians, 5, 10, 15, 167, 186,
197–201, 204–5, 222, 224
"half-orphans," 10, 92, 96–97, 188, 224
Halifax, Lord, 67
Hart, Philip, 149

Hart-Celler Immigration Act (1965), 160, 185

Haxton, Jennie, 54

Hayes, Helen, 29, 44

Hebrew Immigration Aid Society (HIAS), 55, 112, 115–16, 118, 121, 123–24, 147, 152, 159, 171

Hennessy, James, 127, 136

Hennings, Thomas C., Jr., 51

Hennings Mercy Ship, 52

HEW. *See* Department of Health, Education, and Welfare

Hitler, Adolf, 17–18, 25, 41, 51

Holt, Bertha, 98

Holt, Harry, 98

Holtzman, Elizabeth, 180, 226

Homeland Security Act (2002), 210

Honduras, 202, 204, 207, 211; Honduran children, 213–14

Hoover, Herbert, 29

House Appropriations Committee, 149, 155, 159

House Committee on Immigration, 31

Hungarian American "Connecticut Committee," 121

Hungarian National Council, 122

Hungarian Uprising (1956), 131, 172

Huu, Nguyễn D. 195

IATF (Interagency Task Force), 171–75, 177

Illegal Immigration Reform and Immigrant Responsibility Act (1996), 209

immigrants, 2, 8, 10, 15, 19, 22–23, 74, 82, 95, 117, 130, 185, 224, 226–27, 229n1, 230n3; desirable, seen as, 43; from Europe, 35; hostility toward, 5, 14, 135, 213–15, 166, 189, 209, 213–15, 223; from Hungary, 129; "illegal," seen as, 5, 10, 198, 220; from Latin America, 149; from Mexico, 135, 208; non quota immigrants, entering as, 28, 30, 85; permanent status of, 25, 51, 61; quota for, 38, 103; Reform and Control Act impact on, 205; unauthorized entry of, 209–10; from Vietnam, 172; visas for, 61, 85

immigration acts: Immigration Act (1907), 9; Immigration Act (1917), 18, 21; Immigration Act (1924), 28; Hart-Celler Immigration Act (1965), 160, 185; Amerasian Immigration Act (1982), 188

immigration law, U.S., 9, 11–12, 17–19, 21–22, 30, 33, 37, 47, 64, 68, 71, 76; children's best interests in, 225; International Refugee Organization and, 87; liberalization of, 83; National Immigration Law Center, 215; racialized logic of, 217, 221; restrictionists' overhaul of, 93–94, 98, 120, 140, 208–9; U.S. Committee for the Care of European Children's child-saving efforts and, 80–81

Immigration and Naturalization Service, 3, 22–23, 109; Clinton and, 209–10; detention of minors, 206–8; and Displaced Persons Act expansion, 89; and Haitian entrants as strictly "economic" migrants, 201, 205; limitation of admission of refugee minors seen as "anchors," 189, 193–96; placing unaccompanied minors with relatives, 123–27; policies toward Cuban immigrants, 135–36, 139, 141, 146, 156, 158, 199–200; pro-deterrence biases of, 198; and Reagan, 187; and Refugee Act, 185–86; in Thailand, 188; treatment of Vietnamese minors, 174, 176, 180–81; support for Wagner-Rogers Bill, 31

immigration policy, U.S., 1, 4, 12, 18, 28, 40, 93, 104, 121, 159, 217; Truman's impact on, 76; U.S. Committee for the Care of European Children's influence on, 69

Immigration Reform and Control Act (IRCA) (1986), 201, 205

Indochina Migration and Refugee Assistance Act (1975), 173, 178

Indochina Refugee Task Force, 177, 181

Indochinese Refugee Assistance Program (IRAP), 173, 187

INS. *See* Immigration and Naturalization Service

Interagency Task Force (IATF), 171–75, 177

International Refugee Organization (IRO), 80–81, 86–90, 92, 94, 113, 120

International Rescue Committee (IRC), 121, 124, 138, 141, 144–46, 153–54, 171, 178

International Social Service: American branch, 3, 12, 70, 97, 106, 109, 111–12, 114, 116, 123–24, 193, 208, 216; Austrian branch, 111, 114, 122, 125–26; Geneva office, 113; Munich office, 94; partnership with U.S. Committee for the Care of European Children, 78; Vienna office, 120

IRO (International Refugee Organization), 80–81, 86–90, 92, 94, 113, 120

isolationist policies, 19, 34, 37 149

ISS. *See* International Social Service

Ives, Irving, 84

Jackson, Gardner, 34

Javits, Jacob, 84

Javits Bill, 84

JDC (American Jewish Joint Distribution Committee), 24, 60–62, 64, 72

Jewish Americans, child-saving efforts, 11, 14, 18–19, 23, 29, 31, 55, 62, 76, 166, 185, 196, 216; American Jewish Committee and, 18, 20; American Jewish Congress and, 19–20, 22; American Jewish Joint Distribution Committee and, 24, 60–62, 72; Jewish Family and Children Services and, 137, 143–44, 147; public opposition to, 11, 62, 216, 243n39. *See also* European Jewish Children's Aid; German Jewish Children's Aid; National Conference of Jewish Social Workers

Johnson, Lyndon B., 160, 170

Johnson-Reed Act, 18

Joyce Kilmer Reception Center, 3, 103, 105, 114–16, 121, 128

Kennedy, Edward, 169, 180

Kennedy, John F., 142–43, 147, 149–50, 153, 156, 164

Kennedy, Joseph P., 41

Kenworthy, Marion Dr., 27–28, 43

Khmer Rouge, 168, 180, 188; Khmer refugee, 190

Kindertransport, 27, 40

Kirk, William T., 106, 111–12, 114

Kissinger, Henry, 170

Knights of Columbus, 35, 153

Kodakids, 41

Korean War, 89, 95–96, 98–99, 164

Kraus, Eleanor, 31

Kraus, Gilbert, 31–32

Krome North Detention Center, 199; South Detention Center, 200, 205

Ku Klux Klan, 90

Lang, Robert, 65

Larned, Ruth, 62

Latin American immigrants, 5, 133, 139, 147, 164, 187, 197, 202, 204; and fight against communism, 135–36, 205, 211, 220, 225; public hostility toward, 36, 76, 149, 209. *See also* Central America

Laval, Pierre, 61–63

Lehman, Irving, 18

Lenroot, Katharine, 29, 74

Long, Breckenridge, 55, 61

Lost Boys, 15, 203

Luft, Hildegard M., 111

Lutheran organizations, 79, 121; Lutheran Children and Family Service, 183; Lutheran Immigration and Refugee Service, 2, 169, 171, 177, 181, 183, 186, 190, 193, 208; Lutheran Refugee Service, 112, 115–16; Lutheran Social Service, 184; Lutheran World Relief, 72; National Lutheran Council, 79

MacCormack, Daniel, 22

Marcuse, Lotte, 24–25, 58

Mariel Cubans ("Marielitos"), 167, 186, 198–201, 204, 225

Marrs, Theodore, 173

Martin, Graham, 168

McCarran, Pat, 83, 86, 89

McCarran-Walter Act (1952), 93–95, 104

McCollum, Robert S., 123–25

McDermitt, Al, 136

McDowell, John, 51

Mercy Ship, 51, 52

Messersmith, George, 31

Mexico, 5, 34, 38, 55, 78, 204, 212; border between the United States and, 156, 210; child migrants from, 5, 10, 15, 135, 198, 203, 211–13, 220, 222–24; hostility toward immigrants from, 35; immigrants from, 208–9; wall funded by, 214

Miami Association of Black Social Workers, 200

Migration and Refugee Assistance Act (H. R. 8291), 148, 155, 173

Mitchell, William L., 145, 148–49, 152

Mougne, Christine, 195

Mutual Security Act, 103–4, 130, 143, 149

National Association for Vietnamese American Education, 193

National Center for Refugee and Immigrant Children (NCRIC), 212

National Conference of Jewish Social Workers, 20

National Coordinating Committee for Aid to Immigrants and Refugees from Germany, 20

National Lutheran Council, 79

National Refugee Service (NRS), 20

nativist, 22, 209

Nazis, 12, 18–21, 24, 26, 38, 43, 48, 57, 63, 65, 67, 71, 76–77, 180, 216, 232n6; British reaction to, invasion of Poland, 39–40; in France, 60, 62–63; violence against Jews, 18–19, 21–24, 28–31, 44. See also Third Reich

Neutrality Act (1939), 51

neutrality laws, 26, 41, 48

Nguyen, Phuong Tran, 8

Nicaragua, Nicaraguan refugee children, 204–5, 207–8

9/11, 202, 210

Non-Sectarian Committee for German Refugee Children, 28–29, 32, 43, 68

Nuremberg Laws, 24

Obama, Barack, 1, 213–14

"occupation children," 86

O'Connell, William, 35–36

Oetinger, Katherine, 136, 144, 164

Oeuvre de Secours aux Enfants (OSE), 57, 60–62

Office of Refugee and Migration Affairs, 123

Office of Refugee Resettlement (ORR), 2, 185–86, 190, 193, 199–201, 203–4, 210–13. See also Unaccompanied Refugee Minors program

Olsen, Ingeborg, 65, 94

Operation Babylift, 168–69, 172

Operation Mercy, 106–7, 109

Operation Pedro Pan, 5, 140, 152, 162–64

orphanage, 71, 78, 81–82, 93 145, 169

Palestine, 20, 23–26, 72, 87

Passman, Otto, 149, 158–59

Perkins, Frances, 19, 21, 27, 44

Petluck, Ann, 124, 127

Pettiss, Susan, 111, 114

Philippines, 171, 174, 183

Pickett, Clarence, 27–28, 38, 43, 57

Pinegar, Warren A., 113

Pioneers and Rebel Youth, 134

Polier, Justine Wise, 28

Pol Pot, 178, 180, 189

Pond, Peter, 190, 192

Porter, Steven, 7

Powers, Penny, 141, 145–46

President's Advisory Committee on Political Refugees, 44, 57

President's Committee for Hungarian Refugee Relief (PCHRR), 104–6, 112, 114, 115–16, 128–30, 170–72

prima facie, 120, 199

principled opportunism, 12, 39, 56, 68–69, 74

propaganda, 4, 76, 130, 134–35, 218

Proskauer, Joseph, 21

Protestant agencies, and child-saving efforts, 18, 28–29, 79, 87, 111, 121, 135, 143, 145, 147. See also Christianity

Proyecto Libertad, 208

public-private partnership, 13–14, 102, 104, 133, 163

Public Law 85–559, 131

Razovsky, Cecilia, 20, 22, 25, 55

Reagan, Ronald, 187, 194, 201, 204

Red Cross, 49, 60, 107, 157, 159, 175

Refugee Act (1980), 4, 8–9, 14–15, 95, 185, 197–98, 219–20, 222; failure to account for unregulated refugees from the south of the U.S. border, 167–68, 220; inadequacy of the, toward refugee minors' care, 185–86, 206; and racialized logic of deterrence, 196; and Reagan, 187; and Refugee Education Assistance Act, 200; Southeast Asian children, impact on, 166–67, 178, 180, 182; and Trump, 214–15

Refugee Education Assistance Act (1980), 200

Refugee Relief Act (1953), 95–97, 100, 103–5

Refugee Relief Program, 106; Austrian, 113

refugees: admission, 14, 18, 65, 68, 85, 89, 94, 95, 118–19, 170, 177–78, 180, 194, 201–3, 214, 217; advocacy for, 21, 33, 43, 45, 65, 78, 80, 85, 99, 120, 173, 177–78, 182; from Basque Country, 17, 34–36, 38; bills in support of, 8, 95; from Cambodia, 190, 191; camps, 38, 55, 57, 60–61, 63, 112, 181, 191–92; crisis, 40, 57, 82–83, 93, 103, 110, 113, 166–67, 170, 177, 180; from Cuba, 136–37, 139–40, 142–44, 148–49, 160; as different than voluntary immigrants, 95; from Europe, 27, 40, 50, 62, 99; from Germany, 28–29; hostility toward, 5, 14, 61, 173, 196, 223; from Hungary, 103, 107, 111–12, 119, 125, 128, 130, 136; influx of, 173–74, 186; from the Jewish community, 25, 27, 29–30, 32, 40, 43, 47, 54, 64, 151; from Korea, 98; legislation, 8, 82, 84, 86, 94, 96, 100, 130, 155, 158, 166, 204; permanent refugee program and, 136, 160; policy, 4, 6–7, 66, 85, 89, 102–3, 106–7, 120, 131, 167, 177, 185, 187, 219, 225; quotas, 178, 181, 225; relief, 97, 143, 182; resettlement, 13–14, 37, 74–75, 101–2, 106, 119, 133, 138, 142, 171, 175, 178–79, 219; Roosevelt support for, 65; screening, 188; smuggling of, 183; status, 120, 186, 188–89, 199, 120, 210; as students, 192; as teachers, 113; unregulated entry in the U.S., 197; U.S. visas for, 202; from Vietnam, 8, 173, 175–77, 194; from Vietnam, of Chinese origins, 178–79

Reich Agency for Jews in Germany, 19

Reno, Janet, 202

repatriation, 71–72, 75, 87, 113, 119, 128, 145, 194, 210

resettlement services, 178, 185

restrictionism: and the American public, 28, 37, 76, 91, 187, 214; and immigration officials, 222, 224; influence on Reagan's immigration policy, 201; and legislators, 13, 18, 21, 30, 69, 71, 85, 89, 93–95, 104, 120, 167, 204

reunification, 75, 156–57, 162–63, 170, 207, 211

Reynolds, Robert, 30, 33

Ribicoff, Abraham, 143, 148–52

Rodino, Peter, Jr., 180

Rogers, William Pierce, 141

Roosevelt, Eleanor, 28–29, 36, 44, 46, 55, 57

Roosevelt, Franklin Delano, 18–19, 26, 28, 34, 37, 65

RRA (Refugee Relief Act) (1953), 95–97, 100, 103–5

Rusk, Dean, 149

Russia, 57, 61, 130. See also Soviet Union

Save the Children Federation (U.S.), 83, 109

Save the Children Fund (U.K.), 9

Schafer, John Charles, 51

schools, boarding. See education

Semitism, hostility toward. See anti-Semitism

Senate Judiciary Subcommittee, 149, 158–59

Sessions, Jeff, 215

Shakespeare, Geoffrey, 41, 50, 52

Social Security Administration, 137

Southeast Asian refugee children: anti-Asian sentiment toward, 166–67, 180; Asian American children and, 192; limiting immigration of, 18, 93, 95; and U.S. policies, 83, 169, 171

Soviet Union, 4, 34, 38, 72, 76, 82, 87–90, 101, 112, 122, 156, 170, 184, 202, 217–18; anti-Soviet uprising,13, 102, 112; Soviet-aligned states, 87; Soviet-bloc, 95; Soviet-controlled nations, 78, 82, 89–90, 128; Soviet-inspired youth militias, 134; Soviet Jews, 178; Soviet repression, 101; ties with Cuba 133, 194, 202

Spanish Civil War, 17, 33–34, 38, 70, 72
Special Immigrant Juvenile Status
(SIJS), 214
Stratton, William, 82
Stratton Bill, 82
Szilagyi, Nicholas, 107, 109

Temporary Protective Status
(TPS), 214
Thai camps, 180, 187, 192; Cambodia-Thai
border, 180
Third Reich, 33, 37
Thompson, Llewelyn E., 113
trafficking, human, 4, 204, 212
Trafficking Victims Protection Act, 203, 212;
T visa, 203, 214
Trever, John B., 22
Truman, Harry S., 76–77, 79, 81–82, 93,
99, 170
Truman Directive, 77, 79, 81
Trump, Donald J., 214–15
TVPA. See Trafficking Victims
Protection Act

Unaccompanied Refugee Minors program,
4, 7, 14–15, 166–67, 185–86, 193, 196–98,
201–4, 210, 212, 219–20, 223–24. See also
Office of Refugee Resettlement (ORR)
undocumented immigrants, 205, 209, 211,
213, 226
Unitarian Service Committee (USC), 55,
57, 72
United Nations, 3, 7–8, 71, 75, 83, 88, 101–3,
113, 120, 125–26, 182, 195; UN Children's
Fund, 3, 83; UN Convention Relating to
the Status of Refugees, 7, 93, 97, 120; UN
High Commissioner for Refugees, 3, 15,
106, 113, 120, 124,
126–27, 167, 182–84, 188–89, 193–97, 204,
211–12; UN Relief and Rehabilitation
Administration, 71–72, 75, 77–78, 80, 89.
See also Child Welfare Division
Universal Declaration of Human Rights
(1948), 84, 95
UN Relief and Rehabilitation
Administration (UNRRA), 71–72, 75,
77–78, 80, 89

URM program. See Unaccompanied
Refugee Minors program
U.S. Agency for International Development
(USAID), 168
U.S. Border Patrol, 3, 205, 210, 222
U.S. Children's Bureau, 22–23, 29; Black
foster children, views of, 93; German-
Jewish Children's Aid relationship with,
39; Hungarian child placement, 115–16,
131; partnership with U.S. Committee for
the Care of European Children, 48–49,
55, 68, 70, 72–75, 77, 79, 81, 84, 86, 87–90,
93; and social workers, 48–49, 55, 68;
and Southeast Asian unaccompanied
children, 176, 181, 193; and Truman's
executive order, 77; and unattached
Cuban Children, 136, 143–44, 149, 151,
153–54, 159, 163–64; Wagner-Rogers Bill,
support of, 29, 39; and "war orphans," 70,
72–75
USCOM. See U.S. Committee for the Care
of European Children
U.S. Committee for the Care of European
Children, 3, 12, 216–17; Black foster
children, views of, 93; British child
rescue operation, 46–48; child
evacuation in Nazi-occupied France,
61–63; Displaced Persons Act impact
on, 85–86, 90–92, 99; evacuation of
Central European Jewish children,
57; expanding child-saving activities,
64; first evacuation of children, 52;
formation of the, 43–45; foster home
placement, 53–55; and foster parents
clashes, 67; halting British Isles rescues,
56; International Refugee Organization,
tensions with, 87–89; International
Social Service, working with, 94, 106;
licensed war relief agency, becoming a,
60; local affiliates, working with, 49–50;
and the Mercy Ships campaign, 51–52;
1953 retrospective on child-saving efforts
of, 97, 139; partnership with Children's
Bureau, 48; pivot to rescue European
children, 56–57; placement of children,
78–84; post-war preparations, 66;
principled opportunism of, 39–40,

U.S. Committee for the Care of
European Children (*continued*)
68–69; Roosevelt's support of, 65;
Truman's executive order impact on, 77;
and U-boat threats, 50–51, 56; and "war
orphans," 70, 72–75; *We Are Standing By*,
57–59. *See also* Wagner-Rogers Bill
U.S. Customs and Border Protection
(CBP), 210–13, 215, 222
USSR. *See* Soviet Union

Veterans of Foreign Wars, 83
Vichy France, 61–63
Victory in Europe Day (V-E Day), 71–72
Voorhees, Tracy S., 104–6, 110, 129–31,
135–37, 139–40

Wagner-Rogers Bill (1939), 12, 28–33, 36–39,
68. *See also* U.S. Committee for the Care
of European Children
Walsh-Baker program, 142. *See also* Baker,
James

Walsh, Brian O., 3, 136–42, 144–48, 152,
156–57, 163
Walter, Francis, 83, 89, 119, 120, 148–49. *See
also* McCarran-Walter Act (1952)
War Refugee Board, 65
War Relief Control Board, 60, 64
Waters, Alice, 30
Weddell, Justin R., 50
Welfare Planning Council, 136
Welles, Benjamin Summers, 34, 62–63
Wise, Stephen S., 28, 44, 55
World War I, 7, 18, 27, 29
World War II, 2, 6, 12, 38–39, 41, 70, 89, 93,
107, 110, 113, 151, 216, 218

xenophobia, 76

Youth Aliyah, 72
"youth to relatives" program, 124–25,
127–29

Zionism, 20, 25, 44, 72